**From Scrolls to Scrolling**

# Judaism, Christianity, and Islam – Tension, Transmission, Transformation

Edited by Patrice Brodeur, Alexandra Cuffel, Assaad Elias Kattan, and Georges Tamer

## Volume 12

# From Scrolls to Scrolling

Sacred Texts, Materiality, and Dynamic Media Cultures

Edited by Bradford A. Anderson

DE GRUYTER

Die freie Verfügbarkeit der E-Book-Ausgabe dieser Publikation wurde ermöglicht durch den Fachinformationsdienst Jüdische Studien an der Universitätsbibliothek J. C. Senckenberg Frankfurt am Main und 18 wissenschaftliche Bibliotheken, die die Open-Access-Transformation in den Jüdischen Studien unterstützen.

ISBN 978-3-11-064360-2
e-ISBN (PDF) 978-3-11-063444-0
e-ISBN (EPUB) 978-3-11-063146-3
ISSN 2196-405X
DOI https://doi.org/10.1515/9783110634440

This work is licensed under a Creative Commons Attribution-NonCommercial-NoDerivatives 4.0 International License. For details go to http://creativecommons.org/licenses/by-nc-nd/4.0

**Library of Congress Control Number: 2020933703**

**Bibliographic information published by the Deutsche Nationalbibliothek**
The Deutsche Nationalbibliothek lists this publication in the Deutsche Nationalbibliografie; detailed bibliographic data are available on the Internet at http://dnb.dnb.de.

© 2022 Bradford A. Anderson, published by Walter de Gruyter GmbH, Berlin/Boston.
This volume is text- and page-identical with the hardback published in 2020.
The book is published with open access at www.degruyter.com.

Typesetting: Integra Software Services Pvt. Ltd.
Printing and binding: CPI books GmbH, Leck

www.degruyter.com

# Open-Access-Transformation in den Jüdischen Studien

Open Access für exzellente Publikationen aus den Jüdischen Studien: Dies ist das Ziel der gemeinsamen Initiative des Fachinformationsdiensts Jüdische Studien an der Universitätsbibliothek J. C. Senckenberg Frankfurt am Main und des Verlags Walter De Gruyter. Unterstützt von 18 Konsortialpartnern können 2020 insgesamt 8 Neuerscheinungen im Open Access Goldstandard veröffentlicht werden, darunter auch diese Publikation.

Die nachfolgenden wissenschaftlichen Einrichtungen haben sich an der Finanzierung beteiligt und fördern damit die Open-Access-Transformation in den Jüdischen Studien und gewährleisten die freie Verfügbarkeit für alle:

Fachinformationsdienst Jüdische Studien, Universitätsbibliothek J. C. Senckenberg Frankfurt am Main
Staatsbibliothek zu Berlin - Preußischer Kulturbesitz
Universitätsbibliothek der Freien Universität Berlin
Universitätsbibliothek der Technischen Universität Berlin
Universitäts- und Landesbibliothek Düsseldorf
Universitätsbibliothek der Europa-Universität Viadrina Frankfurt (Oder)
Bibliothek der Vereinigten Theologischen Seminare der Georg-August-Universität Göttingen
Niedersächsische Staats- und Universitätsbibliothek Göttingen
Universitäts- und Landesbibliothek Sachsen-Anhalt
Staats- und Universitätsbibliothek Hamburg – Carl von Ossietzky
Gottfried Wilhelm Leibniz Bibliothek – Niedersächsische Landesbibliothek
Hochschule für Jüdische Studien Heidelberg
Universitäts- und Stadtbibliothek Köln
Universitätsbibliothek Mainz
Universitätsbibliothek der Ludwig-Maximilians-Universität München
Universitäts- und Landesbibliothek Münster
Herzog August Bibliothek Wolfenbüttel
Universitätsbibliothek Wuppertal

# Table of Contents

Abbreviations —— IX

Preface —— XI

Bradford A. Anderson
Introduction: Materiality, Liminality, and the Digital Turn: The Sacred Texts of Judaism, Christianity, and Islam in Material Perspective —— 1

## I  Sacred Texts and Material Contexts

Anna Krauß and Friederike Schücking-Jungblut
Stichographic Layout in the Dead Sea Psalms Scrolls: Observations on its Development and its Potential —— 13

Dan Batovici
Reading Aids in Early Christian Papyri —— 35

Asma Hilali
Writing the Qur'ān Between the Lines: Marginal and Interlinear Notes in Selected Qur'ān Fragments from the Museum of Islamic Art, Qatar —— 51

Ben Outhwaite
The Sefer Torah and Jewish Orthodoxy in the Islamic Middle Ages —— 63

Javier del Barco
From Scroll to Codex: Dynamics of Text Layout Transformation in the Hebrew Bible —— 91

Eyal Poleg
Memory, Performance, and Change: The Psalms' Layout in Late Medieval and Early Modern Bibles —— 119

Amanda Dillon
Be Your Own Scribe: Bible Journalling and the New Illuminators of the Densely-Printed Page —— 153

## II Sacred Texts and the Digital Turn

Garrick V. Allen
**Monks, Manuscripts, Muhammad, and Digital Editions of the New Testament —— 181**

Alba Fedeli
**The Qur'ānic Text from Manuscript to Digital Form: Metalinguistic Markup of Scribes and Editors —— 213**

Joshua L. Mann
**Paratexts and the Hermeneutics of Digital Bibles —— 247**

Natalia Suit
**Virtual Qur'ān: Authenticity, Authority, and *Ayat* in Bytes —— 263**

Bradford A. Anderson
**Sacred Texts in a Digital Age: Materiality, Digital Culture, and the Functional Dimensions of Scriptures in Judaism, Christianity, and Islam —— 281**

**Scriptural Index —— 303**

**Subject Index —— 305**

# Abbreviations

| | |
|---|---|
| ANTF | Arbeiten zur neutestamentlichen Textforschung |
| AYB | Anchor Yale Bible |
| BETL | Bibliotheca ephemeridum theologicarum lovaniensium |
| BoCP | Book of Common Prayer |
| BZAW | Beihefte zur Zeitschrift für die alttestamentliche Wissenschaft |
| BZNW | Beihefte zur Zeitschrift für die neutestamentliche Wissenschaft |
| CBGM | Coherence-Based Genealogical Method |
| CSML | Cambridge Studies in Medieval Literature |
| DBS | Digital Biblical Studies |
| DJD | Discoveries of the Judaean Desert |
| *DSD* | Dead Sea Discoveries |
| ECM | *editio critica maior* |
| HOSNME | Handbook of Oriental Studies, The Near and Middle East |
| HThKAT | Herders Theologischer Kommentar zum Alten Testament |
| *HTR* | *Harvard Theological Review* |
| *HTS* | *Harvard Theological Studies* |
| *JBL* | *Journal of Biblical Literature* |
| *JEH* | *Journal of Ecclesiastical History* |
| *JIM* | *Journal of Islamic Manuscripts* |
| *JIS* | *Journal of Islamic Studies* |
| *JQR* | *Jewish Quarterly Review* |
| *JQS* | *Journal of Qur'anic Studies* |
| JSJS | Supplements to the Journal for the Study of Judaism |
| *JSNT* | *Journal for the Study of the New Testament* |
| KHC | Kurzer Hand-Commentar zum Alten Testament |
| LMB | Late Medieval Bible |
| LSTS | The Library of Second Temple Studies |
| MRAT | Medieval and Renaissance Authors and Texts |
| NIGTC | New International Greek Testament Commentary |
| NKJV | New King James Version |
| NovTSup | Supplements to Novum Testamentum |
| NTTSD | New Testament Tools, Studies, and Documents |
| *NTS* | *New Testament Studies* |
| OTE | Old Testament Essays |
| PSAT | Poetologische Studien zum Alten Testament |
| *RdQ* | *Revue de Qumran* |
| RSTC | Alfred W. Pollard et al., *A Short-Title Catalogue of Books Printed in England, Scotland, & Ireland and of English Books Printed Abroad, 1475-1640*, 2nd ed., 3 vols. (London: The Bibliographical Society, 1976) |
| SFIK | Schriften zur Frühen Islamgeschichte und zum Koran |
| StTDJ | Studies on the Texts of the Desert of Judah |
| *TuT* | M. Lembke, et al., eds. *Text und Textwert der griechischen Handschriften des Neuen Testaments. VI. Die Apokalypse*, ANTF 49 (Berlin: de Gruyter, 2017) |
| TUGAL | Texte und Untersuchungen zur Geschichte der altchristlichen Literatur |

| | |
|---|---|
| *TynBul* | *Tyndale Bulletin* |
| WBC | Word Biblical Commentaries |
| WUNT | Wissenschaftliche Untersuchungen zum Neuen Testament |
| WWMW | The Written Word: The Manuscript World |
| *ZAC* | *Zeitschrift für antikes Christentum* |

# Preface

The origins of this volume can be traced back to a symposium held at Dublin City University on the 6th September 2017. Using the "digital turn" as a starting point, the symposium focused on how and why materiality should be a more significant component of our reflection on the sacred texts of Judaism, Christianity, and Islam. The symposium was part of a larger project ("From Scrolls to Scrolling: Sacred Texts, Materiality, and Dynamic Media Cultures") that was funded by the Irish Research Council New Foundations Scheme, and I am immensely grateful to the Research Council for their support. This project included collaboration with colleagues from the University of Heidelberg and the Material Text Cultures research project; I offer sincere thanks to Professor Jan Christian Gertz, Dr Friederike Schücking-Jungblut, and Dr Anna Krauß for the hospitality that was shown during a research visit to Heidelberg. Further financial and administrative support for the symposium came from the DCU School of Theology, Philosophy, and Music, and special thanks are due to Dr Ethna Regan, Dr Garrick Allen, and Dr Jonathan Kearney for their support and encouragement. Additional financial support for the publication of this volume was provided by the DCU Faculty of Humanities and Social Sciences, for which I am very grateful.

I want to thank all of the contributors for their fine scholarship and research, as well as their patience and collegiality during the process. Finally, I offer a special note of thanks to the JCIT editors, as well as Sophie Wagenhofer at de Gruyter, for their encouragement and support in bringing this project to publication.

Bradford A. Anderson<br>
Dublin, Ireland

# Figures

## Stichographic Layout in the Dead Sea Psalms Scrolls: Observations on its Development and its Potential

Fig. 1  *Prose-layout in 11Q5, Col XXIII, 6–12.* Courtesy of The Leon Levy Dead Sea Scrolls Digital Library; Israel Antiquities Authority, photo: Shai Halevi —— **17**

Fig. 2  *A column with two separate stichs: Mas 1e, Col ii and iii.* Courtesy of The Leon Levy Dead Sea Scrolls Digital Library; Israel Antiquities Authority, photo: Shai Halevi —— **20**

## Writing the Qur'ān Between the Lines: Marginal and Interlinear Notes in Selected Qur'ān Fragments from the Museum of Islamic Art, Qatar

Fig. 1  *Bifolio MIA. 67.2007.1.* With kind permission of the museum of Islamic Art, Doha, Qatar —— **56**

Fig. 2  *MIA 2013.16. Folio 8.v.* With kind permission of the museum of Islamic Art, Doha, Qatar —— **57**

Fig. 3  *Detail of marginal reference sign. MIA 2013.16 Folio 8.v.* With kind permission of the Museum of Islamic Art, Doha, Qatar —— **58**

## From Scroll to Codex: Dynamics of Text Layout Transformation in the Hebrew Bible

Fig. 1  Layout 1: A half brick over a half brick, and a whole brick over a whole brick —— **96**
Fig. 2  Layout 2: A half brick over a whole brick, and a whole brick over a half brick —— **96**
Fig. 3  Layout 3: Divided symmetrically in two parts —— **98**
Fig. 4  Layout 4: Layout of The Song at the Sea as described by Maimonides —— **100**
Fig. 5  Layout of The Song at the Sea; LBP: Line before the poem; LAP: Line after the poem —— **104**
Fig. 6  *Paris, BnF, Hébreu 29, fol. 50r.* With permission of the Bibliothèque nationale de France —— **106**
Fig. 7  *Paris, BnF, Hébreu 24, fol. 37v.* With permission of the Bibliothèque nationale de France —— **107**
Fig. 8  *Paris, BnF, Hébreu 28, fol. 37v.* With permission of the Bibliothèque nationale de France —— **108**
Fig. 9  *MS Paris, BnF, Hébreu 19, fol. 49r.* With permission of the Bibliothèque nationale de France —— **109**
Fig. 10 *MS Paris, BnF, Hébreu 8, fol. 75v.* With permission of the Bibliothèque nationale de France —— **111**

Open Access. © 2020 Bradford A. Anderson, published by De Gruyter. This work is licensed under a Creative Commons Attribution-NonCommercial-NoDerivatives 4.0 International License.
https://doi.org/10.1515/9783110634440-205

## Memory, Performance, and Change: The Psalms' Layout in Late Medieval and Early Modern Bibles

**Fig. 1**  *Cantate Domino* – initial to Psalm 110/11 in the de Brailes Bible. Oxford, Bodleian Library, MS Lat. Bib. E. 7, fol. 191v. By permission of The Bodleian Library, University of Oxford —— 123

**Fig. 2**  Late Medieval Bible Layout – Opening of Genesis, Edinburgh University Library MS 2, fols 3v-4r. Edinburgh University Library Special Collections —— 124

**Fig. 3**  Psalm layout (detail); Oxford, Bodleian Library MS Bodl. 959. By permission of The Bodleian Library, University of Oxford —— 128

**Fig. 4**  Wycliffite Psalter (British Library MS Yates Thompson 52, fol. 96v). © The British Library Board —— 130

**Fig. 5**  Great Bible Psalms (*The Byble in Englyshe* [...]) (London: Rychard Grafton and Edward Whitchurch, April 1539), pt 3 fol. 2v. Edinburgh University Library Special Collections —— 137

**Fig. 6**  Grafton 1535 Psalms (*The Bible in Englishe* [...]) (London: Richard Grafton, 1553), fols 188v-189r). Reproduced by kind permission of the Syndics of Cambridge University Library —— 140

**Fig. 7**  Geneva Bible Psalms (*The Bible and Holy Scriptures* [...]) (Geneva: Rouland Hall, 1560), fol. 235v). Edinburgh University Library Special Collections —— 142

**Fig. 8**  Bishops' Bible Psalms (*The. holie. Bible* [London: Richarde Iugge, 1568], pt 3 p.3). Edinburgh University Library Special Collections —— 144

**Fig. 9**  Bishops' 1572 Psalms (*The. holie. Bible* [London: Richarde Iugge, 1572], pt 3 p.3). Edinburgh University Library Special Collections —— 145

## Be Your Own Scribe: Bible Journalling and the New Illuminators of the Densely-Printed Page

**Fig. 1**  Carol Belleau: Deut 11:11–14. With kind permission of the artist —— 167
**Fig. 2**  Salomé Vleeming, Psalm 112:4. With kind permission of the artist —— 171
**Fig. 3**  Salomé Vleeming, Psalm 112:4, detail of lettering. With kind permission of the artist —— 172
**Fig. 4**  Sumayah Hassan, A page of a Qur'an journal featuring Ayah 28 from Surah 21. With kind permission of the artist —— 176

## Monks, Manuscripts, Muhammad, and Digital Editions of the New Testament

**Fig. 1**  GA 2027 (Paris, BnF, gr. 491), Comment on Rev 13:18 (289r). With permission of the Bibliothèque nationale de France —— 190
**Fig. 2**  GA 1732 (Athos, Lavra, A 91) comment on Rev 13:18 (detail, lower margin). Public Domain: Library of Congress Collection of Manuscripts from the Monasteries of Mt. Athos —— 191

**Fig. 3** GA 2073 (Athos, Iviron, 273), Comment on Rev 13:18 (73v). Public Domain: Library of Congress Collection of Manuscripts from the Monasteries of Mt. Athos —— 194

**Fig. 4** GA 051 (Athos, Pantokratoros 44) comment on Rev 13:18 (15r). Public Domain: Library of Congress Collection of Manuscripts from the Monasteries of Mt. Athos —— 196

# The Qur'ānic Text from Manuscript to Digital Form: Metalinguistic Markup of Scribes and Editors

**Fig. 1** Bare consonantal skeleton with homograph base letters: *Arabic MS 11(688) f.23r, detail. John Rylands Library, The University of Manchester.* Copyright of the University of Manchester. Layer extracted by Alba Fedeli —— 226

**Fig. 2** Bare consonantal skeleton with explicit reading of possible homographs: *Arabic MS 11(688) f.23r, detail. John Rylands Library, The University of Manchester. Copyright of the University of Manchester. Layer extracted by Alba Fedeli* —— 226

**Fig. 3** Red vowel-dot level (tuḥraǧūna): *Arabic MS 11(688) f.23r, detail. John Rylands Library, The University of Manchester.* Copyright of the University of Manchester. Layer extracted by Alba Fedeli —— 226

**Fig. 4** Green vowel-dot level (taḥruǧūna): *Arabic MS 11(688) f.23r, detail. John Rylands Library, The University of Manchester.* Copyright of the University of Manchester. Layer extracted by Alba Fedeli —— 227

**Fig. 5** Red and green vowel-dot levels: *Arabic MS 11(688) f.23r, detail. John Rylands Library, The University of Manchester.* Copyright of the University of Manchester —— 227

# Tables

## Stichographic Layout in the Dead Sea Psalms Scrolls: Observations on its Development and its Potential

Table 1   Dating of the Dead Sea psalms scrolls according to paleography —— 21
Table 2   Poetic structure of Ps 118:1–4 (Masoretic text) —— 29
Table 3   Poetic structure of Ps 118:25–26 (Masoretic text) —— 30

## Monks, Manuscripts, Muhammad, and Digital Editions of the New Testament

Table 1   Chronological Distribution of Revelation's Greek Manuscripts —— 199

Bradford A. Anderson
# Introduction

## Materiality, Liminality, and the Digital Turn: The Sacred Texts of Judaism, Christianity, and Islam in Material Perspective

> [Writing] is a maiden with a pen, a harlot in print.
> – Filippo de Strata

The above quotation comes from a fifteenth century Benedictine monk who was not particularly happy with the rise of print culture – a sentiment I suspect he shared with many contemporaries.[1] Technological developments have a long history of disrupting society and culture, and changes to how texts have been produced and transmitted through the centuries have been a large part of such developments. Indeed, from scroll to codex, from manuscript to moveable print, and from book culture to digital contexts, these changes have been monumental in shaping how people communicate.

It is not surprising that sacred texts have been at the heart of many such developments; and yet, the relationship between sacred texts and the material forms in which they are embodied is a complicated one in many traditions. The traditions of Judaism, Christianity, and Islam often describe their respective sacred texts as timeless – indeed, divine – messages. An implication of this "timelessness" is that within these traditions, focus has been placed primarily on the *content* of these texts, while issues of *materiality* have often been taken for granted. From this perspective, scrolls, books, and digital devices are simply receptacles in which the text is housed. However, such thinking masks the fact that these texts are *always embodied* in particular material forms, which emerge in specific times and places, and such embodiment necessarily has implications for the use and reception of these texts.

It is often during times of change that the materiality of objects becomes apparent, and we are living through such a moment.[2] Using the digital turn as a starting point, this volume explores how the materiality of artefacts shapes our knowledge concerning the development and transmission of the sacred texts of Judaism, Christianity, and Islam, as well as the way in which people engage with,

---

[1] Quoted in Keith Houston, *The Book: A Cover-to-Cover Exploration of the Most Powerful Object of Our Time* (New York: W.W. Norton, 2016), 128–29.
[2] See Bruno Latour, *Reassembling the Social: An Introduction to Actor-Network-Theory* (Oxford: Oxford University Press, 2007).

Open Access. © 2020 Bradford A. Anderson, published by De Gruyter. This work is licensed under a Creative Commons Attribution-NonCommercial-NoDerivatives 4.0 International License.
https://doi.org/10.1515/9783110634440-001

use, and perform these texts – that is, how materiality informs our understanding of the interplay of form and function, of production and use. What might it mean to reclaim materiality as a key element of our study of religious traditions and their scriptures? What might materiality and physicality tell us about the use and function of these texts? What is the relationship between material forms of sacred texts and their use, whether for scholars, religious authorities, or lay people? And what can we learn about how and why sacred texts transition between different media forms, including the digital turn which we ourselves are witnessing? Drawing on developments that have taken root in the broader "material turn" – including material philology, book history, and research on the iconic and performative dimensions of sacred texts – this volume explores how issues of materiality factor into the production, use, and interpretation of the scriptures of Judaism, Christianity, and Islam.[3] In doing so, these essays seek to resituate materiality, along with transitions between media forms, as significant for the academic study of sacred texts within and between these religious traditions.

## 1 Key Themes in the Volume

Four key areas are highlighted in this volume. First, the essays give sustained attention to the diverse ways in which materiality has impacted the production and use of sacred texts in Judaism, Christianity, and Islam down through the centuries. From antiquity, those studying the Tanakh, the Bible, and the Qur'ān have focused their attention almost exclusively on proper understanding and interpretation of these collections. This is understandable; after all, it is the *content* of these writings that has most interested readers down through the centuries. As noted above, this has resulted in widespread understanding within these traditions of an abstract, disembodied message, with little thought given to the materiality of such texts. Perhaps unwittingly, these same presumptions have carried over into the academic study of these textual traditions, where the semantic dimension – the content and its interpretation – has received the vast majority of scholarly attention.

---

[3] On the material turn in the study of religion, see S. Brent Plate (ed.), *Key Terms in Material Religion* (London: Bloomsbury, 2015); David Morgan (ed.), *Religion and Material Culture: The Matter of* Belief (Oxford: Routledge, 2010). Examples of research exploring the materiality of sacred texts in particular can be found in Liv Ingeborg Lied and Hugo Lundhaug (eds.), *Snapshots of Evolving Traditions: Jewish and Christian Manuscript Culture, Textual Fluidity, and New Philology*, TUGAL 175 (Berlin: de Gruyter, 2017); and James W. Watts, *Iconic Books and Texts* (Sheffield: Equinox, 2015).

A result of this focus on text and meaning is that there has been relatively little attention given to issues of materiality in the academic study of sacred texts. It is only in recent years that the embodied nature of texts – including scriptures, across traditions – has begun to be taken seriously as an object of critical study. What do issues of materiality tell us about sacred texts and their use? How do elements such as paper and ink, formatting and spacing, or paratexts and reading aids inform our understanding of the transmission and use of such texts? This volume contributes to the burgeoning conversation that places issues of materiality at the forefront of our research into the production and use of sacred texts (see in particular the essays from Krauß and Schücking-Jungblut; Batovici; Hilali; Outhwaite; Poleg; and Dillon).

Second, this volume focuses not only on issues of materiality, but also explores changes and transitions between material forms, including the liminal spaces that emerge from such developments. This, too, is an area that has received limited attention in scholarship, particularly among those scholars who work closely with the texts themselves. Developments in the sociology of translation over the past several decades have made it clear that such transitions are never simply about a change from one format to another. Rather, changes and transitions often carry social and cultural elements that are important parts of such changes.[4] While such media transitions have been formative in Judaism, Christianity, and Islam, beyond the rise of the printing press, little critical attention has been given to analysing such matters. From the scroll to the codex, from manuscript to print culture, from book culture to digital texts: these transitions have shaped in significant ways the religious traditions in question, and the essays in this volume explore a number of such developments (see the contributions from Outhwaite; Poleg; del Barco; Allen; Fedeli; Suit; and Anderson).

Third, this project brings issues of materiality and the digital turn into conversation with one another. Scholars of sacred texts have in recent years begun to shift their attention to issues of materiality, with significant results.[5] Further, there is a growing (if disparate) body of literature on sacred texts and digital culture.[6] Nevertheless, there has been little research done to date – theoretical or otherwise – that attempts to bring these issues together, reflecting on digital texts

---

[4] See, e.g., Bruno Latour, "On Technical Mediation," *Common Knowledge* 3/2 (1994): 29–64; Jonathan Westin, "Loss of Culture: New Media Forms and the Translation from Analogue to Digital Books," *Convergence: The International Journal of Research into New Media Technologies* 19/2 (2012): 129–40.

[5] A fine example is David Stern, *The Jewish Bible: A Material History* (Seattle: University of Washington Press, 2017).

[6] Jeffrey S. Siker, *Liquid Scripture: The Bible in a Digital World* (Minneapolis: Fortress, 2017).

as new instantiations of materiality in which sacred texts are encountered.[7] What issues are raised when we begin to think about digital texts as new forms of materiality? What is lost or gained in such usage? There is much ground still to be ploughed in this area of enquiry, and a number of essays in the present volume do important work on this very subject (see essays from Allen; Fedeli; Mann; Suit; Anderson).

Finally, by exploring the texts of Judaism, Christianity, and Islam in light of materiality, this volume aims to contribute in a unique manner to the ongoing discussion of these traditions and the interrelationships between them. Much work has been done in recent decades on points of convergence and divergence within and among Judaism, Christianity, and Islam.[8] Indeed, this has included important research on the textual traditions of these religions.[9] However, a lacuna in this developing area of study is how the *materiality* of the texts which are sacred to these traditions might inform our understanding of the interrelationship of the traditions – whether formal or informal, intentional or accidental. Again, essays in this collection make important contributions in this regard, suggesting that the traditions in question react, borrow, respond, or indirectly engage with one another around matters of materiality (Outhwaite; Dillon; Allen; Anderson).

## 2 Structure and Content of the Volume

This volume offers a concise entry point to the theme of sacred texts and materiality, and it does so with a broad chronological scope – moving from ancient and medieval contexts to concerns of the contemporary, digital world. Two sections serve to structure the volume: the first section – Sacred Texts and Material Contexts – explores issues such as the relationship of materiality and form, transitions between material forms, paratextual elements, and transmission and use of sacred texts. The second section – Sacred Texts and the Digital Turn – then analyses various aspects related to sacred texts and the contemporary world, including scholarship and the digital humanities, textual authority in the digital age, and socio-cultural elements in the transition from analogue to digital forms.

---

[7] See, recently, Claire Clivaz's work, which touches on these issues: *Ecritures digitales. Digital writing, Digital Scriptures*, DBS 4 (Leiden: Brill, 2019).
[8] Along with volumes in the JCIT series (de Gruyter), see, e.g., Moshe Blidstein, Adam J. Silverstein, and Guy G. Stroumsa, *The Oxford Handbook of the Abrahamic Religions* (Oxford: Oxford University Press, 2015).
[9] F.E. Peters, *The Voice, the Word, the Books: The Sacred Scripture of the Jews, Christians, and Muslims* (Princeton: Princeton University Press, 2007).

Together these essays explore significant questions related to the materiality of sacred texts in the traditions of Judaism, Christianity, and Islam, while also highlighting transitions between various media cultures.

Part One (Sacred Texts and Material Contexts) focuses on questions of materiality, particularly in manuscript and print culture. This section begins with three essays that explore some of the earliest forms of the Jewish, Christian, and Muslim scriptures.

The first contribution is an essay from Anna Krauß and Friederike Schücking-Jungblut exploring the layout of poetic units in the Dead Sea Psalms scrolls ("Stichographic Layout in the Dead Sea Psalms Scrolls: Observations on its Development and its Potential"). Exploring some of the most ancient extant material forms of the Jewish Scriptures, Krauß and Schücking-Jungblut demonstrate how the development of the stichographic layout in certain Psalms – the arrangement of poetical units in stylized lines – can help us better understand how these texts were used and understood in ancient Judaism. As they note,

> material aspects as well as the structure and layout of the writing, helps us to understand the role of text-bearing artefacts as agents in a textual community. In the transition from an oral to a textual culture, texts are reliant on their material embodiment to be preserved. The modes in which a text is recited influences its layout on written artefacts and reciprocally the layout of a written text predetermines its reading, reciting, and interpretation (31–32).

In the second chapter, Dan Batovici explores the complex question of whether or not, and in what way, paratexts functioned as "Reading Aids in Early Christian Papyri". In particular, Batovici complicates the idea that such paratextual features – including *paragraphi*, vacant end lines, *ekthesis*, *diairesis*, breathings and accents, titles and subtitles, enlarged first letter of verse or chapter, spaces, and acute-like text division marker or miscellaneous strokes – can be used to identify a text meant for public or private use. In doing so, Batovici highlights the broader implications of such analysis: "not only do we lack the means of establishing whether a papyrus was meant for public or private reading in the absence of clear testimonies in this sense (e.g. an explicit colophon), but when we draw too clear-cut a distinction between public and private papyri, we run the risk of oversimplifying the reading culture of early and late-antique Christianity" (47–48).

The third chapter turns our attention to Islam, as Asma Hilali explores material aspects of early Islamic fragments and manuscripts ("Writing the Qurʾān Between the Lines: Marginal and Interlinear Notes in Selected Qurʾān Fragments from the Museum of Islamic Art, Qatar"). Annotations within early Qurʾānic manuscripts are rare and unsystematic, as is evidenced by examples of emendations written between the lines as well as in the margins. Such examples, however, are enlightening, in that they point to the transmission of the textual tradition, and may even give us a glimpse of "the first steps towards the scholastic transmission tradition which would later emerge" in Islam (59–60).

The next several chapters in this section begin to explore transitions between material forms, and the material implications of such developments. Ben Outhwaite offers an important exploration of "The Sefer Torah and Jewish Orthodoxy in the Islamic Middle Ages". Drawing on evidence from the Cairo Genizah and other sources, Outhwaite examines the diverse factors that led to the codex being adopted within Judaism. Key issues include the changing conditions of the Jewish community under Islamic rule, and the need for different Jewish groups – Rabbanite and Qaraite, Palestinian and Babylonian – to clearly differentiate themselves from one another.

Javier del Barco's essay continues the discussion regarding the shift from scroll to codex in Judaism ("From Scroll to Codex: Dynamics of Text-Layout Transformations in the Hebrew Bible"). Here del Barco focuses on the implications for the text-layout of the Hebrew Bible in this transition. He examines regulations used for copying Torah scrolls, and how these same guidelines were used (even if irregularly) in the new format of the biblical codex. These textual dynamics, del Barco suggests, have much to tell us about the functional dimensions of these formats, as well as the relationship between scroll and codex after the emergence of the latter.

Eyal Poleg's contribution offers another perspective on text-layout, focusing in particular on the layout of the Psalms in late medieval and early modern Bibles ("Memory, Performance, and Change: The Psalms' Layout in Late Medieval and Early Modern Bibles"). From late medieval pandects to early modern mass-printed books, Poleg demonstrates that new, innovative layouts and revisions were often introduced, only to be rolled back in subsequent editions in favour of traditional divisions, translations, and liturgical elements related to the Psalms. He notes that such "transformations reveal the power of performance and mnemonics" (147), as both clergy and laity encountered and recounted the psalms primarily in liturgical contexts. "Performance remained key to the way the Psalms were presented and recalled" (148).

The final chapter in this section brings us forward to the contemporary period, and hints at a number of issues to be addressed in Part Two of the volume. Nevertheless, Amanda Dillon's essay demonstrates that the materiality of print culture continues to be a powerful force in the contemporary use of sacred texts, and that there is significant continuity between past and present in how users and readers engage with these texts ("Be Your Own Scribe: Bible Journalling and the New Illuminators of the Densely-Printed Page"). Dillon explores a phenomenon known as Bible journalling, an "active and creative engagement with the material books of the Bible," where readers "draw and make typographic designs directly into their

Bibles, illustrating verses and passages that have particular resonance for them" (153). Analysing several examples through the lens of social semiotics, Dillon explores how gender, agency, and materiality all play a significant role in Bible journalling – indeed, investing the Bible "with even greater materiality" (177).

The essays in Part Two of the volume focus on "Sacred Texts and the Digital Turn". This section begins with two chapters that focus on the significant potential of digital scholarship for the academic study of sacred texts.

In his essay "Monks, Manuscripts, Muhammad, and Digital Editions of the New Testament" (winner of the Society of Biblical Literature's 2018 Paul J. Achtemeier Award for New Testament Scholarship), Garrick Allen investigates how the digital turn can help us reconceptualise critical editions. Using Revelation 13 and the number of the beast as a test case, he explores paratexts and interpretive traditions regarding this famous passage that are embedded in the manuscript traditions, but which are ignored by the critical editions. Allen demonstrates how digital critical editions can account for a greater number of factors, including the materiality of manuscripts, and thus can help us better reflect on the complex relationships between textual production, transmission, exegesis, and reception history.

Alba Fedeli's contribution turns our attention to the Qur'ān ("The Qur'ānic Text from Manuscript to Digital Form: Metalinguistic Markup of Scribes and Editors"). Fedeli begins by exploring how early scribes and redactors dealt with the ambiguity of the Arabic script in early Qur'ānic manuscripts of the seventh to tenth centuries CE, including the introduction of vowel systems and other markers. What emerged was a complex text that embodies various readings, and allows for diverse interpretations. The process of digital editing and coding that has developed in recent decades allows scholars to unravel the multi-layered nature of such manuscripts. Further, Fedeli suggests that the markup systems employed in digital scholarship, which are themselves interpretive, have much in common with the strategies used by ancient scribes and editors, which can also be understood as a form of markup on the text. Taken together, we see how issues of materiality are at the centre of textual research, whether the focus is on ancient manuscripts or digital encoding.

In "Paratexts and the Hermeneutics of Digital Bibles", Joshua Mann takes us into the world of contemporary readers of digital scriptures. Following initial reflections on paratextuality and materiality, Mann investigates the YouVersion Bible App, perhaps the most well known and most widely used digital Bible. Mann outlines how paratextual features which often go unnoticed are in fact key elements in the user's engagement with the digital Bible. While digital Bibles lack a binding cover or consecutive pagination that give coherence to the "canonical" collection, other elements such as dropdown menus and versification point to continuity with printed Bibles and a uniform text. However, Mann highlights how digital Bibles have their own unique paratexual elements as well, including social features (connections to social media), terms of use, data collection, a "menu bar" for various uses, and notifications and alerts. What emerges is a picture of how digital texts and paratexts are shaping how users engage with the Bible in both overt and less overt ways.

The penultimate chapter from Natalia Suit likewise focuses on contemporary readers of sacred texts, in this instance the Qur'ān ("Virtual Qur'ān: Authenticity, Authority, and Ayat in Bytes"). Suit offers an ethnographic account of how digital technology, particularly as related to the Qur'ān, is shaping the religious practise of Muslims in Egypt. New electronic forms of the Qur'ān have raised debates about the authority of the text, while also revealing ways in which digital texts can have an impact on gendered engagement with the Qur'ān, particularly around issues of ritual purity. Suit highlights how the digital turn is not a dematerialization of the sacred text, but in fact is opening up new avenues for reflection on materiality.

Bradford Anderson's essay concludes the volume with an exploration of "Sacred Texts in a Digital Age: Reflecting on Materiality, Digital Culture, and the Functional Dimensions of Scriptures in Judaism, Christianity, and Islam". Drawing on the work of James Watts, Anderson explores how the digital turn is impacting the semantic and iconic use of sacred texts in diverse ways. Examples from the media and elsewhere demonstrate that the semantic dimension of scriptural use (content, reading, and interpretation) has been adapted to digital contexts with much greater ease than that of iconicity, which is often bound up with the material form of the codex (swearing of oaths, talismanic properties, book burning, and so on). The essay concludes with some theoretical reflections that help account for the present state of affairs, as well as the coexistence of these material forms.

## 3 Areas for Further Research

A number of significant themes recur in the essays here collected, and point to areas where there is ample room for further reflection and research. The relationship between the materiality of texts (from layout, to paratexts, to ritual purity) and the religious, social, and cultural factors at work in the background of such texts is highlighted in several of the chapters – from the ancient community at Qumran, to medieval monks in Greece, to contemporary Muslims in Egypt (see the essays from Krauß and Schücking-Jungblut; Batovici; Outhwaite; del Barco;

Poleg; Dillon; Suit; Anderson). There is much more work to be done in exploring how the materiality of sacred texts is bound up with social and cultural factors, across the religious traditions in question. Such examples are also a reminder that form and function are intimately connected, and that if we pay close attention only to the semantic dimension of these texts, we run the risk of missing out on significant data related to the production, use, and reception of these scriptures.

Another thread woven throughout the volume is the role and place of paratexts (see Batovici; Hilali; Poleg; Dillon; Allen; Fedeli; Mann). While paratextual elements have begun to receive greater attention in recent years, due in large part to the work of Genette and others,[10] paratexts remain a largely untapped resource for reflection on the use and transmission of sacred texts.[11] Often ignored in favour of the "main" text, paratexts offer a window into the social life of scriptures – their performance, interpretation, and reception. As a number of contributors point out, we now have the capacity to consider paratextual features as part of our standard engagement with the texts and traditions, and we would be wise to heed this call for more robust engagement with such features.

A more subtle theme that finds expression in this volume is the way in which materiality can alert us to the accessibility of sacred texts. Of particular note in this regard are the essays from Dillon and Suit, which highlight the ways in which new material expressions – in this case Bible journalling and digital texts – allow for women to engage with and to have more agency in their use of sacred texts. Further research is needed on how issues of materiality can highlight the ways in which texts are made accessible (or not) to various groups of people.

Finally, these essays demonstrate how materiality – and transitions between material forms – has been a key element in how Judaism, Christianity, and Islam have developed in relationship to one another. While the interplay between scroll and codex, and the socio-cultural issues at work in the adoption or amplification of these forms is the most obvious example of such interaction (see Outhwaite, del Barco, Fedeli), other forms of engagement are also present. These include comparison of the ways in which texts are organised for reading (Batovici), adoption of new techniques gleaned from online communities (Dillon), interpretive traditions that reflect engagement with or response to other traditions (Allen), and the iconic use of scriptures (such as desecration) that reflects larger religious and socio-cultural factors that include but are not limited to religious dimensions

---

[10] Gérard Genette, *Paratexts: Thresholds of Interpretation*, trans. Jane E. Lewin, (Cambridge: Cambridge University Press, 1997).
[11] Martin Wallraff and Patrick Andrist, "Paratexts of the Bible: A New Research Project on Greek Textual Transmission," *Early Christianity* 6 (2015): 237–43.

(Anderson). Further research on how the materiality of sacred texts has played a role in the engagement within and between the traditions of Judaism, Christianity, and Islam will no doubt shed important light on intra- and inter-religious engagement, from antiquity to the present day.

My hope is that this volume will draw attention to the significant role which materiality has played – and continues to play – in the production, use, and reception of the sacred texts of Judaism, Christianity, and Islam. Further, I hope it will inspire continued reflection on materiality, transitions, and liminality within and between these religious traditions, particularly as we witness the continued emergence of digital culture.

## Bibliography

Blidstein, Moshe, Adam J. Silverstein, and Guy G. Stroumsa. *The Oxford Handbook of the Abrahamic Religions*. Oxford: Oxford University Press, 2015.

Clivaz, Claire. *Ecritures digitales. Digital writing, Digital Scriptures*. DBS 4. Leiden: Brill, 2019.

Genette, Gérard. *Paratexts: Thresholds of Interpretation*. Trans. Jane E. Lewin. Cambridge: Cambridge University Press, 1997.

Houston, Keith. *The Book: A Cover-to-Cover Exploration of the Most Powerful Object of Our Time*. New York: W.W. Norton, 2016.

Latour, Bruno. *Reassembling the Social: An Introduction to Actor-Network-Theory*. Oxford: Oxford University Press, 2007.

Latour, Bruno. "On Technical Mediation." *Common Knowledge* 3/2 (1994): 29–64.

Lied, Liv Ingeborg, and Hugo Lundhaug, eds. *Snapshots of Evolving Traditions: Jewish and Christian Manuscript Culture, Textual Fluidity, and New Philology*. TUGAL 175. Berlin: de Gruyter, 2017.

Morgan, David, ed. *Religion and Material Culture: The Matter of Belief*. Oxford: Routledge, 2010.

Peters, F.E. *The Voice, the Word, the Books: The Sacred Scripture of the Jews, Christians, and Muslims*. Princeton: Princeton University Press, 2007.

Plate, S. Brent, ed. *Key Terms in Material Religion*. London: Bloomsbury, 2015.

Siker, Jeffrey S. *Liquid Scripture: The Bible in a Digital World*. Minneapolis: Fortress, 2017.

Stern, David. *The Jewish Bible: A Material History*. Seattle: University of Washington Press, 2017.

Wallraff, Martin, and Patrick Andrist. "Paratexts of the Bible: A New Research Project on Greek Textual Transmission." *Early Christianity* 6 (2015): 237–43.

Watts, James W. *Iconic Books and Texts*. Sheffield: Equinox, 2015.

Westin, Jonathan. "Loss of Culture: New Media Forms and the Translation from Analogue to Digital Books." *Convergence: The International Journal of Research into New Media Technologies* 19/2 (2012): 129–40.

# I  Sacred Texts and Material Contexts

Anna Krauß and Friederike Schücking-Jungblut
# Stichographic Layout in the Dead Sea Psalms Scrolls: Observations on its Development and its Potential

## 1 Introduction

In cultures where means of mass production for written texts were (or are) unknown, unavailable, or uncommon, every script-bearing artifact is in a way unique in realizing the combination of text, writing, and material. Therefore – as has become increasingly acknowledged since the "material turn" within the humanities and social sciences – pre-modern artifacts showing writing should not just be taken as witnesses of the respective text, but as agents in a textual culture. In consequence, interpretation cannot just focus on the content, but has to consider the material features of a script-bearing artifact as well.[1] By combining both aspects, script-bearing artifacts are perceived as the outcome of an artisanal process of production, revealing much more than just the texts.

As part of a broader research project on the writing practices in the Second Temple Period of Ancient Israel, concretely of those scrolls containing "biblical"[2] psalms, the present article deals with one aspect that might be relevant to detect indications of intended or actual practices of reception connected to the psalms manuscripts. Since most – probably all – of the texts collected in the psalms

---

**1** Cf. e.g. Markus Hilgert, "Materiale Textkulturen: Textbasierte historische Kulturwissenschaften nach dem *material culture turn*," in *Materialität: Herausforderungen für die Sozial- und Kulturwissenschaften*, ed. Herbert Kalthoff, Torsten Cress and Tobias Röhl (Paderborn: Fink, 2016): 255–56.
**2** The term "biblical" is anachronistic since an authoritative (Hebrew or Christian) Bible did not exist when the manuscripts were written. Furthermore, some of the psalms scrolls dealt with in this article contain also both apocryphal and formerly unknown compositions. Thus, when the term "biblical" psalms is used, it is referring to psalms that are part of the (later) canonical Psalter. The identification of scrolls which contain both "biblical" and other compositions as "biblical psalms scrolls" is used to distinguish these scrolls from those manuscripts which contain only apocryphal psalms compositions.

**Note:** This article originates from the Heidelberg Collaborative Research Center 933 "Material Text Cultures," sub-project C02, UP 2 "Between Literature and Liturgy – Pragmatics and Practices of Reception of Poetic and Liturgical Writings from the Judean Desert" (2015–2019). The CRC is funded by the German Research Foundation (GRF/DFG).

Open Access. © 2020 Anna Krauß, Friederike Schücking-Jungblut, published by De Gruyter. This work is licensed under a Creative Commons Attribution-NonCommercial-NoDerivatives 4.0 International License.
https://doi.org/10.1515/9783110634440-002

scrolls from the Judean Desert are older than the writing in the extant manuscripts, the production of the concrete script-bearing artifact can already be interpreted as an act of reception and can be analyzed as such. Therefore, the layout of a psalms scroll, dealt with in the following, promises insights both into how the scribes of a certain manuscript understood the texts copied and for what use their scroll was intended. Thus, in the following, a short overview on the materiality and the layout features of the psalms manuscripts from the Judean Desert will be given. After that, we will concentrate on one special feature, the stichographic layout, and analyze its chronological development in a case study on Ps 119 and the potential of its use by the example of Ps 118.

## 2 Preliminary Remarks on the Format of the Psalms Scrolls

The scrolls that are generally referred to as the Dead Sea Psalms Scrolls are in fact a most heterogeneous corpus both in format and content. From the thirty-nine scrolls listed in the index of the major edition of the scrolls (Discoveries of the Judean Desert XXXIX),[3] sixteen are too fragmentary to decide on whether they were real psalms scrolls or just citing a passage from a psalm in a different context.[4] With the exception of 1Q10,[5] these fragments are not part of the following overview and analyses. 1Q10 remains part of this study because its special layout is taken as an indication that this manuscript represents indeed a psalms manuscript.

All psalms manuscripts from the Judean Desert are written on animal skins.[6] The horizontal scrolls are usually made from several sheets of prepared skin sewn together. Their size varies a great deal according to both their height and

---

[3] Emanuel Tov, ed., *The Texts from the Judaean Desert: Indices and an Introduction to the Discoveries of the Judaean Desert Series*, DJD 39 (Oxford: Clarendon, 2002), 173f., 181.
[4] Cf. Eva Jain, *Psalmen oder Psalter? Materielle Rekonstruktion und inhaltliche Untersuchung der Psalmenhandschriften aus der Wüste Juda*, StTDJ 109 (Leiden: Brill, 2014), 217. In addition to the fifteen scrolls listed there, 11Q9 must be assigned to this group, as well, since its only extant fragment is very small and contains just a few hardly readable letters.
[5] The designation of the scrolls in this essay follows the numerical nomenclature as presented in DJD 39.
[6] Cf. Emanuel Tov, *Scribal Practices and Approaches Reflected in the Texts Found in the Judean Desert*, StTDJ 54 (Leiden: Brill, 2004), 32.
The broad discussion on whether it is more suitable to call the material used for the scrolls either "leather" or "parchment" and the related question of which scrolls are made of either the one or the other material, can be left aside for the purposes of this article.

the length of a scroll – and in most cases it can only be partially reconstructed because of the fragmentary state of the scrolls. The scrolls also vary substantially in their content. Some of them, e.g. 5/6Hev 1b, might have contained the psalms 1–150 in the arrangement that we know from the Hebrew Bible. Most, however, comprise only a portion of this psalter. Some arrange the psalms in a different way and again some of these scrolls also add other "biblical" and apocryphal material. The writing – in all cases Hebrew – was carried out with a carbonaceous black ink.[7] In addition, many of the scrolls show horizontal and vertical rulings applied by a sharp instrument ("dry-point-rulings") as a preparation to achieve rather constant columns and lines. However, the concrete sizes of columns and lines vary both within one document and between the individual manuscripts. The type and size of the script also differs from scroll to scroll. The script is often the only possible source to pinpoint the date of inscription for the respective manuscripts. Based on this paleographical dating, it can be shown that psalms manuscripts were produced throughout the timespan covered by the Judean Desert manuscripts. The oldest psalms manuscript, 4Q83, is dated to ca. 150 BCE, the youngest manuscripts (e.g. 4Q85 and 5/6Hev 1b) were most likely inscribed during the second half of the first century CE.

## 3 The Layout of the Psalms Scrolls

Layout can be understood as the "way in which text or pictures are set out on a page."[8] It is an umbrella term that covers all kinds of aspects influencing the layout of a thing – in this case: an inscribed object. Consider for example the decisive role of a manuscript's format with regard to its layout. A codex with separate sheets offers different possibilities for the arrangement of a text and pictures than a vertically inscribed scroll that may even consist of several layers of sheets. This kind of scroll, again, allows for a different layout than horizontally inscribed scrolls like the Dead Sea Scrolls.

The layout can also hint towards modes of reception connected with the respective scroll as in the following examples from the layout features in the Dead Sea psalms scrolls.

---

[7] Cf. Yoram Nir-El and Magen Broshi, "The Black Ink of the Qumran Scrolls," *DSD* 3 (1996): 157–67.
[8] Oxford Living Dictionaries: English, consulted online on 23 May 2018 (https://en.oxforddictionaries.com/definition/layout).

1) The aforementioned format of the individual scrolls, i.e. their physical dimensions which determine the surface that can be written on, can be a first indicator towards the practicability of a scroll.
2) The dimensions of the columns, the number of lines per column, and the question whether the columns and lines were marked by rulings, show the intensity of planning of a scroll. Furthermore, the relation between the rulings, the format of a scroll (e.g. narrower columns towards the end of a sheet), and the textual layout are instructive.
3) The letter size and its connection to the size of the scroll, the columns, and the length of lines can be interpreted as clues for the intended use of a scroll.
4) The arrangement of the text on the scroll, i.e. the representation of the poetical structure of a text in the layout, the marking of individual compositions/psalms, paragraphs, and superscriptions can be evaluated as to their influence on reception.

In the following, the focus will be solely on the representation of the psalms' poetical structure in the layout of the "biblical psalms scrolls" and the possible impacts of a special layout on the reception of psalms.

## 3.1 Different Forms of Layout in the Dead Sea Psalms Scrolls

Contemporary Bible translations almost invariably format poetic texts in some form of structure that sets them apart from prose. Readers of the text today would be forgiven for assuming that such structural formatting has always been a part of the biblical text – but this is not the case. The textual arrangement of "biblical" psalms in the Dead Sea Scrolls varies a great deal, both from one scroll to another, and even within a scroll. The differences show how the scribes were able to represent the poetical structure of psalms in several ways.[9]

---

[9] It is of course correct to say "that taxonomy doesn't tell the full story" (Shem Miller, "Multiformity of Stichographic Systems in the Dead Sea Scrolls," *RdQ* 29 [2017], 243) and that it is necessary to keep an open mind about the living oral culture behind liturgical and poetic texts (ibid., 244f.). However, systematizing a phenomenon like the heterogeneous layout of the Dead Sea psalms scrolls is helpful to gain an overview over the actual range of possibilities, their similarities and differences. Furthermore, it does not exclude one from then zooming into the details and take those aspects of scribal habits and practices into account that are not covered by a systematization. Thus, in the following the textual arrangement will be classified, knowing that this is merely the foreword to the tale of the full story. Another taxonomy can be found in: Emanuel Tov, "The Background of the Stichometric Arrangements of Poetry in the Judean Desert Scrolls," in *Prayer and Poetry in the Dead Sea Scrolls and Related Literature. Essays in Honor of Eileen*

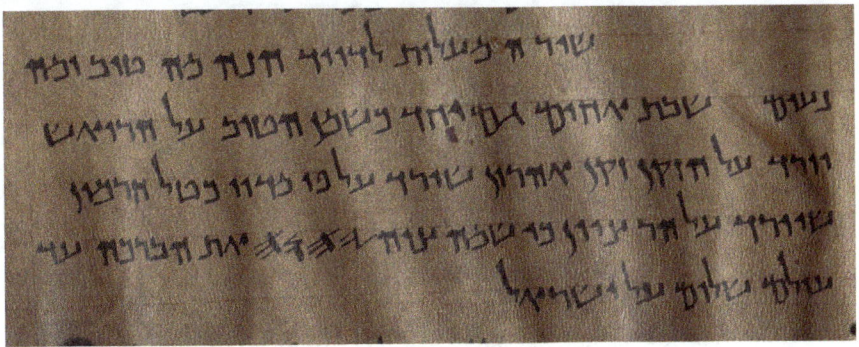

**Fig. 1:** *Prose-layout in 11Q5, Col XXIII, 6–12.* Courtesy of The Leon Levy Dead Sea Scrolls Digital Library; Israel Antiquities Authority, photo: Shai Halevi.

1) In most cases, the scribes did not incorporate the poetical structure of the psalms into the layout. This will be called the "prose-layout" in the following, since the psalms are represented like prose texts without any accentuation of their poetical structure (see Fig. 1). Such a designation, however, is disputed, both since the layout of prose texts may vary and since generally prose should be distinguished from poetry. Yet, other terms are just as much or even more problematic, like e.g. *scriptio continua*. This term does not describe the same phenomenon, because it does not only neglect sense units but also the grouping of single letters to form a word.[10] These considerations are more than mere hair-splitting because most of the "biblical psalms scrolls" – and all the apocryphal[11] – are written in such a way.[12] A fitting description of this phenomenon is, therefore, necessary.

---

*Schuller on the Occasion of Her 65th Birthday*, StTDJ 98, ed. Jeremy Penner, Ken M. Penner and Cecilia Wassen (Leiden: Brill, 2012): 415–17.

**10** Cf. Tiziano Dorandi, "Punctuation I. Greek," in *Brill's New Pauly*, ed. Hubert Cancik, Helmuth Schneider and Christine F. Salazar (2006), consulted online on 23 May 2018 (http://dx.doi.org/10.1163/1574-9347_bnp_e702150).

**11** Cf. Tov, "The Background of the Stichometric Arrangements," 410 with footnote 5.

**12** "Prose-layout" is used exclusively in the following scrolls: 4Q83; 4Q87; 4Q88; 4Q92; 4Q94; 4Q95; 4Q98; 4Q98a; 11Q7; 11Q8. In some other scrolls, the "prose-layout" is predominant with just one psalm each in a stichographic arrangement: 4Q86 (Ps 104); 11Q5 (Ps 119); 11Q6 (Ps 119).

2) When the poetical structure *is* represented in the layout, different strategies are chosen to arrange the text, mainly in order to highlight the verses or stichs[13]:
   a) Once, in Mas 1f, the single stichs are separated by a short *vacat*[14] but the length of the line is not taken into account. Thus, the single lines do not start with a new stich or verse each. This layout seems to be a hybrid of "prose-" and stichographic layout.
   b) Each line begins with a new verse. This type of stichographic layout can be subdivided into such manuscripts that
      a. usually separate the stichs of a verse by a short *vacat*[15] and those that
      b. generally do not separate the single stichs from each other.[16]
   c) Several manuscripts arrange the texts with just one stich per line.[17]

Four conclusions can be drawn from this statistical overview:

Firstly, it must be noted that the textual arrangement of psalms can change within a scroll and even within a single psalm. This includes alterations both from the "prose-layout" to a stichographic arrangement and from a one-verse-

---

[13] A note on the terminology used in this article: A verse of Hebrew poetry can be divided into smaller parts which are called stichs (singular: stich), here. A verse usually consists of two stichs (*bistichon*). Sometimes, a verse contains three stichs (*tristichon*).

[14] This is a blank space of varying length but larger than the usual space between words.

[15] 1Q10 (Ps 119); 4Q85; 5Q5 (Ps 119); 11Q6 (Ps 119); Mas 1e; 5/6Hev 1b. Concerning 1Q10, Tov finds only Ps 119 to have a stichographic layout ("The Background of the Stichometric Arrangements," 411). This is disputed by Miller, who suggests a stichographic arrangement of all psalms of this scroll ("Multiformity of Stichographic Systems," 227f.). See also Dominique Barthélemy and Józef T. Milik, eds., *Qumran Cave 1*, DJD 1 (Oxford: Clarendon, 1955), 69; Peter Flint, *The Dead Sea Psalms Scrolls and the Book of Psalms*, StTDJ 17 (Leiden: Brill, 1997), 31; Armin Lange, *Handbuch der Textfunde vom Toten Meer 1: Die Handschriften biblischer Bücher von Qumran und den anderen Fundorten* (Tübingen: Mohr Siebeck, 2009), 374. Since only the stichographic arrangement of Ps 119 can be identified with certainty, the other psalms of this scroll will not be included in this survey. In 4Q85 some of the verses are longer than the columns provided and continue in the following line. In consequence, the next verse begins in the middle of that line. Nevertheless, the attempt for stichographic layout is clearly visible (see especially 4Q85, fragment 15ii, 7–10).

[16] 4Q84 (Ps 118:1–24); 4Q89 (Ps 119; an interesting case of a scribe ignoring the given layout: instead of writing one stanza per column as indicated by the eight ruled lines per column, the scribe inserts a blank line after each stanza, so that the blank line "wanders" through the columns, in each column one line below the blank line of the preceding column and jumping back to the top line once it has wandered through eight columns); 4Q90 (Ps 119); 11Q5 (Ps 119).

[17] 4Q84 (except Ps 118:1–24); 4Q86 (Ps 104:11ff.); 4Q93 (Ps 104).

per-line to a one-stich-per-line format. The former phenomenon occurs only in connection with Ps 104 and 119,[18] the latter just once.[19]

Secondly, it seems that the choice for a stichographic arrangement of the psalms is made in order to highlight the structure of the text. The visualization of smaller sense units may facilitate the reader's understanding of the psalm.[20] However, at least in one instance, it can be assumed that the layout's aesthetic appeal is more important than the accentuation of the textual structure. Mas 1e is arranged according to the type 2ba-layout, that is: in columns with two separated stichs per line (see Fig. 2). Even when a tristichon occurs, the scribe does not deviate from this strategy.[21] Thus, not every verse begins in a new line but rather shares a line with another verse after every second verse with three stichs. This strict arrangement of columns with two stichs per line does still structure the text in smaller sense units but the larger units – that is: verses – are not visualized through this kind of arrangement. Thus, it seems plausible that in this case the aesthetical appeal of the arrangement is more important to the scribe – or its possible *Vorlage* – than the visualization of the textual structure.

Thirdly, scribes had to adapt to the given space of a line and they did so in different ways, as can be seen in the comparison of Mas 1e with 4Q85.[22] And finally, two psalms seem to be favoured when it comes to a stichographic arrangement of the text.[23] Not only are Ps 104 and 119 among the most prevalent psalms on the psalms scrolls, they can also be written in a special layout while all other psalms on the scroll follow the "prose layout". Psalm 104[24] can be associated with layout type 2c (one stich per line), since it is always arranged in that way when written stichographically. This is the case on the scrolls 4Q93 and 4Q86. The latter scroll witnesses a surprising change from the "prose-layout" to the layout type 2c

---

**18** 4Q86, column III (Ps 104:11); 11Q5, columns VI–XIV (Ps 119); 11Q6, fragment 2 (Ps 119).
**19** 4Q84, columns XXXIV–XXXV (Ps 118:1–24), see below 5.3.
**20** It should be noted that the arrangement in text units according to the stichographic structure of the psalms is already an interpretation of the text's content. Therefore, it is also possible to state that the reader's understanding of the text is influenced by the textual arrangement in a certain way.
**21** A similar phenomenon can be seen in 4Q85, see above footnote 15. This may point to a common practice concerning tristicha in a text arranged according to stichs (separated by short *vacats*). 4Q85 does not, however, seem to be following the pattern as strictly as Mas 1e; see 4Q85, fragment 15iii, 4.
**22** See above, footnotes 15 and 21.
**23** In the case of Ps 104 this connection to stichographic layout may have faded over the course of time. See the chronology, below 3.2.
**24** Preserved on 4Q86, 4Q87, 4Q93, and 11Q5 (as well as on 2Q14 which, however, cannot safely be reconstructed as a proper psalms scroll).

**Fig. 2:** *A column with two separate stichs: Mas 1e, Col ii and iii.* Courtesy of The Leon Levy Dead Sea Scrolls Digital Library; Israel Antiquities Authority, photo: Shai Halevi.

starting with Ps 104:11 (column III). All other scrolls containing Ps 104 arrange this psalm in the "prose-format".[25] Even more striking is the case of Ps 119. No other psalm is preserved by the scrolls as often as this one.[26] More importantly, this psalm is *always* arranged stichographically even when all other psalms on the scroll are not written in a special layout.[27] Furthermore, there is only one scroll, 4Q89, that *certainly* contained just one psalm, and this is Ps 119. It does not come as a surprise that a highly structured text like Ps 119 is arranged according to the type 2b-layout.[28] It is an alphabetic acrostic of 22 stanzas, containing 8 verses each. Other highly structured psalms, however, e.g. Ps 136 or further

---

**25** Jain claims that Ps 104 was always arranged stichographically (*Psalmen oder Psalter?*, 126). This, however, is not correct, since the material evidence for 4Q87, fragments 14–16, and 11Q5, fragment E displays a non-stichographically arranged Ps 104.
**26** At least parts of the psalm are extant on six scrolls, namely: 1Q10; 4Q89; 4Q90; 5Q5; 11Q5; and 11Q6.
**27** See 11Q5 and 11Q6.
**28** Apart from 11Q6 (2ba) always according to the type 2bb.

acrostics like Ps 112, are usually written in the "prose-layout." Such psalms are only arranged in a stichographic layout when the same applies to *all* psalms on the respective scroll.[29] Nowhere are they treated differently from other psalms of the same scroll. Psalm 119, though, seems to be an exception to the rule that psalms (both acrostics and others) are usually written in a "prose-layout" but *can also* be arranged in a special layout.

After this systematic overview on the layout of the psalms manuscripts, the chronology of the psalms scrolls should be taken into account. Psalm 119 will be discussed in more detail in the first case study below.

## 3.2 A Chronology of Special Layouts

**Table 1:** Dating of the Dead Sea psalms scrolls according to paleography.

| Paleographical Dating | Manuscript |
| --- | --- |
| *2nd century BCE* | |
| 1st half 2nd century BCE | |
| mid-2nd century BCE | 4Q83 |
| 2nd half 2nd century BCE | |
| *1st century BCE* | |
| without closer dating | 4Q92 |
| 1st half 1st century BCE | |
| mid-1st century BCE | 4Q86, 4Q88 |
| 2nd half 1st century BCE | 4Q93, 4Q94, 4Q95, Mas 1f |
| "Herodian" (30 BCE to 70 CE) | 4Q90, 4Q98a |
| *1st century CE* | |
| without closer dating | 1Q11, 4Q98, 5Q5 |
| 1st half 1st century CE | 11Q5, 11Q6, 11Q7, Mas 1e |
| mid-1st century CE | 4Q84, 4Q87, 4Q89, 11Q8 |
| 2nd half 1st century CE | 4Q85, 5/6 Hev 1b |

Can the chronology of the psalms scrolls from the Judean Desert (tab. 1) reveal any development in the arrangement of texts? Due to the palaeographic dating of the scrolls, the chronology cannot be fail-safe: first, because paleography does not allow for absolute dating and can only give a time span for each document,

---

**29** E.g. Psalm 112 on 4Q84, see below p.27.

and second, because it can hardly ever be made out whether a scroll is a copy of an older scroll, and if so, whether layout features were strictly copied or could be varied in the process of copying. Nevertheless, some tendencies can be made out:

1) The "prose-layout" seems to have been the standard (not the norm!) layout for poetical texts.[30]
2) The early cases of a special layout – i.e. those from the pre-Christian period – are all somewhat exceptional:
    a. Mas 1f is the aforementioned hybrid of "prose-" and stichographic layout.
    b. All other cases of special layout refer to either Ps 119 or Ps 104 (1Q10, 4Q86, 4Q90, and 4Q93). While all other psalms on 4Q86 are written in a "prose-layout," the same cannot be said with certainty for 4Q90 (Ps 119) and 4Q93 (Ps 104) since no other psalms are extant on these scrolls. Thus, the question of whether these scrolls contained more than just Ps 119 and Ps 104, respectively, and what type of layout would have been chosen for these additional texts remains unanswered.[31]
3) Over the course of time, Ps 119 retains its special role, while Ps 104 seems to lose it.
4) The number of scrolls with all psalms written in a special layout increases.
5) The layout 2ba – that is, one verse per line with (usually two) separate stichs – seems to be more prominent in the younger manuscripts.

To summarize the chronological analysis: it seems to be possible to make out a trend from "prose-layout" to an increasing number of stichographic arrangements of psalm texts with Ps 119 at the centre of the development.[32]

---

**30** The material evidence from Qumran and other sites in the Judean Desert suggests that the "prose-layout" was the standard layout for poetical texts. It should, however, not be called a "norm," both because there is no transmitted rule for the layout of scrolls from the Second temple Period and because the few scrolls with a special layout reveal that it was indeed possible to arrange poetical texts in another way, cf. Klaus Seybold, *Poetik der Psalmen*, Poetologische Studien zum Alten Testament 1 (Stuttgart: Kohlhammer, 2003), 65: "Eine Norm, wie sie die talmudischen Vorschriften und die masoretischen Handschriften zeigen, gab es offenbar im gleichen Maße noch nicht."

**31** For the material reconstruction of these scrolls cf. Jain, *Psalmen oder Psalter?*, 117f., 126f.

**32** This is contrary to Tov's proposition that the evidence – which does also include the poetic units outside the psalms scrolls – suggests a link between the stichographic arrangement and "*scribes writing in the proto-Masoretic tradition*" (Tov, "The Background of the Stichometric Arrangements," 419; italics in the original). He argues that poetic units arranged as running texts do clearly not belong to the (proto-)Masoretic (MT) tradition, whereas texts with a stichographic layout represent the textual tradition of the later MT. Since the textual fluidity within "biblical" psalms is generally rather low and "mostly the variant readings of the Qumran Psalms manuscripts are constrained to minor disagreements such as grammatical differences" (Armin Lange,

## 4 Ps 119 as the Prototype of Stichographic Layout

The peculiarities of Ps 119 have already been mentioned and can be summarized as follows: Ps 119 has been preserved on six different scrolls and is *always* written in a type 2b-layout, irrespective of the other psalms' layout on the same scroll. Furthermore, it is the only psalm certainly known to have been written down without the context of a collection of psalms (4Q89). It has also been mentioned that the acrostic structure of the psalm suits an arrangement of one verse per line (with or without separated stichs), whereas other similarly structured psalms do *not* share this affinity with special layouts. So, the question is: Why is Ps 119 so special in this regard? In an attempt to answer this question, the content of Ps 119 will be taken into account in the following. It might reveal why Ps 119 was so popular, why it has an acrostic structure, and why its connection to a special layout is so strong.

Some modern scholars judged this psalm harshly as monotonous and lacking in content.[33] Psalm 119 is indeed a text that circles around the theme of the study of the Torah using a relatively small vocabulary, thus evoking a feeling of redundancy with the reader. However, the material evidence from Qumran[34] suggests that this psalm was held in a high regard by the recipients collecting the scrolls. This points more toward a high esteem and a reading- or even prayer-practice that regarded Ps 119 as the "golden ABC," an expression coined by Martin Luther. The redundancy in the expressions and the seemingly formalistic structure give the psalm a meditative character somewhat similar to the Rosary. To write the analogy out: reading or reciting Ps 119 is a meditative exercise of praying and the single letters of the alphabet are like the beads leading the praying person

---

"Collecting Psalms in the Light of the Dead Sea Scrolls," in *A Teacher for All Generations 1: Essays in Honor of James C. VanderKam*, ed. Eric F. Mason et al., JSJS 153/1 [Leiden: Brill, 2012]: 301), Tov's complete characterization of the alignment of the scrolls lacks a firm ground. Taking into account not only the textual character but also the order of compositions on a scroll compared to the MT-Psalter, the following can be observed. Not all manuscripts close to MT arrange the psalms stichographically and those that do so display different kinds of stichographic layout. On the other hand, some scrolls deviating from the MT order of psalms use stichographic arrangements – at least for Ps 119 and Ps 104. Therefore, the connection of a special layout for psalms to a certain textual tradition – and an assumed scribal tradition behind it – seems to lack foundation. Both a chronological approach and a look into the special connection of Ps 119 to stichographic arrangements seem to be more promising in tracing the source of special layouts for psalms.

**33** Cf. e.g. Bernhard Duhm, *Die Psalmen*, 2nd ed., KHC 14 (Tübingen: Mohr, 1922), 427f.; referred to by Frank-Lothar Hossfeld and Erich Zenger, *Psalmen 101–150*, HThKAT (Freiburg: Herder, 2008), 350.
**34** There is no evidence of Ps 119 on scrolls found at other locations in the Judean Desert.

through the text. Eight "beads" each form a strophe, which is also marked in the layout of the written text. Yet, the text does not suggest that the act of praying is in fact to be equated to the study of the Torah. There are no concrete contents that would imply an actual process of learning. It is rather an unspecific and comprehensive discourse of the Torah that seems to be subordinated to the actual learning process. The prayer is more an act of realisation and self-assurance of the already familiar subject.

Arranging the content as an alphabetical acrostic and highlighting its single verses and strophes in the layout may have helped to memorize the text.[35] It is even possible that the layout of Ps 119 was stichographic from the very beginning and that scribes never had a *Vorlage* deviating from this schema[36] – thus, the strong connection between Ps 119 and a stichographic layout. Another option would be to say that the layout *reflects* the way in which people memorized the psalm and passed it on in the oral tradition. So, although Ps 119 may have been written down in a "prose-layout" at the beginning, it eventually became closely related to a stichographic arrangement because people basically could not think of it in any other way.

It may even be suggested that Ps 119 was some kind of "prototype" for a stichographic arrangement of poetic texts. As shown above, stichographic arrangement of psalms – and, it may be added, of other poetic texts as well – in the Dead Sea scrolls is the exception, not the rule, and develops only later to a more popular and in the end essential feature of "biblical" poetry. It can also be argued that stichographic layout served first to highlight the textual structure of a poetic unit while later on the focus shifted towards the aesthetics of the textual graphic.[37]

But where does this development start? Looking for a starting point, one must not forget Ps 104 which is also a frequent and early example for special layout among psalms in the Dead Sea manuscripts. Furthermore, there are other poetical texts from outside the Book of Psalms – and even the Hebrew canon – which

---

[35] Seybold denies that the intention of acrostics was an aide for memorizing the texts (*Poetik der Psalmen*, 69). Even if memorization was not the main function of an acrostic, it can nevertheless prove helpful in this process.

[36] Similar Seybold, *Poetik der Psalmen*, 69.

[37] E. Tov thinks that the principle of graphic beauty was not yet reflected in the Dead Sea manuscripts (Emanuel Tov, "Special Layout of Poetical Units in the Texts from the Judean Desert," in *Give Ear to My Words: Psalms and other Poetry in and around the Hebrew Bible: Essays in Honour of Professor N.A. van Uchelen*, ed. Janet Dyk [Amsterdam: Societas Hebraica Amstelodamensis, 1996]: 128). However, as the example of Mas 1e shows, this may well have been the case for some of the scrolls.

display a stichographic layout.[38] In particular, Dtn 32 is frequently and early on arranged according to its stichs. An influence of this – and possibly other – texts on the development of the stichographic arrangement of psalms cannot be excluded. However, none of these texts is *exclusively* connected to a special layout. Only Ps 119 is always represented in a stichographic arrangement and it is also the most frequently found psalm among the Qumran psalms scrolls. The fact that this text is a meditative prayer reflecting the study of the Torah may be the reason why it was so popular among these scrolls. Evidently, not even space was an argument against displaying this longest of all "biblical" psalms with one verse by line and often also separating the stanzas by a blank line. Even if all other psalms on a scroll were arranged in a "prose-layout," this psalm *had* to be arranged stichographically (cf. 11Q5). All other psalms, even Ps 104, are treated with more flexibility when it comes to textual graphics. It has been argued above that memorization practices and perhaps the length of the text made it necessary to display Ps 119 in a special layout from an early stage onwards. It may be assumed that Ps 119 was the prototype for other psalms to be arranged stichographically. What was a necessity for Ps 119 became an option for other psalms and eventually turned into a characteristic feature of "biblical" poetry. Thus, Ps 119 could be called the prototype of stichographic layout.

# 5 The Potential of Stichographic Layout: Considering the Example of Psalm 118 in the Dead Sea Scrolls

## 5.1 Ps 118 in the Dead Sea Scrolls

Whereas Ps 119 is always written down in a stichographic layout within the Dead Sea Scrolls, the second test case, its neighboring psalm in the Masoretic order, Ps 118, appears in rather different shapes concerning both its textual form and its layout. Since there seems to be no general rule for the layout of this psalm, its concrete shape in the individual scrolls is all the more interesting and promises helpful insights in the potential of the stichographic layout.

---

**38** 4Q365 (Ex 15); 1Q5; 4Q29; 4Q30; 4Q44 (all Dtn 32); 4Q102 (Prov 1); 4Q103 (Prov 9); 3Q3 (Lam 3); 2Q18; Mas 1h (both Sir); 4Q521 (Messianic Apocalypse).

Parts of Ps 118 are attested by at least three – maybe four – scrolls from the Judaean Desert: 4Q84, 11Q5, 11Q6 and 4Q87. However, in the case of 4Q87 the assignment to that psalm is less certain. The evidence here is limited to a few letters that could be part of Ps 118:29, because this is the only psalm ending with the formula "כי טוב כי לעולם חסדו" ("for he is good, for his grace endures forever") according to the Masoretic Psalter. But since that formula is widespread in the biblical psalms, its attestation on 4Q87 could also be the end of any other psalm in a textual form slightly varying from its Masoretic shape or a superscription to the following composition, Ps 104.[39] Therefore, 4Q87 will not be taken into account in the following.

## 5.2 11Q5 and 11Q6

11Q5, the so called "great psalms scroll," is the most comprehensive and best-preserved psalms scroll from the Judean Desert. It contains psalms that appear in the fourth and fifth Book of Psalms from the Masoretic Psalter and some additional compositions that are attested in other parts of the Hebrew Bible or other ancient traditions and some that were unknown prior to the discovery of 11Q5. Psalm 118 appears twice in 11Q5, once on fragment E, column i, which contains parts of verses 25–29, and once on the scroll proper in column XVI. Concerning the first appearance, it is not possible to reconstruct the column before and, thus, to find out whether Ps 118 was presented there in entirety.[40] The second version does not comprise the complete psalm, but a catena consisting of verses 1, 15–16, 8–9, a verse similar to the two before but otherwise unknown, and verse 29. Thus, this composition differs decisively from Ps 118 in its Masoretic form – which is also the best explanation for the twofold appearance of one psalm in one single scroll, a phenomenon that is nowhere else to be observed. Thus, the textual character of Ps 118 in 11Q5 is remarkable. Its layout, however, is hardly noteworthy. As shown above, 11Q5 is mainly written in "prose-layout" – with the exception of

---

**39** In DJD 16, the editors identify this line with Ps 118:29 under reserve; cf. Eugene Ulrich et al., eds., *Qumran Cave 4. XI Psalms to Chronicles*, DJD 16 (Oxford: Clarendon, 2000), 81.
For example, in 11Q5, fragment E iii Ps 105 starts with the very same as an addition to the Masoretic form of the psalm; cf. Florentino García Martínez, Eibert J.C. Tigchelaar and Adam S. van der Woude, eds., *Qumran Cave 11. II 11Q2–18, 11Q20–31*, DJD 23 (Oxford: Clarendon, 1998), 35.
**40** If fragment D was immediately followed by fragment E, there would not have been enough space for Ps 118 in its Masoretic form. But there might have been additional columns between the two fragments that would allow for all the verses of the psalm; cf. García Martínez, Tigchelaar and van der Woude, *Qumran Cave 11. II 11Q2–18, 11Q20–31*, 30f.

Ps 119. Accordingly, Ps 118 is presented in "prose-layout" as is all the rest of the scroll. Thus, in the writing there is no representation of the poetical structures – neither concerning the end of the psalm presented in fragment E i, nor concerning the selected verses of the catena in column XVI.

11Q6 shows significant similarities to 11Q5 and is commonly regarded as a parallel manuscript to 11Q5.[41] As far as the extant material allows for reconstruction, its layout features are similar to those of the latter: "prose-layout" is used for most of the scroll, except for a stichographic rendering of Ps 119.[42] Concerning Ps 118, on fragment 3 a few letters can be made out that are to be identified as parts of verse 1 and verses 15–16 immediately following the aforementioned. Since this sequence is identical to the catena version of the psalm in 11Q5, column XVI, it is highly probable that 11Q6, fragment 3 can be seen as another witness of this composition. As in 11Q5, it shows no distinctive poetical layout and is, therefore, interesting especially as a counter-example to the rendering of the psalm in 4Q84 that should be analyzed in more detail.

## 5.3 4Q84

4Q84 belongs to those few psalms scrolls from the Judean Desert that present all their compositions in a stichographic layout. In most parts of the manuscript the system of one stich – i.e. usually three to four words – per line is used (layout type 2c), and the scroll, thus, shows exceptionally small columns of just about 2.5–3.5 cm.[43] A good example of the potential of this layout is the presentation of the alphabetic acrostic Ps 112 in fragment 25 iii. Due to the poetic structure of this psalm, every stich starts with another letter in order of the Hebrew alphabet. The stichographic arrangement, here, puts every poetic unit in a new line. Thus, the alphabet can be read at the right margin of the column – in the extant part the sequence ז - ח ח - ט ט. Whereas twenty-four of the twenty-six partly extant columns are written in that scheme, the third- and second-last columns, those

---

41 Cf. e.g. García Martínez, Tigchelaar and van der Woude, *Qumran Cave 11. II 11Q2–18, 11Q20–31*, 38.

42 To be precise, the stichographic mode varies, since in 11Q6 the two stichs of a verse are separated by a *vacat* (layout-type 2ba) which is not the case in 11Q5 (type 2bb); see above p. 18–20.

43 Cf. the analysis of decisively narrow columns within the Dead Sea Scrolls by Kipp Davis, "Structure, Stichometry, and Standardization: An Analysis of Scribal Features in a Selection of the Dead Sea Psalms Scrolls," in *Functions of Psalms and Prayers in the Late Second Temple Period*, BZAW 486, ed. Mika S. Pajunen and Jeremy Penner (Berlin: Walter de Gruyter, 2017): 155–84. However, Davis fails to note the layout change concerning Ps 118:1–24, since even the broader columns attesting these verses are small compared to the overall corpus of the Dead Sea Scrolls.

attesting Ps 118, show a different layout. The first of these columns presents the beginning of the psalm in a layout with two stichs per line and, thus, lines more or less twice as long as in the rest of the scroll (layout type 2bb). From the analogy of the other columns, it can be assumed that there were 4–6 lines in the column before the initial line of Ps 118, which might or might not have been written in the same layout.[44] The other column then continues with the text of Ps 118, covering the complete column. But astonishingly the fragment comprising the bottom part of that column shows again the scheme of more-narrow columns – one stich per line (type 2c).[45] Such a shift in the stichographic system used within one single scroll is to be observed nowhere else in the Dead Sea Scrolls. Two explanations for this phenomenon might at first come to mind:

1) The fragments of the two respective columns might belong to a different scroll. But several aspects contradict this assumption. The two columns seem to have been written by the same hand, and they show just the same preparation for the act of writing by scored aid lines ("dry-point rulings") as the rest of the scroll – which in their case do not correspond to the written lines and are all the more remarkable. Moreover, the fragments representing the diverging columns do not only show columns with longer lines but indicate the twofold change in column width itself. Fragment 28 shows the bottom part of the previous column with the ending of Ps 116 in a stichographic layout type 2c with one stich per line as well as Ps 118:5–10,12 in the varying scheme 2bb. Fragment 34 adumbrates the change back to the one-stich-per-line rendering by presenting the transition from the first to the second stich of Ps 118:24 in the middle of its first line. Thus, that line should have comprised a complete verse with two stichs and not just one stich as the following lines do. As a result, it is rather unlikely that the two diverging columns should not belong to the scroll. The reason for the change in column width therefore has to be found within the document.

2) There might have been material reasons that would have made the change in layout necessary. But again, this assumption is untenable: the leather in this part is neither better nor worse than in other parts of the scroll, and the scribe would not have saved any space by writing two stichs per line the way

---

**44** Since the order of compositions in 4Q84 is very similar to the Masoretic Psalter, the editors presume that the first line of Ps 118 had been preceded by הללויה *hallelujah* as an ending of Ps 116 (l. 1), one blank line (l. 2), the two verses of Ps 117 written also in the layout of two stichs per line (l. 3–4), another הללויה *hallelujah* finishing Ps 117 set off to its own line (l. 5), and finally another blank line (l. 6; partly extant); cf. Ulrich et al., *Qumran Cave 4. XI Psalms to Chronicles*, 45. However, this reconstruction is not without alternatives.

**45** Cf. Ulrich et al., *Qumran Cave 4. XI Psalms to Chronicles*, 46f.

he does it. Thus, material aspects seem not to be the reason for the change in column width, as well.

Since none of these explanations led to a satisfying solution, the reason for the change in column width might be found in the poetical structure of the respective psalm. Or – to put it the other way round – the attestation of Ps 118 in 4Q84 reveals the potential of the different modes of stichographic layout.

The composition is a highly formalized poem. Its most remarkable feature is the repetition of words and phrases, which starts already in the first verses of the psalm (tab. 2).[46] The first four verses share an identical second stich, namely the hymnic affirmation "כי לעולם חסדו" ("His grace endures forever"). In verses 2–4 the refrain-like second stich is each time preceded by the call to a group to express this hymnic avowal, varying only concerning the addressees, which in consequence leads to a sequence of four verses with very close parallelisms.

**Table 2:** Poetic structure of Ps 118:1–4 (Masoretic text).

| כי לעולם חסדו | הודו ליהוה כי־טוב | Praise Yhwh for he is good! | His grace endures forever. |
| כי לעולם חסדו | יאמר־נא ישראל | Israel should say: | His grace endures forever. |
| כי לעולם חסדו | יאמרו־נא בית־אהרן | The house of Aaron should say: | His grace endures forever. |
| כי לעולם חסדו | יאמרו־נא יראי יהוה | Those who fear Yhwh should say: | His grace endures forever. |

This poetical structure can best be presented by a layout that puts the correlating – respectively identical – stichs exactly below each other. And this applies to the stichographic layout type 2b with one complete verse per line.[47]

In addition to the beginning of the psalm, its last attested verses – the bottom of the second column – are also of interest, as they are presented in the stichographic layout type 2c with one stich per line, as happens elsewhere in the main parts of the scroll. Here again, the poetical structure of the text provides an explanation for the layout-change. In Ps 118:25–26, it is also the repetitive character of the text that strikes the eye (tab. 3). The parts of the two verses extant in fragment 34 show similar endings by twos: an intensified jussive in the first two lines and a construct relation with the name of God as *nomen rectum* in the third and fourth

---

[46] Cf. J. Henk Potgieter, "The structure and intent of Psalm 118," *OTE* 16 (2003): 393.
[47] To be precise, a stichographic layout type 2ba (one verse per line with stichs separated by a *vacat*) would have served the purpose even better than the type 2bb used in 4Q84 (one verse per line without the separation of stichs).

line.⁴⁸ The beginnings of the stichs – that are lost due to material deterioration of the fragment – are even more closely connected: In v. 25 both stichs begin with the invocation "אנא יהוה" – "Please, Lord," in v. 26 both with a form of the verb ברך, "bless". Thus, the parallelisms are no longer on the level of verses but on the level of stichs.⁴⁹

**Table 3:** Poetic structure of Ps 118:25–26 (Masoretic text).

| | |
|---|---|
| אנא יהוה הושיעה נא | Please, Yhwh, save us! |
| אנא יהוה הצליחה נא | Please, Yhwh, grant success! |
| ברוך הבא בשם יהוה | Blessed is he who comes in the name of Yhwh. |
| ברכנוכם מבית יהוה | We bless you from the house of Yhwh. |
| [ב]רֹכֹנוּ אתכם מבית יהוה | |

The layout used within 4Q84 takes up this change in poetic structure and switches to the stichographic arrangement of stichs (= type 2c) from verse 25 onwards. Thus, in both cases, the graphic presentation of the syntactic units supports a rapid perception of their poetic arrangement. While these are the most evident examples, the same can be said for the complete text of Ps 118 as presented by 4Q84.⁵⁰

Paleography dates 4Q84 to the mid first century CE, making it one of the younger of the Dead Sea psalms scrolls.⁵¹ Despite the general uncertainty of chronologies based on paleography, the chronologic arrangement of the scrolls shows that there is an increase of stichographic layout during the time-span represented by the scrolls. If this is more than a coincidence caused by the fragmentary transmission, 4Q84 can be explained as representing an advanced stage of stichographic arrangement of poetical texts – a stage in which the correspondence between linguistic structure and graphic arrangement is valued higher than the optical uniformity of a manuscript.

---

**48** Concerning line four, there is a small textual variance between the received text of the Masoretic tradition and the text extant in 4Q84, fragment 34 (cf. tab. 3): the object – second person plural – is once reflected by a suffix attached directly to the verb (MT) and once by an additional object-marker with the respective suffix (4Q84); cf. Cf. Ulrich et al., *Qumran Cave 4. XI Psalms to Chronicles*, 47.
**49** Cf. the analysis by Erich Zenger in Hossfeld and Zenger, *Psalmen 101–150*, 330f., which, however, does not note the similarities in the structure of the two verses.
**50** See e.g. the parallel openings of verses 6 and 7, and verses 8 and 9 that are also supported by the layout used here.
**51** See above section 3.2.

# 6 Conclusion

Trying to reconstruct modes of production and reception of psalms scrolls in the late Second Temple Period of Ancient Israel, the present article sheds some light on the materiality and layout of the scrolls, especially by asking if and how poetical structures of the texts were represented in the writing. In total, five modes of layout can be discerned within the Dead Sea psalms scrolls. Whereas the first, the "prose-layout," is used the most, it is the exceptions, the various forms of stichographic layout, that are dealt with in the main part of this essay. Summarizing the analyses of the layout of the psalms scrolls in general and the two case studies Ps 119 and 118 as attested in the Dead Sea scrolls, three major results can be noted:

1) The varying layout of the scrolls – which goes far beyond the stichographic arrangement covered in this paper – along with other features diverging between the scrolls requires us to interpret each scroll and its pragmatics individually.
2) In general, it is highly probable that a stichographic arrangement is chosen to highlight the linguistic structure of a text. As such, stichographic layout predetermines the reading of a poetic text and, therefore, can be interpreted as an act of authority. At the same time, this layout feature supports the text comprehension and the readability of the scroll and is geared to serving the intended reader.
3) If the chronology is more than a coincidence, it can be observed that the scribes of the Dead Sea psalms scrolls increasingly considered the linguistic structure of the poetic texts and tried to reflect it in the layout of their writing, thus making use of the different modes of stichographic layout between the individual scrolls – and in the exceptional case of 4Q84 within one scroll. As a prototype for this layout feature, Ps 119 can be identified, since its poetical structure matches the stichographic arrangement of verses very well and it is never attested in a different shape within the scrolls from the Judean Desert. It is easily conceivable that scribes applied the same or a similar layout to other psalms – and even complete psalm scrolls – because they knew about their advantages from documents bearing Ps 119. The increasing relevance of the layout of texts can be further followed up in the manuscripts and editions of the biblical psalms from late antiquity and medieval times and influenced interpretation and translations down through the centuries (see also the chapter from Poleg in the present volume). Thus, this material feature is a key aspect in the reception of the psalms as poetic literature.

In summary, it can be seen from analysis such as that presented in this essay that considering materiality, that is, material aspects as well as the structure and layout of the writing, helps to understand the role of text-bearing artifacts as agents in a textual community. In the transition from an oral to a textual culture, texts are reliant on their material embodiment to be preserved. The modes in which a text is recited influences its layout on written artifacts and, reciprocally, the layout of a written text plays a role in predetermining its reading, reciting, and interpretation.

# Bibliography

Barthélemy, Dominique, and Józef T. Milik, eds. *Qumran Cave 1*. DJD 1. Oxford: Clarendon, 1955.

Davis, Kipp. "Structure, Stichometry, and Standardization: An Analysis of Scribal Features in a Selection of the Dead Sea Psalms Scrolls." In *Functions of Psalms and Prayers in the Late Second Temple Period*. BZAW 486, edited by Mika S. Pajunen and Jeremy Penner, 155–84. Berlin: Walter de Gruyter, 2017.

Dorandi, Tiziano. "Punctuation I. Greek." In *Brill's New Pauly*, Antiquity volumes edited by Hubert Cancik and Helmuth Schneider, English edition by Christine F. Salazar. Consulted online on 23 May 2018 (http://dx.doi.org/10.1163/1574-9347_bnp_e702150), 2006.

Duhm, Bernhard. *Die Psalmen*. KHC 14. Tübingen: Mohr, ²1922.

Flint, Peter. *The Dead Sea Psalms Scrolls and the Book of Psalms*. StTDJ 17. Leiden: Brill, 1997.

García Martínez, Florentino, Tigchelaar, Eibert J.C., and Adam S. van der Woude, eds. *Qumran Cave 11. II 11Q2–18, 11Q20–31*. DJD 23. Oxford: Clarendon, 1998.

Hilgert, Markus. "Materiale Textkulturen: Textbasierte historische Kulturwissenschaften nach dem *material culture turn*." In *Materialität: Herausforderungen für die Sozial- und Kulturwissenschaften*, edited by Herbert Kalthoff, Torsten Cress and Tobias Röhl, 255–67. Paderborn: Fink, 2016.

Hossfeld, Frank-Lothar, and Erich Zenger. *Psalmen 101–150*. HThKAT. Freiburg: Herder, 2008.

Jain, Eva. *Psalmen oder Psalter? Materielle Rekonstruktion und inhaltliche Untersuchung der Psalmenhandschriften aus der Wüste Juda*. StTDJ 109. Leiden: Brill, 2014.

Lange, Armin. *Handbuch der Textfunde vom Toten Meer 1: Die Handschriften biblischer Bücher von Qumran und den anderen Fundorten*. Tübingen: Mohr Siebeck, 2009.

Lange, Armin. "Collecting Psalms in the Light of the Dead Sea Scrolls." In *A Teacher for All Generations 1: Essays in Honor of James C. VanderKam*. JSJ.S 153/1, edited by Eric F. Mason et al., 297–308. Leiden: Brill, 2012.

Miller, Shem. "Multiformity of Stichographic Systems in the Dead Sea Scrolls." *RdQ* 29 (2017): 219–45.

Nir-El, Yoram, and Magen Broshi. "The Black Ink of the Qumran Scrolls." *DSD* 3 (1996): 157–67.

Oxford Living Dictionaries: English. Consulted online on 23 May 2018 (https://en.oxforddictionaries.com).

Potgieter, J. Henk. "The structure and intent of Psalm 118." *OTE* 16 (2003): 389–400.

Seybold, Klaus. *Poetik der Psalmen*. Poetologische Studien zum Alten Testament 1. Stuttgart: Kohlhammer, 2003.

Tov, Emanuel. "Special Layout of Poetical Units in the Texts from the Judean Desert." In *Give Ear to My Words: Psalms and other Poetry in and around the Hebrew Bible: Essays in Honour of Professor N.A. van Uchelen*, edited by Janet Dyk, 115–28. Amsterdam: Societas Hebraica Amstelodamensis, 1996.

Tov, Emanuel, ed. *The Texts from the Judaean Desert: Indices and an Introduction to the Discoveries of the Judaean Desert Series*. DJD 39. Oxford: Clarendon, 2002.

Tov, Emanuel. *Scribal Practices and Approaches Reflected in the Texts Found in the Judean Desert*. StTDJ 54. Leiden: Brill, 2004.

Tov, Emanuel. "The Background of the Stichometric Arrangements of Poetry in the Judean Desert Scrolls." In *Prayer and Poetry in the Dead Sea Scrolls and Related Literature. Essays in Honor of Eileen Schuller on the Occasion of Her 65th Birthday*. StTDJ 98, edited by Jeremy Penner, Ken M. Penner and Cecilia Wassen, 409–20. Leiden: Brill, 2012.

Ulrich, Eugene, et al., eds. *Qumran Cave 4. XI Psalms to Chronicles*. DJD 16. Oxford: Clarendon, 2000.

Dan Batovici
# Reading Aids in Early Christian Papyri

## 1 Introduction

This contribution offers a discussion of the issues related to the function of reading aids in early Christian papyri, in view of the role assigned to these elements in recent scholarship. To that end, it will briefly introduce the question in the context of early Christian studies, discuss in some detail a recent proposal with regard to reading aids in canonical gospels papyri, and present some further data from apocryphal and apostolic fathers papyri, before offering a number of considerations in conclusion.

The background for this is the fact that "the scholarly interest in early Christian (and in particular New Testament) manuscripts as artifacts has witnessed a remarkable growth in the last couple of decades alongside a parallel increase in the attention paid to materiality and material practices in the study of religious phenomena more broadly conceived."[1] In this context, various paratextual features such as the distribution and execution of titles and subtitles, the use of paragraphing and punctuation, the existence of corrections and glosses, as well as potential lectional signs are often taken as possible indicators of how early Christians treated and used their texts.[2] Alternatively, such factors are taken as clues for tracing the history of the transmission and reception of early Christian texts copied in the papyri.[3] Indeed, the fact that we have Christian manuscripts

---

[1] Giovanni Bazzana, "'Write in a Book What You See and Send It to the Seven Assemblies:' Ancient Reading Practices and the Earliest Papyri of Revelation," in *Book of Seven Seals: The Peculiarity of Revelation, its Manuscripts, Attestation, and Transmission*, ed. Thomas J. Kraus and Michael Sommer, WUNT 363 (Tübingen: Mohr Siebeck, 2016): 11–31, at 11.

[2] See, for instance, Larry W. Hurtado, *The Earliest Christian Artifacts: Manuscripts and Christian Origins* (Grand Rapids, MI: Eerdmans, 2006), 34–41 and 81–83; Larry Hurtado, "The Greek Fragments of the Gospel of Thomas as Artefacts: Papyrological Observations on Papyrus Oxyrhynchus 1, Papyrus Oxyrhynchus 654 and Papyrus Oxyrhynchus 655," in *Das Thomasevangelium: Entstehung – Rezeption – Theologie*, ed. J. Frey, E.E. Popkes and Jens Schröter, BZNW 157 (Berlin: de Gruyter, 2008): 19–32; AnneMarie Luijendijk, "Reading the *Gospel of Thomas* in the Third Century: Three Oxyrhynchus Papyri and Origen's *Homilies*," in *Reading New Testament Papyri in Context/Lire les papyrus du Nouveau Testament dans leur contexte*, ed. C. Clivaz and J. Zumstein, BETL 242 (Leuven: Peeters, 2011): 241–67.

[3] A recent example is available in Peter Malik, "The Greek Text of Revelation in Late Antique Egypt: Materials, Texts, and Social History," *ZAC* 22 (2018): 400–21. See also Dan Batovici, "The Apostolic Fathers in Codex Sinaiticus and Alexandrinus," *Biblica* 97 (2016): 581–605, or Bazzana, "Ancient Reading Practices," 11–31, and Juan Chapa, "Su demoni e angeli: Il Salmo 90 nel suo

from the second and third centuries means that we have in them artefacts which were copied and used by actual Christians, and as such bear the promise of a glimpse into the life and habits of early Christians, a notion which, unsurprisingly, has attracted significant attention in recent years from scholars of early Christianity.

Of course, early and late-antique Christianity is not the only manuscript culture where research has been done on the ways in which texts are organized and adapted for reading. In Arabic manuscript studies there is also a growing interest in studying the witnesses as artefacts and not only for the texts they carry. For instance, Adam Gacek's *Vademecum for Readers* includes entries on abbreviations and abbreviations symbols, book titles, calligraphy and penmanship, chapter and section headings, conjunction marks, glosses and scholia, marginalia, textual dividers and paragraph marks,[4] as well as other paratextual features in early Qur'ānic texts which point to what is a very developed and complex phenomenology of reading and copying (for more on this, see the chapter from Fedeli in the present volume). There is also a growing literature on scribal practices in Hebrew manuscript culture, especially on the Dead Sea Scrolls fragments. The seminal work of Emanuel Tov, for instance, includes chapters on writing practices, sections on titles of compositions and headers of sections, word and small sense unit division, scribal marks and procedures, as well as appendices on characteristic features of the Qumran scribal practices, and on scribal features of biblical manuscripts,[5] reflecting a multifaceted, reader-oriented, manuscript culture (see the chapter from Krauß and Schücking-Jungblut in this volume).

While such connections are interesting and illuminating, the background for early Christian Greek papyri, however, is formed for the most part in relation to the larger Greek papyrus culture, and especially the papyri of classical literature. The few pages devoted to the topic in E.G. Turner's introduction to his important *Greek Manuscripts of the Ancient World*, first published in 1971 then revised by P.J. Parsons a decade later, are perhaps the most cited when the classical background

---

contesto," in *I papiri letterari Cristiani: atti del Convegno internazionale di studi in memoria di Mario Naldini. Firenze, 10–11 giugno 2010*, ed. Guido Bastianini and Angelo Casanova, Studi e Testi di Papirologia N.S. 13 (Firenze: Instituto Papirologico "G. Vitelli," 2011): 59–90.

4 Adam Gacek, *Arabic Manuscripts: A Vademecum for Readers*, HOSNME 98 (Leiden: Brill, 2009), respectively at 2–6, 37–38, 43–47, 57–58, 81, 114–17, 156, 268–270.

5 Emanuel Tov, *Scribal Practices and Approaches Reflected in the Texts Found in the Judean Desert*, STDJ 54 (Leiden: Brill, 2004). For a more focused approach, see Stephen Reed, "Physical Features of Excerpted Torah Texts," in *Jewish and Christian Scripture as Artifact and Canon*, ed. Craig A. Evans and H. Daniel Zacharias, LSTS 60 (London: Bloomsbury, 2009): 82–104.

of Christian Greek papyri is mentioned.⁶ Therein several paratextual features are introduced and discussed, and these still inform the current treatments of early Christian papyri. After a brief mention of the relevance of the width of the column of copied text, the various ways in which a text in *scriptio continua* can be segmented are discussed one after another: the rare practice of forming word groups, oblique strokes as (again, rather rare) markers of phrases or individual words, abbreviations, apostrophe, punctuation as a later invention, rarely used and in the absence of a standardized system beyond working as separators, *ekthesis* (the projection of a first word or letter in the left margin), *eisthesis* (an indentation, in fact the opposite of an *ekthesis*), blank spaces to separate sentences, *paragraphi* as horizontal strokes below the line which is so marked, the double dot, high dot, and middle dot, *diairesis*, breathings and accents, *coronis* (by which he means a *paragraphus* with further lines at one end as, for instance, the so-called forked *paragraphus* > – ), titles and subtitles, the *diple* (>), *nomina sacra*, and various ways to perform corrections.⁷ Turner's description still provides the current working terminology and typology for research on early Christian papyri from this perspective.

More recently, an important collective volume was published with the aim of updating our knowledge on paratextual signs in the Greco-Roman world by way of a comparative approach from papyri to inscriptions, and from Greek to Latin.⁸ It offers sixteen contributions on the Greek and Roman background of signs found in manuscripts and inscriptions and should therefore inform future developments on early Christian papyri. Kathleen McNamee's chapter on "Sigla in Late Greek Literary Papyri" is particularly interesting in that it offers a wide-ranging discussion of paratextual signs in late-antique Classical literary papyri,⁹ from old signs with old uses, to and old signs with new uses, to altogether new sigla. Among the inherited paratextual features which keep their older use, McNamee discusses the *diple* (>) which, while normally placed at the beginning of the line, still signals quotations, the diagonal slash (/), which is still used inconsistently for various reasons, such as marking errors or the beginning of a new section or passages which are interesting in some way, and

---

**6** E. G. Turner, "Introduction," in *Greek Manuscripts of the Ancient World*, second edition revised and enlarged, ed. P.J. Parsons (London: Institute of Classical Studies, 1987): 1–23.
**7** Turner, "Introduction," 7–17.
**8** Gabriel Nocchi Macedo and Maria Chiara Scappaticcio, eds., *Signes dans les textes, textes sur les signes: Érudition, lecture et écriture dans le monde gréco-romain*, Papyrologica Leodiensia 6 (Liège: Presses Universitaires de Liège, 2017).
**9** Kathleen McNamee, "Sigla in Late Greek Literary Papyri," in Nocchi Macedo and Scappaticcio, *Signes dans les textes, textes sur les signes*, 127–41.

the dot (*stigme*), which is placed, in her examples, in the margin to indicate "a textual peculiarity in a line" or between a lemma and its comment.[10] Among the old sigla which were put to new use in late antiquity, McNamee includes the *paragraphus* and the *diple obelismene* (> – , described by Turner as a forked *paragraphus*, and as a particular type of *coronis*), which "continues to be written in the left margin, between lines, to indicate a new section of text," but which is now also used to separate "material *within* the line."[11] The author concludes with a description of new and newly proliferating sigla. For instance, the older, more austere, signs employed to "articulate parts of a text," such as "the horizontal *paragraphus*, *diple obelismene*, and (at the conclusion of a piece) a *cornis* of fairly standard shape," make way in late antiquity for more developed forms of *coronis* and more elaborate as well as variate *paragraphi*, as can be found, for instance, in Codex Sinaiticus.[12] She also notes the use of larger *diplae* (>) with the function of a *paragraphus* in as much as "they do not mark individual lines but are written, instead, between lines or after sections of text."[13] All in all, McNamee draws attention to the lack of similar studies on the Christian Latin, Greek and Coptic manuscripts.[14]

## 2 Reading Early Christian Papyri in Early Christian Studies

A peculiarity of the assessment of reading aids in Christian papyri is the fact that they have been set in relation to ongoing debates concerning the history and development of early and late-antique Christianity, notably with regard to the development of the New Testament canon.

In relatively recent scholarship we can find, for instance, the argument that the three Greek papyri of the Gospel of Thomas – P.Oxy. 1, 654, and 655 – do not "reflect a regard for this text as "scripture" to be read in worship and treated

---

**10** McNamee, "Sigla in Late Greek Literary Papyri," 128–30, quotes from 130.
**11** McNamee, "Sigla in Late Greek Literary Papyri," 131, emphasis added. What follows is also interesting, because in samples the variety of contexts in which it is used: "Among later classical texts, > – separates medical prescriptions, sections of a medical catechism, Hippocratic aphorisms, passages of dense marginalia, and perhaps parts of a commentary on Aristophanes *Pax* (unless here it is a space filler at the end of the line)."
**12** McNamee, "Sigla in Late Greek Literary Papyri," 131.
**13** McNamee, "Sigla in Late Greek Literary Papyri," 132.
**14** McNamee, "Sigla in Late Greek Literary Papyri," 128.

somehow authoritative for faith."[15] The argument is based on the format, appearance and the comparative quality, or lack thereof, of these manuscripts. This would depend, of course, on the level of uniformity that we presuppose existed with early Christianity. It is not clear how one could rule out either – especially the latter. The conclusion of this particular argument is that the three papyri offer "strong reasons" to doubt that those who used them considered them "scriptural". One wonders whether there is any reason at all, let alone strong ones to reach such a conclusion. Is it impossible that those Christians considered the text "scriptural" but also used a "private" papyrus of it (however one chooses to define "private")? To take a more extreme case, it is hard to imagine why an amulet, or a writing exercise, or a miniature papyrus with verses from the Gospel of John would indicate that those who used them as such did not consider it "canonical".

Indeed, taking a different approach with regard to the same P.Oxy. 654 of the Gospel of Thomas, AnneMarie Luijendijk has noted, for instance, that, "inscribed with reader's aids, the Thomas roll appears intended for reciting," suggesting further that it "might have been used in a liturgical setting," or it "may have been intended for reading out loud in a different context, for instance in an educational setting," or else "the scribe might have copied the punctuation from the *Vorlage*," which would also point to an exemplar "intended for declamation."[16] Therefore, there are scholarly takes which try to situate such papyri not only with respect to their probable use in early Christianity, but also in relation to the history of the formation of the New Testament canon.

In a recent contribution, Dan Nässelqvist too offers a discussion of how paratextual features of early Christian papyri might have influenced public reading of papyri.[17] However, his argument is that, when "pragmatics of reading" are considered, "abbreviations and lectional signs [in early New Testament papyri] were employed infrequently, unsystematically, and at times in ways that render public reading more difficult."[18] In claiming this, he is challenging the notion that early Christian paratextual features were "lectional signs" meant to aid public reading,

---

15 Hurtado, *Early Christian Artifacts*, 34, reacting specifically to the title of Bentley Layton, *The Gnostic Scriptures: A New Translation with Annotations and Introductions* (New York: Doubleday, 1987).
16 Luijendijk, "Reading the *Gospel of Thomas* in the Third Century," 253–54.
17 Dan Nässelqvist, *Public Reading in Early Christianity: Lectors, Manuscripts, and Sound in the Oral Delivery of John 1–4*, NovTSup 163 (Leiden: Brill, 2016), 17–62.
18 Nässelqvist, *Public Reading in Early Christianity*, 322.

while also suggesting that they are perhaps more likely to have worked as "reader's aids" for the private reader.[19]

As such, the interest raised by paratextual features in early Christian papyri taken as possible reading aids has brought about a scholarly discussion concerning a posited distinction between public and private use of these papyri. Generally speaking, whether a manuscript is or is not meant for private use is a fairly common sort of estimation in most areas of manuscript studies, where it is normally taken in a neutral manner. However, this becomes quite a sharp distinction precisely when the underlining presupposition is that public reading in early Christian churches might indicate canonical status.

## 3 Public and Private: Charlesworth's *Early Christian Gospels*

The most developed attempt so far to situate paratextual features as reading aids is arguably that by Scott Charlesworth in his 2016 book on the production and transmission of *Early Christian Gospels*, which aims to compare the papyri of the canonical and non-canonical gospels.[20] The author proceeds by picking a literary genre, that is the gospel genre, and then draws a comparison across the clear-cut categories of canonical and non-canonical, largely on two levels: from the point of view of codicology and palaeography on the one hand, and from the perspective of textual stability on the other.

In the following, Charlesworth's codicological and palaeographical discussion is particularly of interest, as it addresses in the process the related issue of establishing whether a papyrus is meant for private or public use. This matter is covered in the second chapter of his book – entitled "Public and Private: Early Christian Codicological Conventions" – which is an attempt to describe and systematise reading aids in papyri of the four canonical gospels.[21] In view of this, the starting point is the assumption that "early canonical gospel MSS were used in two general settings – publicly in corporate worship, and privately by indi-

---

[19] Nässelqvist, *Public Reading in Early Christianity*, 323.
[20] Scott D. Charlesworth, *Early Christian Gospels: Their Production and Transmission*, Papyrologica Florentina 47 (Firenze: Edizioni Gonnelli, 2016).
[21] Charlesworth, *Early Christian Gospels*, 31–92, which is a developed version of Scott D. Charlesworth, "Public and Private: Second- and Third-Century Gospel Manuscripts," in *Jewish and Christian Scripture as Artifact and Canon*, ed. Craig A. Evans and H. Daniel Zacharias, LSTS 70 (London: Bloomsbury, 2009): 148–75.

viduals." The general argument is that "the majority of *second-century* canonical gospel manuscripts (MSS) can be designated 'public,' in the sense that they were intentionally produced to be read aloud by lectors in Christian meetings."[22]

Commendably, the author is cautious when mentioning that "it is important to recognize that the categories of 'public/controlled' and 'private/uncontrolled' should not be seen as inflexible classifications to be imposed on the evidence."[23] At the same time, he maintains that "nonetheless, the manuscript evidence clearly supports the notion that early canonical gospel MSS were used and produced in broad 'public/controlled' and 'private/uncontrolled' settings."[24]

Charlesworth then proposes four categories of early papyri of the canonical gospels, based on the size and format of codices, script (whether copied by a bookhand, or a more informal hand, or documentary) and – of relevance for the present contribution – "types of text division and/or punctuation": the presence (or lack thereof) of *paragraphi*, vacant line ends, *ekthesis*, enlarged first letter, space, medial or high point, dicolon, apostrophe, diple as line filler and "acute-like text division marker or miscellaneous stroke."[25] The fourfold categorisation is therefore based on paratextual features and goes as follows: (a) controlled production of "public" canonical gospels, (b) probable and possible "public/controlled" manuscripts, (c) uncontrolled production of "private" canonical gospels, and (d) probable and possible "private/uncontrolled" manuscripts.[26] As it were, Charlesworth proposes two main categories – public and controlled manuscripts, opposed to private and uncontrolled – and two additional ones with manuscripts which are close to either of the main two, but not enough to make it in. With these categories as framework, the general characterisation of non-canonical gospels papyri is then that they are, as the title of the corresponding chapter puts it, "private and marginal."[27]

The analysis of the data is thorough and interesting, and its main result is that it puts in the spotlight the differences in terms of size, scribal hand, and paratextual features among New Testament gospel papyri up to the fourth century. Yet the reconstruction proposed on the basis of the analysis invites some scrutiny. For instance, Charlesworth's proposal, which was initially formulated in the terms that "most [major manuscripts] were copied in controlled settings where

---

[22] Charlesworth, *Early Christian Gospels*, 31.
[23] Charlesworth, *Early Christian Gospels*, 31.
[24] Charlesworth, *Early Christian Gospels*, 31.
[25] Charlesworth, *Early Christian Gospels*, 35–36.
[26] Charlesworth, *Early Christian Gospels*, 40. The full description of the four categories then follows on pages 42–84.
[27] Charlesworth, *Early Christian Gospels*, 121.

policy dictated some aspects of production,"[28] has already met some criticism from scholars for whom this notion is "without basis and stands at odds with papyrological evidence,"[29] mostly because "unfortunately, we have hardly any information about the production sites of Christian texts in this period."[30]

Indeed, the proposed way of categorising canonical gospel papyri invites a number of considerations. In particular, one wonders whether setting these categories – controlled and public, uncontrolled and private, and the two grey areas for each – is really more than just to say that there are differences from one manuscript to another, and that they can be grouped according to these differences: papyri with many reading aids, others with a smaller number of such features, others still with scarcely any paratextual features. Beyond that, claiming that they are "public/controlled" or "private/uncontrolled" comes in the form of an undemonstrated assumption.

To illustrate, in the introduction of the chapter the author indicates programmatically that "paucity or irregularity of text division, punctuation and lectional aids will be taken to be an indication that a MS was produced for private rather than public use, especially when coupled with a documentary hand," and then announces that the "analysis of the 3rd century evidence will show that the lack of such features can often be traced to an uncontrolled production stetting."[31] Indeed, it would be great to be able to trace down any production setting for early Christian papyri. However, the book does not offer external evidence to corroborate the proposal, as both the uncontrolled and the controlled production setting are presupposed. Instead, what we get as conclusion at the end of the analysis of one particular manuscript is, for instance, that "the cursive tendency of the hand, the use of a roll, and absence of text division, denote uncontrolled/private production for private use."[32]

It is important, then, to stress the point that whether (or not) these features are indicators of private rather than public use is precisely the question, and therefore it cannot also be the answer. Charlesworth may well be right that that particular manuscript was meant for private use, but this is not proven in his book. It is simply presupposed from the outset. The author documents – in great,

---

[28] Scott D. Charlesworth, "Consensus Standardization in the Systematic Approach to *Nomina Sacra* in Second- and Third-Century Gospel Manuscripts," *Aegyptus* 86 (2006): 37–68, at 66.

[29] Kim Haines-Eitzen, "Social History of Early Christian Scribes," in *The Text of the New Testament in Contemporary Research: Essays on the Status Quaestionis*, ed. Bart D. Ehrman and Michael W. Holmes, NTTSD 42 (Leiden: Brill, 2013): 479–95, at 491.

[30] Luijendijk, "Reading the *Gospel of Thomas* in the Third Century," 255, n. 58.

[31] Charlesworth, *Early Christian Gospels*, 34–35.

[32] Charlesworth, *Early Christian Gospels*, 75.

and often interesting, detail – just how well a manuscript is adorned with reading aids compared to other manuscripts which have barely any reading aids, and are poorly written. Perhaps most of all this emphasizes once again the fragmentary and scarce nature of the available evidence, and the limitations that come with the reconstructions we attempt. We have some manuscripts which are larger, more competently copied, and with more paratextual features than others, and we indeed can and should categorize those accordingly. But the reconstructions we can attempt starting from "reading aids" seem to remain riddled with limitations and blind spots.

Similarly, with regard to the comparison between canonical and non-canonical gospels papyri, Charlesworth's description of the latter as "private and marginal,"[33] rather than telling us something about their use as artefacts read by early Christians, tells us simply what we already know: there are far more and better copied papyri of the canonical gospels. But it does so in a detailed manner and from a fresh perspective, and future studies will certainly profit from it.

## 4 Reading Other Early Christian Papyri

Judging from the surviving papyri, early Christians read and copied texts other than the canonical gospels as well.[34] Indeed, as mentioned, Charlesworth includes in his treatment not only canonical, but also non-canonical gospels, and it is of course generally suitable for the purpose of a comparison to select papyri of the same genre across the canonical border. However, the definition of the gospel genre (apart from the four canonical ones) is notoriously problematic.[35] Moreover, for several non-canonical gospel papyri, as Charlesworth recognizes,[36] it is

---

[33] Charlesworth, *Early Christian Gospels*, 121.
[34] Most recently, see Lincoln H. Blumell and Thomas A. Wayment, *Christian Oxyrhynchus: Texts, Documents, and Sources* (Baylor: Baylor University Press, 2018). Other important contributions are Lincoln H. Blumell, *Lettered Christians: Christians, Letters, and Late Antique Oxyrhynchus*, NTTSD 39 (Leiden: Brill, 2012); AnneMarie Luijendijk, *Greetings in the Lord: Early Christians and the Oxyrhynchus Papyri*, HTS 60 (Cambridge, MS: Harvard University Press, 2008); Kim Haines-Eitzen, *Guardians of Letters: Literacy, Power and the Transmitters of Early Christian Literature* (Oxford: Oxford University Press, 2000).
[35] See, for instance, the discussion in Lorne R. Zelyck, "Identifying the Extra-Canonical Gospels," in his *John among the Other Gospels*, WUNT 2/347 (Tübingen: Mohr Siebeck, 2013), 3–12. The same goes for the category of apocrypha in general. See Christopher Tuckett, "What is Early Christian Apocrypha?", in *The Oxford Handbook of Early Christian Apocrypha*, ed. Andrew Gregory and Christopher Tuckett (Oxford: Oxford University Press, 2015): 3–12.
[36] E.g. Charlesworth, *Early Christian Gospels*, 135.

not clear at all whether they contain gospel texts proper, or gospel-like texts, or fragments of exegetic or homiletic works, or exercises of some kind, to the effect that the non-canonical gospels sample may be too small to serve this purpose. Outside this sample, however there are papyri with known apocryphal works of other genres which are better represented, for instance the Apocryphal Acts, or the Protoevangelium of James.[37] There are also papyri of other texts for which there are claims that they might have been at some point candidates for canonical status, such as the Didache and the Shepherd of Hermas, some of which also survived in comparatively bigger numbers.

Based on my research exploring a sample of forty-nine continuous Greek literary papyri of apocrypha and apostolic fathers,[38] the study of paratextual features yields a host of possible reading aids ranging from *diaeresis*, breathings and accents, apostrophes, to *ekthesis* (protruding the beginning of a sentence in the margin), enlarged letters, *paragraphus*, *diple*, dots, blank spaces, and oblique lines above the text. Much like in other papyri, more often than not these are employed inconsistently throughout this sample of papyri, acting more like sense separators in an otherwise continuous text – differing in this respect, for example, from the consistently deployed, sense-unit delimiting function of modern punctuation.

However, it is important to outline the fact that not all paratextual features function in the same way with regard to the manner in which they might aid reading. The diaeresis over initial ι and υ is a fairly common paratextual feature, just as in other papyri, among the apocryphal and apostolic fathers papyri and can be found in P.Egerton 2 + P.Köln VI 255, P. Oxy. LXXVI 5072, P.Oxy. II 210, P.Oxy. X 1224, P.Oxy. I 1, P.Oxy. IV 654, P.Oxy. LXIX 4706, P.Mich. II 2.129, P.Mich. II 2.130, P. Oxy. LXIX 4707, P.Bodmer 38, BKT VI 2.2, P.Mich. 1317 + P.Mich. 3788 + P.Berol 13893, P.Hamburger 1, P.Bodmer 10, P.Oxy. L 3525, P.Ryl. III 463, Bodl. Ms Gr. tb. f. 4 [P] + P.Vindob.G 39756, Greek Papyrus JE 85643, PSI I 6, P.Bodmer 5 and P.Grenf. I 8. Just like breathings and accents – found, for instance, in P.Oxy. V 840, P.Ryl. III 463, and P.Mich. II 2.130 – diareses can hardly be construed as lectional

---

[37] A useful reference tool is now Thomas A. Wayment, *The Text of the New Testament Apocrypha (100–400)* (New York: Bloomsbury, 2013).

[38] Bodl. Ms Gr. tb. f. 4 [P] + P.Vindob.G 39756, BKT VI 2.2, Greek Papyrus JE 85643, P.Antinoopolis I 13, P.Ashmolean inv. 9, P.Berol 13272, P.Bodmer 5, P.Bodmer 10, P.Bodmer 38, P.Egerton 2 + P.Köln VI 255, P.Grenf. I 8, P.Hamburger 1, P.Hamburg inv. 24, P.Harris I 128, P.Oxy. I 1, P.Oxy. II 210, P.Oxy. III 404, P.Oxy. IV 654, P.Oxy. IV 655, P.Oxy. V 840, P.Oxy. VI 849, P.Oxy. VI 850, P.Oxy. VIII 1081, P.Oxy. X 1224, P.Oxy. XIII 1599, P.Oxy XIII 1602, P.Oxy. XV 1782, P.Oxy. XV 1783, P.Oxy. XV 1828, P.Oxy. L 3524, P.Oxy. L 3525, P.Oxy. L 3526 + P.Oxy. IX 1172, P.Oxy. L 3527, P. Oxy. LX 4009, P. Oxy. LXIX 4705, P.Oxy. LXIX 4706, P.Oxy. LXIX 4707, P.Oxy. LXXVI 5072, P.Merton II 51, P.Mich. II 2.129, P.Mich. II 2.130, P.Mich. 1317 + P.Mich. 3788 + P.Berol 13893, P.Prag. I 1 + P. Weill I 96, P.Ryl. III 463, P.Schøyen I 21, PSI I 6, PSI VII 757, P.Vindob.G 2325, and P.Vindob.G 39756 [49].

aids. Dan Nässelqvist, for instance, describes these as "lectional signs that guide pronunciation."³⁹ But even if they are to be taken as reading aids, they are so in a different way than the rudiment of paragraphing by the means of *ekthesis*. Similarly, apostrophes which mark elision and some geminate consonants, as in P.Egerton 2 + P.Köln VI 255, P.Oxy. II 210, P.Mich. 1317 + P.Mich. 3788 + P.Berol 13893, or P.Oxy. XIII 1599, look more like a writing convention than anything meant to help reading.

Indeed *ekthesis* – a letter protruded in the left margin at the beginning of a line, for instance in P. Oxy. LX 4009, PSI VII 757, or P.Oxy. L 3524 – can mark the beginning of a quotation or a new section in the narrative. Enlarged letters can mark the beginning of a sentence, as in P.Merton II 51 or P.Oxy. IV 654, but can also appear in the middle of paratactical constructions, where today we would have a modern comma, for instance in P.Egerton 2 + P.Köln VI 255. *Paragraphi* can be found in several apocryphal and apostolic fathers papyri, sometimes preceding a subtitle (P.Mich. II 2.129, P. Oxy. LXIX 4707, P.Bodmer 38), other times in the middle of a paragraph, seemingly marking for instance the shift in the narrative from the voice of a character to that of another (Bodl. Ms Gr. tb. f. 4 [P] + P.Vindob.G 39756), or even the shift from one explanation to another within the speech of the same character (P.Mich. II 2.129).

*Diplae* (>) appear in several papyri, in various positions. They can be line-fillers as in P.Oxy. I 1 and P.Oxy. IV 655, or they can be in the margin of a column marking a quotation or a passage distinct in some other way, as in P.Bodmer 5. It can even occur at the end of the line but in the middle of a word, as in P.Oxy. V 840, in which case its purpose is less clear. Dots in various positions (low, mid, high, or in pairs as dicolon) and blank spaces of various sizes seem ubiquitous, but their function is not always clear, as they can appear in the middle of a word, for instance in Bodl. Ms Gr. tb. f. 4 [P] + P.Vindob.G 39756). Otherwise, such dots can precede the adversative ἀλλά within the same sentence (P.Antinoopolis I 13), separate sentences, or coordinate parts of a sentence, being present where nowadays you would have a question mark or dicolon, for instance in P.Egerton 2 + P.Köln VI 255.

Overall, this material confirms the view according to which "abbreviations and lectional signs were employed infrequently, unsystematically, and at times in ways that render public reading more difficult."⁴⁰ These can be construed as lectional signs to the extent that they might have been meant to assist the act of reading. They can also be taken to be scribal markings if they reflect the scribes' effort or habit to make sense of the text they are transcribing. Of course, they can

---

39 Nässelqvist, *Public Reading in Early Christianity*, 25.
40 Nässelqvist, *Public Reading in Early Christianity*, 322.

be seen both as reading aids and scribal markings, in as much as the activity of the scribe presupposes both acts. None of these markings is applied consistently in the same way punctuation (e.g. space) is used in English in any one manuscript – where enough of it has survived to make an informed judgement on the matter. Their main feature is that they are occasional in nature and therefore do not strictly mark sense units, a notion which would presuppose delimitations with both a beginning and an end. Indeed, it is rarely that they mark both the beginning and the end of a word, syntagm, sentence, or paragraph. These signs point to interruptions more than to "sense units" with a beginning and an end. In the most general sense, such para-textual signs mark a shift in the narrative, which, as seen, can be a new sentence, a new action, a shift from a character's voice to that of another, and so on. Especially blank spaces and dots (in all positions) can function in largely the same manner, interchangeably, separately or combined. But most of these signs can be used in the middle of the words as well, which further complicates the image.

## 5 Concluding Remarks

Perhaps expectedly, virtually all reading aids discussed by Charlesworth as part of the canonical gospel papyri – *paragraphi*, vacant end lines, *ekthesis*, enlarged first letter of verse or chapter, space, medial or highpoint, dicolon, *diplae* use as line filler or in other ways, and acute-like text division marker or miscellaneous stroke[41] – do appear in other apocrypha papyri and in those of the apostolic fathers. While I would agree that the paratextual features listed above are one way or another meant to assist the act of reading, the question remains as to what extent the available data allows us to distinguish with any degree of confidence that they are meant for public reading and not for private reading – or even loud as opposed to silent reading.[42]

---

**41** Charlesworth, *Early Christian Gospels*, 121
**42** For a recent re-assessment of the question of reading habits in antiquity, challenging the notion that only loud reading was the custom, see R. W. McCutcheon, "Silent Reading in Antiquity and the Future History of the Book," *Book History* 18 (2015): 1–32, esp. 3–17, where evidence from Augustine (on Ambrose, in *Confessions* 6.3.3), Dionysius of Halicarnassus (*De compositione verborum* 25), Lucian (*Adv. Ind.* 2), Quintilian (*Inst. Or.* 1.1.34, 10.1.8–10, 11.3.2–4), Ovid (*Heroides* 21.3–4), Plutarch (on Caesar, in *Brut.* 5.2–3), Euripides (*Hipp.* 874–875), Aristophanes (*Kn.* 115–128), Cicero (*Tusc.* 5.116), Ptolemy (*Judic.* 5.2), Josephus (*Vita* 793), Ptolemy (*Judic.* 5.2), and the scholarly debates on these are presented and discussed.

Recent studies offer new insights, admittedly, complicating things further. From the perspective of public reading in general – thus without the aggravations produced by introducing the canonical divide into the topic – Nässelqvist shows how our best papyri do not actually lend themselves to easy reading, and documents the need and presence, in early communities, of lectors, which were needed to make sense of the papyri and perform the content. They as well would have needed time to prepare the reading, as opposed to reading it on the spot.[43] Also recently, Alan Mugridge, in an important book on *Copying Early Christian Texts*, argues that early Christian papyri were more likely copied by non-Christian scribes than by Christians, which would have been more or less professional copyists who would copy what we call Christian features like *nomina sacra* upon request, or from the exemplar along with everything else.[44] This new proposal might not convince everyone, and it is not impossible that many will remain persuaded that it is more likely that they were copied by Christians. But what this proposal does is to move the discussion from the widely accepted, virtually unchallenged, presupposition that they were copied by Christians, to a question of likelihood. For all intents and purposes, "it is more likely" is quite different from "it is clear" when discussing whether or not early Christian papyri were written by Christians.

A very recent critique of the limitations of the public/private binary, in relation to previous claims that some Revelation papyri would have been "private", notes: "I fail to see why, in the third century C.E., a church cannot have employed a reused manuscript for purposes of communal worship – whatever form that communal worship may have taken," drawing attention to the weakness of a case that "rests on the assumption that a church could not have used a manuscript produced so 'economically.'"[45] In a sense, the persistence of associating the quality of a papyrus with the importance of the text on it is surprising since already in 1979 C. H. Roberts was noting that "not all text written on improvised material need have been private. It may have been a paper shortage or just poverty that led one church to economize by sticking together sheets of papyrus already written on one side, fold them, and so form a makeshift codex out of the unwritten side."[46]

Indeed, not only do we lack the means of establishing whether a papyrus was meant for public or private reading in the absence of clear testimonies in this

---

[43] Nässelqvist, *Public Reading in Early Christianity*, 322.
[44] Alan Mugridge, *Copying Early Christian Texts: A Study in Scribal Practice*, WUNT 362 (Tübingen: Mohr Siebeck, 2016), 144–54.
[45] Malik, "The Greek Text of Revelation in Late Antique Egypt," 405, n. 21.
[46] Colin H. Roberts, *Manuscript, Society and Belief in Early Christian Egypt: The Schweich Lectures 1977* (Oxford: Oxford University Press, 1979), 9–10, also quoted in this regard in Malik, "The Greek Text of Revelation in Late Antique Egypt," 405, n. 21.

sense (e.g. an explicit colophon), but when we draw too clear-cut a distinction between public and private papyri, we run the risk of oversimplifying the reading culture of early and late-antique Christianity. Just how uniform an early Christianity should we envisage? Can we not imagine a poor church community using a smaller and poorly written canonical gospel papyrus, or a well-off individual with many excellently looking New Testament codices? Or should we imagine there were no poor churches at all in late-antique Christianity? One might wonder what we are left with if we drop this apparently very attractive yet deceitful assumption. We are left with no small thing: reading aids in manuscripts become once again a very interesting and complex issue which still provides a window into the material culture of early and late-antique Christians, and at the same time into the reception history of the text so marked, which should indeed invite further – but perhaps less essentialized – study.

# Bibliography

Batovici, Dan. "The Apostolic Fathers in Codex Sinaiticus and Alexandrinus." *Biblica* 97 (2016): 581–605.
Bazzana, Giovanni. "'Write in a Book What You See and Send It to the Seven Assemblies:' Ancient Reading Practices and the Earliest Papyri of Revelation." In *Book of Seven Seals: The Peculiarity of Revelation, its Manuscripts, Attestation, and Transmission*, edited by Thomas J. Kraus and Michael Sommer, 11–31. WUNT 363. Tübingen: Mohr Siebeck, 2016.
Blumell, Lincoln H. *Lettered Christians: Christians, Letters, and Late Antique Oxyrhynchus*. NTTSD 39. Leiden/Boston: Brill, 2012.
Blumell, Lincoln H. and Thomas A. Wayment, *Christian Oxyrhynchus: Texts, Documents, and Sources*. Baylor: Baylor University Press, 2018.
Chapa, Juan. "Su demoni e angeli: Il Salmo 90 nel suo contesto." In *I papiri letterari Cristiani: atti del Convegno internazionale di studi in memoria di Mario Naldini. Firenze, 10–11 giugno 2010*, edited by Guido Bastianini and Angelo Casanova, 59–90. Studi e Testi di Papirologia N.S. 13. Firenze: Instituto Papirologico "G. Vitelli," 2011.
Charlesworth, Scott D. *Early Christian Gospels: Their Production and Transmission*. Papyrologica Florentina 47. Firenze: Edizioni Gonnelli, 2016.
Charlesworth, Scott D. "Public and Private: Second- and Third-Century Gospel Manuscripts." In *Jewish and Christian Scripture as Artifact and Canon*, edited by Craig A. Evans and H. Daniel Zacharias, 148–75. LSTS 70. London: Bloomsbury, 2009.
Charlesworth, Scott D. "Consensus Standardization in the Systematic Approach to Nomina Sacra in Second- and Third-Century Gospel Manuscripts." *Aegyptus* 86 (2006): 37–68.
Gacek, Adam. *Arabic Manuscripts: A Vademecum for Readers*. HOSNME 98. Leiden: Brill, 2009.
Haines-Eitzen, Kim. "Social History of Early Christian Scribes." In *The Text of the New Testament in Contemporary Research: Essays on the Status Quaestionis*, edited by Bart D. Ehrman and Michael W. Holmes, 479–95. NTTSD 42. Leiden: Brill, 2013.

Haines-Eitzen, Kim. *Guardians of Letters: Literacy, Power and the Transmitters of Early Christian Literature*. Oxford: Oxford University Press, 2000.

Hurtado, Larry W. "The Greek Fragments of the Gospel of Thomas as Artefacts: Papyrological Observations on Papyrus Oxyrhynchus 1, Papyrus Oxyrhynchus 654 and Papyrus Oxyrhynchus 655." In *Das Thomasevangelium: Entstehung – Rezeption – Theologie*, edited by J. Frey, E.E. Popkes and Jens Schröter, 19–32. BZNW 157. Berlin: de Gruyter, 2008.

Hurtado, Larry W. *The Earliest Christian Artifacts: Manuscripts and Christian Origins*. Grand Rapids, MI: Eerdmans, 2006.

Layton, Bentley. *The Gnostic Scriptures: A New Translation with Annotations and Introductions*. New York: Doubleday, 1987.

Luijendijk, AnneMarie. "Reading the *Gospel of Thomas* in the Third Century: Three Oxyrhynchus Papyri and Origen's *Homilies*." In *Reading New Testament Papyri in Context/Lire les papyrus du Nouveau Testament dans leur contexte*, edited by C. Clivaz and J. Zumstein, 241–67. BETL 242. Leuven: Peeters, 2011.

Luijendijk, AnneMarie. *Greetings in the Lord: Early Christians and the Oxyrhynchus Papyri*. HTS 60; Cambridge, MS: Harvard University Press, 2008.

Malik, Peter. "The Greek Text of Revelation in Late Antique Egypt: Materials, Texts, and Social History." *Zeitschrift für antikes Christentum* 22.3 (2018): 400–21.

McCutcheon, R.W. "Silent Reading in Antiquity and the Future History of the Book." *Book History* 18 (2015): 1–32.

McNamee, Kathleen. "Sigla in Late Greek Literary Papyri." In *Signes dans les textes, textes sur les signes: Érudition, lecture et écriture dans le monde gréco-romain*, edited by Gabriel Nocchi Macedo and Maria Chiara Scappaticcio, 127–41. Papyrologica Leodiensia 6. Liège: Presses Universitaires de Liège, 2017.

Mugridge, Alan. *Copying Early Christian Texts: A Study in Scribal Practice*. WUNT 362. Tübingen: Mohr Siebeck, 2016.

Nässelqvist, Dan. *Public Reading in Early Christianity: Lectors, Manuscripts, and Sound in the Oral Delivery of John 1–4*. NovTSup 163. Leiden: Brill, 2016.

Nocchi Macedo, Gabriel and Maria Chiara Scappaticcio (eds.). *Signes dans les textes, textes sur les signes: Érudition, lecture et écriture dans le monde gréco-romain*. Papyrologica Leodiensia 6. Liège: Presses Universitaires de Liège, 2017.

Reed, Stephen. "Physical Features of Excerpted Torah Texts." In *Jewish and Christian Scripture as Artifact and Canon*, edited by Craig A. Evans and H. Daniel Zacharias, 82–104. LSTS 60. London: Bloomsbury, 2009.

Roberts, Colin H. *Manuscript, Society and Belief in Early Christian Egypt: The Schweich Lectures 1977*. Oxford: Oxford University Press, 1979.

Tov, Emanuel. *Scribal Practices and Approaches Reflected in the Texts Found in the Judean Desert*. STDJ 54. Leiden: Brill, 2004.

Tuckett, Christopher. "What is Early Christian Apocrypha?" In *The Oxford Handbook of Early Christian Apocrypha*, edited by Andrew Gregory and Christopher Tuckett, 3–12. Oxford: Oxford University Press, 2015.

Turner, E.G. *Greek Manuscripts of the Ancient World*. Second edition revised and enlarged, edited by P.J. Parsons. London: Institute of Classical Studies, 1987.

Wayment, Thomas A. *The Text of the New Testament Apocrypha (100–400)*. New York: Bloomsbury, 2013.

Zelyck, Lorne R. *John among the Other Gospels*. WUNT 2.347. Tübingen: Mohr Siebeck, 2013.

Asma Hilali
# Writing the Qur'ān Between the Lines: Marginal and Interlinear Notes in Selected Qur'ān Fragments from the Museum of Islamic Art, Qatar

## 1 Introduction

Exploring selected fragments from the collection of the Museum of Islamic Art, Doha, Qatar (MIA), this essay offers a snapshot of marginal and interlinear annotations in Qur'ān fragments dated to the seventh-ninth centuries.[1] It reflects on the methods that scribes deployed when annotating Qur'ān fragments, and explores the relationship between the marginal and interlinear annotations and the Qur'ān passages to which they refer. The information that such annotations convey about the context of transmission of the text are crucial in this research. This study aims to identify the types and functions of the corrections, additional material, and independent annotations in the Qur'ān fragments, while also highlighting the significance of materiality in the study of the Qur'ān and its transmission. This essay is part of a larger project focusing on the channels of transmission of the Qur'ān text outside the framework of a final work such as the Qur'ān codex.[2]

---

[1] This paper has been written on the basis of my research stay in The Museum of Islamic Art in Doha, Qatar (MIA). My work has been accomplished with the collaboration of Dr. Mounia Chekhab Boudayya, the Curator for North Africa and Iberia – Museum of Islamic Art – Doha. My research trip to MIA in May 2017 was possible thanks to the support of the *Institute of Ismaili Studies*, London, I thank Dr. Omar Ali de-Unzaga, the head of the department of research and publications at the *Institute of Ismaili Studies* for his encouragement. Finally, I thank David Hollenberg for correcting my English. This paper is the second of a series of contributions about the marginal and interlinear annotations in Qur'ān manuscripts; I have presented the first paper on this topic in the international symposium "Before the Printed Word: Texts, Scribes, and Transmission," which took place at *The Institute of Ismaili Studies*, London, 12–13 October, 2017. That paper was about the marginal and interlinear annotations in the Qur'ān manuscripts kept in the Ismaili collection of the Library of the *Institute of Ismaili Studies*. I shared some of the results of my project in lectures and courses in the University of Hamburg, Germany, in April 2018 and in *École Pratique des Hautes Études*, Section des sciences religieuses, Paris, in Autumn 2018. I thank the colleagues and students who took part in my reflection.

[2] The project includes the study of the Qur'ān fragments held in the Ismaili collection in the *Institute of Ismaili Studies* and in the collection of "The Laboratory of Conservation and preservation of Manuscripts in Raqqāda", Qayrawān, Tunisia.

∂ Open Access. © 2020 Asma Hilali, published by De Gruyter. This work is licensed under a Creative Commons Attribution-NonCommercial-NoDerivatives 4.0 International License.
https://doi.org/10.1515/9783110634440-004

## 2 Context and Methodological Reflections

My stay in the Museum of Islamic Art in Doha was planned two years ago when I decided to study the marginal and interlinear notes in ancient Qur'ān manuscripts in the libraries of the Islamic world: Qayrawan, Raqqqada (Tunisia) and Doha (Qatar). The project dovetails with my study of the transmission of religious texts in early and medieval Islam.[3] My interest with marginal and interlinear annotations in ancient Qur'ān fragments originates in my work on the collections of Qur'ān fragments from *Dar al-Makhṭūṭat* Ṣan'a', the so called the "Sanaa palimpsest".[4] In that study, I demonstrated that marginal annotations are crucial to understanding the use of the text.[5]

A few methodological points are important before addressing the topic of marginal and interlinear annotations in Qur'ān fragments dated to the seventh-ninth centuries CE.[6] By marginal and interlinear annotations, I mean the annotations written in the margins of the text and sometimes between the lines.[7] These annotations are occasional and fragmentary; they refer to specific Qur'ān

---

[3] Asma Hilali, "Compiler, exclure, cacher. Les traditions dites forgées dans l'Islam sunnite (VIe/XIIe siècle)," *Revue de l'histoire des Religions* 2 (2011): 163–74; Asma Hilali, "Coran, hadith et textes intermédiaires. Le genre religieux aux débuts de l'islam," *Mélanges de l'Université Saint Joseph* 64 (2014): 29–44.

[4] Asma Hilali, *The Sanaa Palimpsest: The Transmission of the Qur'ān in the Seventh Century AH* (Oxford: Oxford University Press/The Institute of Ismaili Studies, 2017).

[5] Asma Hilali, "Le palimpseste de Ṣan'ā' et la canonisation du Coran: Nouveaux éléments," *Cahiers du Centre Gustave Glotz* 21 (2010): 443–48; Asma Hilali, "Was the Ṣan'ā' Qur'ān Palimpsest a Work in Progress?," in *The Yemeni Manuscript Tradition*, ed. Sabine Schmidtke, David Hollenberg, and Christoph Rauch (Leiden: Brill, 2015): 12–27; Hilali, *The Sanaa Palimpsest*, 39–40; cf. Behnam Sadeghi and Mohsen Goudarzi, "Ṣan'ā'1 and the Origins of the Qur'ān," *Der Islam* 87 (2012): 1–129 (here at p. 53, n. 157); Elisabeth Puin, "Ein früher Koran palimpsest aus Sanaa II (DAM 01-27.1). Teil II," in *Vom Koran zum Islam*, ed. Markus Groß and Karl-Heinz Ohlig, Schriften zur Frühen Islamgeschichte und zum Koran, Band 4 (Berlin: Hans Schiler, 2009): 523–681 (547). The reading instruction consists on the sentence "Do not say on the name of God" inserted before the beginning of a specific Qur'ān chapter (IX), a chapter that some traditional accounts consider as not being part of the Qur'ān corpus. See Hilali, *The Sanaa Palimpsest*, 39–40.

[6] For the dating of similar early *ḥijāzī* Qur'ān manuscripts, see for example, François Déroche, *La transmission écrite du Coran dans les débuts de l'islam. Le codex Parisino-petropolitanus* (Leiden: Brill), 2009; Alba Fedeli, "Mingana and the Manuscript of Mrs. Agnes Smith Lewis, One Century Later," *Manuscripta Orientalia* 11.3 (2005): 3–7; Alba Fedeli, "Early Qur'ānic Manuscripts, their Text, and the Alphonse Mingana Papers Held in the Department of Special Collections of the University of Birmingham" (PhD Dissertation, University of Birmingham, 2015); Sadeghi and Goudarzi, "Ṣan'ā'1 and the Origins of the Qur'ān."

[7] On the use of the margins in Arabic manuscripts, see Annie Vernay-Nouri, "Marges, gloses et décor dans une série de manuscrits arabo-islamiques," *Revue des Mondes Musulmans et de la*

passages and have various functions such as correcting[8] the passage or inserting additional material such as Qur'ānic variants and readings.[9] Thus, the marginal and interlinear annotations studied here are occasional and fragmentary. They are unlike the parallel systematic translation or commentary of the BnF Arabe 384 discussed by Déroche.[10] The second methodological point focuses on the textual composition of the fragment. By textual composition, I mean the organization of the material within the writing space and the way it indicates the context of transmission of the manuscript. From the textual composition, I explore the following issues: What is the dynamic between the marginal or interlinear notes and the Qur'ān passage as a whole?[11] Who composed the annotations and how do they take into consideration the reader? What does the organization of the writing space tell us about the intended reader of the manuscript? Were the fragments copied in a didactic context? In other words, were they works in progress for which annotations served as an enterprise of rewriting?[12]

In short, this paper aims to offer some keys for reflection on the materiality of Qur'ānic manuscripts, namely, writing the Qur'ān between the lines, its technique, and its relevance; this facilitates understanding to which use the manu-

---

*Méditerranée*, special issue La tradition manuscrite en écriture arabe, ed. Geneviève Humbert, 99–100 (2002): 117–31.

**8** For the corrections in the Qur'ān manuscripts, see, Adam Gacek, "Taxonomy of Scribal Errors and Corrections in Arabic Manuscripts," in *Theoretical Approaches to the Transmission and Edition of Oriental Manuscripts: Proceedings of a Symposium Held in Istanbul March 28-30, 2001*, ed. Judith Pfeiffer and Manfred Kropp (Beirut: Ergon Verlag Wurzburg in Kommission, 2007): 217–36; Adam Gacek, "Technical Practices and Recommendations Recorded by Classical and Post-classical Arabic Scholars Concerning the Copying and Correction of Manuscripts," in *Les Manuscrits du Moyen-Orient. essais de codicologie et de paléographie. Actes du colloque d'Istanbul*, ed. François Déroche (Istanbul and Paris: Bibliothèque Nationale, 1989): 51–60; see more recently, Daniel Alan Brubaker, *Corrections in Early Qur'ān Manuscripts: Twenty Examples* (London: Think and Tell, 2019). On the corrections of the Qur'ān from a theoretical perspective, see Behnam Sadeghi, "Criteria for Emending the Text of the Qur'ān," in *Law and Tradition in Classical Islam. Studies in honor of Hossein Modarressi*, ed. Michael Cook, Najam Haider, Intisar Rabb, and Asma Sayeed (New York: Palgrave Macmillan, 2013): 21–41.

**9** Alba Fedeli, "Relevance of the Oldest Qur'ānic Manuscripts for the Readings Mentioned by Commentaries: A Note on Sura 'Ṭā-Hā'," *Manuscripta Orientalia* 15.1 (2009): 3–10.

**10** Jozé Martinez Gazquez and François Déroche, "Lire et traduire le Coran au Moyen Âge. Les gloses latines du manuscrit arabe 384 de la BnF," *Comptes rendus des séances de l'académie des Inscriptions et Belles-Lettres* 154 (2010): 1021–40.

**11** I dedicated an independent reflection to the issue of the fragment *vs.* the whole within the textual composition in Islamic religious literature in Asma Hilali and S.R. Burge, eds., *The Making of Religious Texts in Islam: The Fragment and the Whole* (Berlin: Gerlach, 2019).

**12** I have investigate the hypothesis of a work in progress as the status of some manuscript such as the Ṣanā' palimpsest in Hilali, "Was the Ṣanʿā' Qur'ān Palimpsest a Work in Progress?," 12–27.

script is dedicated. On the basis of my interest in the marginal and interlinear annotations in the Qur'ān fragments dated to the seventh-ninth centuries CE, this paper displays and discusses two samples from the collection of MIA that show samples of the phenomena in question.[13] My research investigates the following points:

a) I identify the Qur'ān passages for each fragment in order to discover whether there is a continuity in the text and then I conclude whether it is a continuous text. From this I suggest it is a Qur'ān fragment or Qur'ān fragment within another text.
b) I Identify the passages containing marginal or interlinear annotations.
c) I study the writing in order to determine whether the scribe is him/herself the author of the marginal or interlinear annotation.
d) I note the erasure and determine the category of erasure, *i.e.* palimpsesting or crossing out.
e) Where possible, I decipher the marginal and interlinear annotations in order to confirm whether they are Qur'ānic text or other material such as an exegetical text, for example.
f) I study the function of marginal and interlinear annotations vis-à-vis the text (completion, addition, comment, etc.).

## 3 Example Fragments from the MIA, Qatar

There are important examples of manuscripts with marginal and interlinear annotations in MIA. If we take into consideration manuscripts dated to the tenth century CE and even later, in addition to the examples studied in this paper, a few other cases contain interesting samples of interlinear material and marginal comments, including MS. MIA. 189, 474, 480, 227, 466, 718. Moreover, if we take into consideration rewriting on the basis of palimpsesting as a way of bypassing interlinear and marginal additions, we can find numerous examples, such as MIA. 465, 466, 467, 468, 469, 504. In this paper, I limit my observations to two samples of manuscripts. In the first, I show an interlinear correction; in the second, I present an example of a marginal annotation with a reference-sign in the main body of the Qur'ān text referring to the margin.

---

[13] Other samples of Qur'ān manuscripts dated to the seventh century CE from the collection of the Museum of Islamic Art, Doha, and from other collections can be seen in Brubaker, *Corrections*.

The following analysis is not meant to be an exhaustive codicological description. It is rather, focused on the way in which the scribe – and sometimes the successive scribes – organized the Qur'ān text. Thus, the objectives are, as noted above, investigating the various uses of both texts: the original text and the annotations (for more on "layers" within Qur'ānic texts, see the essay from Fedeli [chapter 9] in the present volume; on marginal additions and other paratexts in Christian literature see the contributions from Batovici [chapter 2] and Allen [chapter 8]).

## 3.1 Example 1: MIA. 67. 2007. 1. Bifolio

Qur'ān parchment bifolio in *ḥijazī* script, dated to the seventh-eighth century CE. Length: 33, 6 cm/ Width: 24 cm.

This bifolio contains passages from chapter 5 of the Qur'ān, *al-Ma'ida* ("The Feast")[14] from Q. 5: 88 to Q. 5: 107 (Fig. 1). An interlinear annotation occurs in the right folio between the lines fourteen and fifteen at the level of the verse Q. 5: 93. The annotation consists on the following sentence: {وعملوا الصالحات ثم اتقوا وآمنوا} *wa 'amilū al-ṣaliḥat ṯumma ittaqū wa āmanū* ("and do good deeds, then are mindful of God and believe").[15] According to the Standard Qur'ān, that is, the Cairo edition of the Qur'ān published in 1924, the verse as presented in MIA. 67. 2007.1 misses precisely the fragment quoted above; the annotation between lines fourteen and fifteen thus seems to be a correction, adding this missing clause. The interlinear annotation seems to have been added by the same scribe, the one who wrote the entire passage Q.5: 88–107 in the bifolio.[16]

The absence of suitable space in the margin might explain the choice of the scribe to insert the fragment between lines fourteen and fifteen. As for a reference-sign that might guide the reader to the correction, there is none. However, the way the correction is written shows that the writing starts at its initial place in the verse, that, is, at the end of the verb {آمنوا}*āmanū* ("they believe").[17] As for the end of the correction, there is no reference-sign indicating it; the reader is expected go back somehow to reading line fifteen after the end of the inserted fragment. The

---

[14] The English translation of the Qur'ān referred to is: M.A.S. Abdel Haleem, *The Qur'ān: A new translation* (Oxford: Oxford University Press, 2004–2005).
[15] Abdel Haleem, *The Qur'ān: A New Translation*, 77.
[16] See Brubaker, *Corrections*, 49.
[17] This choice might explain the confusion between the *alif al-wiqāya* of the verb *'amilū* and the *hamza* of *ittaqū* in the line underneath. See the comment of Brubaker on the same *alif* in Brubaker, *Corrections*, 49.

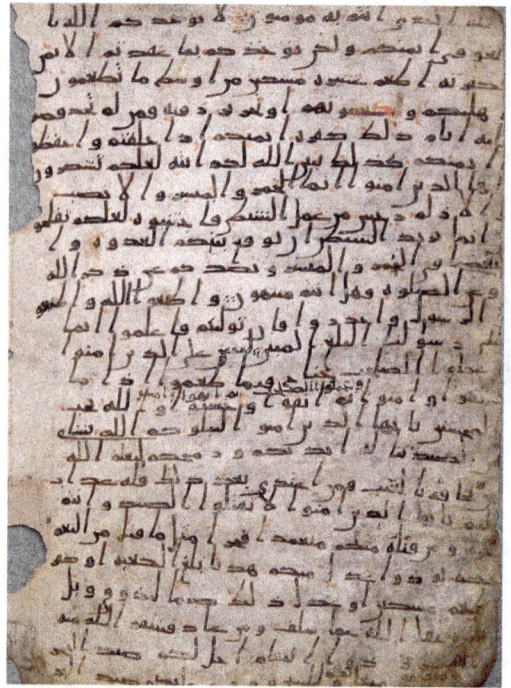

**Fig. 1:** *Bifolio MIA. 67.2007.1.* With kind permission of the museum of Islamic Art, Doha, Qatar.

aim of the placement of the interlinear annotation is to designate the exact place of the correction; this indicates that the scribe has an available oral or written version of the "correct" version of the Qur'ān passage; the lack of clear indication of the way the reader should consider the interlinear annotation might suggest that the corrector is taking the note for his/her own usage.

## 3.2 Example 2: MIA. 2013.16. Folio 8v.

Folio 8v. from thirteen Qur'ān folios in Kūfic script, dated to the eighth-ninth century CE. Length: 16, 5 cm/ Width: 25,5 cm.

This folio contains passages from chapter 7, *al-Aʿrāf* ("The Heights") from Q.7: 73 to Q.7: 83. The marginal annotation occurs in verse Q.7: 77, line 8 of the folio 8v. (Fig. 2). However, the annotation barely appears as it is half damaged because of the disintegration of the parchment on the edges of the right margin. Nevertheless, we can decipher the following clause: {عن أمر} *ʿan amr*, an incomplete sentence suggesting the action of misappropriation and the diversion from an order and a commandment. This clause is part of the Qur'ānic verse written in line 8 but which is missing in the body of the text. The following passage is the transcription of the verse with the missing clause underlined: {و عقروا الناقة و عتوا عن أمر ربّهم} *wa ʿaqarū al-nāqa waʿataw ʿan ʿamr rabbihim* ("and then they hamstrung the camel. They defied their Lord's commandment").

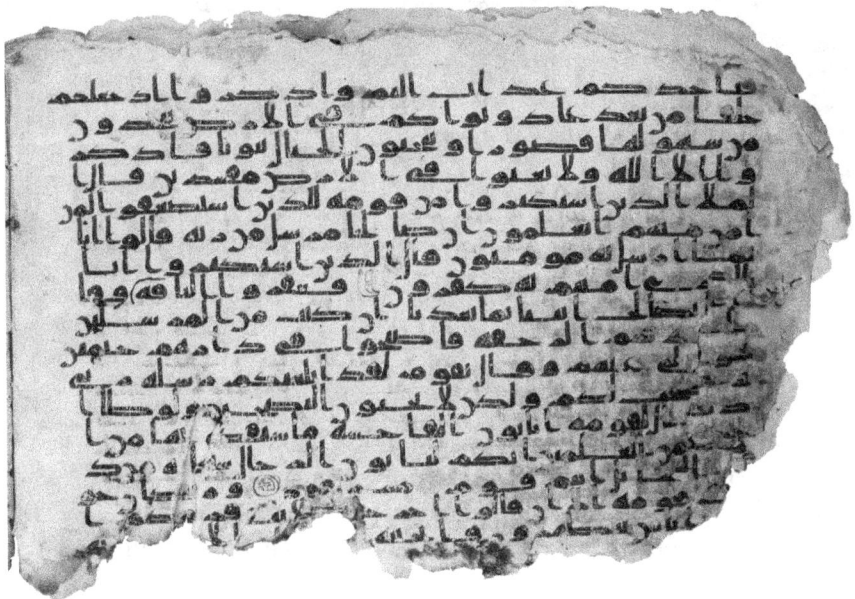

**Fig. 2:** *MIA 2013.16. Folio 8.v.* With kind permission of the museum of Islamic Art, Doha, Qatar.

A scribe different from the one who wrote the main Qur'ān text in the thirteen leaves seems to have added the marginal annotation that apparently postdates considerably the original script given the darker ink of the writing and of the reference sign and given the different handwriting between the body of the text and the marginal clause. However, apart from the marginal annotation, what is striking in this example is the reference-sign that appears at the end of the word *al-nāqa* and which refers to the right margin of the folio where the marginal annotation is placed (Fig. 3). This suggests that the whole missing fragment from the verse was written in the margin before the damage of the parchment, *i.e.* {عتوا عن أمر ربّهم} *waʿataw ʿan ʿamr rabbihim* ("They defied their Lord's commandment"), a sentence from which only remains the few words we deciphered above, {عن أ مر} ("from the commandment").

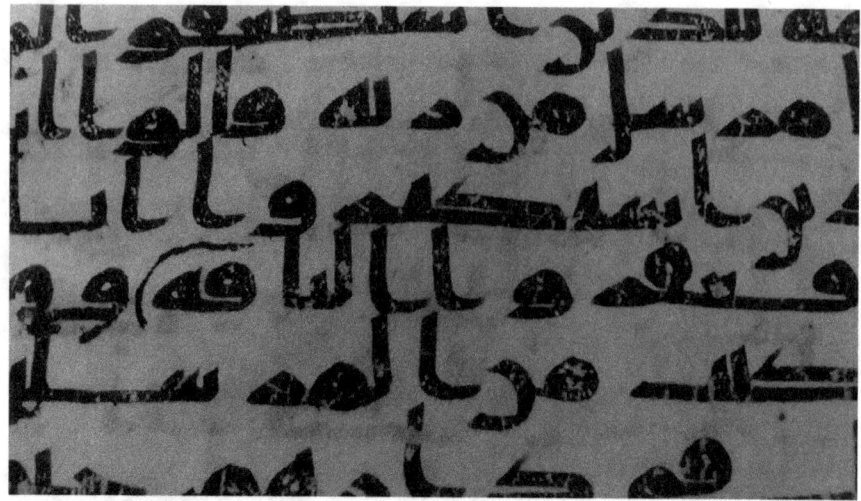

**Fig. 3:** *Detail of marginal reference sign. MIA 2013.16 Folio 8.v.* With kind permission of the Museum of Islamic Art, Doha, Qatar.

As is the case within the interlinear annotation studied in Example 1, the marginal annotation in Example 2 aims to correct the verse, and, more precisely, adds the sentence omitted in the verse by the original scribe. The reference-sign aims to catch the eye of the reader and direct him/her to the right margin of the folio. The technique of reporting to the margin in order to read the corrected version of the Qur'ān fragment seems to be executed in a random way. Despite the damage of the parchment in the margin, one can attest that the clause written in the margin is not clear and the space allowed in the margin does not seem sufficient. Moreover, there is enough space in the left margin which is closer to the mistake but which has not been used by the corrector. All the choices made by the corrector indicate that he/she is not inserting his/her correction in a careful way, i.e, a way that makes him/her sure the correction is considered by the reader. The organization of the few words we decipher in the right margin shows a superimposition of the letters and the absence of a linear and clear writing of the missing fragment or any technique that might guarantee a correct consideration of the inserted correction.

Similar to Example 1, the example of the marginal annotation underlines the absence of a clear technique of adding missing words and sentences. The method of the corrector shows his appropriation of the Qur'ān text and suggests that we are dealing with a copy that is destined to a restricted usage that is probably limited to the corrector's personal usage. Despite the absence of other corrections in the rest of the thirteen folios of the manuscript MIA 2013.16, there are a few aspects that show incompleteness of the writing: for example, some versifications are missing in the Qur'ān text such in folio 8v. such as Q. 7:82. The versification is not reported in Spitaler's list of variations among the different schools of versification.[18] However, we consider this as an additional sign that we are dealing with a copy of the Qur'ān text that has been submitted to an enterprise of correction that does not follow a clear method, nor is the correction based on a systematic technique.

# 4 Conclusion

This essay has outlined two examples of early Qur'ān manuscripts which highlight different methods of annotating the Qur'ānic text. The first example showed an interlinear fragment; the second showed the insertion of a marginal annotation. Both of these emendations seem to be inserted in a subjective and rather non-representative way and the objective of being readable does not prevail. It seems to be possible that this reflects a personal text that is not meant for other readers.

Various interpretations might explain such particular interventions. For example, the multiplicity of errors in private copies of the Qur'ān text might have motivated the owners of these Qur'ān manuscripts to limit their circulation to private spheres, while also explaining their submission to non-expert or non-professional corrector hands.[19] Another explanation might be that, in the writing context in which these manuscripts emerged, scribes did not normally use the margins, and thus the need for a reference-sign to guide the reader to the marginal addition.

Unlike manuscripts dated to the historical period when the scholastic manuscript Islamic tradition is operative (tenth century CE and later), early manuscripts such as those discussed above show limited use of the margins as well as of the interlinear space. When such interventions are found in the Qur'ān manuscripts in the early period, these appear to be personal, subjective, and unsystematic. In this sense, these emendations were perhaps the first steps towards the

---

[18] Anton Spitaler, *Die Verszählung des Koran nach islamischer Überlieferung* (Munich: Verlag der Bayerischen Akademie der Wissenschaften, 1935), 37.

[19] Elisabeth Puin considers that the important number of errors in the lower text of the Ṣanʿā' palimpsest motivated the decision to scratch the parchment and to reuse it. See Elisabeth Puin, "Ein früher Koranpalimpsest aus Sanaa II (DAM 01-27.1). Teil. III: 'Eine nicht-ʿutmānischer Koran'," in *Die Entstehung einer Weltreligion I: Von der Koranischen Bewegung zum Frühislam*, ed. Markus Groß and Karl-Heinz Ohlig, Schriften zur frühen Islamgeschichte und zum Koran, Band 5 (Berlin: Hans Schiler, 2010): 233–305 (258).

scholastic transmission tradition which would later emerge. In other words, these early steps, graphically, set up a framework which would be developed further into forms such as the certificates of transmission (*sama'* pl. *sama'at*), glosses, the commentaries, and the Qur'ānic variants and readings (*qira'at* pl. *qira'at*), and so on. Accordingly, investigating the techniques of annotating early Qur'ānic texts can help facilitate a reconstruction of the transmission of the Qur'ān in its earliest contexts.

To conclude: taking seriously the material forms of early Qur'ānic texts – and their annotations in particular – is a reminder that exploring the material dimensions of texts such as the Qur'ān is an important and necessary aspect of understanding sacred texts, their use, and their transmission.

## Bibliography

Brubaker, Daniel Alan. *Corrections in Early Qur'ān Manuscripts: Twenty Examples*. London: Think and Tell, 2019.

Déroche, François. *La transmission écrite du Coran dans les débuts de l'islam. Le codex Parisino-petropolitanus*. Leiden: Brill, 2009.

Fedeli, Alba. "Mingana and the Manuscript of Mrs. Agnes Smith Lewis, One Century Later." *Manuscripta Orientalia* 11.3 (2005): 3–7.

Fedeli, Alba. "Relevance of the Oldest Qur'ānic Manuscripts for the Readings Mentioned by Commentaries: A Note on Sura 'Ṭa-Ha'." *Manuscripta Orientalia* 15.1 (2009): 3–10.

Fedeli, Alba. "Early Qur'ānic Manuscripts, their Text, and the Alphonse Mingana Papers Held in the Department of Special Collections of the University of Birmingham." PhD Dissertation, University of Birmingham, 2015.

Gacek, Adam. "Taxonomy of Scribal Errors and Corrections in Arabic Manuscripts." In *Theoretical Approaches to the Transmission and Edition of Oriental Manuscripts. Proceedings of a Symposium Held in Istanbul March 28–30, 2001*, edited by Judith Pfeiffer and Manfred Kropp, 217–36. Beirut: Ergon Verlag Wurzburg in Kommission, 2007.

Gacek, Adam. "Technical Practices and Recommendations Recorded by Classical and Post-classical Arabic Scholars Concerning the Copying and Correction of Manuscripts." In *Les Manuscrits du Moyen-Orient. essais de codicologie et de paléographie*, edited by François Déroche, 51–60. Istanbul and Paris: Bibliothèque Nationale, 1989.

Gazquez, Jozé Martinez, and François Déroche. "Lire et traduire le Coran au Moyen Âge. Les gloses latines du manuscrit arabe 384 de la BnF." In *Comptes rendus des séances de l'académie des Inscriptions et Belles-Lettres* 154 (2010): 1021–40.

Haleem, M.A.S. Abdel. *The Qur'ān: A New translation*. Oxford: Oxford University Press, 2004–2005.

Hilali, Asma. "Le palimpseste de Ṣan'a' et la canonisation du Coran: Nouveaux éléments." *Cahiers du Centre Gustave Glotz* 21 (2010): 443–48.

Hilali, Asma. "Compiler, exclure, cacher. Les traditions dites forgées dans l'Islam sunnite (VIe/XIIe siècle)." *Revue de l'histoire des Religions* 2 (2011): 163–74.

Hilali, Asma. "Coran, hadith et textes intermédiaires. Le genre religieux aux débuts de l'islam." *Mélanges de l'Université Saint Joseph* 64 (2014): 29–44.

Hilali, Asma. "Was the Ṣanʿaʾ Qurʾān Palimpsest a Work in Progress?" in *The Yemeni Manuscript Tradition*, edited by Sabine Schmidtke, David Hollenberg, and Christoph Rauch, 12–27. Leiden: Brill, 2015.

Hilali, Asma. *The Sanaa Palimpsest: The Transmission of the Qurʾān in the Seventh Century AH*. Oxford: Oxford University Press/The Institute of Ismaili Studies, 2017.

Hilali, Asma, and S.R. Burge, eds. *The Making of Religious Texts in Islam: The Fragment and the Whole*. Berlin: Gerlach, 2019.

Puin, Elisabeth. "Ein früher Koranpalimpsest aus Ṣanʿāʾ II (DAM 01-27.1). Teil II." In *Vom Koran zum Islam*, edited by Markus Groß and Karl-Heinz Ohlig, 523–81. Schriften zur Frühen Islamgeschichte und zum Koran 4. Berlin: Hans Schiler, 2009.

Puin, Elisabeth, "Ein früher Koranpalimpsest aus Ṣanʿāʾ II (DAM 01-27.1). Teil. III: 'Eine nicht-ʿuṯmanischer Koran'." In *Die Entstehung einer Weltreligion I: Von der Koranischen Bewegung zum Frühislam*, edited by Markus Groß and Karl-Heinz Ohlig, 233–305. Schriften zur frühen Islamgeschichte und zum Koran 5. Berlin: Hans Schiler, 2010.

Sadeghi, Behnam. "Criteria for Emending the Text of the Qurʾān." In *Law and Tradition in Classical Islam: Studies in Honor of Hossein Modarressi*, edited by Michael Cook, Najam Haider, Intisar Rabb, and Asma Sayeed, 21–41. New York: Palgrave Macmillan, 2013.

Sadeghi, Behnam, and Mohsen Goudarzi. "Ṣanʿāʾ1 and the Origins of the Qurʾān." *Der Islam* 87 (2012): 1–129.

Spitaler, Anton. *Die Verszählung des Koran nach islamischer Überlieferung*. Munich: Verlag der Bayerischen Akademie der Wissenschaften, 1935.

Vernay-Nouri, Annie. "Marges, gloses et décor dans une série de manuscrits arabo-islamiques." In *Revue des Mondes Musulmans et de la Méditerranée*. Special issue La tradition manuscrite en écriture arabe, edited by Geneviève Humbert, 99–100 (2002): 117–31.

Ben Outhwaite
# The Sefer Torah and Jewish Orthodoxy in the Islamic Middle Ages

## 1 Introduction

Between the period of the Second Temple and the early Middle Ages, reflected in the two great collections of the Dead Sea Scrolls and the Cairo Genizah, a change happens in Judaism's transmission of its scripture. The texts from Qumran reflect a society necessarily wedded to the scroll as the medium for transmitting the Hebrew Bible (for more on the Qumran materials, see Chapter 1 from Krauß and Schücking-Jungblut). In the ensuing centuries, even as surrounding cultures adopted the codex, this necessity was fixed, regulated and formalized into a set of halakhic prescriptions for the copying and reading of the Torah scroll, the only acceptable medium for the recitation of God's law in rabbinic Judaism of late antiquity (on this, see the essay from del Barco in the present volume). Yet, by the Middle Ages, the Cairo Genizah reveals a Jewish community that had embraced the codex with an impressive enthusiasm, evidenced by the tens of thousands of leaves from books big and small that were deposited into the genizah chamber of the Synagogue of the Jerusalemites in al-Fusṭāṭ. What occasioned such a shift in the Jewish relationship to the book? Does the heterogeneous manuscript evidence of the Genizah provide a clear answer, or did the medieval Judaism of the Islamic east, divided as it was between Rabbanite and Qaraite, Palestinian and Babylonian, possess a complex relationship with the new medium?

## 2 The Sefer Torah

The Torah scroll, the Sefer Torah, occupies a pre-eminent position in Judaism's cultural consciousness by dint of long tradition and frequent repetition of codified rites. Reverence and sanctity have accrued to it as a physical object, and respect is paid to it during its useful lifetime and even on its "death". The synagogue congregation stand in the Sefer Torah's presence. One should not produce a Torah scroll thoughtlessly, but with careful and full intent; nor needlessly sell one. Public reading from the scroll marks not only the passing of weeks, and the celebration of holy and high holy days, but also cements an individual's transition into adulthood. In antiquity, public reading of the Torah scroll was a sign of authority enjoyed by Jewish kings and high priests (Mišna Soṭa 7:8; Yoma

϶ Open Access. © 2020 Ben Outhwaite, published by De Gruyter. This work is licensed under a Creative Commons Attribution-NonCommercial-NoDerivatives 4.0 International License.
https://doi.org/10.1515/9783110634440-005

7:1); with the dispersion, and the rise of the synagogue, possession of a Sefer Torah denoted a congregation, and thereby a community. In the synagogue, the Torah scroll stands at the centre of the principal rite, the reading of the weekly portion of the Pentateuch, and special prayers accompany its introduction into the service, and its subsequent withdrawal from it.[1] Some congregations raise and lower the scroll, before or after the reading, receiving a scriptural response in reply; other practices have grown up over time.[2] In late antiquity the main Jewish legal sources, the Mišna and Talmuds, discussed the correct form, treatment and disposal of the Sefer Torah. A scroll's creation, from the production of the parchment to the ornamenting of the letters, is set out in dedicated treatises such as Sofrim or the minor tractate Sefer Tora. Failure to follow these prescriptions can result in a scroll that is פסול (*pasul*), "blemished, defective", i.e., liturgically invalid. Even scrolls that are at the end of their useful life retain their sanctity and must be treated appropriately: ואמר רבא ספר תורה שבלה גונזין אותו אצל תלמיד חכם, "And Rava said: 'A Sefer Torah that is worn out should be interred with a scholar'" (Babylonian Talmud Megilla 26b). The Torah's sanctity gives the scroll a totemistic value: the Mišna decrees that a king heading off to fight should take along his Torah scroll (Mišna Sanhedrin 2:4). According to the historian Josephus, the Romans turned this back on the Jews by parading a captured scroll as plunder through Rome, following the legions' victory in the Great Revolt, a detail which perhaps Josephus added as embellishment to underline the definitive nature of the Jewish defeat.[3]

These cumbersome rolls of animal skins derive their prestige from their weighty contents, the Law of Moses, the first five books of the Hebrew Bible. In Rabbinic Judaism the Sefer Torah was "the only suitable and appropriate receptacle of the Holy Writ,"[4] and it was expected to contain the entire text of the Hebrew Pentateuch, unchanged and unabbreviated. Any suspicion that this might not be the case could render a scroll invalid, for instance, if it had been purchased from a non-Jew or there were too many errors or erasures.[5] Manuscript discoveries suggest that this rabbinic stipulation was probably not

---

**1** Ismar Elbogen, *Jewish Liturgy: A Comprehensive History*, trans. Raymond P. Scheindlin (Philadelphia: Jewish Publication Society; Jewish Theological Seminary of America, 1993), 158–63.
**2** Elbogen, *Jewish Liturgy*, 142.
**3** Simon Schama, *The Story of the Jews: finding the words, 1000 BCE–1492 CE* (London: Vintage Books, 2014), 153–54.
**4** Menahem Haran, "Bible Scrolls in Eastern and Western Jewish Communities from Qumran to the High Middle Ages," *Hebrew Union College Annual* 56 (1985): 22.
**5** Elbogen, *Jewish Liturgy*, 142. Aaron Rothkoff and Louis Isaac Rabinowitz, "Sefer Torah," in *Encyclopaedia Judaica*, ed. Fred Skolnik and Michael Berenbaum (Detroit: Macmillan Reference USA, 2007): 243.

operative in the period of the Dead Sea Scrolls (to ca. second century CE), since the biblical scrolls from the Judean Desert are mostly single-book scrolls, with only a very few exceptions with two or possibly three books.[6] Even the later En Gedi Leviticus scroll, which probably dates from the third-fourth century CE, was probably just a scroll of Leviticus and not the whole Torah.[7] Several centuries later, by the time of the Babylonian Talmud, the liturgical use of scrolls containing only a portion of the Torah was expressly forbidden: אין קוראין בחומשין בבית הכנסת משום כבוד צבור, "one should not read from *ḥumašin* in the synagogue out of respect for the congregation" (Babylonian Talmud Giṭṭin 60a). In the era of the Talmud חומשין (*ḥumašin*) were scrolls that contained only a single biblical book. The pre-eminence of the Sefer Torah for public reading was thus firmly established in the Oral Torah, the oral law, as transmitted by the sages. In the twelfth century, the scholar Moses Maimonides stated in his law code that one may copy an individual book of the Torah, but it does not have the same sacred status as a Sefer Torah: מותר לכתוב התורה כל חומש וחומש בפני עצמו ואין בהן קדושת ספר תורה, "It is permissible to write the Torah as separate books (*ḥumaš ve-ḥumaš*), but these do not have the sanctity of a Torah scroll (*sefer tora*)" (Mišne Tora Hilḵot Təfillin, Məzuza ve-Sefer Tora 7:14). These single biblical books and excerpted texts are usable for study or for teaching children but not the liturgy. Even with the shift in worship from a single holy site, the Temple in Jerusalem, to synagogues scattered across the Jewish world, the strict rules governing the production and use of Torah scrolls remained and, indeed, multiplied. Regional and chronological variations emerged, which were then recorded in new halakhic compendia. Strict adherence to a standard was still necessary, even when the number of scrolls vastly increased. Maimonides regularized those rules in his Mišne Tora: there should be לא פחות משמונה וארבעים ולא יתר על ששים, "not less than 48 and not more than 60" lines on a scroll (Mišne Tora Hilḵot Təfillin, Məzuza ve-Sefer Tora 7:10), for instance, as opposed to the earlier, looser standard of "42 and 98" given in tractate Sofrim.[8] But Maimonides still stipulated that attentive adherence to the traditional form remained the essential mark of quality, and thereby of liturgical rectitude; he despaired at the decline in the standard of Sifre Torot that he consulted while in Egypt (Mišne Tora, Hilḵot Təfillin, Məzuza və-Sefer Tora 8:4).

---

[6] Emanuel Tov, *Textual Criticism of the Hebrew Bible*, Second Revised Edition (Minneapolis: Fortress, 2001), 203–04.

[7] Gary A. Rendsburg, "The World's Oldest Torah Scrolls," *ANE Today* 6:3 (March 2018). http://www.asor.org/anetoday/2018/03/Worlds-Oldest-Torah-Scrolls (accessed 14 October 2019).

[8] Michael Higger, מסכת סופרים ב ונלוו עליה מדרש מסכת סופרים (מסכת סופרים) (Jerusalem: Maqor, 1970), §2:11 116–17.

As the medium for God's word in antiquity, the scroll was deployed early on as a divine metaphor by the poets and prophets of the Hebrew Bible. We can read about scrolls directly performing God's will as His instruments of divine power – flying through the air dispensing justice in Zechariah, ואשוב ואשא עיני ואראה והנה מגלה עפה, "Then I turned, and lifted up mine eyes, and looked, and behold a flying roll (məgilla ʿafa)" (Zech 5:1–2), or literally forcing prophecies in the form of "lamentations, mourning and woe" down Ezekiel's throat (Ezek 2:8–3:3). The scroll is a repository for God's law and His instrument for spreading it. Ownership or production of a scroll became a requirement for Jews, fixing through an act of writing the bond between the nation and God's word. The Babylonian Talmud, in the name of the sage Rava (Abba ben Joseph bar Ḥama, d. 352 CE), quotes Deut 31:19, ועתה כתבו לכם את־השירה הזאת ולמדה את־בני ישראל, "Now therefore write ye this song for you, and teach it the children of Israel," as underpinning a commandment for every Jew to write a Torah scroll (Babylonian Talmud Sanhedrin 21b). Maimonides' Mišne Tora decrees (Hilkot Təfillin, Məzuza və-Sefer Tora 7:1) that it is a necessity (a מצות עשה, a positive commandment) for "each and every man of Israel" (כל איש ואיש מישראל) to write for himself a Torah scroll, a Sefer Torah. If he is not capable of the task, then it is acceptable to get someone else to write it on his behalf. A Jewish king should therefore have two scrolls: one a personal scroll, which he would already have owned before becoming king, and one produced for his kingship. The former is put into storage, while the latter should accompany him in battle, when he sits in a court of law and at mealtimes, all of which Maimonides takes from Deut 17:19, והיתה עמו וקרא בו כל־ימי חייו, "And it shall be with him, and he shall read it all the days of his life."

The requirement to produce a personal Sefer Torah is an exacting and, for most people, an impractical task. According to the Masoretic notes at the end of the book of Deuteronomy (f. 120a) in the manuscript Russian National Library Evr. I B19a, known popularly as Codex Leningrad and the earliest complete codex of the Hebrew Bible, there are 5845 verses, 79,856 words, and 400,045 letters in the Pentateuch. Even an expert scribe can take many months to copy all that with the requisite care into a Torah scroll. The cost of the parchment alone would place the production beyond the means of most members of the Jewish community in the Middle Ages. Like many of the laws codified from the Mišna onwards, these commandments reflect ideals, the conditions for which might never obtain in ordinary life. They can be grouped with those governing the behaviour of Jewish royalty or the sacrifices in the temple, neither of which had relevance after the temple's destruction and the demise of the kingdom of Judaea, but which are preserved as historically important or potentially relevant in the future. On the other hand, halakhists have always been capable of showing ingenuity in coming up with ways to obey the strict letter of the law. Today members of a congregation can observe the commandment to write their own Torah scroll by the act of completing a scroll, each member writing, or even filling in the outline of, just a single letter, in a ceremony known as סיום התורה (*siyyum ha-tora*), "completion of the Torah."[9] This action was anticipated by Maimonides who wrote "and anyone who corrects a Torah scroll, even a single letter, it is as if he wrote all of it" (Mišne Tora, Hilkot Təfillin, Məzuza və-Sefer Tora 7:1). In the Middle Ages, the completion of another's scribal work is recorded as a meritorious act. The Cairo Genizah fragment Cambridge University Library T-S A42.3 is the colophon of a large-format Bible, written on parchment. The colophon comes at the end of the book of Deuteronomy, indicating that this was probably originally a manuscript of the whole Torah. It reads:

אני יצחק המלמד בן הרב ר׳ עמרם גן נוחו ועדן מנוחו השלמתי חסרון זה הספר ונקדתי אתו ביד אלהי הטובה
עלי וגמרתי אתו ביום רביעי בחדש כסליו בתשעה בו שנת אתקין לשטרות סימן טוב אמן

"I, Isaac the Teacher son of the Rav R. Amram – his rest be in the garden and his repose in Eden – have completed the missing part of this *sefer*, and I have vocalised it, with my God's bountiful hand upon me, and I finished it on Thursday, on the ninth of Kislev, in the year 1560 of the Era of Documents. A good sign. Amen."

The dating, which uses the Seleucid Era, corresponds to 1248 CE. A note above the colophon, in a different hand, indicates that the volume was subsequently dedicated to the Synagogue of the Palestinians in al-Fusṭāṭ, which was the synagogue in which the Cairo Genizah was discovered. Both the completion and the dedication were regarded as meritorious acts, and a great many colophons in tenth–thirteenth century Bibles mark their dedication to a synagogue or community.[10]

## 3 Scrolls and Codices

What is notable about this Pentateuch manuscript, T-S A42.3, and many others produced in the Near East during the same period of the high Middle Ages, is that

---

**9** Rothkoff and Rabinowitz, "Sefer Torah," 243.
**10** There are many in the Cairo Genizah Collections, e.g., T-S NS 248.28, a bifolum from a smaller format parchment codex, containing Genesis, with a note dedicating it לכנסת אלשאמין, "to the Synagogue of the Palestinians." Paul Kahle gives a number of examples from the Firkovich Collection in the Russian National Library. See, e.g., RNL Evr. II B225, which was dedicated to עדת בעלי הקראים השוכנים בירושלים, "the community of Qaraites who dwell in Jerusalem"; Paul Kahle, *Masoreten des Westens* (Stuttgart: Kohlhammer, 1927), 67–68.

they are books, codices, and not scrolls of the Torah. The Hebrew Bible itself extols the scroll, the *sefer* (ספר) or *megilla* (מגלה), and rabbinic sources similarly discuss scrolls of the Torah. In origin, and particularly in the compound Sefer Torah (ספר תורה), the noun ספר (*sefer*, pl. *səfarim*) refers solely to a scroll. From the Middle Ages onwards, and certainly in Modern Hebrew, *sefer* comes to mean "book". This can lead to ambiguity. Moses Maimonides' statement in the Mišne Tora that he has seen much confusion in all the *səfarim* he has consulted is just such a case, in fact, one of the more egregious examples. His use of *səfarim* is traditionally translated as "scrolls", e.g., in the Moses Hyamson edition, "As in all the scrolls I have seen, I noticed serious incorrectness in these regards."[11] However, we could equally take this to mean "books" in its broadest sense, copies of the Bible in all formats, perhaps more like the way the word *kitāb* is used in Arabic, which was, after all, Maimonides' native language.[12] The ambiguity of Maimonides' Hebrew formulation is on open display in the passage of the Mišne Tora that discusses the correct layout of the "open and closed sections" (the *parašiyyot sətumot* and *pətuḥot*) of the Masoretic text. He states that he has relied on a famous copy of the Bible, well-known in Egypt, for the correct writing of them:

> ולפי שראיתי שיבוש גדול בכל הספרים אלו וכן בעלי המסורת שכותבין ומחברין להודיע הפתוחות והסתומות נחלקים בדברים אלו במחלוקת הספרים שסומכין עליהם ראיתי לכתוב הנה כל פרשיות התורה הסתומות והפתוחות וצורת השירות כדי לתקן עליהם כל הספרים ולהגיה מהם וספר שסמכנו עליו בדברים אלו הוא הספר הידוע במצרים שהוא כולל ארבעה ועשרים ספרים שהיה בירושלים מכמה שנים להגיה ממנו הספרים ועליו היו הכל סומכין לפי שהגיהו בן אשר ודקדק בו שנים הרבה והגיהו פעמים רבות כמו שהעתיקו ועליו סמכתי בספר התורה שכתבתי כהלכתו

And because I have seen great confusion in all these *səfarim*, and indeed the Masoretic authorities who write and produce compositions to proclaim the open and closed sections are themselves divided in these matters due to the lack of concord in the *səfarim* that they rely on, I have thought it fit to write here all the open and closed sections of the Torah, and the format of the songs, in order that all the *səfarim* may be corrected and carefully checked against them. And the *sefer* on which we relied in these matters is the *sefer* well-known in Egypt, which contains the twenty-four *səfarim*, that was used in Jerusalem some years ago to check *səfarim* and on which everyone used to rely because Ben Asher had checked it and closely studied it over many years, and he checked it many times whenever it was copied from. And I myself relied on it for the *Sefer Torah* that I wrote according to the *halaka* (Mišne Tora, Hilkot Təfillin, Məzuza və-Sefer Tora 8:4).

---

[11] Moses Hyamson (ed.), *Mishneh Torah: The Book of Adoration by Maimonides*, edited according to the Bodleian (Oxford) Codex with an English Translation (Jerusalem: Boys Town Jerusalem Publishers, 1965), 131b.

[12] Johannes Pedersen and Geoffrey French, *The Arabic Book* (Princeton, NJ: Princeton University Press, 1984), 12.

Maimonides caused the confusion here himself, because he chose to write his great codification of Jewish law in a deliberately archaising Hebrew, the language of the Rabbis who transmitted the Oral Torah. Rabbinic Hebrew, especially in the form in which Maimonides reimagined it, lacked a nuanced vocabulary for the different forms of writing medium that had become available even long before Maimonides' day.[13] Traditional Rabbinic Judaism knew only the scroll for the communication of its religious texts. Hence, in this quite crucial passage, which has provoked considerable interest over time, he uses the noun *sefer* in singular and plural to refer to (a) a codex of the whole Hebrew Bible; (b) a biblical book as a literary unit; (c) scrolls or codices of the Bible in general; and (d) a Torah Scroll, which he had copied, in particular. This passage is well known and frequently cited because the codex that Maimonides sets up as the model for all to follow is believed by tradition, and now by most modern scholarship, to be the famous Aleppo Codex, which documentary evidence can place in Egypt in Maimonides' day and which is held to be the work of the last, great Masorete, Aaron ben Moses ben Asher.[14]

Had Moses Maimonides written his testimonial for the Aleppo Codex in Judaeo-Arabic, in which most of his other compositions were written, then perhaps alongside the word כתאב (*kitāb*) for "book" in a general sense, he would have used a number of different nouns for the varying types of *sefer* that he was describing. A clear contrast can be seen in a Judaeo-Arabic letter written in 1100 CE, a half-century before Maimonides' work, following the capture of Jerusalem in the First Crusade. This letter draws a clear distinction between scrolls and books, quite unlike the uniform *sefer/səfarim* of Maimonides' text. Written at a time of immense crisis, it details how the Jewish community of Ashqelon had coped with the fall of Jerusalem and the arrival of the soldiers of the First Crusade on their doorstep.[15] The community had fallen into debt by ransoming captive Jews back from the Crusaders. Ashqelon was well fortified and remained in Fāṭimid hands while the rest of the Holy Land fell to the sudden onslaught of the invading "Franks". After taking Jerusalem, they came to what was their new border with the Islamic world and traded the captives they had taken for dinars. The ransoming of prisoners was a necessary and righteous act in Jewish

---

**13** Cf. Saul Lieberman, *Hellenism in Jewish Palestine: Studies in the Literary Transmission, Beliefs and Manners of Palestine in the I Century B.C.E.–IV Century C.E.* (New York: Jewish Theological Seminary of America, 1962), 206.
**14** David Stern, *The Jewish Bible: A Material History* (Seattle: University of Washington Press, 2017), 64; Jordan Penkower, "Maimonides and the Aleppo Codex," *Textus* 9 (1981): 39–129.
**15** Shelomo Dov Goitein, "Contemporary Letters on the Capture of Jerusalem by the Crusaders," *Journal of Jewish Studies* 3 (1952): 168–75.

eyes, but the letter also reveals the purchasing of sacred texts that the invaders had plundered, and from which the Franks also profited. Alongside the details of the debt incurred through ransoming prisoners, the writers talk about the debt incurred פי אבתיאע מאיתין ותלתין מצחף ומאיה דפתר וכ׳ ותמניה ספרי תורות גמיע דלך קודש, "in the purchasing of two hundred and thirty codices [of the Bible], one hundred quires etc, and eight Torah scrolls, all of them holy [=consecrated public property]" (Cambridge University Library T-S 20.113).[16] The language is Judaeo-Arabic, the written vernacular of the Jews of the Fāṭimid realm, although "Torah scrolls" is the Rabbinic Hebrew compound plural ספרי תורות (*sifre torot*). The noun מצחף (*muṣḥaf*) is Arabic for "codex" and is used in the Judaeo-Arabic of this period to denote codices of the Bible. Having originally referred in Arabic to Qur'an codices,[17] it was borrowed into Jewish Arabic to refer to codices of their holiest book, and was subsequently hebraised as מִצְחָף (*miṣḥaf*). The noun דפתר (*daftar, diftar*), a Greek loan into Arabic, denotes a book-type distinct from *muṣḥaf*, referring here probably to partial or unbound books, i.e., volumes, fascicles or quires.[18] Arabo-Islamic sources have a relatively large number of words for such book-like structures, including *juzʾ*, "fascicle, part", and *karrāsa*, "volume", reflecting the sophistication of the Arabic book trade.[19] The prime liturgical object, the Torah scroll, retains its Hebrew identity, however, even in an Arabic document, whereas the vocabulary denoting books, no matter how "holy" they are too by dint of the sacred text they carry, is Arabic. The cause of this discrepancy is a lack of an existing, embedded Hebrew vocabulary for the codex, which necessarily reflects the late period of the writing medium's adoption by Judaism.

It is generally accepted by scholarship that Judaism, as an institution, adopted the codex much later than the cultures around it, centuries after the technology's introduction into the Hellenistic world and long after its adoption by Christianity. In his recent material history of the Jewish Bible, David Stern put it so: "[I]t is clear that it took Jews at least four hundred years longer to adopt the new writing platform than most everyone else in the Mediterranean world."[20]

---

**16** The manuscript can be viewed online at https://cudl.lib.cam.ac.uk/view/MS-TS-00020-00113/1 (accessed 14 October 2019).
**17** Pedersen and French, *The Arabic Book*, 101–02.
**18** Malachi Beit-Arié, *Hebrew Codicology: Historical and Comparative Typology of Hebrew Medieval Codices based on the Documentation of the Extant Dated Manuscripts using a Quantitative Approach*, Preprint internet English version 0.3+ (August 2019), 41. https://web.nli.org.il/sites/NLI/English/collections/manuscripts/hebrewcodicology/Documents/Hebrew-Codicology-continuously-updated-online-version-ENG.pdf (accessed 14 October 2019).
**19** Doris Behrens-Abouseif, *The Book in Mamluk Egypt and Syria (1250–1517): Scribes, Libraries and Market* (Leiden–Boston: Brill, 2019), 50–52.
**20** Stern, *The Jewish Bible*, 66.

Beit-Arié writes similarly: "The Jews, on the other hand, adopted the codex much later [than the Christians], not before the Muslim period and the beginning of the Geonic literary activity, and presumably no earlier than the eighth century."[21] By "Jews", in both cases, I think we have to understand "Judaism", for reasons which will become clear below. Medieval Jewish sources would generally agree with these statements. The French commentator Rashi (Solomon ben Isaac, d. 1105) remarked in his notes on the liturgical reading of the Scroll of Esther (Babylonian Talmud Megilla 19a) that ספרים שהיו בימי חכמים כולן בגיליון כספר תורה שלנו, "the 'books' they had in the time of the Sages were all in roll (*gilayon*) form, like our Torah scroll."[22] The failure of the codex to make a significant inroad into late antique Jewish culture can be partly attributed to the Torah scroll's weighty position as the pre-eminent sacred object and the concomitant manner in which prayer was conducted in the early synagogue – led by expert readers, with limited participation of the wider congregation. The continued required presence of the Torah scroll in the synagogue today is evidence that this position was not displaced by the book in the liturgical sphere. But the codex, as a multi-leaved and easily portable media carrier, did manage to enter Jewish life, and not just in the private realm of personal prayer, contemplation and study, where the Torah scroll does not hold sway, but also into the public liturgical space.

Proofs of the late adoption of the codex by Jews may be sought in codicological-archaeological evidence, although the poor survival of Jewish manuscripts from the period between the Dead Sea Scrolls to the earliest medieval manuscripts, i.e., from the end of the second century CE to the beginning of the tenth century, means that this is mostly an argument from silence. The earliest explicitly dated Hebrew codex is from the Cairo Genizah, where a few fragments survive of a small horizontal-format copy of the Bible, resembling in shape an ʿAbbāsid-era Qurʾān. On one surviving bifolium (T-S NS 246.26.2) there is a colophon stating that Joseph b. Nimorad copied the text in the town of Gunbad-i-Mallgan, in Iran, in the year 1215.[23] Although Joseph did not indicate which system of dating he was employing, it can only reasonably be the Seleucid, "Era of Documents", and hence equates to 903–904 CE. This is the earliest that is dated explicitly and genuinely. The Cairo Codex of the Prophets, a large format Bible with striking Masoretic notes, has a colophon in the name of the Masorete Moses b. Asher and is

---

21 Beit-Arié, *Hebrew Codicology*, 39.
22 Beit-Arié, *Hebrew Codicology*, 39.
23 Ben Outhwaite, "Bifolium from a Biblical Codex," in *In the Beginning: Bibles before the Year 1000*, ed. Michelle P. Brown (Washington, D.C.: Freer Gallery of Art and Arthur M. Sackler Gallery, Smithsonian Institution, 2006): 252. The manuscript can be viewed online at https://cudl.lib.cam.ac.uk/view/MS-TS-NS-00246-00026-00002/1 (accessed 14 October 2019).

dated 894–895 CE. It has for some time now been recognised that the Cairo Codex itself is a product of a later period, probably the eleventh century, and the Moses b. Asher colophon was written by the same hand as wrote other, later colophons in the book.[24]

Although this casts doubt on the authenticity of the biblical text and especially its vowels, accents, and Masoretic notes, which cannot be a faithful copy of the work of Moses b. Asher, the text of the colophon could be genuine. It was probably copied from an authentic source, even if the Bible text to which it was added was copied from another manuscript. The colophon is thus secondary evidence of an early, pre-tenth century, biblical codex, since it states: אני משה בן אשר כתבתי זה המחזור שלמקרא, "I, Moses b. Asher, have written this codex of the Bible" (Cairo Codex of the Prophets, f. 575). The word מחזור (*maḥzor*) appears to have been coined in the Islamic period as a Hebrew term for the Arabic *muṣḥaf* (Glatzer 1989, 260–263). It is usual to find writers of Hebrew in the early Islamic Middle Ages avoiding Arabic terms, either through repurposing older Hebrew words or creating neologisms.[25] By the late tenth-eleventh century, *maḥzor* is sometimes still used for "codex", but by then the word מצחף had become thoroughly hebraised and can be found in otherwise purely Hebrew colophons. Russian National Library Evr. I B19a (Codex Leningrad), which dates to the first decade of the eleventh century, perhaps reflects a period of transition, since it uses both: זה המחזור מקרא שלם נכתב ונגמר בנקודות ובמוסרות ומוגה יפה במדינת מצרים, "This codex (*maḥzor*) of the complete Bible was written, furnished with vocalisation and masora, and carefully checked in Fusṭāṭ" (the plain colophon, f. 1r) and אני שמואל בן יעקב כתבתי ונקדתי ומס׳ זה המצחף לכבוד רבנא מבורך הכהן, "I, Samuel b. Jacob, have written, vocalised and provided the masora of this codex (*miṣḥaf*) for the honour of our master Mevorak ha-Kohen" (star-shaped carpet page colophon, f. 474r).[26] Later the word *maḥzor* takes on a specialised meaning of "prayer-

---

[24] Stern, *The Jewish Bible*, 226 n. 15; Colette Sirat, *Hebrew Manuscripts of the Middle Ages*, trans. Nicholas de Lange (Cambridge: Cambridge University Press, 2002), 42–44.

[25] Ben Outhwaite, "Lines of communication: Medieval Hebrew letters of the 11th century," in *Scribes as Agents of Language Change*, ed. Esther-Miriam Wagner, Ben Outhwaite and Bettina Beinhoff (Berlin: De Gruyter, 2013): 5–6.

[26] For a translation and discussion of B19a's plain colophon, see Ben Outhwaite, "Beyond the Leningrad Codex: Samuel b. Jacob in the Cairo Genizah," in *Studies in Semitic Linguistics and Manuscripts: A Liber Discipulorum in Honour of Professor Geoffrey Khan*, ed. N. Vidro, R. Vollandt, E.-M. Wagner and J. Olszowy-Schlanger (Uppsala: University of Uppsala Press, 2018): 320–40; for the illuminated colophon, see Ben Outhwaite, "Samuel ben Jacob: the Leningrad Codex B19a and T-S 10J5.15," *Genizah Research Unit's Fragment of the Month*, January 2016. https://www.lib.cam.ac.uk/collections/departments/taylor-schechter-genizah-research-unit/fragment-month/fragment-month-5 (accessed 14 October 2019).

book for the festivals," perhaps because its original base meaning of "codex", as opposed to scroll, had been usurped by the Arabic loanword. It was hard for neologisms to thrive in the sort of linguistic environment that Hebrew faced in the Islamic period.[27] Further earlier but undated evidence is possibly found in a papyrus codex of liturgical poetry (T-S 6H9–21) – poems that embellished the reading of the Bible in the synagogue –, made from a single gathering, and also from the Cairo Genizah. This may on codicological grounds be from the eighth century, but that leaves it still a product of the Islamic world.[28]

## 4 Literary Evidence of Book Use

In contrast to the lack of physical evidence prior to the Islamic era, there are literary traces attesting to the knowledge and use of the book format by Jews. The codex developed as an evolution of the wooden writing tablet, and Saul Lieberman has pointed to the frequency of the Rabbinic Hebrew term פנקס (*pinqas*) in the Jewish sources, a loanword from Greek πίναξ (*pinax*), "tablet".[29] While in origin the Hebrew word refers indeed to the classical wax writing-tablet, it is evident from the sources that in practice such tablets could have multiple "leaves" or be of different types of material. In Mišna Kelim 24:7 we find laws relating to the uncleanness of פנקסיות (*pinqasiyyot*) – "tablets" – either holding wax, "smooth" *pinqasiyyot*, or even *pinqasiyyot* made of papyrus. Thus by the end of the second century CE, when, by tradition, the Mišna was codified by Rabbi Judah ha-Nasi, the Rabbis were recording purity laws for the use of clearly codex-like writing supports. These supports appear to have been used principally for holding personal and business records, e.g., Mišna Šəvuʿot 7:5 where the shopkeeper states זה כתוב על פנקסי שאתה חיב לי מאתים, "It is written in my account book (*pinqasi*) that you owe me two hundred *zuz*." In the ensuing period, which is covered by the legal discussions documented in the Babylonian and Palestinian Talmuds, these notebooks came to be used for the recording of legal decisions, rabbinic apothegms and the like, e.g., Babylonian Talmud Šabbat 156a records that various legal opinions were "written in Ze'eiri's notebook" (כתיב אפינקסיה דזעירי), "written in Levi's notebook" and "written in Rabbi Joshua b. Levi's notebook," using the Babylonian Aramaic version of the word. In this, they were like

---

[27] Ben Outhwaite, "Lines of communication: Medieval Hebrew letters of the 11th century," 196–97.
[28] Beit-Arié, *Hebrew Codicology*, 40 n.8.
[29] Lieberman, *Hellenism in Jewish Palestine*, 203.

the writing tablets of Greece, which, as Roberts and Skeat point out, were used for texts of an "impermanent nature – letters, bills, accounts, school exercises, memoranda."[30] We cannot be sure of the materials used, but it is evident that the scroll or other forms of roll, such as the rotulus, were giving way to new kinds of writing medium in the Hellenistic Jewish world. This technological shift was occurring principally among Jews in the secular sphere, but showing a gradual move – from shopkeepers to rabbis (the distinction is not necessarily great in that period) – into Judaism's more specifically religious environment. There is no real evidence in the sources, however, for the tablet's or the notebook's entry fully into the liturgical realm, and the codex is not seen as a suitable container for "Holy Writ" itself. The Written Torah was still the exclusive bailiwick of the scroll. However, its use by religious leaders and functionaries for their notes and legal decisions, as described in the Talmud, suggests that it was encroaching on the other, equally important religio-legal realm of Judaism, the Oral Torah, itself, since the codification of the Mišna in 200 CE, a tradition that was increasingly transmitted in writing.

Although the manuscript record is largely silent for the late Byzantine to early Islamic era, it is undeniable that by the time of the high Middle Ages (950–1250 CE), not only Jews but also Judaism had wholly embraced the codex, despite any earlier perceived reluctance. The magnificent Bible codices of the tenth and eleventh centuries, such as Aleppo, Codex Leningrad and the Cairo Codex of the Prophets, are tangible, imposing, expensive evidence of advanced book production in Egypt and Palestine, and they take pride of place in libraries of Judaica today for their accuracy and beauty. Leaves from similar prestige codices may be found in the Cairo Genizah collections, in dismembered or fragmentary states, suggesting that hundreds of such books were in circulation in Egypt and environs in the Middle Ages. On the other hand, the great strength of the Genizah Collection is its copious evidence of everyday book production, through the tens of thousands of leaves from less prestigious, user-produced books, such as pages from "Common Bibles," personal prayer books and other more "popular" examples of the codex format in use. A number of social-economic factors must have contributed to the comparative explosion in the manuscript record from Syria-Palestine and Egypt that we see in the tenth-eleventh centuries. These include the prosperity brought to Egypt by its incorporation into the burgeoning Fāṭimid Empire towards the end of the tenth century, together with the tolerant attitude of the authorities towards Jewish education – which produced a predominantly literate populace – and the practice

---

**30** Colin H. Roberts and Theodore C. Skeat, *The Birth of the Codex* (London: Published for the British Academy by the Oxford University Press, 1983), 11.

of the Jewish religion, which was largely centered on the study, promulgation and recitation of the written word. The society revealed through the Cairo Genizah is one that was literate in at least two languages – Hebrew and Arabic, the latter mainly in the form of Judaeo-Arabic, with significant knowledge of Aramaic, for religious reasons, and Persian, for cultural reasons, too. It was also a community that had a practice of or aspiration towards book ownership, revealed through the booklists and colophons of Genizah manuscripts, and one that extended beyond those with a clear occupational need such as jurisconsults or physicians. An additional driver for the popularisation of the codex format was the introduction of paper, which is found on sale in Egypt as early as 848 CE.[31] Access to paper reduced the price of purchased books or enabled much cheaper production by users themselves; the results of this can be seen in the huge number of fragments from Jewish paper codices of the eleventh century onwards that the Cairo Genizah, almost uniquely, has preserved.

In addition to socio-economic factors, changes in the theological landscape may also have led to a changing Jewish attitude to the codex. While Christianity may not have been responsible for the introduction of the codex, or even for the promulgation of the format, its enthusiastic adoption of the book for the transmission of Christian works evidently led to the association in non-Christian eyes of Christians with codices.[32] Such an association would have been problematic for Jews, but there are no explicit statements in Jewish sources that testify to a theological rejection of the codex as a Christian object or even, in Stern's words, as "a non-Jewish writing platform."[33] The *halakot* that reinforce the role of the scroll as the holder of holy writ, and which enforce its position in Rabbinic Judaism as the holiest of objects, do mostly date from the Christian period – the Jerusalem and Babylonian Talmuds, the tractate Sofrim.[34] But the foundation of those roles dates from the biblical period of Ezra, and the evidence of the Mišna and Dead Sea Scrolls is already of an established set of scribal prescriptions regarding scrolls of the Torah. Beit-Arié makes a suggestion that the Jews may have harboured theological suspicions: "One may presume that the diffusion of the codex among the Christians elicited a counter-response from the Jews, who must have been reluctant to adopt this book-form because of its associations with

---

[31] Maya Shatzmiller, "An Early Knowledge Economy: The Adoption of Paper, Human Capital and Economic Change in the Medieval Islamic Middle East, 700–1300 AD," *Centre for Global Economic History Working Papers Series* no. 64 (2015): 4.
[32] Roger S. Bagnall, *Early Christian Books in Egypt* (Princeton and Oxford: Princeton University Press, 2009), 71–73.
[33] Stern, *The Jewish Bible*, 67.
[34] Stern, *The Jewish Bible*, 31–32.

Christianity."³⁵ This is probably the best that we can do, but the underlying lack of evidence should caution against promoting it to any more than a presumption. Other assumptions, such as the essentially conservative nature of Judaism and Jewish observance, may well be equally valid. In any case, from the tenth century onwards, the block is removed and Jewish codices abound, filling libraries and *genizot*. Was the incorporation of eastern Judaism into the Islamic world the principal factor behind this adoption of the codex? Undoubtedly it was a major mechanistic factor: the widespread use of the codex in the Islamic world provided a ready source of materials, artisans and knowledge to those who wanted to use the format. Most Hebrew nouns for the book, in all its different grades, are derived from or through Arabic or Persian; exceptions appear to be neologisms from the Islamic period. But the question of motivation remains necessarily obscure. The Islamic world's flaunting of the Qurʾān in codex form would have been impossible to ignore, particularly as the physical size of such codices increased enormously from the ʿAbbāsid to Fāṭimid eras. The appearance of the Islamic book on the cultural scene may have dispelled, in non-Christian eyes, the Christian clergy's apparent monopoly on the codex. But again, this is just supposition, as we have no explicit statements to that effect from contemporary Jewish sources. The presumption that Islam was the crucial factor is ingrained: "The material form of the codex came to the Jews from without, from the larger Islamic world."³⁶ The facts plainly testify to the period and the cultural milieu in which the technological exchange took place, but these should not also be confused with the motivation behind it, which remains obscure.

By the classical genizah period, which is handily equivalent to the high Middle Ages, 950–1250 CE, when the Fāṭimids and Ayyūbids governed in Egypt, the abundance of evidence from the Jewish community for the take-up of the codex is overwhelming. Individual book ownership is evidenced by the huge number, variety and diverse quality of parchment and paper codices of smaller format. Like the rabbis and shopkeepers of earlier generations, the Jewish merchants and court clerks of the Genizah period employed the *pinqas*, now a small, unbound paper notebook, for the recording of commercial activity and legal affairs. Halakhic monographs, such as Halaḵot Gedolot, circulated in book form, sometimes of quite impressive size, e.g., T-S K6.193, which is a parchment leaf from such a book, 30cm high.³⁷ These existed alongside more impromptu, personal collections of practical *halaḵot* in notebooks. Poetry, religious and secular,

---

35 Beit-Arié, *Hebrew Codicology*, 42.
36 Stern, *The Jewish Bible*, 7.
37 The manuscript can be viewed online at https://cudl.lib.cam.ac.uk/view/MS-TS-K-00006-00193/1 (accessed 14 October 2019).

was copied as the *dīwān* of a single poet or incorporated into compendia of festival poems: e.g., the book-list T-S K3.28, which includes דיואן יהודה הלוי כראבים, "the *dīwān* of Judah ha-Levi in [several] volumes," and מעמד כיפור, "service for Yom Kippur."[38] There are personal prayer-books, *siddurim*, in great number, alongside all manner of secular, philosophical, scientific, mathematical and even magical works in codex form – a veritable explosion of books. This is remarkable in itself given the Jewish reticence towards the codex of an earlier age, but in a significant development for Judaism we also now find, from at least the first half of the tenth century, and probably a century before that, the use of the codex for purely biblical text.

There are approximately 25,000 biblical fragments on paper and parchment in the Taylor-Schechter Genizah Collection at Cambridge.[39] Around only 1500 of those originally derived from scrolls. A small number are single-page writing exercises by children or trainee scribes. This leaves probably more than 20,000 pieces from codices of the Bible, including "Great Codices" of two or three columns, Bibles with the Aramaic targum or with Judaeo-Arabic translation, and collections of prophetic readings (the *hafṭarot*) or edifying snippets intended for homilies or poetry. A great proportion of the 25,000 biblical fragments come from smaller format biblical texts, which can include psalters and collections of *hafṭarot* or other subdivisions of the complete Bible. Among books of this type, Goshen-Gottstein distinguished "study codices", those which showed an assiduous commitment to correct transmission of the text, from "listener's codices", which were intended, in his eyes, for everyday use.[40] He chose the latter name because they were to support the congregation in its listening, not its reading, functioning as "little more than hearing aids."[41] He suggested that "listener's codices" made up more than half of the biblical fragments in the Elkan Nathan Adler Collection in the Jewish Theological Seminary in New York. Goshen-Gottstein's observation as to the purpose of the biblical texts is useful, but at this remove in time, and given the fragmentary nature of the evidence, we cannot often be sure as to the producer's purpose at the time of creation or the owner's at the time of purchase (on similar concerns in relation to early Christian documents, see the essay from Batovici in this volume). Colette Sirat's term "Common Bibles" is a more useful one, given

---

**38** The manuscript can be viewed online at https://cudl.lib.cam.ac.uk/view/MS-TS-K-00003-00028/1 (accessed 14 October 2019).
**39** Malcolm C. Davis and Ben Outhwaite, *Hebrew Bible Manuscripts in the Cambridge Genizah Collections. Vol. 4: Taylor-Schechter Additional Series 32–255 with addenda to previous volumes* (Cambridge: Cambridge University Press, 2003), ix.
**40** Moshe Goshen-Gottstein, "Biblical Manuscripts in the United States," *Textus* 2 (1962): 38–41.
**41** Goshen-Gottstein, "Biblical Manuscripts in the United States," 41.

that it describes format alone, and not use. She distinguishes them from Great Bibles (multi-columned Masoretic works) and various types with translation and/or commentary.⁴² Taking the broadest definition, Common Bibles can range from parchment codices, produced by scribes and with a fully vocalised and cantillated text, to very scrappy pamphlet-type paper codices with only a partially or fully unvocalised Hebrew text, and evidently the work of the owner-user of the book.⁴³ Their purposes may have been for study, or for practice or as an aide-memoire or as an adornment, a "lap" or "hand" Bible, in the synagogue. But it is equally likely that they shared a number of purposes, and we should not strictly define them as a single-use item: members of the Jewish community clearly liked to own a book, and for many people, following the halakhic directive to produce a Torah of their own, this was a Bible. What these Common Bibles all share is that they represent evidence of Bible ownership across the whole community, rich and poor, scholarly and ignorant, professionals and amateurs.

The Cairo Genizah contains not only the direct physical evidence for numerous codices on parchment and paper, but the documentary evidence of the book trade, book production, book ownership and the coveting of books over the high Middle Ages.⁴⁴ Cambridge University Library T-S NS J53, for example, a twelfth of thirteenth century list of books on a folded piece of paper has 57 titles on it, all of which probably belonged to a single owner.⁴⁵ Synagogue inventories from the Genizah show just how many books were in public ownership – as communal property, the הקדש (*heqdeš*) – in the eleventh and twelfth centuries. The Synagogue of the Palestinians in al-Fusṭāṭ lists 80 codices, of which 68 are the Torah, in an inventory from 1186 CE, with terse listings such as, for example, מצחף תורה בג׳ דפאת מצחף גאמע ללמקרא, "a codex of the Torah in 3 columns; a codex of the whole Bible" (Bodl. MS Heb. f56.49 line 7).⁴⁶ All of these books were in public

---

**42** Sirat, *Hebrew Manuscripts of the Middle Ages*, 42–50.
**43** Ben Outhwaite, "The Tiberian Tradition in Common Bibles from the Cairo Genizah," in Geoffrey Khan and Aaron Hornkohl (eds). *Semitic Vocalization and Reading Traditions* (Cambridge: University of Cambridge and Open Book Publishers, 2020).
**44** Shelomo Dov Goitein, *A Mediterranean Society: The Jewish Communities of the World as Portrayed in the Documents of the Cairo Geniza*. Vol. 2: *The Community* (Berkeley–Los Angeles–London: University of California Press, 1971), 189, 206, 239–240; Nehemya Allony, *The Jewish Library in the Middle Ages: Book Lists from the Cairo Genizah*, ed. by Miriam Frenkel, Haggai Ben-Shammai, with the participation of Moshe Sokolow [Hebrew] (Jerusalem: Ben-Zvi Institute for the Study of Jewish Communities in the East Yad Izhak Ben-Zvi and the Hebrew University of Jerusalem, 2006).
**45** Allony, *The Jewish Library in the Middle Ages*, 35–38. The manuscript can be viewed online at https://cudl.lib.cam.ac.uk/view/MS-TS-NS-J-00053/1 (accessed 14 October 2019).
**46** Allony, *The Jewish Library in the Middle Ages*, 303–05.

ownership, some apparently having been written expressly to be given to the synagogue, e.g., a book-list of 1181–2 CE, for the Synagogue of the Iraqis (Jews of Babylonian heritage or affiliation) in al-Fusṭāṭ, has מצחף תורה גדיד אסתנסכתה אם תנא ואקדשתה ללכניסה אלמדכורה, "a new codex of the Torah that Umm Tanna commissioned ("caused to be copied") and dedicated to the aforementioned synagogue" (Bodl. MS Heb. f56.50 lines 37–38).⁴⁷ Many other copies of the Bible, big and small, reveal similar evidence of having passed into public hands, through the addition of public ownership notes inside the body of the book in the manner of library stamps, e.g., a bifolium from a beautiful tenth-eleventh century parchment codex in two columns has a note at the end of the book of Job, קדש ליהוה אלהי ישראל לא ימכר ולא יגאל, "Holy to the LORD God of Israel, not to be sold or redeemed (i.e., pawned)"; it also has קדש ליהוה written in large square letters across the top of the columns (Cambridge University Library and Bodleian Libraries, Oxford, Lewis-Gibson Bible 6.88).⁴⁸ This kind of addition is very frequent in large- and medium-format Bibles in the Genizah Collection.

I have cautioned above against trying to ascertain the purpose of biblical manuscripts – Common Bibles in particular – on the grounds that without documentary evidence it can just remain speculation. The physical evidence alone cannot, for the most part, explain their purpose, although we may reasonably suspect that a Bible of the size of Aleppo or Leningrad was unlikely to be used as a "hand Bible" by a member of the congregation as they listened to the service. Purpose could be, in any case, a misleading concept, because their production might have been, first and foremost, an act of observance in and of itself, fulfilling the commandment to produce and own a Torah scroll, just in its more modern form of a Torah book – something that Maimonides' use of the term ספר certainly allows. Or, given the evidence of book ownership that the Genizah presents us, their production might have been an acquisitive act of book ownership, as an essentially luxury item that the wealthier congregants might have aspired to. In this way, the creation of the object or the acquisition of it might trump any subsequent purpose to which it is put. In some cases, however, we do have documentary evidence as to how Hebrew Bible miṣḥafim were used, and, while scarce, this provides an illuminating illustration of the Jewish dichotomy of scroll versus book in action in the liturgical sphere.

---

47 Allony, *The Jewish Library in the Middle Ages*, 299–302.
48 The manuscript can be viewed online at https://cudl.lib.cam.ac.uk/view/MS-LG-BIBLE-00006-00088/1 (accessed 14 October 2019).

## 5 Scriptural Codices and the Influence of Qaraism

The Cairo Codex of the Prophets, which I have mentioned above, is a problematic manuscript, given its erroneous attribution to the Masorete Moses b. Asher himself.[49] However, the text of its colophons, dedications and ownership notes has provided a number of interesting details concerning the use of it as a book. On f. 581 there is a dedication note (repeated elsewhere in the volume), which reads in part:

> זה הדפתר שמונה נביאים שהקדיש אותו יעבץ בן שלמה בירושלם עיר הקדש אלהים יכוננה עד עולם סלה
> לקראין העושים את המועדים על ראית הירח יקראו בו כלם בשבתות ובחדשים ובמועדים

> "This volume of the Eight Prophets that Yaʻbeṣ b. Solomon has dedicated in Jerusalem, the Holy City – God establish it forever, *sela* – to the Qaraites who perform the festivals at the sighting of the (new) moon, for them all to read from it on Sabbaths, on New Moons and on festivals."[50]

The implication of this colophon is that the book was used liturgically by the Qaraite community of Jerusalem at all the points in the calendar when the Bible was read in the service.

Qaraism was a movement, or, more properly a *madhab*, a "school" in the Islamic sense, of Judaism that arose in the ninth century.[51] It appears to have formed from various groups in the early Islamic period, of whom the followers of ʻAnan b. David, a member of the Babylonian exilarchic family, were most prominent.[52] What bound the original groups was a shared dissent from the standard Rabbinic tradition. A rejection of the Oral Torah, or at least an uncritical acceptance of it, therefore came to define the movement.[53] Qaraism accrued many followers, and following emigration from the homelands of Iraq and Persia, Qaraite

---

**49** See, e.g., Paul Kahle, *The Cairo Geniza* (London: Oxford University Press, 1947), 56–57. When faced with the problems of two contrasting colophons (both in the same hand), Kahle chose to interpret the common phrase ועשה אותו לעצמו uniquely, as meaning that Yaʻbeṣ b. Solomon had "prepared the parchment for the codex" (taking the earlier mention of *daftar* to mean "parchment"), thereby avoiding the problem of two different people taking credit for producing the same biblical codex. Subsequent scholars have similarly tied themselves up in knots trying to justify the authenticity of the Moses b. Asher attribution.
**50** See Kahle, *The Cairo Geniza*, 112–13, for the text of this colophon.
**51** Marina Rustow, *Heresy and the Politics of Community: The Jews of the Fatimid Caliphate* (Ithaca, NY: Cornell University Press, 2008), xxvii–xxix.
**52** Moshe Gil, *A History of Palestine, 634–1099*, trans. Ethel Broido (Cambridge: Cambridge University Press, 1992), 777–84.
**53** Rustow, *Heresy and the Politics of Community*, 25.

centres in Egypt and Jerusalem arose in the ninth-tenth centuries.⁵⁴ In Palestine, Qaraite scholars took a very close interest in the Tiberian Masoretic tradition, though the exact relationship between Qaraism and the Masoretes of Tiberias remains unclear. To understand the colophon in the Cairo Codex of the Prophets and similar colophons we find in other Bibles, we need to consider the Qaraites' relationship to the Bible. With their distrust of the Oral Torah, the Qaraites placed the Hebrew Bible at the centre of their spiritual and liturgical life. Qaraite *halaka* was taken, wherever possible, solely from the Bible, prayers were derived from the Psalms. Nehemiah Allony gathered evidence, from both colophons and mostly later (sixteenth-nineteenth centuries) literary sources that Qaraites preferred or advocated the liturgical reading of the Bible from codices and not scrolls.⁵⁵ In doing so, they were rejecting the Torah scroll-centrism of the Rabbanite movement. Given that it is the Oral Torah that prescribes the correct writing and reading of the Torah Scroll, this is not only feasible for the Qaraite movement, but actually desirable, or even essential, as it sought to distance itself from mainstream Rabbanism. It is in light of this that Allony read the colophon of the Cairo Codex, as evidence of the Qaraites' preference for the *miṣḥaf* over the *sefer*, in the tenth-eleventh centuries. Given that the Cairo Codex of the Prophets is just that – of the Former and Latter Prophets, the book of Joshua through to the book of the Twelve Minor Prophets – one can argue that the colophon only reveals that the Qaraites were reading their *hafṭarot* – the prophetical readings that follow the reading of the weekly section (*paraša*) of the Torah – from a book. This would not be surprising, as it became acceptable even within Rabbanite circles to read the *hafṭarot* from a codex, although many scrolls of *hafṭarot* are found in the Cairo Genizah.⁵⁶ Allony also pointed to the evidence from the greatest of Great Bibles, the Aleppo Codex, the book that Maimonides seems to have esteemed so highly. Damaged in the Aleppo riots of 1948, the colophons of that important Bible are lost, but fortunately they had been studied or copied several times in the preceding centuries.⁵⁷ S. D. Cassuto's notes on the Aleppo Codex, which he made in 1943, before the book was damaged, were discovered and published by Yosef Ofer. They

---

54 Rustow, *Heresy and the Politics of Community*, 23–24.
55 Nehemya Allony, "ספר התורה והמצחף בקריאת התורה בציבור בעדת הרבנים ובעדת הקראים," *Beit Mikra: Journal for the Study of the Bible and its World* 78 (1979): 321–34.
56 Elbogen, *Jewish Liturgy*, 145–146. A good example from the Cairo Genizah is T-S A41.37, a very fragmentary scroll of Zech 14 and 1 Kgs 8, which are *hafṭarot* for the festivals of Sukkot and Šəmini ʿAṣeret. The scroll has an Aramaic colophon beginning ספרא הדין, "this scroll", in case its current physical state should give any doubt to its original format.
57 Geoffrey Khan, *A Short Introduction to the Tiberian Masoretic Bible and its Reading Tradition*. 2nd ed. (Piscataway, NJ: Gorgias Press, 2013), 9–10.

reveal his reading of a very similar dedicatory colophon, which begins זה המצחף השלם של עש׳ וארבעה ספרים, "This complete codex of the twenty-four books," and goes on to specify how the book should be used:

> כדי שיוציאוהו אל המושבות והקהלות שבעיר הקדש בשלשה רגלים חג המצות וחג השבועות וחג הסוכות לקרות בו ולהתבונן וללמד ממנו כל אשר יחפצו
>
> "In order that they should bring it out to the meeting-places and the congregations that are in the Holy City on the three Pilgrim festivals, the festival of Unleavened Bread, and the festival of Šavuʿot, and the festival of Sukkot, to read in it, and to reflect [on it] and study it, whoever would desire to."[58]

Importantly here we are dealing with a complete copy of the Hebrew Bible, all 24 books (though sadly, it is no longer complete, having been badly damaged in the riots). The colophon reveals that the book is in the care of the Qaraite leadership, the two Qaraite Nesi'im, Josiah and Hezekiah,[59] and that it should be read on the major festivals, which is to say at the principal liturgical occasions in the Jewish calendar. It appears that the Qaraites were deliberately setting themselves apart from their Rabbanite competitors by promoting in the meeting-places – *mošavot*, a calque of Arabic *majlīs*, which served Qaraite congregations for synagogues[60] – the public reading of the Law from a codex. Objections could be raised to details of this interpretation, aside from the fact that the colophon is no longer extant to check its details and authenticity more thoroughly. The very special nature of the Aleppo Codex itself might make this more an occasion of parading a talismanic object, a public progress for the leadership and their centrepiece. But the explicit mention of reading from it, and the connection with the major liturgical occasions support Allony's interpretation.

The Cairo Genizah, which is the storeroom of the Palestinian, Rabbanite, synagogue of al-Fusṭāṭ, has, over the years of its investigation, provided a fair number of manuscripts which originally emanated from the Qaraite community of Egypt. This is surprising but not unexpected, given that the rules of genizah state that all holy texts (*kitve qodeš*) should be safely stored away, no matter what language they are in or no matter whether they are read in the congregation or not, and this includes the deliberate putting out of sight of harmful or sectarian texts.[61] It should not be too surprising, therefore, that it can provide

---

**58** Joseph Offer (Yosef Ofer), "M. D. Cassuto's Notes on the Aleppo Codex" (Hebrew), *Sefunot* 19 (1989): 287–88.
**59** Gil, *A History of Palestine, 634–1099*, 792–93.
**60** Gil, *A History of Palestine, 634–1099*, 179–81, 810.
**61** Stefan C. Reif, *A Jewish Archive from Old Cairo: The History of Cambridge University's Genizah Collection* (Richmond, Surrey: Curzon, 2000), 11–14.

some documentary evidence of the Qaraites' practice of reading the Bible in the Middle Ages. A paper bifolium containing a Fāṭimid-era Shi'ite text in Arabic script, T-S Ar.51.86a, was reused in the twelfth of thirteenth century, and a liturgical text with clearly Qaraite features has been written, in Judaeo-Arabic and Hebrew, between the lines.[62] The text consists of instructions in Judaeo-Arabic to perform the prayers, and includes the instruction תמת צלאה בקר וצהרים ותפתח אלמצאחף ותקרא אחרי מות, "at the end of the morning and afternoon prayer, open the codices and read 'After the death'" (T-S Ar.51.86a P3v). The instruction is to read the *paraša* אחרי מות, Leviticus 16:1–18:30, from the annual reading cycle of the Torah, and to read it from *maṣāḥif*, "codices" – not an ambiguous *sefer*. This is not the reading of *hafṭarot*, where a *ḥumaš*-style (partial text of the Bible) book might be used by a non-Qaraite congregation, but is a core liturgical reading of the Torah. Taken together with the colophons' evidence of Great Bibles forming the centrepiece of Qaraite festival liturgies, we can see that in the Middle Ages it became Qaraite practice to read the Torah from codices, thereby distinguishing themselves in a very visible manner from their Rabbanite brethren.

If for the Qaraites, the use of a codex signalled an independence from the mainstream, then for Rabbanites we might expect to see a greater prominence for the Torah Scroll as their sacred object and a marker of orthodoxy. A literary account of a ceremony of excommunicating the Qaraite nation en masse can be found in Abraham ibn Dā'ūd's Sefer ha-Qabbala ("Book of Tradition", c. 1161 CE), which is also a defence of orthodoxy against the Qaraites, whom he refers to throughout as "heretics". Abraham's version – he did not witness the ceremony himself – describes it so:

וכשהיו ישראל חוגגים חג הסוכות בהר הזתים היו חונים בהר מחנות מחנות אוהבים אלו את אלו ומברכין אלו את אלו. והמינין חונים כנגדם כב׳ חשיפי עזים. והרבנין היו מוציאין ספר תורה ומחרימים שמות המינים בפניהם והם שותקים כמו כלבים אלמים.

"When the Jews used to celebrate the festival of Tabernacles on the Mount of Olives, they would encamp on the mountain in groups and greet each other warmly. The heretics would encamp before them like two little flocks of goats. Then the rabbis would take out a scroll of the Torah and pronounce a ban on the heretics right to their faces, while the latter remained silent like dumb dogs."[63]

---

**62** Esther-Miriam Wagner and Mohamed Ahmed, "T-S Ar. 51.86a: Shi'ite and Karaite – a Fatimid Melange," *Genizah Research Unit's Fragment of the Month*, December 2017. https://www.lib.cam.ac.uk/collections/departments/taylor-schechter-genizah-research-unit/fragment-month/fotm-2017/fragment-6 (accessed 14 October 2019).

**63** Gerson D. Cohen, *A Critical Edition with a Translation and Notes of the Book of Tradition (Sefer Ha-Qabbalah) By Abraham Ibn Daud* (Philadelphia: The Jewish Publication Society of America, 1967), 94, and Hebrew section 68.

The Torah scroll is a necessary part of a formal excommunication, which usually in that period took place in the synagogue, but the symbolism inherent in brandishing it in the Qaraites' faces, while on one of the holiest sites in Jerusalem, is profound. Ibn Dā'ūd's story is embellished; the excommunication was not a regular occurrence; the numerous and powerful Qaraites of Jerusalem would not have cowered before the threadbare members of the Palestinian Academy; but it does have its origins in Rabbanite-Qaraite friction, particularly at the popular level, in eleventh century Palestine, which resulted in an attempted public excommunication on the Mount of Olives in 1029 CE (Rustow 2008, 201).[64]

In al-Fusṭāṭ in the Classical Genizah period, there were two main synagogues, the Synagogue of the Palestinians (or of the Jerusalemites), which served the congregation who looked to Jerusalem as their spiritual centre and the Palestinian Gaon as their leader, and the Synagogue of the Iraqis (of the Babylonians), which looked to the Yešivot (Academies) of Iraq for their guidance. Although the Palestinian congregation had been dominant in the Jewish community of Egypt, the increasing arrival of Jewish immigrants from Babylon and North Africa from the ninth century onwards had eroded their position.[65] By the tenth century, most of the Jewish world had adopted the customs and *halaḵot* of the Babylonian Academies, recognising the primacy of the Babylonian Talmud, adopting an essentially Babylonian liturgy, and the custom of reading the Torah through in a single year.[66] The Palestinian congregation of al-Fusṭāṭ, however, continued with a number of their ancestral customs, the most discernible of which was the liturgical reading of the Torah in three years, the triennial reading cycle.[67] The congregation of the Palestinian synagogue thus read the *seder*, rather than the *paraša*, and followed it with different *hafṭarot* to those read in the Iraqi synagogue and much of the rest of the Jewish world. This custom continued in Moses Maimonides' day, and he noted it in the Mišne Tora: ויש מי שמשלים את התורה בשלש שנים ואינו מנהג פשוט, "And there are those who complete the Torah in three years, but this is not a common custom" (Tefilla u-Virkat Kohanim 13:1). Following attempts by Maimonides and his son, Abraham, to eradicate the divergent custom and impose the annual reading cycle and other Babylonian orthodoxies across the whole community, the Palestinian congregation resisted and sought to cement their traditional rites in a formal declaration in Judaeo-Arabic written in 1211 CE. A copy of this decla-

---

**64** Rustow, *Heresy and the Politics of Community*, 201.
**65** Elinoar Bareket, *Fustat on the Nile: The Jewish Elite in Medieval Egypt* (Leiden: Brill, 1999), 16–18.
**66** Robert Brody, *The Geonim of Babylonia and the Shaping of Medieval Jewish Culture* (New Haven: Yale University Press, 1998), 113–121.
**67** Elbogen, *Jewish Liturgy*, 133.

ration, preserved in a Cairo Genizah manuscript (Bodl. MS Heb. b13.41), set out the custom followed in the כניסה אלשאמיין (Kanīsat al-Šāmiyīn), the Palestinian Synagogue, and it acknowledged a number of distinctively Palestinian practices, including the regular reading of Psalms, and of the Ten Commandments as well as the reading פי ספר תורה אלסדר אלדי ואפק דלך אלסבת ואפטאראתה, "from the Sefer Torah the *seder* which corresponds to that Sabbath and its *hafṭara*."[68] The declaration asserts not only the reading of the triennial lection, but also that it should be from a Torah scroll, a fact that perhaps could have been taken as read, were it not for the earlier assertion that it is also their regular practice to read the *paraša*, of the (Babylonian) annual reading cycle: וקראה אלפרשה פי אלמצאחף, "and the reading of the *paraša* from codices" – *maṣāḥif*. Out of respect for the dominant Babylonian community's custom, and probably out of a minority's sensitivity for inter-communal relationships, the Palestinian congregation acknowledged the Babylonian reading of the Torah, with a "double reading of the Torah."[69] But whereas the Palestinian *seder* was read as it should be from the Torah scroll, the added, extra-halakhic, reading of the *paraša* was from a book, marking its non-liturgical status in the Palestinian synagogue, its second-class standing.

# 6 Conclusion

From late antiquity to the Middle Ages, the Torah scroll stood as a symbol of orthodoxies within Judaism. The histories of Josephus and Ibn Dā'ūd, separated by a thousand years, show the powerful status that the Sefer Torah held in their eyes. One used it as a momentous symbol of Jewish defeat and the other wielded it as a potent weapon against the heretics. Beyond the imagination of these medieval historians, we can see through the frictions of Qaraite versus Rabbanite, and Palestinian versus Babylonian, the symbolic role of the liturgical medium, book versus scroll and scroll versus book – giving new resonance to Solomon Schechter's famous observation in the London Times that the Genizah was "a battlefield of books."[70] The pre-eminent position of the Torah scroll in observance of Jewish rites, ensconced in the Oral Law and codified in Mišna, Talmud, extra-talmudic tractates and the medieval codes ensured that it could not be displaced, or its position even significantly eroded in mainstream rabbinic Judaism. Perhaps this,

---

**68** Ezra Fleischer, *Eretz-Israel Prayer and Prayer Rituals as Portrayed in the Geniza Documents* [Hebrew] (Jerusalem: The Magnes Press, the Hebrew University, 1988), 219–22.
**69** Fleischer, *Eretz-Israel Prayer and Prayer Rituals*, 293–320.
**70** Solomon Schechter, "A Hoard of Hebrew MSS.," *The Times*, 3 August 1897, 13.

more than a Jewish distrust of Christian influence, kept the Jewish liturgical space clear of the codex for hundreds of years. Where the codex did infiltrate Judaism, it was through the Jews' use of it for non-liturgical purposes, so that it was neither an unknown nor an especially foreign technology by late antiquity. Following the Islamic conquests, the existing communities of the Near East found themselves surrounded by an Islamic culture that had, with the enthusiasm of new converts, wholeheartedly adopted the codex for their sacred text. The Jewish take-up of the codex for scripture began in earnest thereafter, perhaps initially through prayer-books and poetry, before reaching its apogee in the magnificent Great Bibles of the tenth-eleventh centuries, which themselves were emulated by the general public, to varying degrees of quality and workmanship, in their thousands with the Common Bible. What caused this dramatic shift of the "Holy writ" from scroll to codex in the Middle Ages? At this stage of our knowledge, and with the severe lack of evidence in the immediately preceding period, answers can only be speculative. The Qaraites are, however, likely to have played a leading role. From their arrival in the ninth-tenth centuries in the Holy Land, they took a great interest in the accurate copying and transmission of the Bible, to the point that Qaraism and the Masoretic tradition of Tiberias has become intertwined. An examination of Great Bible colophons from the early Middle Ages shows again and again that Qaraites were the owners and commissioners of these magnificent codices. RNL Evr. I B19a, Codex Leningrad, was commissioned and initially owned by a rich merchant of Egypt called Mevorak̲ b. Joseph b. Netan'el, known as Ibn Yazdād ha-Kohen, a Qaraite of Persian extraction.[71] It is a luxury volume, with rich carpet pages and extensive Masora, and was produced by one of the leading scribes of al-Fusṭāṭ. Perhaps for Ibn Yazdād it served as the central liturgical focus for his Qaraite *majlīs*, just as the Aleppo Codex did for the Qaraites of Jerusalem, and the Cairo Codex of the Prophets for its congregation. The physical and documentary evidence that places the book at the heart of the medieval Qaraite service must reflect the fundamental influence the Qaraites had on the proliferation of the Bible codex in the early Middle Ages.

---

[71] Outhwaite, "Beyond the Leningrad Codex," 328–29. Note too (p. 326) that the book subsequently passed into the ownership of the Palestinian Ga'on Maṣliaḥ, a Rabbanite. As with Maimonides and the Aleppo Codex, the books' origins in the Qaraite community were no barrier to their use by Rabbanites.

# Bibliography

Allony, Nehemya. "ספר התורה והמצחף בקריאת התורה בציבור בעדת הרבנים ובעדת הקראים." *Beit Mikra: Journal for the Study of the Bible and its World* 78 (1979): 321–34.

Allony, Nehemya. *The Jewish Library in the Middle Ages: Book Lists from the Cairo Genizah*, ed. by Miriam Frenkel and Haggai Ben-Shammai, with the participation of Moshe Sokolow. Hebrew. Jerusalem: Ben-Zvi Institute for the Study of Jewish Communities in the East Yad Izhak Ben-Zvi and the Hebrew University of Jerusalem, 2006.

Bagnall, Roger S. *Early Christian Books in Egypt*. Princeton and Oxford: Princeton University Press, 2009.

Bareket, Elinoar. *Fustat on the Nile: The Jewish Elite in Medieval Egypt*. Leiden: Brill, 1999.

Behrens-Abouseif, Doris. *The Book in Mamluk Egypt and Syria (1250–1517): Scribes, Libraries and Market*. Leiden–Boston: Brill, 2019.

Beit-Arié, Malachi. *Hebrew Codicology: Historical and Comparative Typology of Hebrew Medieval Codices based on the Documentation of the Extant Dated Manuscripts using a Quantitative Approach, Preprint internet English version 0.3+* (August 2019). https://web.nli.org.il/sites/NLI/English/collections/manuscripts/hebrewcodicology/Documents/Hebrew-Codicology-continuously-updated-online-version-ENG.pdf

Brody, Robert. *The Geonim of Babylonia and the Shaping of Medieval Jewish Culture*. Paperback ed., with a new preface and an updated bibliography. New Haven and London: Yale University Press, 1998.

Cohen, Gerson D. *A Critical Edition with a Translation and Notes of the Book of Tradition (Sefer Ha-Qabbalah) By Abraham Ibn Daud*. Philadelphia: The Jewish Publication Society of America, 1967.

Davis, Malcolm C., and Ben Outhwaite. *Hebrew Bible Manuscripts in the Cambridge Genizah Collections*. Vol. 4: *Taylor-Schechter Additional Series 32–255 with addenda to previous volumes*. Cambridge: Cambridge University Press, 2003.

Elbogen, Ismar. *Jewish Liturgy: A Comprehensive History*. Trans. Raymond P. Scheindlin. Philadelphia: Jewish Publication Society; Jewish Theological Seminary of America, 1993.

Fleischer, Ezra. *Eretz-Israel Prayer and Prayer Rituals as Portrayed in the Geniza Documents*. Hebrew. Jerusalem: The Magnes Press, the Hebrew University, 1988.

Gil, Moshe. *A History of Palestine, 634–1099*. Trans. Ethel Broido. Cambridge: Cambridge University Press, 1992.

Glatzer, Mordechai. "The Aleppo Codex: Codicological and Paleographical Aspects." Hebrew. *Sefunot* NS 19 (1989): 167–276.

Goitein, Shelomo Dov. "Contemporary Letters on the Capture of Jerusalem by the Crusaders." *Journal of Jewish Studies* 3 (1952): 162–77.

Goitein, Shelomo Dov. *A Mediterranean Society: The Jewish Communities of the World as Portrayed in the Documents of the Cairo Geniza*. Vol. 2: *The Community*. Berkeley–Los Angeles–London: University of California Press, 1971.

Goshen-Gottstein, Moshe. "Biblical Manuscripts in the United States." *Textus* 2 (1962): 28–59.

Haran, Menachem. "Bible Scrolls in Eastern and Western Jewish Communities from Qumran to the High Middle Ages." *Hebrew Union College Annual* 56 (1985): 21–62.

Higger, Michael. ב סופרים מסכת: מסכת סופרים ונלוו עליה מדרש מסכת סופרים ב. Jerusalem: Maqor, 1970.

Hyamson, Moses, ed.. *Mishneh Torah: the Book of Adoration by Maimonides, edited according to the Bodleian (Oxford) Codex with an English Translation*. Jerusalem: Boys Town Jerusalem Publishers, 1965.

Kahle, Paul. *Masoreten des Westens*. Stuttgart: Kohlhammer, 1927.
Kahle, Paul. *The Cairo Geniza*. London: Oxford University Press, 1947.
Khan, Geoffrey. *A Short Introduction to the Tiberian Masoretic Bible and its Reading Tradition*. 2nd Ed. Piscataway, NJ: Gorgias Press, 2013.
Lieberman, Saul. *Hellenism in Jewish Palestine: Studies in the Literary Transmission, Beliefs and Manners of Palestine in the I Century B.C.E.–IV Century C.E.* New York: Jewish Theological Seminary of America, 1962.
Offer, Joseph. (Yosef Ofer) "M. D. Cassuto's Notes on the Aleppo Codex." Hebrew. *Sefunot* 19 (1989): 277–344.
Outhwaite, Ben. "Bifolium from a Biblical Codex." In *In the Beginning: Bibles before the Year 1000*, ed. Michelle P. Brown, 252. Washington, D.C.: Freer Gallery of Art and Arthur M. Sackler Gallery, Smithsonian Institution, 2006.
Outhwaite, Ben. "Lines of communication: Medieval Hebrew letters of the 11th century." *Scribes as agents of language change*, ed. In Esther-Miriam Wagner, Ben Outhwaite and Bettina Beinhoff, 183–98. Berlin: De Gruyter, 2013.
Outhwaite, Ben. "Samuel ben Jacob: the Leningrad Codex B19a and T-S 10J5.15." *Genizah Research Unit's Fragment of the Month*, January 2016. https://www.lib.cam.ac.uk/collections/departments/taylor-schechter-genizah-research-unit/fragment-month/fragment-month-5
Outhwaite, Ben. "Beyond the Leningrad Codex: Samuel b. Jacob in the Cairo Genizah." In *Studies in Semitic Linguistics and Manuscripts: A Liber Discipulorum in Honour of Professor Geoffrey Khan*, ed. N. Vidro, R. Vollandt, E.-M. Wagner and J. Olszowy-Schlanger, 320–40. Uppsala: University of Uppsala Press, 2018.
Outhwaite, Ben. "The Tiberian Tradition in Common Bibles from the Cairo Genizah." In Geoffrey Khan and Aaron Hornkohl (eds). *Semitic Vocalization and Reading Traditions*. Cambridge: University of Cambridge and Open Book Publishers, forthcoming 2020.
Pedersen, Johannes, and Geoffrey French. *The Arabic Book*. Princeton, New Jersey: Princeton University Press, 1984.
Penkower, Jordan. "Maimonides and the Aleppo Codex." *Textus* 9 (1981): 39–129.
Reif, Stefan C. *A Jewish Archive from Old Cairo: the history of Cambridge University's Genizah Collection*. Richmond, Surrey: Curzon, 2000.
Rendsburg, Gary A. "The World's Oldest Torah Scrolls." *ANE Today* 6:3 (March 2018). (http://www.asor.org/anetoday/2018/03/Worlds-Oldest-Torah-Scrolls).
Roberts, Colin H. and Theodore C. Skeat. *The Birth of the Codex*. London: Published for the British Academy by the Oxford University Press, 1983.
Rothkoff, Aaron, and Louis Isaac Rabinowitz. "Sefer Torah." In *Encyclopaedia Judaica*, ed. Fred Skolnik and Michael Berenbaum, 241–43. Detroit: Macmillan Reference USA, 2007.
Rustow, Marina. *Heresy and the Politics of Community: the Jews of the Fatimid Caliphate*. Ithaca, NY: Cornell University Press, 2008.
Shatzmiller, Maya. "An Early Knowledge Economy: The Adoption of Paper, Human Capital and Economic Change in the Medieval Islamic Middle East, 700–1300 AD." *Centre for Global Economic History Working Papers Series* no. 64 (2015).
Schama, Simon. *The Story of the Jews: Finding the Words, 1000 BCE–1492 CE*. London: Vintage Books, 2014.
Schechter, Solomon. "A Hoard of Hebrew MSS." *The Times*, 3 August 1897: 13.
Sirat, Colette. *Hebrew Manuscripts of the Middle Ages*. Trans. Nicholas de Lange. Cambridge: Cambridge University Press, 2002.

Stern, David. *The Jewish Bible: A Material History*. Seattle: University of Washington Press, 2017.
Tov, Emanuel. *Textual Criticism of the Hebrew Bible*. Second Revised Edition. Minneapolis: Fortress, 2001.
Wagner, Esther-Miriam, and Mohamed Ahmed. "T-S Ar. 51.86a: Shi'ite and Karaite – a Fatimid Melange." *Genizah Research Unit's Fragment of the Month*, December 2017. https://www.lib.cam.ac.uk/collections/departments/taylor-schechter-genizah-research-unit/fragment-month/fotm-2017/fragment-6.

Javier del Barco
# From Scroll to Codex: Dynamics of Text Layout Transformation in the Hebrew Bible

## 1 The Adoption of the Codex in Judaism

We know very little about the process by which late-antique and early-medieval Jewish communities adopted the codex for copying and transmitting their fundamental texts (for more on these matters, see the chapter in this volume from Outhwaite). This is due mainly to the fact that there is a long hiatus during which we have very few texts written in Hebrew, between the second century of the Common Era – the date of the latest scrolls and the documents found in several places around Qumran and the Dead Sea[1] – and the ninth and tenth centuries,[2] the date of the first more or less complete Bible codices that are extant today, which were copied in Palestine, Syria, Egypt, Iraq, and Iran.[3] There are many reasons that

---

[1] For detailed palaeographical dates for the different groups of documents from the Judaean Desert, ranging from the third century BCE to the second century CE, see Emanuel Tov, *Scribal Practices and Approaches Reflected in the Texts Found in the Judean Desert*, STDJ 54 (Leiden: Brill, 2004), 5–6. See also Chapter 1 in this volume.

[2] There is only a very small number of Bible fragments that can be dated with certainty to before the ninth century CE. See Judith Olszowy-Schlanger, "The Hebrew Bible," in *The New Cambridge History of the Bible*, vol. 2, *From 600 to 1450*, ed. Richard Marsden and E. Ann Matter (Cambridge: Cambridge University Press, 2012): 19–40, esp. 20, and Colette Sirat, *Hebrew Manuscripts of the Middle Ages* (Cambridge: Cambridge University Press, 2002), 27–29 and 34–36.

[3] The oldest dated codex, now lost, is that of the Prophets from the Karaite Mussa Dar'i Synagogue in Cairo, which had a colophon that mentioned the date corresponding to 894/895 CE. Nonetheless, there is some doubt about the authenticity of the colophon, and some scholars date the codex a century later, i.e., at the end of the tenth century or beginning of the eleventh. Cairo Geniza fragments of a Bible codex copied in Gunbad-i-Mallgàn (Iran) are dated with certainty to 903/904 CE. See Malachi Beit-Arié, Colette Sirat, and Mordechai Glatzer, *Codices hebraicis litteris exarati quo tempore scripti fuerint exhibentes – Otsar ha-mitsḥafim ha-ivriyim : kitve-yad bi-khetav ivri mi-yeme ha-benayim be-tsiyune ta'arikh.*, vol. 1, *Jusqu'à 1020*, Monumenta Paleographica Medii Aevi. Series hebraica (Turnhout: Brepols, 1997), § 1–2 (pp. 25–41).

---

**Note:** Research on this topic is possible thanks to the collaborative research project entitled "Legado de Sefarad II. La producción material e intelectual del judaísmo sefardí bajomedieval," which is based at the ILC-CSIC in Madrid and funded by the Plan Nacional de I+D+i (FFI2015-63700–P).

have been suggested for this hiatus,⁴ but none of them provides any details about when or how Jews began to adopt the format of the codex for copying texts in Hebrew. Nevertheless, there are two widely accepted ideas about the adoption of the codex by Jewish communities. One is that, during the early centuries of Christianity, the codex was largely rejected since it was the main format in which Christian religious texts circulated.⁵ The second is that the codex was not adopted until after the spread of Islam,⁶ following the assimilation of the Eastern Jewish communities into the new dominant culture, particularly the practices of Islamic book production, which used the codex as its main format.⁷

What we do know is that, as the codex was being adopted, both the horizontal and the vertical scroll (*rotulus*) continued to be used, and the different functions and kinds of texts conveyed by each were not fixed definitively until at least the eleventh century CE. Thus, vertical scrolls, or *rotuli*, were frequently used up to that date to transmit different kinds of texts, as Judith Olszowy-Schlanger has shown.⁸ The horizontal scroll, which was the format used going back to ancient times, gradually became specialized for transmitting the sacred text used for liturgical purposes in the synagogue. In this way, the ritual reading of the Pentateuch, as well as other sections of the Hebrew Bible, was performed using scrolls produced and copied according to strict rules drawn from traditional rabbinical literature. This functional specialization of the scroll continues to this day in traditional synagogue liturgy as a fossilized remnant of a format passed down from antiquity. However, even if the scroll continues to be used, the fact is that, beginning sometime between the seventh and the ninth centuries CE, Eastern Jewish

---

**4** One possible reason has to do with the fact that the teaching of the text of the Bible was an eminently oral activity during this period. See David Stern, "The First Jewish Books and the Early History of Jewish Reading," *JQR* 98/2 (2008): 163–202, esp. 178–81; "appreciating the fact that the rabbis' knowledge of the Bible was acquired from auditory experience, we can better understand certain features of midrash that otherwise are largely inexplicable" (180).
**5** See Irven M. Resnick, "The Codex in Early Jewish and Christian Communities," *Journal of Religious History* 17/1 (1992): 1–17, and Sirat, *Hebrew Manuscripts of the Middle Ages*, 35.
**6** Other than a doubtful reference by Saint Augustine to the use of codices by Jews, the first mention comes from the Islamic period, in the eigth century. See Judith Olszowy-Schlanger, "The Anatomy of Non-Biblical Scrolls from the Cairo Geniza," in *Jewish Manuscript Cultures: New Perspectives* (Berlin: De Gruyter, 2017): 49–88, esp. 52, and Sirat, *Hebrew Manuscripts of the Middle Ages*, 35.
**7** François Déroche, *Manuel de codicologie des manuscrits en écriture arabe*, Études et recherches (Paris: Bibliothèque nationale de France, 2000), 13.
**8** Olszowy-Schlanger, "The Anatomy of Non-Biblical Scrolls," esp. table 1, pp. 55–61.

communities largely adopted the codex, even though the new format coexisted with other, preexisting forms such as horizontal scrolls, *rotuli*, and *pinkasim*.[9]

Indeed, the transition from the scroll to the codex took place gradually over a long period, and during this process all formats continued to be used. The *rotuli* that have been mentioned, as well as fragments of horizontal scrolls from the Cairo Geniza, lead us to question the traditional hypothesis that the scroll was rapidly replaced by the codex, except in the liturgical context,[10] and that therefore many of these fragments should be dated to before the Islamic conquest. As Olszowy-Schlanger asserts, "different book forms co-existed in the non-biblical sphere for much longer than previously believed."[11] Therefore, only an exhaustive codicological and paleographic analysis of the scroll fragments can provide a dating that is not based on traditional, *a priori* assumptions, which should be rejected.

One of the most useful aspects of a formal comparative analysis for understanding the dynamics of the transition from the scroll to the codex is the text layout used for the Bible in the two formats. The term "text layout" is mostly concerned with the planning of the pages in a codex or sheets in a scroll where a text is to be copied, including the organization of spaces and the choice of typographical features, before the text is copied. P. Andrist, M. Maniaci, and P. Canard have recently defined text layout as follows:

> L'ensemble des stratégies que le copiste (éventuellement en collaboration avec d'autres artisans) met en œuvre pour distribuer un contenu sur l'ensemble des pages destinées à l'accueillir, de façon à le rendre correctement (et aisément) accessible à ses lecteurs.
>
> [The set of strategies that the copyist (possibly in collaboration with other craftsmen) implements to distribute a text on all the pages intended to accommodate it, so as to render it correctly (and easily) accessible to its readers.][12]

---

**9** Sing. *pinkas* (פִּנְקָס), from Greek *pinaks* (πίναξ), "writing tablet." They consisted of several tablets attached altogether, i.e., each tablet attached to the ones that preceded and followed it, in a concertina-like way. They were used for jottings and ephemera, and are mentioned in the Mishnah. See Olszowy-Schlanger, "The Anatomy of Non-Biblical Scrolls," 51.
**10** See Israel Yeivin, *Introduction to the Tiberian Masorah*, trans. E. J. Revell, Masoretic Studies 5 (Missoula, Montana: Scholars Press, 1980), § 5 (p. 7): "The scroll was the only accepted format for a Jewish book until the end of the Talmudic period (c. 600 CE) … The codex form … does not seem to have been used until about 700 CE. As commonly occurs, the older form continued to be used for religious purposes."
**11** Olszowy-Schlanger, "The Anatomy of Non-Biblical Scrolls," 54.
**12** Patrick Andrist, Paul Canart, and Marilena Maniaci, *La syntaxe du codex: Essai de codicologie structurale*, Bibliologia: elementa ad librorum studia pertinentia 34 (Turnhout: Brepols, 2013), 58.

It is important to point out that the concept of text layout is not tied to the organization of a specific page but rather affects a group of pages (or sheets) on which a textual unit is arranged. Thus, the choices – or requirements – for the size of the text, the script type and mode, the placement of certain words or phrases, and the hierarchization of texts are among the text layout strategies and do not depend – at least not solely – on the organization of the writing space on one specific page.

Therefore, in this chapter I am going to focus on the dynamics behind the transformations in text layout in Bible manuscripts that accompanied the transition from scroll to codex, as a way to understand how the text layout specifications conceived and codified for the copying of Bible scrolls were transformed and adapted for the copying of Bible codices. We will look closely at how the implementation of these specifications, which rabbinic literature had already standardized, is negotiated with different factors that will transform the end product in the codex. Among these factors are the adaptation to a new spatial unit for copying – the page; the degree of faithfulness in codices to the norms established for copying the text of the Bible in scrolls; factors related to geo-cultural traditions (that is, aspects of the text layout that vary according to the geo-cultural area in which the codex was copied: Ashkenaz, Sepharad, Italy, Byzantium, the Orient)[13]; and lastly, aesthetic factors related to the particular time period when the copy was made (the fashion of the day) or the tastes of the commissioner or the scribe.

## 2 Copying Torah Scrolls: Transmission and Tradition

The text layout specifications conceived for copying Bible scrolls are codified in several places in the rabbinical literature (both Babylonian and Palestinian Talmudim, *Massekhet Soferim*), as well as in certain works by medieval authors who gradually established the details of these specifications, notably Maimonides (1135–1204), Meir Abulafia (1170–1244), and Menahem ha-Meiri (1249–1310). Specifications regarding the text layout of Hebrew Bibles that affect the resulting page layout in a codex include the following:

---

[13] For codicological Jewish geo-cultural areas, see Malachi Beit-Arié, *Hebrew Codicology: Tentative Typology of Technical Practices Employed in Hebrew Dated Medieval Manuscripts* (Paris: Institut de recherche et d'histoire des textes, 1977), 17.

- The בי"ה שמ"ו rule, according to which the following words should be copied at the beginning of a column: בראשית ("In the beginning," Gen. 1:1), יהודה ("Judah," Gen 49:8), הבאים ("that came," Exod 14:28), שמר ("Observe," Exod 34:11), מה טובו ("How goodly," Num 24:5), and ואעידה ("and I will call to witness," Deut 31:28)[14];
- The distinctive features of some letters[15];
- The use of blank spaces and lines in open and closed sections (*petuḥot* and *setumot*)[16] and at the end of each book, and to divide the text into pericopes (*parashiyyot*) and other paragraph divisions[17];
- The layout of the text in the poetic sections of the Bible and in the poetic books (*Sifre EMeT*) – Job, Proverbs, and Psalms.[18]

The specifications relating to the layout of the poetic sections are particularly relevant, since even though they do not need to be followed in codices, many of them will be adhered to, and they will pose many challenges for transposing the text to the codex format.

In *b. Meg.* 16b, a mention of the text layout for the list of the sons of Haman (Esth 9:7–9) in the copying of the Esther scrolls declares

> All the songs are written in the form of a half brick over a whole brick, and a whole brick over a half brick, with the exception of this one [the list of the sons of Haman] and the list of

---

**14** Yeivin, *Introduction to the Tiberian Masorah*, § 75 (p. 43), mentions that there was some disagreement regarding these words, and therefore the convention was not always followed in codices.

**15** Christian D. Ginsburg, *Introduction to the Massoretico-Critical Edition of the Hebrew Bible* (New York: Ktav Publishing House, 1966), 318–45, lists the following: the fifteen extraordinary points, suspended letters, and inverted *nuns*. Yeivin, *Introduction to the Tiberian Masorah*, § 79 to § 86 (pp. 44–48), mentions dotted words, inverted *nun*, suspended letters, large letters, small letters, and other unusual letter forms. See also Manfred R. Lehmann, "Further Study of the Pe'in Lefufot," in *Proceedings of the Eleventh Congress of the International Organization for Masoretic Studies (IOMS), Jerusalem, June 21–22, 1993*, ed. Aron Dotan (Jerusalem: World Union of Jewish Studies, 1994): 41–46. He lists the distinctive features as follows: "Extraordinary Points, Isolated Letters, Suspended Letters, Large and Small letters, and Other Odd Letters such as the *waw* with a crack in the middle, the crooked *nun*, and the 'winding *peh*' [*peh lefufah*]" (41). On the use of large letters in particular, see María Josefa de Azcárraga, "Las 'ôtiyyôt gedôlôt en las compilaciones masoréticas," *Sefarad* 54/1 (1994): 13–29.

**16** The sections or paragraphs that the pericopes (*parashiyyot*) of the Pentateuch are divided into are named – *petuḥah* ("open") and *setumah* ("closed") – for how the blank space between the end of one section and the beginning of the next should look. See Yeivin, *Introduction to the Tiberian Masorah*, § 74 (pp. 40–41).

**17** Yeivin, *Introduction to the Tiberian Masorah*, § 72 to § 75 (pp. 39–43).

**18** Yeivin, *Introduction to the Tiberian Masorah*, § 77 (pp. 43–44). See below.

the Kings of Canaan (Josh. 12:9–24), which are written in the form of a half brick over a half brick, and a whole brick over a whole brick.[19]

This mention is important, because it establishes two kinds of formats for poetic sections of the Bible. On the one hand we have "the form of a half brick over a half brick, and a whole brick over a whole brick," that is, lines in which the words line up one above the other, leaving blank spaces in between that also line up one over the other (Fig. 1). This is the arrangement of the text containing the list of the sons of Haman and the text containing the list of the kings of Canaan:

**Fig. 1:** Layout 1: A half brick over a half brick, and a whole brick over a whole brick.

On the other hand, there is "the form of a half brick over a whole brick, and a whole brick over a half brick," in which the words and spaces alternate from one line to the next (Fig. 2):

**Fig. 2:** Layout 2: a half brick over a whole brick, and a whole brick over a half brick.

This second arrangement is the one that, according to b. Meg. 16b, the rest of the poetic sections of the Bible should adopt, including the Song at the Sea (Exod 15) and the Song of Moses (Deut 32) in the Pentateuch and the Song of Deborah (Judg 5) and the Song of David (2 Sam 22) in the Prophets. However, this typical arrangement of alternating bricks, or "brick pattern," is not the only arrangement

---

**19** English translations of b. Meg. are taken from David Kantrowitz, *The Soncino Talmud*, version 3.0.8 (Davka Corp. and Judaic Press, 2004).

found in medieval codices for all the poetic texts. Other arrangements of the text can be found for the poetic sections other than the brick pattern and, within the Pentateuch, there are arrangements that differentiate the Song at the Sea from the Song of Moses. *Massekhet Soferim*, one of the Minor Tractates of the Babylonian Talmud, prescribes a more specific arrangement of the text for the Song of Moses, the Song at the Sea, and the Song of Deborah. In chapter 12, it states

> A mnemonic sign for the beginnings of the lines [of the Song of Moses] is the following [it gives the first word in every line, the total number of lines being seventy] ... The Song at the Sea and the Song of Deborah are written in the form of a half-brick over whole brick, and a whole brick over half-brick. The Song at the Sea consists of thirty lines [it gives the first word in every line].[20] The mark for the Song of Deborah is sixty-four lines [it gives the first word in every line].[21]

It seems that, according to *Massekhet Soferim*, the arrangement of the text in a brick pattern would apply only to the Song at the Sea and the Song of Deborah, since no specific prescription is provided concerning the layout of the Song of Moses. Only a list is given with the words that should be placed at the beginning of each line. By counting these line beginnings, we can deduce that the Song of Moses should be arranged in seventy lines, plus two additional blank lines, one coming before the poem and the other after it, as is indicated in the same chapter: "[The Song of Moses] must also be provided with the space of a full line above it and of a full line below it."[22] Despite these details, *Massekhet Soferim* does not specify any other requirements pertaining to the text layout that should be used for the Song of Moses. Neither does it include that poem in the same group with the Song at the Sea and the Song of Deborah, for which it does specify an arrangement of the text following the well-known brick pattern. We can conclude, therefore, that for *Massekhet Soferim* the Song of Moses should be arranged in scrolls differently than the other two poems, as was customary, for example, in the medieval Sephardi tradition.

In chapter 13, *Massekhet Soferim* mentions what is described as the most common practice followed by scribes when copying the text of the Song of David and the poetic books of Psalms, Job, and Proverbs: "A skilled scribe," it states, "spaces [the lines] out symmetrically according to the beginnings, the middle

---

[20] In *Massekhet Soferim*, the first word in line 30 is מי ("waters"), from את מי הים ("waters of the sea") in Exod 15:19. This is not the tradition mentioned by Maimonides. See below.

[21] English translations of *Massekhet Soferim* are taken from Abraham Cohen, ed., *Hebrew-English Edition of the Babylonian Talmud: Minor Tractates* (London: Soncino Press, 1948).

[22] The practice of leaving blank lines before and after the poem is also used in the text of the Song at the Sea.

pauses, and the endings of the verses." This would result in an arrangement of the text in which each verse would be divided symmetrically in two parts (Fig. 3):

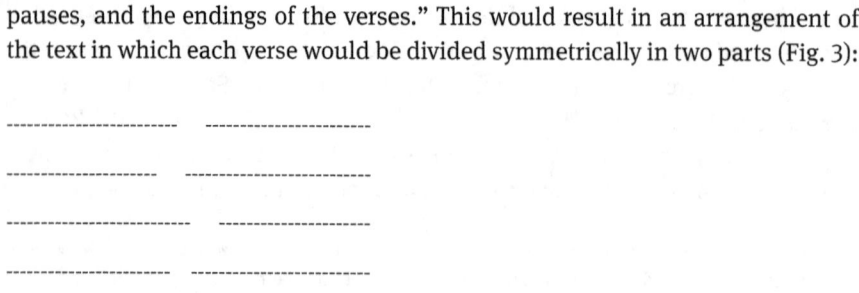

**Fig. 3:** Layout 3: Divided symmetrically in two parts.

This layout, with secondary variations, is characteristic, for example, of the books of Psalms, Job, and Proverbs in the medieval Sephardi manuscript tradition. However, this prescription is far from being universally followed in medieval codices of the Bible for the Song of David.

The prescription given in *y. Meg.* 3:7 is very similar to what we have just seen in *Massekhet Soferim*. It establishes that "the Song at the Sea and the Song of Deborah are written in the manner of setting bricks, that is, two halves of a brick over a whole brick, and a whole brick over half-bricks," and it adds – like *Massekhet Soferim* 13, and also like *b. Meg.* 16b – that "the names of the ten sons of Haman and the Kings of Canaan are written with a half-brick over a half-brick and a whole brick over a whole brick, for no building could stand if built that way."[23] It says nothing, however, about the copying of other poetic sections such as the Song of Moses or the Song of David.

Maimonides, in his *Mishne Torah, Hilkhot Sefer Torah*, defines the arrangement of the text of both the Song at the Sea and the Song of Moses according to the Ben Asher tradition.[24] Maimonides had access to this tradition in Egypt by consulting authoritative Masoretic codices, which he claims to have used for a copy he himself made of a Torah Scroll.[25] According to him:

---

**23** English translations of *y. Meg.* are taken from Jacob Neusner, trans., *The Talmud of the Land of Israel: A Preliminary Translation and Explanation*, vol. 19, *Megillah*, Chicago Studies on the History of Judaism (Chicago, London: The University of Chicago Press, 1987).

**24** Aaron b. Moses ben Asher and Moses b. David ben Naftali are considered the last two Masoretes of the school of Tiberias. See Yeivin, *Introduction to the Tiberian Masorah*, § 154 (p. 141), and Ángel Sáenz-Badillos, *A History of the Hebrew Language* (Cambridge: Cambridge University Press, 1996), § 4.5 (pp. 105–11). For Masorah and Masorete, see below.

**25** "... the scroll [meaning the codex] well known in Egypt containing the twenty-four books, which was in Jerusalem until recently, and which was used to check other scrolls. All relied on it, since Ben Asher corrected it ... I relied on it when I wrote a correct Torah Scroll." Maimonides, *Mishne Torah: Sefer Ahavah, Hilkhot Sefer Torah*, chap. 8. English translation in Menahem

> This is the form of the poem *Ha'azinu* (The Song of Moses): every line has a blank space in the middle, like the shape of a closed paragraph, so that every line is divided in half. It is to be written in 70 lines.²⁶ Here are the words at the beginning of each line [the list of words follows, which is the same as the one given in *Massekhet Soferim*].²⁷

This means that for Maimonides the Song of Moses is to be copied with a layout very similar to that of the list of the sons of Haman and the list of the kings of Canaan (Fig. 1). Concerning the Song at the Sea, he sets out the following:

> The Song at the Sea is written in thirty lines. The first line is normal [i.e., there are no blank spaces in the line], while the rest are as follows: one line has an empty space in the middle, while the next line has two empty spaces, so that the line is divided into three and so that there is space opposite each written part, and writing opposite each space.²⁸

Immediately after, as can be seen in a copy of the *Mishne Torah* corrected according to Maimonides's original,²⁹ he offers the text of the poem in the form that it should take when copied. Maimonides not only takes up the ancient tradition of laying the text out in a brick pattern (Fig. 2) but also specifies the number of blank spaces that each line should have, one in one line, starting with line 2, and two in the next, and so on (Fig. 4).

---

Kellner, trans., *The Code of Maimonides: Book Two; The Book of Love*, Yale Judaica Series 32 (New Haven: Yale University Press, 2004), 100. It is interesting that Maimonides is copying a Torah Scroll from a codex ("the scroll… containing the 24 books" was without a doubt a codex, as no scroll contained the twenty-four books), thus reflecting a practice that persisted throughout the Middle Ages; see below.

26 The number of lines in medieval manuscripts of the Hebrew Bible varies between 67–73, according to different traditions of dividing the text into lines, 70 being the rule observed by Maimonides. The Aleppo Codex (Jerusalem, Makhon Ben Tzvi, MS 1), dated ca. 930 CE, arranges the Song of Moses in 67 lines. The Leningrad Codex (St. Petersburg, National Library of Russia, MS EBP. I B 19a), dated to 1008, arranges this song in 37 lines, each line roughly corresponding to two lines in codices presenting the text in 67–73 lines, except for the last line (36 x 2 +1 = 73). See descriptions of both codices in Beit-Arié, Sirat, and Glatzer, *Codices hebraicis*, § 6 and 17 (pp. 65–72 and 114–31).

27 Kellner, *The Code of Maimonides: Book Two; The Book of Love*, 101.

28 Ibid., 101–2.

29 Oxford, Bodleian Library, MS Hunt. 80. Copied in Egypt (Fostat?), between 1181 and 1204. See Adolf Neubauer and A. E. Cowley, *Catalogue of the Hebrew Manuscripts in the Bodleian Library and in the College Libraries of Oxford*, 2 vols. (Oxford: Clarendon Press, 1886–1906), and Malachi Beit-Arié, R. A. May, and Adolf Neubauer, *Catalogue of the Hebrew Manuscripts in the Bodleian Library: Supplement of Addenda and Corrigenda to Vol. 1 (A. Neubauer's Catalogue)* (Oxford: Clarendon Press, 1994), no. 577.

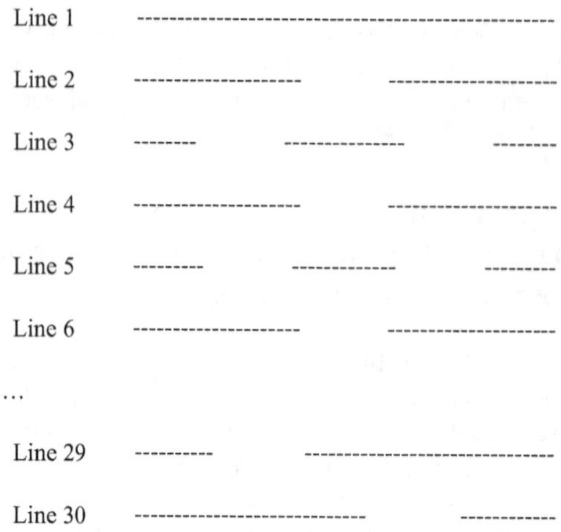

```
Line 1      ----------------------------------
Line 2      --------------------    --------------------
Line 3      ---------    ---------------    ---------
Line 4      --------------------    ---------------------
Line 5      ---------    ---------------    ---------
Line 6      --------------------    ---------------------
...
Line 29     ----------    --------------------------------
Line 30     ----------------------------    -----------
```

**Fig. 4:** Layout 4: Layout of The Song at the Sea as described by Maimonides.

As for lines 29–30,[30] Maimonides does not give any direct indication about how they should be copied, but the model of the poem as presented in the *Mishne Torah* manuscript displays lines 29–30 with one space each, line 29 with a space towards the end, and line 30 with a space towards the beginning (Fig. 4). This is the tradition followed by most medieval Eastern codices of the Hebrew Bible.[31]

In addition to these guidelines, Maimonides mentions other scribal practices that also concern the text layout of the Song at the Sea and the Song of Moses:

> Other practices not mentioned in the Talmud, which scribes customarily do according to their traditions: that the five lines preceding the Song at the Sea begin with the words: הבאים, ביבשה, יהוה, מת, במצרים ; that the five lines following the Song at the Sea begin with the words: ותקח, אחריה, סוס, ויצאו, ויבואו ; that the six lines preceding the Song Ha'azinu begin with: ואעידה, אחרי, הדרך, באחרית, להכעיסו, קהל ; that the five lines following the Song Ha'azinu begin with: ויבא, לדבר, אשר, הזאת, אשר.[32]

---

**30** Lines 29 and 30 are the most unstable with respect to their form and to the distribution of text. Different traditions and regional variants can be traced through the Middle Ages. See Michèle Dukan, *La Bible hébraïque: Les codices copiés en Orient et dans la zone séfarade avant 1280*, Bibliologia: elementa ad librorum studia pertinentia 22 (Turnhout: Brepols, 2006), 46–49.
**31** The first word in line 30 according to Maimonides is את, from את מי הים ("waters of the sea"), in Exod. 15:19. This tradition is also followed in almost all medieval Eastern manuscripts of the Hebrew Bible, including Aleppo and Leningrad, as well as in some Sephardi manuscripts from the thirteenth century. See Dukan, *La Bible hébraïque*, 49.
**32** Maimonides, *Mishne Torah: Sefer Ahavah, Hilkhot Sefer Torah*, chap. 8; Kellner, *The Code of Maimonides: Book Two; The Book of Love*, 97.

These practices are not mandatory and failing to follow them does not make a scroll faulty for liturgical purposes. In fact, medieval codices of the Hebrew Bible present divergent traditions, and sometimes these practices are not followed at all. However, they will often be observed in the copy of Bible codices as if they were as important as other requirements needed to make a scroll suitable for the synagogue service. In Bible codices that adhere to them, these additional scribal practices will have repercussions for the page layout.

## 3 A New Spatial Unit – the Page

When we open a medieval codex of the Hebrew Bible and we compare it to a Torah Scroll, the thing that strikes us most is something that is generally found in the codex but not in the Torah Scroll – the vocalization of the consonantal text (Heb., *nikkud*), the cantillation marks (Heb., *ṭeʿamim*), and, frequently, the paratext in micrography in the margins surrounding the biblical text, generally called the Masorah.[33] Both the Masorah and the graphical innovations that developed in order to ensure that the text was read and transmitted correctly (vocalization and cantillation marks) were gradually adopted over a period of several centuries[34] that coincides roughly to the period in which Judaism adopted the codex. The tradition of copying Torah Scrolls for liturgical use, which was firmly established much earlier and codified in the Talmud, did not provide the most favorable conditions for incorporating these elements into scrolls, since the prescriptions of the *halakhah* (Jewish religious law) were very strict in this regard. Nonetheless, the new codex format was not subject to these prescriptions since it had no liturgical

---

[33] Yeivin, *Introduction to the Tiberian Masorah*, § 63 (p. 34), defines the Masorah as "the collected body of instructions used to preserve the traditional layout and text of the Bible unchanged." It is traditionally believed that the writing and compiling of the Masorah ended in the tenth century, although it is now being debated whether the copyists of the Masorah after that date limited themselves to merely copying it uncritically and without innovations. The compilers and, to a certain degree, the authors of this body of instructions are called Masoretes. The bibliography on the Masorah and its study is vast, and therefore, besides Yeivin, who was cited previously, I will mention here only the most-general manuals: Page H. Kelley, Daniel S. Mynatt, and Timothy G. Crawford, *The Masorah of Biblia Hebraica Stuttgartensia: Introduction and Annotated Glossary* (Grand Rapids, Michigan: William Beerdmans Publishing Company, 1998); Elvira Martín Contreras and Guadalupe Seijas de los Ríos-Zarzosa, *Masora: La transmisión de la tradición de la Biblia hebrea*, Instrumentos para el estudio de la Biblia 20 (Estella: Verbo Divino, 2010).

[34] Sixth–ninth centuries, approximately. See Sáenz-Badillos, *A History of the Hebrew Language*, § 4.1 (p. 77); Ernst Würthwein, *The Text of the Old Testament* (London: SCM Press, 1979), 21, pushes the date for the beginning of this activity back to the fifth century.

function, and even if it did, it was at least not used exclusively for this purpose.[35] Thus, very early on, the Masorah and the graphical innovations for vowels and cantillation marks found a place in the codices of the Hebrew Bible.

The new format made it possible to design a text layout without the constraints imposed by liturgical prescriptions, and there were limitless possibilities for the page layout as well, since it did not have to conform to the scroll's arrangement into columns. Nonetheless, as was already mentioned, many of the requirements that were obligatory for scrolls were also conformed to in codices, to varying degrees. And the arrangement of the text into columns, as was done in scrolls, was also largely observed in codices.[36]

In their transposition to the codex, the columns of Torah Scrolls had to be adapted to the space on the page, which is why the vast majority of Bibles use a page layout consisting of either two or three columns per page – depending on the tradition, the size of the codex and letter size.[37] In the copying of scrolls, the number of columns per sheet into which the scrolls are divided is governed by the Talmud, which states that this number must be between three and eight.[38] Emmanuel Tov has shown that this was already the case in the Dead Sea Scrolls, save a few exceptions, with three or four columns being the most common.[39] A codex with either two or three columns per page, when lying open – a two-page spread being the basic visual unit of a medieval manuscript – would have four or six columns, which is within the parameters established by the Talmud for a sheet in scrolls. The width of a column is also prescribed in the Talmud, though this can vary depending on the letter size and the number of columns that are copied on each sheet.[40] According to Michèle Dukan, the width of the columns in Torah

---

**35** Some rabbis believed that it was acceptable to read the Torah from a codex for liturgical purposes, especially if a community did not have a Torah Scroll. See Dukan, *La Bible hébraïque*, 40–41.

**36** Codices were also copied with the text of the Bible running the entire width of the text block (in a single column). There are several extant examples and many Geniza fragments of this kind of Bible, which was probably more common in small-format codices intended for individual daily use, often lacking the Masorah. See esp. the catalogue of the Bible fragments in the Geniza, M.C. Davis, H. Knopf, and Ben Outhwaite, *Hebrew Bible Manuscripts in the Cambridge Genizah Collections*, 4 vols. (Cambridge: Cambridge University Press, 1978–2003).

**37** The oldest Eastern codices – including Aleppo, Leningrad, and London, British Library, MS Or. 4445, dated 920–50 CE – often arrange the text in three columns per page. This tradition was also followed in European codices, though the two-column layout was widely used as well.

**38** *b. Menaḥ.* 30a, *y. Meg.* chap. 1.71c–d, *Massekhet Soferim* chap. 2.10.

**39** Tov, *Scribal Practices*, 80–81.

**40** *b. Menaḥ.* 30a: "Our Rabbis taught: A man should use sheets [of parchment] which contain from three to eight columns; he should not use one which contains fewer columns or more. And he should not put in too many columns for it would look like an epistle, nor too few columns for

Scrolls from the Islamic period[41] ranges from 60 mm to 110 mm, with an average of 85 mm.[42] This variation, together with the use of the margins in the design of the *mise en page* – and moreover, as we have seen, the option of copying two or three columns per page – made it possible for codex scribes to adapt the columns to the space on the page without any great difficulty, in accordance with their individual way of organizing the page layout.

However, the columns in the poetic sections of the Bible are much more standardized. As we have seen, the Talmud establishes norms for the arrangement of these sections, as well as the words that have to go at the beginning of each line. We have also seen how Maimonides adopts other traditions that add new norms for how the text of the poetic sections should be copied. Although following these other norms was not mandatory, they nonetheless became common in Torah Scrolls. Thus, the columns with the poetic sections of the Pentateuch (the Song at the Sea and the Song of Moses) have a different width than the rest of the scroll, generally equivalent to one and a half columns.

Using the data provided by Dukan on column width in Torah Scrolls we can calculate that, in the Islamic period, a column measuring approximately 130 mm, on average, would be required to copy the Song at the Sea. Of course, each scroll has specific measurements that do not necessarily coincide with that number, but the average gives us an idea of the available width for each line of the Song of the Sea to be copied using the same letter size, text density, and spacing between words as were used in the rest of the text, all the while respecting the requirements of the text layout, especially the requirement that each line begin with a particular word.

Keeping in mind the rules given by Maimonides that were mentioned above, a column with the Song at the Sea must have the following structure (Fig. 5): The column must start with the word הבאים ("that came," Exod 14:28), in accordance with the בי"ה שמ"ו rule. The next four lines before the beginning of the poem must also start with the prescribed words (ביבשה, יהוה, מת, במצרים, respectively). The poem itself (Exod 15:1–19) must take up thirty lines, as we have seen. Following the poem, the next five lines of text also must begin with the prescribed words (ותקח, אחריה, סוס, ויצאו, ויבאו, respectively), which makes a total of 42 lines for the whole section, since before and after the poem there has to be a blank line.[43]

---

the eyes would wander, but [the width of the columns should equal] the word *le-mishpeḥotekhem* (למשפחותיכם) written three times." See also Yeivin, *Introduction to the Tiberian Masorah*, § 78 (p. 44).
41 Produced mostly in Egypt and the Near East between the tenth and the thirteenth centuries.
42 Dukan, *La Bible hébraïque*, table 6, p. 33.
43 In fact, there is a tendency in Pentateuch scrolls from the Islamic period for the number of lines per column to be 42 in the entire scroll, enabling the arrangement of the Song at the Sea

| LBP 1 | -------------------------------------------------- |
| LBP 2 | -------------------------------------------------- |
| LBP 3 | -------------------------------------------------- |
| LBP 4 | -------------------------------------------------- |
| LBP 5 | -------------------------------------------------- |

[Blank line]

| Line 1 | -------------------------------------------------- |
| Line 2 | --------------------      -------------------- |
| Line 3 | --------    ---------------    -------- |
| Line 4 | --------------------       -------------------- |
| Line 5 | ---------    --------------    --------- |
| Line 6 | --------------------       -------------------- |

...

| Line 29 | ----------       ------------------------------ |
| Line 30 | ----------------------------       ------------ |

[Blank line]

| LAP 1 | -------------------------------------------------- |
| LAP 2 | -------------------------------------------------- |
| LAP 3 | -------------------------------------------------- |
| LAP 4 | -------------------------------------------------- |
| LAP 5 | -------------------------------------------------- |

**Fig. 5:** Layout of The Song at the Sea; LBP: Line before the poem; LAP: Line after the poem.

---

in one single column, with the five lines of text preceding and following the poem in the same column. Some rabbis considered the number 42 to have special significance since it is the sum of the number of days during which the Torah was given to Moses (40) plus the number of the tables of the law (2). See Dukan, *La Bible hébraïque*, p. 29, n. 26, and table 6, p. 33. The importance of the number 42 was carried over into the codex. Some Bible codices have a page layout with 21

Thus, the specific regulations for the Song at the Sea establishes the exact text in each of the thirty lines that make up the poem, along with the five lines of text that precede it, and the five lines that follow it. These lines before and after, in addition to the first line of the poem – which, according to Maimonides, is the only one that does not have any blank spaces – are what dictate the width of the poem in its entirety, as long as the norms are observed. As has been noted, the column containing the Song at the Sea is generally wider than an ordinary column, but too narrow to occupy the space of a complete page in a codex of medium size. In addition, the 42 lines that make up the poem's column are often too many to be copied in one column on a single page of a codex. As a result, scribes who followed these specifications were obliged to devise new strategies for creating a page layout that would maintain the tradition while simultaneously producing a graphically balanced and aesthetically pleasing page.

As can be easily imagined, these copying traditions posed a challenge to scribes, which was dealt with in a variety of ways. In MS Paris, BnF, Hébreu 29 (Fig. 6),[44] the scribe opted to use a column width that is the same as the length of the lines that precede the poem, and this length is determined by the amount of text that is prescribed and by the letter size used in copying the codex. Since the width of the page's text block is larger,[45] the scribe designed the page layout to accommodate a supplementary column with non-poetic text that precedes the word הבאים ("that came," Exod 14:28). In this way, the scribe follows the בי"ה שמ"ו rule and copies the requisite amount of text in each line, without needing to have recourse to other strategies to manage the text.

---

lines, half a 42-line column, allowing the complete poem of the Song at the Sea to be arranged symmetrically on two facing pages. See Dukan, *La Bible hébraïque*, 52.

**44** Castile? Approx. 1470–80, 3 cols., 224 x 182 mm. See Hermann Zotenberg, *Manuscrits orientaux: Catalogues des manuscrits hébreux et samaritains de la Bibliothèque impériale* (Paris: Imprimerie impériale, 1866), no. 29; Javier del Barco, *Bibliothèque nationale de France: Hébreu 1 à 32; Manuscrits de la bible hébraïque*, Manuscrits en caractères hébreux conservés dans les bibliothèques publiques de France 4 (Turnhout: Brepols, 2011), 188–94; Gabrielle Sed-Rajna and Sonia Fellous, *Les manuscrits hébreux enluminés des bibliothèques de France*, Corpus of illuminated manuscripts 7, Oriental series 3 (Leuven: Peeters, 1994), no. 36; Katrin Kogman-Appel, *Jewish Book Art between Islam and Christianity: The Decoration of Hebrew Bibles in Medieval Spain*, The Medieval and Early Modern Iberian World 19 (Leiden: Brill, 2004), 218–19.

**45** By "text block" I mean the space on the pages of a codex that is reserved *prior to copying* for a certain text. There is almost always a fixed proportion between text block and page margins, which varies from codex to codex depending on codex size and cultural and regional traditions; see Colette Sirat, *Writing as Handwork: A History of Handwriting in Mediterranean and Western Culture*, Bibliologia. Elementa ad librorum studia pertinentia 24 (Turnhout: Brepols, 2006), 169–75.

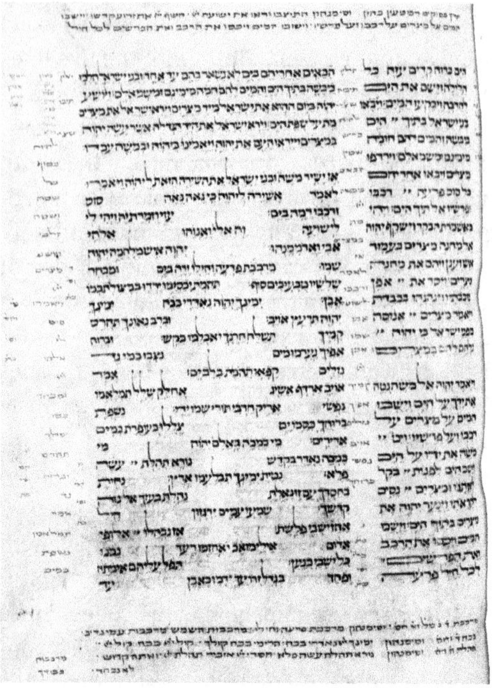

**Fig. 6:** Paris, BnF, Hébreu 29, fol. 50r.

In MS Paris, BnF, Hébreu 24 (Fig. 7),[46] the copyist also kept the column width the same as the length of the lines that precede the poem. However, in this case, the choice was made to design the page layout in such a way that the column containing the poem would be positioned in the middle of the page.[47] The resulting

---

**46** Castile? Approx. 1250–1300, 3 cols., 293 x 251 mm. See Zotenberg, *Catalogues des manuscrits hébreux et samaritains*, no. 24; Del Barco, *Bibliothèque nationale de France: Hébreu 1 à 32*, 150–53; Sed-Rajna and Fellous, *Les manuscrits hébreux enluminés des bibliothèques de France*, no. 21; Michel Garel, *D'une main forte: manuscrits hébreux des collections françaises* (Paris: Seuil, Bibliothèque nationale, 1991), no. 38.

**47** Moreover, the copyist took into account the total number of lines occupied by the poem and preceding and following it (42) and fit half of them (21) on each of two facing pages. The result is thus a symmetrical and aesthetically balanced double page, with the book lying open, presenting the Song at the Sea by itself according to Maimonides's prescriptions. This tradition can also be found in other Sephardic codices. See Javier del Barco, "Shirat ha-Yam and Page Layout in Late Medieval Sephardi Bibles," in *Sephardic Book Art of the 15th Century*, ed. Luís U. Afonso and Tiago Moita, Studies in Medieval and Early Renaissance Art History (Turnout: Harvey Miller, 2020): 107–20.

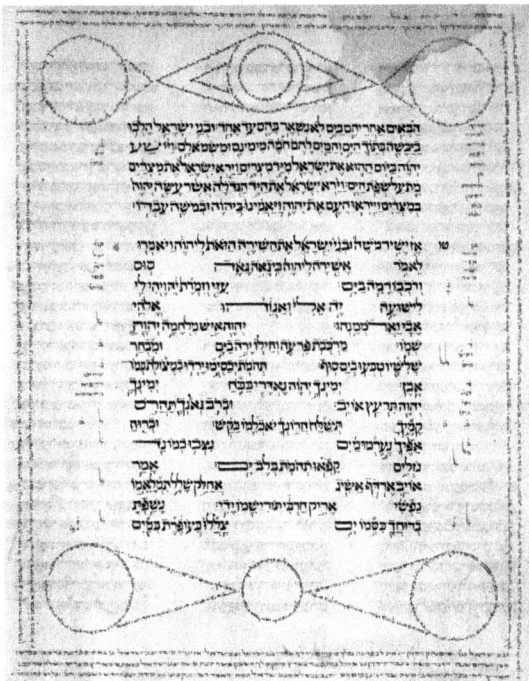

Fig. 7: Paris, BnF, Hébreu 24, fol. 37v.

margins, which are much wider than in the rest of the manuscript, give the copyist space to include sections of the Masorah adopting figurative forms.

In MS Paris, BnF, Hébreu 28 (Fig. 8),[48] different strategies were adopted. The copyist copied the five lines preceding the poem according to the tradition transmitted by Maimonides, such that each of these lines begins with the prescribed word. The resulting width of these lines is, therefore, the width that the entire poem should have. However, we can see that this is not what was done. The text of the poem, which is recognizable because it has been arranged according to the brick pattern model, was copied by adjusting the width to the size of the text block, which is larger than that of the lines preceding the poem. When copying

---

[48] Iberian Peninsula, 1344, 2 cols., 218 x 172 mm. See Zotenberg, *Catalogues des manuscrits hébreux et samaritains*, no. 28; Del Barco, *Bibliothèque nationale de France: Hébreu 1 à 32*, 182–185; Colette Sirat and Malachi Beit-Arié, *Manuscrits médiévaux en caractères hébraïques: portant des indications de date jusqu'à 1540 – Otsar kitve-yad 'ivriyim mi-yeme-ha-benayim: be-tsiyune ta'arikh 'ad shenat 5300*, vol. 1. (Paris and Jerusalem: Centre National de la Recherche Scientifique, Ha-Akademyah ha-Le'umit ha-Yisra'elit le-Mada'im, 1972), no. 30; Sed-Rajna and Fellous, *Les manuscrits hébreux enluminés des bibliothèques de France*, no. 136.

**Fig. 8:** Paris, BnF, Hébreu 28, fol. 37v.

the poem, the copyist opted to use the entire width of the page provided by the text block, which meant that he was forced to disregard the prescribed words for the beginning of each line of the poem. And this meant, in turn, that each line contains more text than would have been the case if the prescribed first words had been adhered to. Thus, the complete poem occupies only 21 lines, compared to the 30 that it would occupy if Maimonides's norms had been followed. This also made it possible for the whole poem to be copied on a single page, in such a way that the unit of meaning (the poem) coincides with the smallest unit of textual organization (the page). However, it should be pointed out that the scribe copied the text of the poem using the brick pattern arrangement, so that it would be visually recognizable and have at least the *appearance* of a poetic text.

In MS Paris, BnF, Hébreu 19 (Fig. 9),[49] we observe strategies for managing the text that are different from the ones above. As in the preceding case, the scribe

---

[49] Northern France? Approx. 1275–1325, 3 cols., 456 x 337 mm. See Zotenberg, *Catalogues des manuscrits hébreux et samaritains*, no. 19; Del Barco, *Bibliothèque nationale de France: Hébreu 1 à 32*, 106–9; Sed-Rajna and Fellous, *Les manuscrits hébreux enluminés des bibliothèques de France*, no. 64.

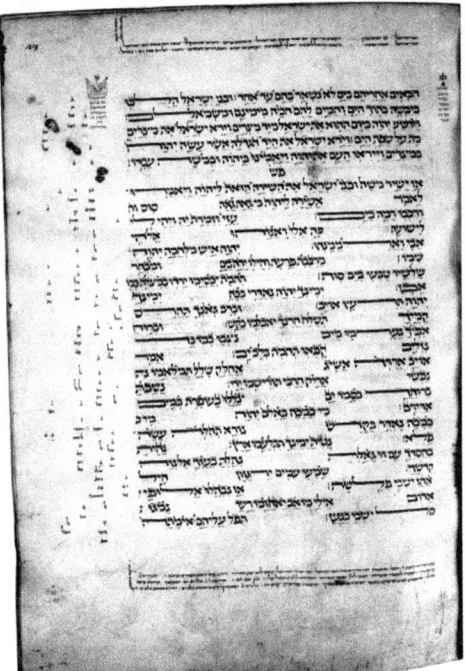

**Fig. 9:** MS Paris, BnF, Hébreu 19, fol. 49r.

copied the five lines that precede the poem following the tradition transmitted by Maimonides, and each of them begins with the prescribed words except line 3.[50] Below, the scribe fit the text of the poem on 30 lines, each of which also begins with the prescribed words. The resulting text block is of the same width as the rest of the manuscript. That is, the page does not have margins that are any wider than usual. To achieve this page layout, the scribe had to resort to using stretched-out or elongated letters, a common device used by Jewish scribes to manage line length.[51] Elongated letters are used in this example both in the five lines that precede the poem and in the lines of the poem itself, so that the text occupies the entire width of the text block without leaving additional space in the side margins.

---

[50] The Talmud and Maimonides both prescribe that line 3 should start with the word יהוה ("God"), from ויושע יהוה ("Thus God saved," Exod 14:30). Here, this line starts with ויושע, the word that comes before it in the same verse.

[51] Using stretched-out or elongated letters is one of the devices that Jewish scribes used to make columns justified on the left. See Malachi Beit-Arié, *Unveiled Faces of Medieval Hebrew Books: The Evolution of Manuscript Production – Progression or Regression?* (Jerusalem: Magnes Press, 2003), chap. 2, "Copying Dynamics: Line Management," 32–48.

Nonetheless, the variety of forms taken by Hebrew Bible codices, especially during the late Middle Ages,[52] meant that scribes had to make more and more decisions about the text layout in the manuscript as a whole and about the page layout to adopt for the specific pages on which the Song at the Sea and other poetic sections were copied. For example, beginning in the thirteenth century, Hebrew Bible codices started to appear in Ashkenaz that had, in addition to the Hebrew text, the Aramaic paraphrase, or Targum, and Rashi's commentary (Shelomo ben Yitzhak de Troyes, 1040–1105).[53] This accretion of texts would have been unthinkable for copies of Pentateuch scrolls, but the codex format could be adapted to new functions, new modes of reading, and different exegetical traditions. Thus, both the form and the function of the Hebrew Bible codex gradually moved away from those of Pentateuch scrolls.

In MS Paris, BnF, Hébreu 8 (Fig. 10),[54] the scribe copied the Hebrew text and its paraphrase in Aramaic for the entire Pentateuch. As a text layout strategy, the choice was made to copy the two texts verse by verse, using the same letter type and size for both. As a result, it is not possible to differentiate one from the other by visual means. For the page on which the Song at the Sea appears, the scribe maintained this same text layout strategy in the poem, such that following each verse in Hebrew is the corresponding Aramaic. In order to do this, the scribe gave up on following the prescriptions given by the Talmud and Maimonides. The page does not obey the בי"ה שמ"ו rule, the text preceding the poem is not arranged into five lines beginning with the prescribed words, and the lines of the poem itself do not start with the prescribed words either. The scribe also failed to follow Maimonides's instructions regarding the spaces that there should be in each line of the poem (one or two), and due to the considerable page width (320 mm), the choice was made to insert two or three spaces in each line. In the end, the only

---

**52** For a preliminary typology and genres of the medieval Hebrew Bible, see David Stern, "The Hebrew Bible in Europe in the Middle Ages: A Preliminary Typology," *Jewish Studies: An Internet Journal* 11 (2012): 235–322; and David Stern, *The Jewish Bible: A Material History*, Samuel and Althea Stroum Lectures in Jewish Studies (Seattle: University of Washington Press, 2017), 88–131. I am presently preparing a monograph about form and function in medieval manuscripts of the Hebrew Bible in the late Middle Ages.

**53** See Stern, "The Hebrew Bible in Europe," 71–77; Stern, *The Jewish Bible*, 119–26; and Javier del Barco, "The Ashkenazi Glossed Bible," The Polonsky Foundation Catalogue of Digitised Hebrew Manuscripts, *Articles* (blog), 2016, http://www.bl.uk/hebrew-manuscripts/articles/theashkenazi-glossed-bible.

**54** Ashkenaz, 1300–1305, 3 cols., 447 x 319 mm. See Zotenberg, *Catalogues des manuscrits hébreux et samaritains*, no. 8; Del Barco, *Bibliothèque nationale de France: Hébreu 1 à 32*, 54–59; Sirat and Beit-Arié, *Manuscrits médiévaux en caractères hébraïques*, vol. 1, no. 28; Sed-Rajna and Fellous, *Les manuscrits hébreux enluminés des bibliothèques de France*, no. 72.

**Fig. 10:** MS Paris, BnF, Hébreu 8, fol. 75v.

device used by the scribe to distinguish the poem from the rest of the text is the brick pattern arrangement, used for both the Hebrew text as well as the paraphrase in Aramaic.

The manuscripts from which the examples we have looked at up to now are taken come from different geo-cultural areas (Sepharad and Ashkenaz) and cover a broad chronological range, from the end of the thirteenth century to the end of the fifteenth. They do not represent, therefore, tendencies or characteristics that can be attributed to a particular time in a particular place; rather, they provide an initial overview of the repertoire of strategies that Jewish scribes used in the late Middle Ages to accommodate a text, the Song at the Sea, that had to comply with a series of specific requirements that were part of the text layout of the Bible in the scroll format. How these strategies developed and spread, the contexts in which they were used, and to what degree they succeeded and helped to create models for copying codices of the Hebrew Bible are questions that have been largely ignored up to now.[55]

---

[55] Dukan, *La Bible hébraïque*, pp. 44–54, makes a preliminary attempt to deal with the variety of ways that the Song at the Sea is arranged in Eastern and Sephardi codices prior to 1280, and

## 4 Teaching the Tradition: From Codex to Scroll

It was mentioned earlier that Maimonides copied a Torah Scroll taking as a model a codex that was famous in Egypt for its authoritativeness and fidelity to tradition. What is interesting about this quotation from Maimonides about the fact of copying from a model is that it reflects what seems to have become a common practice after the adoption of the codex as a valid format for copying the text of the Bible. It became customary at that point to copy codices and scrolls consulting a revised and authoritative codex (*sefer muggah*),[56] that is, a model or exemplar codex for the correct copy of the biblical text according to the *halakhah*. Although this is something that has not been much studied in late medieval codices, the Masorah in some of these codices includes very precise instructions regarding things that relate specifically to the layout of the biblical text. These instructions, copied into the margins of the codices, must have served in many cases as reminders, or a sort of instruction manual, for scribes who had to copy a Torah Scroll. It is difficult to know whether any of these codices served specifically and exclusively as exemplar codices, since we know very little at this point about the specific function or functions of the different types of medieval codices of the Hebrew Bible. Nonetheless, it is common in Bible codices with Masorah to find references to certain readings and spellings that come from the same group of codices, including the famous Hilleli codex, the Yerushalmi codex, the Zambuki codex, and others.[57] These doubtless must have served as exemplar codices for copying other codices, and they were possibly used for copying Torah Scrolls as well.

Other manuscripts whose margins have precise instructions about the layout of the biblical text might also have served as exemplar codices, though they may have been used in other contexts as well. This was possibly the case of MS Paris, BnF, Hébreu 65.[58] This codex of the Hebrew Bible consistently indicates the differences between Maimonides and the work called *Sefer tagi* relating to the open and closed sections of the Pentateuch. Maimonides and *Sefer tagi* transmit different

---

to establish some copying traditions. See also Del Barco, "Shirat ha-Yam and Page Layout in Late Medieval Sephardi Bibles," for a preliminary study of the arrangement of the Song at the Sea in the Sephardi tradition.

**56** On the term *sefer muggah*, see Yeivin, *Introduction to the Tiberian Masorah*, § 152 (p. 138); and Kelley, Mynatt, and Crawford, *The Masorah of Biblia Hebraica Stuttgartensia*, s. v. מוגה, p. 133.

**57** On these references, see Ginsburg, *Introduction to the Massoretico-Critical Edition of the Hebrew Bible*, 429–41; Yeivin, *Introduction to the Tiberian Masorah*, § 152 (p. 138); and more recently, M. Teresa Ortega Monasterio, "Los códices modelo y los manuscritos hebreos bíblicos españoles," *Sefarad* 65 (2005): 353–83.

**58** Northern Italy, around 1400, 1 col., 335 x 224 mm. See Zotenberg, *Catalogues des manuscrits hébreux et samaritains*, no. 65; Garel, *D'une main forte*, 79.

traditions regarding the starting and ending points and whether the sections are open or closed within each pericope of the Pentateuch, and all these discrepancies are indicated in the margins of MS Paris, BnF, Hébreu 65. This kind of information is relevant for copying Torah Scrolls and in itself might suffice for this manuscript to be defined as an exemplar codex. However, there are other marginal notes that would seem to corroborate this possible function of the codex, in particular some that specify how certain features of the text layout should appear in Torah Scrolls, which is something that is not always specified in medieval codices of the Hebrew Bible. Some of these annotations are the following:

- On folio 201v, one of the cases where there is a prescribed word that must be at the beginning of the column (according to the בי"ה שמ"ו rule) is indicated in the following way: לספר תורה כותבי' שמר ושמעת בראש הדף ובראש' השטה ("[Instruction] for Sefer Torah: we write 'Observe and obey' (Exod 34:11) at the beginning of the sheet and at the beginning of the line").
- On folio 223r, the same instruction is given regarding ואעידה ("and I will call to witness," Deut 31:28), which precedes the Song of Moses, also according to the בי"ה שמ"ו rule. Here, as in Maimonides, the prescribed words at the beginning of each of the six lines of text that precedes the Song of Moses are also indicated, in the following way: לספ' תורה כותבי' לפני שירת האזינו ו' ראשי שיטין ואעידה בראש הדף ובראש השיט' אחרי הדרך באחרית להכעיסו קהל ("[Instruction] for Sefer Torah: we write before the poem 'Give ear' (the Song of Moses) [the following] six beginnings of lines: 'and I will call to witness' at the beginning of the sheet and at the beginning of line, 'after,' 'the way,' 'in the latter,' 'to provoke him to anger,' and 'the congregation' [at the beginning of the line]").
- On folio 226r, there is an annotation about a tradition, also transmitted by Maimonides, for copying Torah Scrolls, regarding the last line of the Pentateuch[59]: לספר תורה כותבין לעיני כל ישראל בסוף הדף ומש"ל באמצע השטה אחרונה ("[Instruction] for Sefer Torah: we write 'in the sight of all Israel' (Deut 34:12) at the end of the sheet, and also in the middle of the last line"). Unlike the other two annotations, this instruction is not reflected in the way this codex dealt with the verse in question. Indeed, the fact that this instruction is provided here but is not applied to the copy of the text confirms that it is not describing how the text was copied in this codex but *how it should be copied in a Torah Scroll*. Thus, we can affirm that this Bible functions as a model or exemplar codex.

---

**59** Maimonides, *Mishne Torah: Sefer Ahavah, Hilkhot Sefer Torah*, chap. 7.7; Kellner, *The Code of Maimonides: Book Two; The Book of Love*, 96.

These and other indications in this manuscript that address text layout must have been used as an instruction manual by scribes copying Torah Scrolls. This is true as well of MS Paris, BnF, Hébreu 19, mentioned above, where among other things we find indications about the text layout of the five lines that precede the Song at the Sea. In the margins of folio 49r there are two highly precise annotations about the prescriptions that govern the copying of these lines. In the right margin we read: הבאים בראש עמוד בספר תורה וסי׳ ביה שמו ("[the word] 'that came' (Exod 14:28) [should be written] at the beginning of the column in a Torah Scroll, and the [mnemonic] indication is בי"ה שמו" [in reference to the בי"ה שמו rule]"). In the left margin, the note specifies: והן כתובין בה׳ שיטין הבאים ביבשה ויושע מת במצרים ("And this [text preceding the poem] is copied in five lines [whose beginnings are] 'that came,' 'dry land,' 'thus [God] saved,' 'dead,' and 'upon the Egyptians'"). As noted before, the word at the beginning of line 3 in this manuscript is not יהוה ("God"), as it should be according to the בי"ה שמו rule (the letter י in בי"ה stands for יהוה), but the preceding word, ויושע. However, the scribe gives the בי"ה שמו rule for the copying of Torah Scrolls in the right margin, and seems to find no contradiction in giving also the indication of the first word in line 3 (ויושע) in the annotation in the left margin. That is, the use of the word ויושע at the beginning of line 3 in this case is not due to ignorance of the בי"ה שמו rule, but rather perhaps to the use of a local tradition that was different from the dominant tradition. It remains to be seen whether this tradition is documented in other Ashkenazi codices and, more significantly, if it was followed in the coping of Ashkenazi Torah Scrolls, which might be the focus of further research in the future.

On folio 49v of this same manuscript we find similar annotations about line 30 of the Song at the Sea and about the five lines that follow the poem. In the right margin, we read: מי בראש שיטה ("[the word] 'waters' at the beginning of [this] line [which is line 30 in the poem]").[60] On the same folio, in the blank space of the open section after the five lines that follow the poem, we read the following indication: אלו חמשה ראשי שיטין ותקח אחריה סוס ויצאו ויבאו ("These are the words at the beginning of the five lines [after the poem]: 'took,' 'after her,' 'the horse,' 'they went out,' and 'and when they came'"). Thus, in this manuscript we find precise instructions for copying the lines that precede and follow the Song at the Sea according to tradition, as well as for copying line 30 of the poem, about whose first word there were different traditions, as was mentioned above.

The cases that we have just seen indicate, in my opinion, that there was a close relationship between codices of the Hebrew Bible and Torah Scrolls when

---

**60** This is the prescribed word according to *Massekhet Soferim*, which is different from the tradition transmitted by Maimonides. See above.

it came to copying the latter. This does not necessarily mean that the scribes who made Torah Scrolls copied the text *directly* from a codex but rather that they probably used certain codices as study manuals for copying and as reference and revision guides for both the text and the text layout. The fact that these indications do not appear in all Bible manuscripts that also contain the Masorah, but only in certain codices of the Hebrew Bible, thus seems to point to the function that these codices may have had as model or exemplar codices in the communities in which they were copied and used.

# 5 Conclusion

As was recalled at the beginning of this chapter, the period of transition from the scroll – whether vertical or horizontal – as the only format for Hebrew texts to the codex as the main format had to have been more prolonged than what has traditionally been maintained. During this lapse of time, the adoption of the codex brought with it a distribution of functions between the scroll and the codex, and as those functions belonging to the former decreased, those belonging to the latter increased. This process of distributing functions must have happened gradually, until the scroll was finally relegated almost exclusively to the function of the liturgical reading of the Pentateuch and Esther in the synagogue,[61] which is the role that it continues to have still today. Meanwhile, the codex, because of its ease of use, assumed the rest of the functions that had previously been performed by the scroll and gained priority in all spaces except for the synagogue.

Therefore, codices were copied for daily reading, for studying, for carrying around, as gifts, as works of art, and for other purposes. We can discern some of these functions from the features in Bible codices, as we were able to see with the exemplar codices. However, this does not mean that any given codex did not have multiple functions or that these did not change over time. An in-depth study of the possible functions of Bible codices relative to their formal characteristics is then an important direction for future research.

In the end, Judaism's adoption of the codex did not mean that it abandoned the scroll as a medium for reading and transmitting the text of the Bible. The

---

[61] The reading of the weekly pericope of the Pentateuch from a Torah Scroll continues to be one of the most important moments in the liturgy of the Sabbath and, to a lesser degree, on Mondays and Thursdays, when an excerpt from the pericope corresponding to the following Sabbath is read. Likewise, the reading of the book of Esther from a scroll continues to be the most important moment in the liturgy for the Purim holiday.

relationship between the two formats underlies the dynamics of text layout transformation, as has been shown in some examples of Bible codices. It also explains the marginal notes that we find in some codices, which provide precise specifications for copying special sections of the Pentateuch, according to traditional scribal practices. A systematic study of medieval and early modern Torah Scrolls, which still remains to be undertaken, will be able to shed light on the impact that the adoption of the codex had on these scrolls and will provide more details about the interaction and coexistence of the two different formats.

# Bibliography

Andrist, Patrick, Paul Canart, and Marilena Maniaci. *La syntaxe du codex: Essai de codicologie structurale*. Bibliologia: elementa ad librorum studia pertinentia 34. Turnhout: Brepols, 2013.

Azcárraga, María Josefa de. "Las 'ôtiyyôt gedôlôt en las compilaciones masoréticas." *Sefarad* 54/1 (1994): 13–29.

Beit- Arié, Malachi. *Hebrew Codicology: Tentative Typology of Technical Practices Employed in Hebrew Dated Medieval Manuscripts*. Paris: Institut de recherche et d'histoire des textes, 1977.

Beit- Arié, Malachi. *Unveiled Faces of Medieval Hebrew Books: The Evolution of Manuscript Production – Progression or Regression?* Jerusalem: Magnes Press, 2003.

Beit-Arié, Malachi, R. A. May, and Adolf Neubauer. *Catalogue of the Hebrew Manuscripts in the Bodleian Library: Supplement of Addenda and Corrigenda to Vol. 1 (A. Neubauer's Catalogue)*. Oxford: Clarendon Press, 1994.

Beit- Arié, Malachi, Colette Sirat, and Mordechai Glatzer. *Codices hebraicis litteris exarati quo tempore scripti fuerint exhibentes – Otsar ha-mitsḥafim ha-ivriyim: kitve-yad bi-khetav ivri mi-yeme ha-benayim be-tsiyune ta'arikh*. Vol. 1, *Jusqu'à 1020*. Monumenta paleographica Medii Aevi. Series hebraica. Turnhout: Brepols, 1997.

Cohen, Abraham, ed. *Hebrew-English Edition of the Babylonian Talmud: Minor Tractates*. London: Soncino Press, 1948.

Davis, M.C., H. Knopf, and Ben Outhwaite. *Hebrew Bible Manuscripts in the Cambridge Genizah Collections*. Cambridge University Library Genizah Series 2. Cambridge: Cambridge University Press, 1987.

Del Barco, Javier. "The Ashkenazi Glossed Bible." The Polonsky Foundation Catalogue of Digitised Hebrew Manuscripts. Articles (blog), 2016. http://www.bl.uk/hebrew-manuscripts/articles/the-ashkenazi-glossed-bible.

Del Barco, Javier. *Bibliothèque nationale de France: Hébreu 1 à 32; Manuscrits de la bible hébraïque*. Manuscrits en caractères hébreux conservés dans les bibliothèques publiques de France 4. Turnhout: Brepols, 2011.

Del Barco, Javier. "Shirat ha-Yam and Page Layout in Late Medieval Sephardi Bibles." In *Sephardic Book Art of the 15th Century*, edited by Luís U. Afonso and Tiago Moita, 107–120. Studies in Medieval and Early Renaissance Art History. Turnout: Harvey Miller, 2020.

Déroche, François. *Manuel de codicologie des manuscrits en écriture arabe*. Études et recherches. Paris: Bibliothèque Nationale de France, 2000.

Dukan, Michèle. *La Bible hébraïque: Les codices copiés en Orient et dans la zone séfarade avant 1280*. Bibliologia: elementa ad librorum studia pertinentia 22. Turnhout: Brepols, 2006.
Garel, Michel. *D'une main forte: manuscrits hébreux des collections françaises*. Paris: Seuil, Bibliothèque nationale, 1991.
Ginsburg, Christian D. *Introduction to the Massoretico-Critical Edition of the Hebrew Bible*. New York: Ktav Publishing House, 1966.
Kantrowitz, David. *The Soncino Talmud* (version 3.0.8). Davka Corp. and Judaic Press, 2004.
Kelley, Page H., Daniel S. Mynatt, and Timothy G. Crawford. *The Masorah of Biblia Hebraica Stuttgartensia: Introduction and Annotated Glossary*. Grand Rapids, Michigan: William Beerdmans Publishing Company, 1998.
Kellner, Menahem, trans. *The Code of Maimonides: Book Two; The Book of Love*. Yale Judaica Series 32. New Haven: Yale University Press, 2004.
Kogman-Appel, Katrin. *Jewish Book Art between Islam and Christianity: The Decoration of Hebrew Bibles in Medieval Spain*. The Medieval and Early Modern Iberian World 19. Leiden: Brill, 2004.
Lehmann, Manfred R. "Further Study of the Pe'in Lefufot." In *Proceedings of the Eleventh Congress of the International Organization for Masoretic Studies (IOMS), Jerusalem, June 21–22, 1993*, edited by Aron Dotan, 41–46. Jerusalem: World Union of Jewish Studies, 1994.
Martín Contreras, Elvira, and Guadalupe Seijas de los Ríos-Zarzosa. *Masora: La transmisión de la tradición de la Biblia hebrea*. Instrumentos para el estudio de la Biblia 20. Estella: Verbo Divino, 2010.
Neubauer, Adolf, and A.E. Cowley. *Catalogue of the Hebrew Manuscripts in the Bodleian Library and in the College Libraries of Oxford*. 2 vols. Oxford: Clarendon Press, 1886–1906.
Neusner, Jacob, trans. *The Talmud of the Land of Israel: A Preliminary Translation and Explanation*. Vol. 19, *Megillah*. Chicago Studies on the History of Judaism. Chicago: The University of Chicago Press, 1987.
Olszowy-Schlanger, Judith. "The Anatomy of Non-Biblical Scrolls from the Cairo Geniza." In *Jewish Manuscript Cultures: New Perspectives*. Berlin: De Gruyter, 2017.
Olszowy-Schlanger, Judith. "The Hebrew Bible." In *The New Cambridge History of the Bible*. Vol. 2, *From 600 to 1450*, edited by Richard Marsden and E. Ann Matter, 19–40. Cambridge: Cambridge University Press, 2012.
Ortega Monasterio, M. Teresa. "Los códices modelo y los manuscritos hebreos bíblicos españoles." *Sefarad* 65 (2005): 353–83.
Resnick, Irven M. "The Codex in Early Jewish and Christian Communities." *Journal of Religious History* 17/1 (1992): 1–17.
Sáenz-Badillos, Ángel. *A History of the Hebrew Language*. Cambridge: Cambridge University Press, 1996.
Sed-Rajna, Gabrielle, and Sonia Fellous. *Les manuscrits hébreux enluminés des bibliothèques de France*. Corpus of illuminated manuscripts 7, Oriental series 3. Leuven: Peeters, 1994.
Sirat, Colette. *Hebrew Manuscripts of the Middle Ages*. Cambridge: Cambridge University Press, 2002.
Sirat, Colette. *Writing as Handwork: A History of Handwriting in Mediterranean and Western Culture*. Bibliologia. Elementa ad librorum studia pertinentia 24. Turnhout: Brepols, 2006.
Sirat, Colette, and Malachi Beit-Arié. *Manuscrits médiévaux en caractères hébraïques: Portant des indications de date jusqu'à 1540 – Otsar kitve-yad 'ivriyim mi-yeme-ha-benayim:*

be-tsiyune ta'arikh 'ad shenat 5300, vol. 1. Paris: Centre National de la Recherche Scientifique, 1972.

Stern, David. "The First Jewish Books and the Early History of Jewish Reading." *JQR* 98/2 (2008): 163–202.

Stern, David. "The Hebrew Bible in Europe in the Middle Ages: A Preliminary Typology." *Jewish Studies: An Internet Journal* 11 (2012): 235–322.

Stern, David. *The Jewish Bible: A Material History*. Samuel and Althea Stroum Lectures in Jewish Studies. Seattle: University of Washington Press, 2017.

Tov, Emanuel. *Scribal Practices and Approaches Reflected in the Texts Found in the Judean Desert*. STDJ 54. Leiden: Brill, 2004.

Würthwein, Ernst. *The Text of the Old Testament*. London: SCM Press, 1979.

Yeivin, Israel. *Introduction to the Tiberian Masorah*. Translated by E. J. Revell. Masoretic studies 5. Missoula, Montana: Scholars Press, 1980.

Zotenberg, Hermann. *Manuscrits orientaux: Catalogues des manuscrits hébreux et samaritains de la Bibliothèque impériale*. Paris: Imprimerie impériale, 1866.

Eyal Poleg
# Memory, Performance, and Change: The Psalms' Layout in Late Medieval and Early Modern Bibles

## 1 Introduction

The Psalms are a foreign element within the Bible.[1] Their poetry stands against the prose of other biblical books; their archaic vocabulary and imagery, narrating the prayers of the sinner or referring to an anthropomorphic deity, is sometimes at odds with monotheistic worship and diverges from the tone of historical narrative, prevalent across both Old and New Testament. Rather than hindering their reception, the Psalms' idiosyncrasies have contributed to their overwhelming popularity. Their detachment from biblical history and their personal voice have enabled men and women to relate to them and to embed them into their own prayers. They became the cornerstone of divine worship, and accommodated the devotions of Jews and Christians, monks and nuns, Lutherans and Calvinists.

As Jews and Christians have been performing and meditating on the Psalms for over two millennia, the layout of their books has undergone major transformations. Based on extensive research, this article follows the evolution of biblical books in England for over four centuries. Across the rise of moveable-type print and Reformation, it unfolds how manuscripts and printed books have mediated the biblical text through choice of script and ink, illumination and size. Such features are indicative of the theological stance of editors and stationers, while aiming to accommodate diverse audiences. The Psalms are an outstanding testcase for such an investigation. No other biblical book has been engaged with so ardently and for such differing goals. The Psalms were heavily glossed by scholars and exegetes, punctuated lives in medieval monasteries and nunneries, and were chanted by lay men and women in homes and workshops. The complexity of their structure has led editors and stationers to decide on what to highlight, to marginalise, or to omit altogether, shedding light on their priorities and worldviews.

---

[1] Psalm numbers are presented in the Vulgate (Septuagint) and Hebrew sequences in the following format: Vulgate/Hebrew; Middle- and early modern English quotations have been modernized.

Monastic Psalters, lay Books of Hours and Primers, and the late sixteenth-century *Whole Book of Psalmes*, were all among the most popular books of the Middle Ages and early modernity. In order to efficiently assess the uniqueness of the Psalms' layout and minor variants to their appearance, these books are used only as auxiliary evidence in this essay. Rather, it explores how the Book of Psalms was embedded into full Bibles, a corpus which supports comparison between the Psalms' layout and that of other biblical texts. The introduction sets the scene by briefly charting the Psalms' appearance from the Dead Sea Scrolls to the High Middle Ages, enumerating a number of unique features related to the materiality of the Psalms which will be explored throughout the essay. The essay then explores the rise of the single-volume Bible at the beginning of the thirteenth century, with the Psalms being a major exception to its standardised layout. In Wycliffite Bibles, the first full translation of the Bible into English, the Psalms emerge as sites of competing mnemonics, evidencing the gap between heretical origins and a more orthodox reception. Bible production resumed in England only towards the end of Henry VIII's reign. The layout of the period's Bibles reveals a turbulent break from Rome, when the impact of Church reformers collided with Henry's unease with lay access to Scripture. The last section follows Bibles of more reformed reigns: the new liturgy ushered at the reign of Edward VI and the two seemingly opposing Bibles printed during Elizabeth I's reign. The conclusion reveals a new phenomenon across four centuries, unfolding the dynamics of reform and conservatism which shaped the layout of late medieval and early modern Psalters.

Books of Psalms are among the earliest witnesses to the Hebrew Bible. They take a prominent place among the Dead Sea Scrolls. As the analysis of Anna Krauß and Friederike Schücking-Jungblut in the current volume demonstrates, even these early samples present the Psalms in a layout distinct from other biblical books.[2] While the majority of biblical texts are written as continuous texts, the Psalms are gradually depicted in lines of meaning, at times further divided into stichs. This followed their poetical structure, in which each verse comprises of a distinct unit, and grew to be depicted as such in biblical manuscripts. The earliest evidence reveals a link between performance, contents and layout as the novel layout was first applied to Psalm 118/19, whose "reading or reciting [...] is a meditative exercise of praying".[3]

---

[2] See Chapter 1 in the present volume: Anna Krauß and Friederike Schücking-Jungblut, "Stichographic Layout in the Dead Sea Psalms Scrolls: Observations on Its Development and Its Potential."

[3] Krauß and Schücking-Jungblut, "Stichographic Layout," 23.

The superscriptions (also known as *superscripts* or *tituli*) are short verses affixed to individual Psalms, and are arguably the least stable feature of the Book of Psalms. Whereas the Psalms are typically a-historical devotional hymns, the superscriptions identify specific moments in biblical history, Temple worship or Israelite literature. Their connection to the text of the Psalms is at times tenuous, and their language enigmatic. There is evidence to suggest that already in the second century BC the translators of the Septuagint had found their vocabulary challenging; their position in the Dead Sea Scrolls is unclear, and biblical scholars nowadays debate their dating and function.[4] The superscriptions have remained a distinct textual unit from inception to the present day. They are often separated from the body of the Psalm by diverse means and to the best of my knowledge have not been chanted in Jewish or Christian worship. In many liturgical manuscripts, therefore, the superscriptions are omitted. The Psalms are commonly identified, in Jewish and Christian sources alike, by their opening line following the superscriptions.

The Psalms attracted and challenged emerging Christian communities in Late Antiquity. As Christians embraced the Psalms as the foundation of divine worship, they developed means of accommodating them to new dogma. Church Fathers employed allegorical and Christological exegesis in linking the Psalms to events from the life of Christ, as well as from Church or salvation history.[5] Mirroring Jewish practice, the Psalms became the cornerstone of church liturgy, influencing their layout in medieval manuscripts.[6] Much like earlier Hebrew manu-

---

[4] Lesley McFall, "The Evidence for a Logical Arrangement of the Psalter," *Westminster Theological Journal* 62 (2000): 223–56, with a bibliography of previous scholarship; Sam Mirelman, "Contrafactum in the Ancient near East," in *Herausforderungen Und Ziele Der Musikarchäologie: VorträGe Des 5. Symposiums Der Internationalen Studiengruppe Musikarchäologie Im Ethnologischen Museum Der Staatlichen Museen Zu Berlin, 19.–23. September 2006 = Challenges and Objectives in Music Archaeology: Papers from the 5th Symposium of the International Study Group on Music Archaeology at the Ethnological Museum, State Museums Berlin, 19–23 September 2006*, ed. A.A. Both, et al. (Rahden/Westfalen: M. Leidorf, 2008): 99–110.

[5] In manuscripts from the early and high Middle Ages these took the form of *Tituli* (or *titles*), short verses which summarized exegetical works to replace the superscriptions in prefacing the Psalms with means of connecting them to established dogma. See: Pierre Salmon, *Les "Tituli Psalmorum" Des Manuscrits Latins*, Collectanea Biblica Latina (Roma: Abbaye Saint-Jérome, 1959).

[6] Paul Saenger, "The Impact of the Early Printed Page on the Reading of the Bible," in *The Bible as Book: The First Printed Editions*, ed. Paul Saenger and Kimberly Van Kampen (London: British Library in association with The Scriptorium: Center for Christian Antiquities, 1999): 31–51; A useful introduction to the structure of medieval Psalters is Elizabeth Solopova, *Latin Liturgical Psalters in the Bodleian Library: A Select Catalogue* (Oxford: Bodleian Library, University of Oxford, 2013).

scripts, the Psalms were typically written in lines of poetry. In earlier manuscripts they were written *in lines of meaning*, spaciously representing their poetical structure, and the way they were chanted in churches. In later manuscripts scribes adopted a less parchment-wasteful layout. They marked the beginning of each verse with a minor capital, which, by the thirteenth century, was often in alternating red and blue initials (Fig. 1). A *puctus elevatus* (inverted semicolon) separated the stichs. This layout accorded with the performance of the Psalms: they were often chanted with each verse as an independent unit, followed by a short doxology; a distinct pause followed each stich, and was discussed in liturgical and musical commentaries.[7] Like other liturgical texts, the Psalms were known by their incipit, or their opening line in the Vulgate text (omitting the superscription). Thus, the first Psalm was known as *Beatus vir* ("Blessed is the man"), the second *Quare turbabuntur gentes* ("Why have the Gentiles raged") and so forth. The entire book of Psalms was chanted by monks and nuns in weekly or bi-weekly cycles. To facilitate this, key Psalms were signalled-out in medieval manuscripts.[8] In the high and later Middle Ages historiated initials were deployed to identify these Psalms, often depicting the Christological interpretation of the Psalms, or alluding to their liturgical performance. Thus, for example, the initial to Psalm 110/11 ("The Lord said to my lord: sit thou on my right") often depicts the Trinity, while that to Psalm 97/8 ("O sing unto the Lord"), commonly depicts monks in the course of chanting the Psalms (Fig. 1).

## 2 The Later Middle Ages

In the early Middle Ages, very few libraries possessed a full Bible, and single-volume Bibles (known as pandects) were a rarity. Bible were typically a multi-volume affair: heavy, expensive, and befitting the libraries of large and well-endowed religious establishments, or the wealthy aristocracy. This situation underwent a radical transformation in the first three decades of the thirteenth century. Then, the creation of new universities joined with a rising lay book-trade and the establishment of the mendicant orders (primarily the Franciscans and the Dominicans) to bring

---

**7** S.J.P. van Dijk, "Medieval Terminology and Methods of Psalm Singing," *Musica Disciplina* 6 (1952): 7–26; John Harper, *The Forms and Orders of Western Liturgy from the Tenth to the Eighteenth Century: A Historical Introduction and Guide for Students and Musicians* (Oxford: Clarendon Press, 1991), 67–72.
**8** This was commonly a seven-fold division, with Psalm 1 the first Psalm on Matins on Sundays, Psalm 26/7 on Mondays, Psalm 38/9 on Tuesdays, etc.

**Fig. 1:** *Cantate Domino* – initial to Psalm 110/11 in the de Brailes Bible. Oxford, Bodleian Library, MS Lat. Bib. E. 7, fol. 191v. By permission of The Bodleian Library, University of Oxford.

about the production and dissemination of single-volume, small and portable Bibles.[9] By 1250, pandects became the norm across medieval Europe. Although copied laboriously by hand, these often-minute volumes (with many measuring less than 20 cm in length) adhered to a uniform layout, and as such should be seen against the backdrop of the late medieval mass-communication revolution.[10] The proliferation of pandects was accompanied by the introduction of a highly efficient navigation and retrieval system, encoded in a layout of great longevity, which has influenced the appearance of Bibles ever since. A typical example is seen in Fig. 2, in which running titles in red and blue identify the biblical book. The biblical text is written in two columns, and divided into numerical chapter divisions. These chapter divisions were the hallmark of the Late Medieval Bible (LMB), and are still

---

[9] Eyal Poleg and Laura Light, eds., *Form and Function in the Late Medieval Bible*, WWMW (Leiden: Brill, 2013).
[10] David d'Avray, "Printing, Mass Communication and Religious Reformation: The Middle Ages and After," in *The Uses of Script and Print, 1300–1700*, ed. Julia C. Crick and Alexandra Walsham (Cambridge: Cambridge University Press, 2004): 50–70.

**Fig. 2:** *Late Medieval Bible Layout – Opening of Genesis, Edinburgh University Library MS 2, fols 3v-4r.* Edinburgh University Library Special Collections.

employed (with minor variation) in Bibles nowadays. (Verse division was introduced to Bibles only in the sixteenth century.)

The new pandects became an immediate success. They emerged from centres of learning in Northern France, South-East England and Northern Italy, to spread rapidly throughout Europe. Their uniform layout is witnessed nowadays in hundreds of manuscripts. The uniformity of the layout did not apply, however, to all biblical books. The Psalms were the most notable exception and in the overwhelming majority of LMBs were devoid of the key features of the abovementioned innovative layout.[11] Like earlier manuscripts, their layout reflected the performance of the liturgy, and the way the Psalms were retained in the memory of the clergy who chanted them day and night, the same clergy who were also the prime audience of the LMB. The Psalms were not subjected to the numerical chapter division, characteristic of other biblical text. Rather, they were still

---

[11] A more in-depth discussion of the Psalms in LMBs is Eyal Poleg, *Approaching the Bible in Medieval England*, Manchester Medieval Studies (Manchester: Manchester University Press, 2013), 129–38.

known and identified by their incipit. Major initials were employed to identify key Psalms, while minor initials marked the beginning of each verse in alternating red and blue. The link between performance and the LMB, however, is far from evident. Laura Light has recently explored the use of these Bibles within the liturgy, revealing a small group of Bibles containing Mass-texts, or Bibles used within the Divine Office.[12] The initial in Fig. 1, however, demonstrates a gap between liturgical ideals and practicalities. The image depicts monks in the course of liturgical chant, following a book open on the lectern. As this initial precedes Psalm 97/8, one can imagine they are singing the Psalms. However, the book containing the image, the c.1250 de Brailes Bible, is a small pocket Bible, and one which would be ill suited for placing on a lectern or reading from afar. It was suitable for facilitating individual worship (the type of worship often suggested in Light's research), while still depicting the ideal of communal Psalmody.

One key element draws us away from seeing the Psalms in LMBs merely as mirroring liturgical rites. In the overwhelming majority of LMBs the Psalms are preceded with superscriptions, which follow Jerome's translation of the biblical superscriptions in the Vulgate (in the Gallican version). At odds with liturgical manuscripts and performance, the superscriptions brought the complex nature of the Psalms to the mind of readers, reminding them of a function beyond chant. The superscriptions were not integrated into the body of the Psalms, but were signalled out and separated from the body of the Psalm, noted in red ink. The superscriptions' integration evidences an interest in the literal sense of Scriptures, and in the Bible's original languages, predating Humanists and Reformers alike. Like the most common addendum to the LMB – a glossary of Hebrew and Aramaic biblical names known as the *Interpretations of Hebrew Names* – the superscriptions brought to mind elements of Jewish worship and archaic Hebrew vocabulary. They attest to the origins of the LMB among biblical exegetes, who remained one of its prime users.

A small group of LMBs, primarily of mendicant origins, evidences new modes of thinking about the Psalms, as well as about liturgy more widely.[13] The Psalms emerge in this group as sites of conflicting mnemonics. Their layout replicates that of liturgical manuscripts and earlier Bibles, reflecting the performance of the

---

[12] Laura Light, "Thirteenth-Century Pandects and the Liturgy," in *Form and Function in the Late Medieval Bible*, ed. Eyal Poleg and Laura Light (Leiden: Brill, 2013): 185–215; Laura Light, "What Was a Bible For? Liturgical Texts in Thirteenth-Century Franciscan and Dominican Bibles," *Lusitania Sacra* 34 (2016): 165–82.
[13] This group is explored in my *A Material History of the Bible, England 1200–1553* (Oxford: Oxford University Press, 2020).

Psalms. They also, however, incorporate the numerical chapter divisions, subjecting the Psalms to the common layout of the LMB, and to a form of knowledge that did not rely on the Psalms' incipits.[14] This layout accords with the treatise of Hugh of St Victor (†1142), who had advocated memorizing the Psalms not as chanted liturgical text, but rather visually, placing them on a numerical grid and thus retaining the ability to recall then out of sequence.[15] This distinct layout of the Psalms remained an exception among biblical manuscripts, with the majority of Bibles keeping to the more liturgical, and traditional, means of presenting and recalling the Psalms.

The appeal of the Psalms extended beyond Latin Bibles and clerical readership. Nuns and lay brothers, as well as lay men and women, were presented with the Psalms in a variety of ways. First among them were Books of Hours, which simplified monastic liturgy to facilitate lay devotions.[16] Psalm translations also engaged with new audiences. As explored by Annie Sutherland, the English Psalms have been central to vernacular devotion throughout the Middle Ages.[17] The Psalms emerge once more as sites of conflicting mnemonics, now with the added difficulty of navigating between English translation and (primarily) Latin performance. Different strategies for presenting and engaging with the Psalms are evident in manuscripts of the Wycliffite Bible – the first translation of the

---

[14] A preliminary list includes: Cambridge, CUL Ee.1.16; Cambridge, Fitzwilliam Museum, McLean 16 (Dominican); Cambridge, Gonville and Caius MS 350/567 (Oxford, second quarter of thirteenth century); Cambridge, Pembroke 303 (Dominican); Cambridge, Trinity B.10.21 (Dominican); Edinburgh, UED MS 313; London, BL Add 35085 (Dominican); London, BL, Add. 31830 (Dominican, Naples c.1253); London, BL, Arundel 303 (Dominican, Oxford); London, BL, Royal MS 1.D.i (Mendicant, Oxford); London, Lambeth 534 (with the Dominicans of Arklow [Ireland] in the fifteenth century); Oxford, Bod., Auct. D.4.11 (Franciscan, Oxford); Oxford, Bod., Auct. D.5.9 (in Lincoln Cathedral by the fourteenth century); Oxford, Bod., Lat. bibl. e. 7 (Dominican, Oxford c.1250); Paris, BnF, MS lat. 163 (Dominican and later Franciscan); San Marino, California, Huntington Library, HM 51.

[15] William M. Green, "Hugo of St. Victor: De Tribus Maximis Circumstantiis Gestorum," *Speculum* 18 (1943): 484–93; Hugh of St. Victor, "The Three Best Memory Aids for Learning History," in *The Medieval Craft of Memory: An Anthology of Texts and Pictures*, ed. Mary Carruthers and Jan M. Ziolkowski (Philadelphia: University of Pennsylvania Press, 2002): 32–40; For discussion see Mary Carruthers, *The Book of Memory: A Study of Memory in Medieval Culture*, CSML (Cambridge: Cambridge University Press, 1992), 121–27.

[16] On Books of Hours and their use: Eamon Duffy, *Marking the Hours: English People and Their Prayers 1240–1570* (New Haven: Yale University Press, 2006); Kathryn M. Rudy, *Piety in Pieces: How Medieval Readers Customized Their Manuscripts* (Cambridge: Open Book Publishers, 2016).

[17] Annie Sutherland, *English Psalms in the Middle Ages, 1300–1450* (Oxford: Oxford University Press, 2015).

entire Bible into English at the end of the fourteenth century.[18] The Wycliffite Bible originated among the followers of John Wyclif (†1384), whose rejection of the established Church had led to the Church condemnation of Wycliffites (or Lollards) as heretics; the centrality they placed on lay access to Scriptures had resulted in Constitutions of Archbishop Arundel in 1407/09, which prohibited unauthorised vernacular translations of Scriptures. The manuscript culture of the Wycliffite Bible, however, presents a different narrative, with survival rates akin to orthodox Bibles on the Continent (ca. 250 manuscripts) and a general lack of heterodox texts in the vast majority of surviving manuscripts.

In Wycliffite Bibles the Psalms by and large replicate the layout of the LMB, with its verse identification and major initials for key liturgical Psalms. This was seen by Anne Hudson as evidence for the gravitational pull exerted by the Book of Psalms, arguing that Wycliffite Bibles "seem [...] to have been unable to escape from the traditional high regard for this book of the Old Testament."[19] An in-depth examination of key manuscripts sheds light on how this process took place. Oxford, Bodleian Library MS Bodley 959 is well known among scholars of the Wycliffite Bible. One of its earliest manuscripts, this text has been mined as evidence to the course of the translation project.[20] Unnoticed by scholars, however, is a moment frozen in the evolution of the Wycliffite Bible. The original scribe of the Psalms had transferred the common layout of the Latin Psalms into the English. He had also noted the Psalms' numbers in the margins in a mixture of Arabic and Roman numerals (as was done with other biblical books). His work was followed by another scribe (a rubricator), who preceded each Psalm with a three-line red capital and noted down the superscriptions in red, reflecting the appearance of the LMB (Fig. 3).

---

**18** On the Wycliffite Bible: Mary Dove, *The First English Bible: The Text and Context of the Wycliffite Versions*, CSML 66 (Cambridge: Cambridge University Press, 2007); Elizabeth Solopova, ed., *The Wycliffite Bible: Origin, History and Interpretation*, MRAT (Leiden: Brill, 2016). On its dependency on the Latin Bible: Eyal Poleg, "Wycliffite Bibles as Orthodoxy," in *Instructing the Soul, Feeding the Spirit and Awakening the Passion: Cultures of Religious Reading in the Late Middle Ages*, ed. Sabrina Corbellini (Turnhout: Brepols, 2013): 71–91; Anne Hudson and Elizabeth Solopova, "The Latin Text," in *The Wycliffite Bible: Origin, History and Interpretation*, ed. Elizabeth Solopova (Leiden: Brill, 2016): 107–32.
**19** Anne Hudson, *The Premature Reformation: Wycliffite Texts and Lollard History* (Oxford: Oxford University Press, 1988), 182.
**20** For short description and summary of bibliography see Elizabeth Solopova, *Manuscripts of the Wycliffite Bible in the Bodleian and Oxford College Libraries*, Exeter Medieval Texts and Studies (Liverpool: Liverpool University Press, 2016), 88–92. The Psalms in the manuscript have also been central to Sutherland, *English Psalms in the Middle Ages, 1300–1450*, 112–19; Sutherland, "The Wycliffite Psalms," in *The Wycliffite Bible: Origin, History and Interpretation*, ed. Elizabeth Solopova (Leiden: Brill, 2016): 183–201 (187–92).

**Fig. 3:** *Psalm layout (detail); Oxford, Bodleian Library MS Bodl. 959.* By permission of The Bodleian Library, University of Oxford.

Translating the Psalms into English affected their identification. Recalling the Psalms through their Latin incipit no longer applied to the English Psalter, with its differing opening lines. The original production team had avoided the link with Latin Psalmody altogether, and the Psalm's number became their only means of identification. This, however, was soon to change. Shortly after the scribe and rubricator had concluded their labours, another reader added the Latin incipits as means of Psalm-identification beyond those offered by the original creators. The timing of this addition can be ascertained by a close examination of the manuscript (Fig. 3). The hand of the annotation is contemporaneous with that of the original scribes. Its ink, however, is on top of the capital letter, clearly indicating that this took place after the rubricator had finished his role. The original stage of production thus presented a fully English Psalter, which left little place to Latin mnemonics. The gap between inception and reception was quickly filled, and the manuscript reveals how the Psalms' layout was made to accommodate common mnemonics and Latin chant. A similar phenomenon is evident in Cambridge University Library MS Add. 6681, another manuscript from the earlier strata of the Wycliffite Bible in which an early reader/scribe had provided the Latin incipits.

The omission of the Latin incipit in the earliest strata of the Wycliffite Bible, and its insertion shortly afterwards, is part of a wider phenomenon, evident across the manuscript culture of the Wycliffite Bible. A move away from reformed ideal and heterodoxy and into more orthodox use of the Bible comes to the fore when examining the addenda to the Wycliffite Bible. As explored by Matti Peikola, tables of lections to the Wycliffite Bible, which link biblical readings with a given liturgical feast, gradually aligned with common liturgical use by incorporating non-biblical saints, frowned upon by Wyclif and his followers.[21] The most overt

---

[21] Matti Peikola, "'First Is Writen a Clause of the Bigynnynge Therof': The Table of Lections in Manuscripts of the Wycliffite Bible," in *Form and Function in the Late Medieval Bible*, ed. Eyal Poleg and Laura Light (Leiden: Brill, 2013): 351–78.

link between the translation project and heterodoxy is the General Prologue, a treatise discussing Bible and translation, which opposes the established Church. This treatise, however, exists only in a fraction of Wycliffite Bibles.[22] The majority of Wycliffite Bibles are therefore devoid of any link to heterodox thought, and their layout, especially that of the Psalms, links them to orthodox, Latin, worship.

The Psalms emerge as a major arena for the forces of heterodoxy and orthodoxy, Latin and English. The multiple layers of the Psalms – text, superscription, incipit, number – forced editors, stationers and readers to omit and highlight, to take a stance on importance and audience. Annie Sutherland's work on medieval English Psalters has highlighted the competing linguistic spheres of Latin and English, and revealed that, across different translations and manuscripts, "incipits are almost universally preserved."[23] Marked in red, they became one of the most distinct features of the Psalms' layout, and central means in their identification.[24] The Psalms were recalled performatively, experienced through their chanting in the liturgy. Here I veer from Sutherland's analysis. Sutherland argues that "It is, in fact, no exaggeration to say that the translated psalms formed the backbone of intercessory experience in the late Middle Ages".[25] The manuscript culture, however, suggests the Psalms were encountered primarily through the Latin of the performed liturgy. Not only in monastic and church worship, but Books of Hours, commonly owned by lay men and women (and overwhelmingly in Latin) attest to the way the Psalms were encountered in the later Middle Ages.

One should not hasten to place a boundary between lay and clerical, Latin and vernacular Psalmody. The layout of the Psalms in Wycliffite Bibles seems to merge, rather than oppose, linguistic spheres. Latin and English cohabitate the space of Wycliffite Psalters, with multiple layers of information – chapter number, Latin incipit, biblical superscription – presented one next to the other. This cohabitation is most evident in a liturgically oriented Psalter, where each verse of the Psalms is preceded with its Latin opening words (Fig. 4).[26] This manuscript merges Latin and English Psalmody, but did not constitute a bilingual

---

[22] Mary Dove, ed., *The Earliest Advocates of the English Bible: The Texts of the Medieval Debate* (Exeter: University of Exeter Press, 2010), 3–85; For analysis see Kantik Ghosh, "The Prologues," in *The Wycliffite Bible: Origin, History and Interpretation*, ed. Elizabeth Solopova (Leiden: Brill, 2016): 162–82.
[23] Sutherland, *English Psalms in the Middle Ages, 1300–1450*, 264.
[24] Sutherland's view of red as denoting hierarchy is at odds with the use of red across Latin manuscripts, and especially with the presentation of the Superscription in the LMB.
[25] Sutherland, *English Psalms in the Middle Ages, 1300–1450*, 274.
[26] Other Psalters are London, British Library MSS Yates Thompson 52, Add. 10,047, and Add. 31,044.

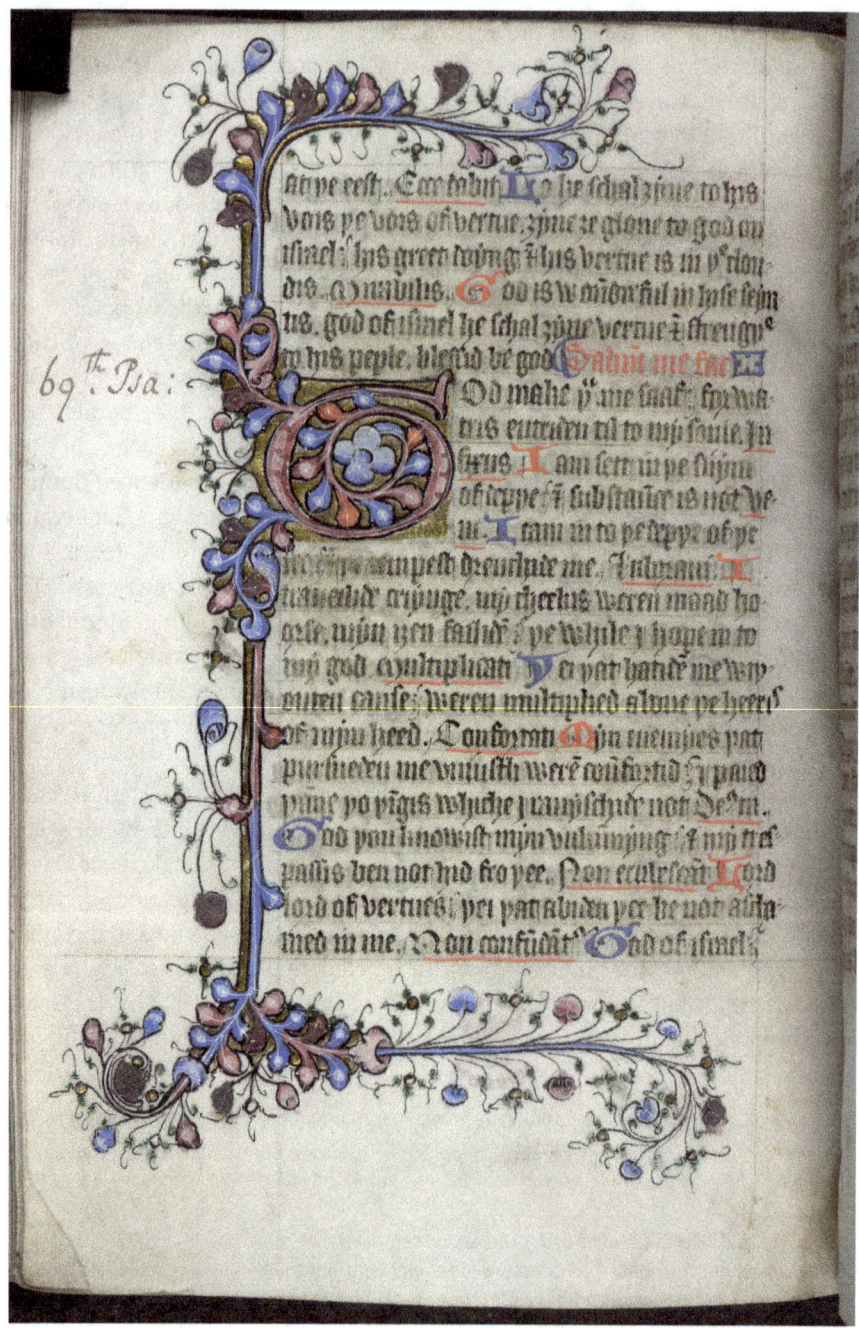

**Fig. 4:** *Wycliffite Psalter (British Library MS Yates Thompson 52, fol. 96v).* © The British Library Board.

Psalter. Rather, it enabled readers to employ the book of Psalms in the course of Latin Psalmody, or alongside a Latin Psalter. It also cued the memory of readers versed in the Latin Psalms to the English translation. Scholars often regard vernacular manuscripts as linked with the laity and Latin illiteracy. Such Psalters, however, were not aimed at the uninitiated. Rather, previous knowledge of Latin Psalter is necessary to decipher the truncated Latin incipits, and their layout suggests these were created for readers embedded within Latin Psalmody.

A glimpse into the function and readership of Wycliffite Psalters is revealed in a few explicit statements made by translators and editors. The General Prologue makes clear that although the Psalter "teaches plainly the mysteries of the Trinity, and of Christ's incarnation, passion, rising again [..] and the coming of the Antichrist [...] and often rehearses the stories of the Old Testament," it was nevertheless most challenging to understand as "No book in the Old Testament is harder to understand to us Latins."[27] An additional prologue made clear the role of the superscriptions in unfolding the mysteries of the Psalter and its links with biblical history. It argues for a two-tier understanding of the Psalter: the superscriptions mark events from biblical history, while the Psalms themselves are more prophetic, following events from the life of Christ and Church history. The link between Psalms and biblical history was also expanded in other means.

Short glosses are often incorporated into Wycliffite Bibles, placed before individual Psalms to create "mini-prologue", marked-off in red or brown underline.[28] These build on the superscriptions in connecting the Psalms to the life of David and Jewish history (e.g., the gloss to the second Psalm: "A gloss. The second Psalm that has no title in Hebrew and in Jerome's translation; was made of David as the Apostles witnessed in iiij that of deeds [Acts 4:25]")[29]; they also provide a more allegorical understanding of the Psalter, linking Psalms to the life of Christ and the history of salvation (e.g. Psalm 40, depicting a man who is persecuted and then risen by God, is preceded by "A gloss. This Psalm is expounded of Christ's passion and rising again"; Psalm 95, a song of glory to God who comes to judge the earth, is preceded by "This Psalm has no title, neither in Hebrew nor in Jerome. This Psalm speaks of the time of Christ, that began properly at the beginning of the preaching of the Gospel."). The glosses helped align Psalms with Christian dogma. They commonly appear in the margins, but at times were integrated into the textual column, merging text and interpretation. They were not noted in the

---

27 Dove, *Earliest Advocates*, 58.
28 Dove, *First English Bible*, 157–59; Michael P. Kuczynski, "Glossing and Glosses," in *The Wycliffite Bible: Origin, History and Interpretation*, ed. Elizabeth Solopova (Leiden: Brill, 2016): 346–67; Sutherland, "The Wycliffite Psalms."
29 BL Additional MS 10,046 fol. 5r.

abovementioned Wycliffite Psalters. In these manuscripts, which befitted liturgical use, superscriptions and glosses were omitted altogether, putting aside means of unfolding the literal sense in favour of liturgical practice.

## 3 Henry the Eighth's Bibles

Bibles were printed on the Continent from the very beginning of moveable-type printing. Gutenberg's celebrated 42-line Bible replicated the appearance of the LMB, albeit on a much grander scale, and most incunabula followed suite. Gradually, however, printers employed new techniques to innovate in size and layout. English printing lagged behind the Continent for much of the period, with books typically shorter and less sophisticated than their Continental counterparts. This, combined with a general unease with vernacular theology following Arundel's fifteenth-century Constitutions, had led to a lack of any printed Bible in England for nearly a century after Gutenberg's innovation.[30] By the 1530s, however, the wheels were clearly moving in the direction of an English Bible. Reforming ideals took hold among English scholars, and on the Continent William Tyndale was publishing biblical books to fill his plan of putting an English Bible in the hands of every ploughboy. In England, Henry VIII's active engagement with Christian theology, and complex relationship with the Roman curia, sowed the seeds for a national Bible.

The hesitant beginning of the English Bible came to partial fruition in 1535, with the publication of two Bibles. The first Bible printed in England was in Latin. Ill fitted for histories of the English Reformation, it has received little scholarly attention.[31] It was printed by Thomas Berthelet, the King's Printer, and the book's "Epistle to the Reader" links the project to Henry himself. However, it was not

---

[30] This lacuna has not been adequately explored. Thus, in a recent volume of *The New Cambridge History of the Bible*, the chapter on English Bibles begins at 1520, and the lack of English Bibles is only briefly mentioned in Andrew Pettegree, "Publishing in Print: Technology and Trade," in *The New Cambridge History of the Bible: Volume 3: From 1450 to 1750*, ed. Euan Cameron (Cambridge: Cambridge University Press, 2016): 159–86. For a survey of English printing and its dependence on the Continent: Lotte Hellinga, "Printing," in *The Cambridge History of the Book in Britain Volume 3: 1400–1557*, ed. Lotte Hellinga and J.B. Trapp (Cambridge: Cambridge University Press, 1999): 65–108.

[31] It is presented in Peter W.M. Blayney, *The Stationers' Company and the Printers of London 1501–1557*, 2 vols. (Cambridge: Cambridge University Press, 2013), 352–56; and discussed at length in Eyal Poleg, "The First Bible Printed in England: A Little Known Witness from Late Henrician England," *JEH* 67 (2016): 760–80.

endorsed by Henry, and its modest appearance is far removed from a majestic tome. Attesting to Berthelet's limited capacities, the Bible is a selection of biblical books. The preface promises a second volume, which never saw the light of day, nor, in my eyes, was ever realistically intended. Berthelet's book is comprised of the "best of" the Bible: the Pentateuch, Joshua, Judges, the Psalms, Proverbs, Wisdom and the entire New Testament. This peculiar amalgamation followed Berthelet's Continental models, while according with the gist of salvation history and liturgical performance. The Psalms are noteworthy in Berthelet's choice. Being the longest book of the Bible, their inclusion made the volume more complex, long and expensive, and was clearly paramount for Berthelet and his intended audience.

The layout of the Psalms in Berthelet's Bible owed much to the limited abilities of his print shop. By 1535 European Bibles were printed in a range of sizes, with a variety of aids and addenda, and accompanied by specially commissioned woodblocks, charts and diagrams. This was hardly the case for Berthelet's Bible, which mainly recycled materials from earlier, non-biblical, prints. The Psalms, like other books of the Bible, are presented in two thick textual columns in Gothic type (or Black Letter), with little marginal annotations or additional apparatus. Each verse begins on a new line, starting with a minor capital; the Psalms are numbered and the superscriptions signalled-out, written in Roman type (used in other biblical books for the scant marginal references). This spans the entire length of Berthelet's technological capacities. However, it sufficed to create a layout similar to LMBs and Wycliffite Bibles alike. By using a different typeface for the superscriptions, Berthelet replicated the rubrication of these texts in earlier manuscripts and incunabula. The superscriptions are presented as a distinct textual component. Identifying the Psalms by their incipits was eased by using three-line initials for each chapter, directing one's attention to its opening words and tying-in with current knowledge of the Psalms. Combined with identification of chapter numbers, it reflects Wycliffite Bibles and Continental prints in presenting two parallel systems of retrieval. Readers' annotations reveal that these books were indeed used by diverse audiences – by scholars and exegetes, as well as in church services.

In the very same year, the first complete Bible in English was printed on the Continent. Unlike Berthelet's Bible, its novelty and reformed ideology have attracted considerable scholarly attention.[32] Compiled by Miles Coverdale, it was

---

[32] RSTC§2063. For scholarship see: Blayney, *Stationers' Company*, 344–51; S.L. Greenslade, *The Coverdale Bible, 1535* (Folkestone: Wm. Dawson & Sons, 1975); James Frederic Mozley, *Coverdale and His Bibles* (London: Lutterworth Press, 1953); Gwendolyn Verbraak, "William Tyndale and the Clandestine Book Trade: A Bibliographical Quest for the Printers of Tyndale's New

based on Luther's German translation, as well as the Vulgate, rather than the original Hebrew and Greek. The circumstances of its creation are encoded in the layout of the Psalms. Much like the earliest strata of the Wycliffite Bible, Coverdale presented the Psalms in a way similar to other biblical texts. Like other biblical books the Psalms are numbered and their number is the sole means of identification, appearing on the heading alongside a running title. The superscriptions are modified into generic identifier of speaker, and merged with the Psalm number into a Psalm title (e.g. *The II. A Psalme of Dauid; The XLVI. A Psalme for the children to Corah*). As any other biblical text, the Psalms are subjected to an alphabetical sub-division and composed in continuous textual blocks with verses distinguished only by short spaces. The Psalms' Latin incipit are omitted, drawing the Bible away from Latin Psalmody, as well as from earlier Latin and English Bibles. Coverdale's list of corrections (pt 3, fol. 52r) indeed refers to the Psalms according to their numerical value ("In the Psalter. | Upon the xxxv. leaf, the second side, in the cxxxvi. psalm, the second verse [...]").

Coverdale's engagement with the Psalms was multifaceted. Much like his *Goostly psalmes and spirituall songes*,[33] published possibly the very same year, Coverdale's Bible contained no reference to Latin psalmody, rejecting the way the Psalms had been known and recalled by laity and clergy for centuries. This reflected Coverdale's isolated position on the Continent. It was also the work of a Church reformer, wishing to mould a new understanding of the Bible. Coverdale's knowledge of Latin Psalmody from his past as an Augustinian canon cannot be doubted. His Psalter, however, followed that of Luther, whose 1534 Bible (Coverdale's role model) likewise omitted all Latin incipits. For Coverdale the Psalms were to serve as a conduit of personal devotion. This is made clear in his prologue *(Unto the Christen reader*, sig. ⚓[.vi].r), as well as in an interpretative note at the end of the Psalms: "In the Psalter this word sela comes very often. And (after the mind of the interpreters) it is as much to say as, always, continually, for ever, forsooth, verily, a lifting up of the voice, or to make a pause and earnestly to consider, and to ponder the sentence" (pt 3, fol. 37v). This note encapsulates the differing strands of understanding the Psalms: exegetical, performative, and meditative. It is the latter, however, that was key to Coverdale's Psalms.

The layout of Coverdale's Bible was quickly transformed, attesting to the turmoil of the English Church in the last decade of Henry's reign and the reigns

---

Testament," in *Infant Milk or Hardy Nourishment? The Bible for Lay People and Theologians in the Early Modern Period*, ed. W. Francois and A. A. den Hollander (Leuven: Peeters, 2009): 167–89.
**33** RSTC§5892.

of his offspring. Coverdale's 1535 Bible was created with royal approval in mind. This is evident in its title page, depicting the majestic Henry distributing Bibles, en-par with biblical monarchs.³⁴ When the Royal approval became a reality, production quickly changed. James Nicholson of Southwark printed anew its preliminary leaves, sidelining its association with Luther and inserting a dedication to Henry (sig. ✠.ii.r-✠.iiii.r), which made explicit the appeal of the Bible to the monarch. This prefaced the quires printed abroad, with the abovementioned Psalm layout. While scholars typically focus on the first edition, the Psalms' layout did not remain unchanged as the Bible was reprinted. In all subsequent editions of the Coverdale Bible printed in England, the Psalms underwent further transformations.³⁵ The most important of these was the re-integration of the Psalms' Latin incipits, moving these books further away from Coverdale's reformed ideals and closer to English audience and common means of navigating the Psalter.

Coverdale remained a major actor in the production of English Bibles. The landscape of the Bible in England was now transforming on a much grander scale. Up until then, the vast majority of parish churches in England did not have a full Bible, nor were they required to.³⁶ Thomas Cromwell (†1540), Henry's chief minister and royal vicegerent, or vicar-general, was affiliated with the reformed cause, and strongly supported the dissemination of English Bibles. In August 1536 he mandated that every parish church was to have a Bible.³⁷ This injunction, reaffirmed in subsequent years, had led to the creation of a new Bible on a national scale, commonly known as the Great Bible. Cromwell lent his considerable support for the project, while Coverdale was to amend the translation. Royal approval was paramount to the project, and, as explored by Tatiana String, the title page to the Great Bible distilled Henry's view of a national Bible: A majestic Henry is portrayed disseminating Bibles to priests and nobles (assisted

---

**34** Tatiana C. String, *Art and Communication in the Reign of Henry VIII* (Aldershot: Ashgate, 2008), 88–91.
**35** 1537 RSTC§2064; 1537 RSTC§2065; 1550 RSTC§2080; 1553 RSTC§2090
**36** Poleg, *Approaching the Bible*, 67–69.
**37** At first a Latin and English Bible: Walter Howard Frere and William McClure Kennedy, eds., *Visitation Articles and Injunctions of the Period of the Reformation. Vol. 2: 1536–1558*, Alcuin Club Collections (London: Longmans, Green, 1910), 9. In 1538 this was modified to an English Bible alone: Paul L. Hughes and James F. Larkin, eds., *Tudor Royal Proclamations: Vol. 1, the Early Tudors, 1485–1553* (New Haven: Yale University Press,1964), 296–98; For a reappraisal of the time of the injunctions: Paul Ayris, "Reformation in Action: The Implementation of Reform in the Dioceses of England," *Reformation & Renaissance Review: Journal of the Society for Reformation Studies* 5 (2003): 27–53; refuted by Richard Rex, *Henry VIII and the English Reformation*, 2nd ed., British History in Perspective (Basingstoke: Palgrave Macmillan, 2006), 190–91, n. 28.

by Cromwell and Thomas Cranmer [†1556], Archbishop of Canterbury), with the population at the bottom of the page calling 'Long live the King'.[38] This reflected the Epistle of Berthelet's 1535 Bible, as well as the title page of Coverdale's Bible. The Great Bible, however, surpassed all earlier English Bibles in its materiality, printed on high-grade paper in royal folio.

The Great Bible ushered in an era of English Bibles and English psalmody. Its size, alongside the omission of most marginal annotations, led to a clear and spacious layout (Fig. 5). The Psalms are introduced by the Psalm number, a Latin incipit, and the biblical superscription. A three- or four-line capital letter marks the beginning of the text of the Psalm itself. Typographically, the Latin incipit is the most distinct feature of the Psalms' layout, printed in Roman capitals on the background of Black Letter. Unlike Coverdale's or the Wycliffite Bible, this was not meant to be a reformed Bible, but rather a continuation of past practices. It was to facilitate – at least in theory – the liturgy in every parish church, as well as in cathedrals and collegiate churches (where liturgy was still performed in Latin). It linked the English Psalms, new to many, with past knowledge of the Psalms, which was still predominantly oral and performative.[39] This emphasis is also reflected in the liturgical addenda to the Bible, containing a table of liturgical lessons according to the Use of Sarum, similar to that found in many Wycliffite Bibles. The Great Bible was printed in seven successive editions (the last in December 1541), with minimal alterations to the layout of the Psalms or its liturgical addendum.

The layout of the Great Bible contains traces of a controversy surrounding its inception and influencing its reception. Manicules, or pointing hands, appear throughout the biblical text (Fig. 5).[40] The Prologue to the Bible (sig. *.[v.]v) explicates that these were meant to be accompanied by explanatory notes, which, unfortunately, had not been printed due to lack of time and the need for approval. Correspondence between members of the production team reveals the notes to be the most controversial element within the Bible, with Coverdale assuring Cromwell repeatedly of their value and un-contentious nature. Cromwell, the patron of the Great Bible, supported the type of lay access to Scripture that was facilitated by such annotations. His hesitation reveals other forces at play. The annotations never saw the light of day, and in subsequent editions the manicules themselves were removed, furthering the need for clerical mediation. Henry's unease with lay access to Scripture quickly came to the fore. In 1543 Henry's *Act*

---

**38** String, *Art and Communication*, 96–98.
**39** As the Great Bible adopted the Hebrew numbering of the Psalms, which differed from that of the Vulgate, the Latin incipits were even more important as means of linking the Psalms with past knowledge.
**40** On the manicules to the Great Bible see Poleg, *A Material History of the Bible*, pp. 133–8.

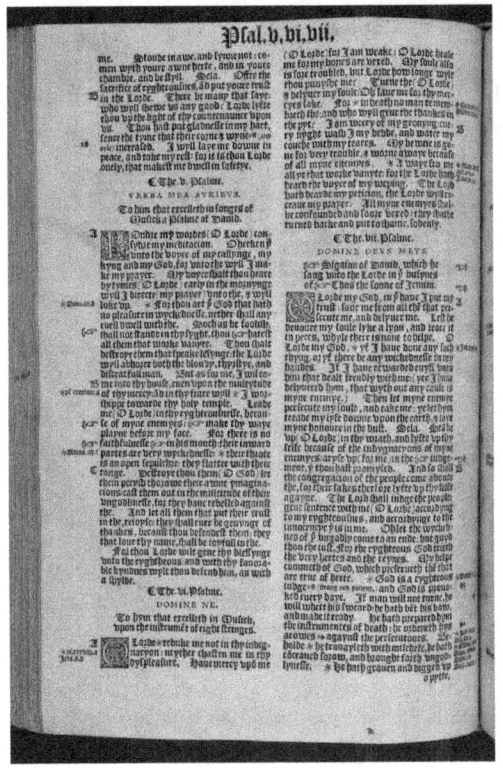

**Fig. 5:** *Great Bible Psalms (The Byble in Englyshe [...]* (London: Rychard Grafton and Edward Whitchurch, April 1539), pt 3 fol. 2v. Edinburgh University Library Special Collections.

*for the Advancement of True Religion* joined with the *King's Book* to curb unrestricted lay access to Scripture, forbidding private and public reading by women of the lower classes, artificers, prentices, journeymen, yoemen and under.[41] As the layout of the Psalter in the Great Bible reveals, it was a book caught between reformed ideals and a more hesitant monarch.

---

**41** *The Statutes of the Realm, Printed by Command of His Majesty King George the Third, in' Pursuance of an Address of the House of Commons of Great Britain from Original Records and Authentic Manuscripts.* (London: Eyre and Strahan, 1817; reprint, 1963), 3:894–97. For the original draft, analysis and reappraisal see Blayney, *Stationers' Company*, 550–55. For the King's Book: Henry VIII, "The King's Book: Or, a Necessary Doctrine and Erudition for Any Christian Man, 1543," in *Church Historical Society New series*, ed. T.A. Lacey (London: Society for Promoting Christian Knowledge, 1932): 5–6. For analysis: Alec Ryrie, *The Gospel and Henry VIII: Evangelicals in the Early English Reformation*, Cambridge Studies in Early Modern British History (Cambridge: Cambridge University Press, 2003), 44–54; Richard Rex, "The Crisis of Obedience: God's Word and Henry's Reformation," *The Historical Journal* 39 (1996): 863–94. As demonstrated by Ryrie (*The Gospel and Henry VIII: Evangelicals in the Early English Reformation*, 49–50), there is little to suggest the law had ever been enforced.

## 4 The Bibles of Edward VI and Elizabeth I

No other Bible was printed for the remainder of Henry's reign. Following his death in 1547 and the accession of the young Edward VI, reformers were once more at the helm. During Edward's short reign, Bible printing proliferated, with eleven full Bibles printed in diverse formats and by different printers.[42] Liturgy also underwent a major transformation. Thomas Cranmer, the Archbishop of Canterbury, was able to implement his plans for reforming the liturgy, which had been foiled under the previous reign. This led to the introduction of the Book of Common Prayer (BoCP), printed in 1549 and in a revised edition in 1552.[43] It was meant to replace all other liturgical books by providing a uniform and simplified liturgy across the realm. The Bible was to serve as the backbone of the new liturgy, with the entire Bible read throughout the year, the New Testament three times, and the Psalter chanted every month. Cranmer made this explicit in the Preface to the book, negating the medieval past in advocating a simplified, and more biblically oriented, worship:

> the ancient fathers had devised the psalms into seven portions: whereof every one was called a nocturne: now of late time a few of them have been daily said (and oft repeated) and the rest utterly omitted. Moreover, the number & hardness of the rules called the pie [Ordinale], and the manifold changings of the service, was the cause, that to turn the book only, was so hard and intricate a matter, that many times, there was more business to find out what should be read, then to read it when it was found out. [sig. A.ii.r]

In the book itself, 'THE ORDRE how the Psalter is appointed to be read' (sig. A.iii.v-A.iiii.r) elucidates the way of reading the Psalms in monthly cycles, including how to manage longer or shorter months. Intentionally and explicitly, it breaks away with common Psalmody and Psalms' mnemonics. The seven-fold division of the Psalms, which facilitated chant in monasteries and cathedrals, and depicted in Latin and English manuscripts alike, is put aside in favour of a simplified monthly cycle. The Latin incipits are once more removed. Like other Church reformers, from the earlier Wycliffite Bibles to Coverdale's Bible, Cranmer

---

[42] For a study of these Bibles see: Poleg, *A Material History of the Bible*, esp. ch. 5, "Into Fast Forward: The Bibles of Edward VI".

[43] RSTC II:87–90; "The Book of Common Prayer: The Texts of 1549, 1559, and 1662," ed. Brian Cummings (Oxford: Oxford University Press, 2011); Bryan Spinks, "The Bible in Liturgy and Worship, C. 1500–1750," in *The New Cambridge History of the Bible: Volume 3: From 1450 to 1750*, ed. Euan Cameron (Cambridge: Cambridge University Press, 2016): 563–78; Aude de Mézerac-Zanetti, "A Reappraisal of Liturgical Continuity in the Mid-Sixteenth Century: Henrician Innovations and the First Books of Common Prayer," *Revue française de civilisation britannique* 22, no. 1 (2017), http://rfcb.revues.org/1218.

did away with the common way the Psalms were retained in the memory of priests and the laity. This extended also to the numbering of the Psalms. Akin to Continental Reformers, the BoCP follows the numbering of the Great Bible, and hence is incompatible with the Vulgate and its differing numbering. Cranmer, however, was unable to escape past knowledge of the Psalter altogether. Within the book itself, Psalms and hymns are identified by their Latin incipit. Thus, for example, in Matins (fol. ii.r) it is noted that "After the first lesson shall follow *Te deus laudamus* in English, daily throughout the year, except in Lent, all the which time in the place of *Te deum* shalbe used *Benedicite omnis opera Domini Domino*, in English as follows [...]".

The ideals of reform were likewise not fully embraced by printers, and the layout of Bibles from the reign often incorporates more traditional means of identifying the Psalms. This fluctuated between printers. Bibles printed by new printers typically omit the Latin incipits, while those printed abroad, or by Whitchurch or Grafton (the merchants behind the printing of the Great Bible), preface the Psalms with the Latin incipits.[44] The last Bible printed in the reign of Edward reveals that Latin incipits were not seen as opposed to reformed liturgy, but rather as complementing it. This innovative Bible was printed by Richard Grafton in 1553, most likely after Edward had been taken ill.[45] It was the smallest single-volume English Bible printed hitherto, and the strongest amalgamation between biblical layout and the new liturgy. Marginal notes throughout the Bible identify the time for each biblical reading, following the sequence of the BoCP. In the Psalter, the notes identify the time of the month and morning or evening prayer, when the Psalms were to be read. Thus, as can be seen in Fig. 6, the First Psalm is linked to the first day at matins; Psalm 6 at evensong; Psalm 9 to the second day at matins; and so on. This, however, was accompanied by the integration of the Latin incipits. Alongside the Psalm number (by now an indispensable means of identifying the Psalm, facilitating the monthly cycle of Psalmody) the Latin incipit is integrated into the title preceding each Psalm. The biblical superscriptions are omitted altogether, attesting to the liturgical nature of the Psalter, if not to a rushed production.

Grafton's Bible constitutes the zenith of the link between Bible and new liturgy. It also marks its temporary end. The death of Edward and the Accession of Mary had moved the realm away from reform. Liturgy reverted back to Latin,

---

**44** Including the incipits are Incipits: RSTC§2079; RSTC§2080; RSTC§2081; RSTC§2019; RSTC§2092; Omitting the incipits are the Bibles printed by John Day (with William Seres) and William Hill (with Thomas Raynolds): RSTC§2077; RSTC§2078; RSTC§2083–6; RSTC§2088. The exception is RSTC§2089, printed by Hill and containing the Latin incipits, as well as the BoCP.
**45** RSTC§2092.

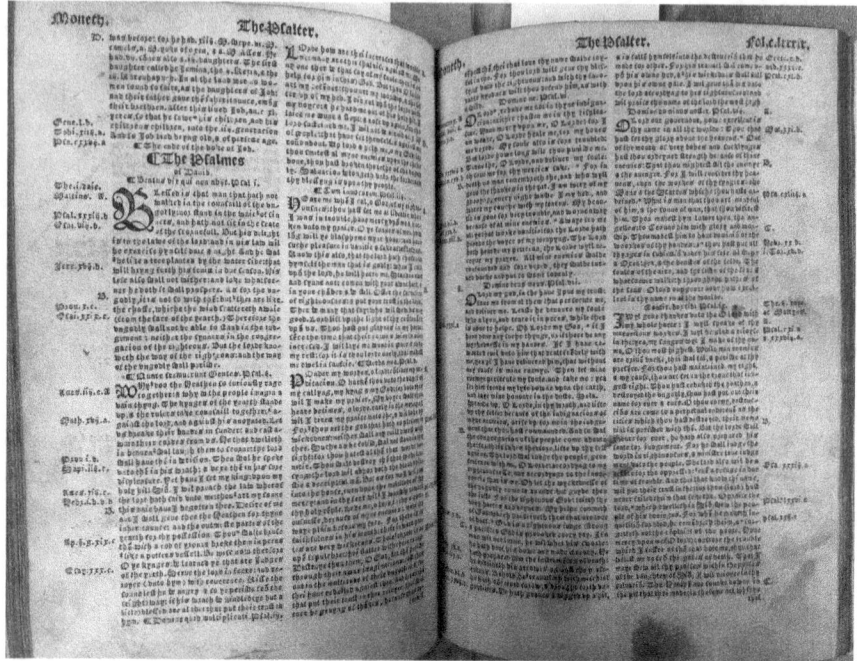

**Fig. 6:** *Grafton 1535 Psalms (The Bible in Englishe [...]* (London: Richard Grafton, 1553), fols 188v-189r). Reproduced by kind permission of the Syndics of Cambridge University Library.

and reformers fled the country to find refuge in Protestant strongholds. Some settled among the Calvinists of Geneva, where a new edition of the Bible was prepared, tapping into cutting-edge Continental theology and technology. This resulted in arguably the most influential Bible of early modern England. Created by a team of scholars and translators (including Coverdale), it was published in 1560, already after Elizabeth I's accession. The Geneva Bible became an overwhelming success and was printed in c.140 editions, surviving even the introduction of the King James Version in 1611.[46] The first edition of the Geneva Bible

---

[46] RSTC§2093. For facsimile and introduction see: Lloyd E. Berry, ed., *The Geneva Bible, a Facsimile of the 1560 Edition* (Madison: University of Wisconsin Press, 1969); Maurice S. Betteridge, "The Bitter Notes: The Geneva Bible and Its Annotations," *The Sixteenth Century Journal* 14 (1983): 41–62. An in-depth examination of subsequent prints, editions, and reception are: Ian Green, *Print and Protestantism in Early Modern England* (Oxford: Oxford University Press, 2000), 42–100, esp. ch. 2, "English Bibles and Their Owners"; Femke Molekamp, "Using a Collection to Discover Reading Practices: The British Library Geneva Bibles and a History of Their Early Modern Readers," *The Electronic British Library Journal* (2006); Molekamp, "Genevan Legacies: The Making of the English Geneva Bible," in *The Oxford Handbook of the Bible in England, C.*

is surprisingly modest. Unlike Berthelet's 1535 Bible, this was matter of choice rather than necessity. Printed in quarto on thin paper kept costs down, befitting the production team's ideology of disseminating the Bible far and wide across the social spectrum.

The Geneva Bible emulated Continental models to become the first English Bible printed in Roman type, and the first to integrate verse division (Fig. 7). Applying verse numbers across the Bible diminished one of the unique features of the Psalms' layout, as all books of the Bible were now written in identifiable lines of meaning. Unlike the Psalms' layout in earlier Bibles, the new division was not made to facilitate or mirror liturgical performance. Rather, the address to the reader [sig.*∴*.iiii.r-v] depicted this new division as "most profitable for memory," and useful for biblical study. Once more, typically of reformed Bibles, the Psalms' layout took the form of any other biblical book. Extensive marginal annotations provided readers with commentary on the biblical text. The Psalms are preceded by a short summary (or argument) and the biblical superscription. Both are printed in italic typeface, which had a dual effect: detaching the superscription from the text of the Psalm, while equating it with the argument, which emulates the spirit of the superscriptions by connecting the Psalms to events from the life of David or the tenets of Christian faith.[47] Many arguments reflect the experience of the community of exiles in Geneva, and its memories of persecution. Thus, for example, the argument to Psalm 4 alludes to Saul's persecution of David; the note to the superscription of Psalm 29/30 refers to the dedication of David's house, "After that Absalóm had polluted it with most filthy fornication." Other arguments and notes seamlessly embed theological stands. The note to the superscription of Psalm 31/32 identifies David's instructions to "the free remission of sins, which is the chiefest point of our faith," with subsequent notes expounding on the reformed ideal of Justification by Faith. The note to Psalm 44/45:17 facilitates a clear Christological reading ("This must only be referred to Christ and not to Salomón"). An additional interpretative layer is incorporated into the running titles, which provide succinct allegorical interpretations, as, for example, in the title to Psalm 55/6 *The tears of the Saints* or 74/5 *The Church afflicted prays* (both reflecting Genevan perceptions). Much like

---

*1530–1700*, ed. Kevin Killeen, Helen Smith, and Rachel Willie (Oxford: Oxford University Press, 2015): 38–53; Thomas Fulton, "Toward a New Cultural History of the Geneva Bible," *Journal of Medieval and Early Modern Studies* 47 (2017): 487–516.

**47** Molekamp, "Genevan Legacies"; Erica Longfellow, "Inwardness and English Bible Translations," in *The Oxford Handbook of the Bible in England, C. 1530–1700*, ed. Kevin Killeen, Helen Smith, and Rachel Willie (Oxford: Oxford University Press, 2015): 626–39; Fulton, "Toward a New Cultural History of the Geneva Bible".

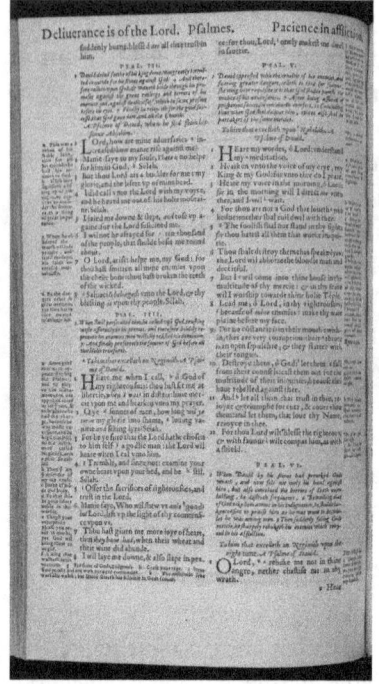

**Fig. 7:** *Geneva Bible Psalms (The Bible and Holy Scriptures [...] (Geneva: Rouland Hall, 1560), fol. 235v).* Edinburgh University Library Special Collections.

the glosses to the Wycliffite Bible, arguments and titles are presented as a form of biblical summary, rendering the editors' interpretation inseparable from the literal sense of the biblical text.

Given the reformed nature of the Geneva community, it is hardly a surprise that Latin incipits do not appear in the Geneva Bible. The Psalms are detached not only from Latin Psalmody, but from performance more widely. The introduction to the Psalter lacks any reference to their performance, but only praises their meditative and edifying value. The reader is asked to "seek" and "know", rather than chant. This is reiterated in the argument of the first Psalm, which explicitly sees the Psalter's goal "to exhort all godly men to study, and meditate the heavenly wisdom" (fol. 235.r). No chanting nor performance, but study and devotion. One should not assume that the Genevan community shied away from chanting the Psalms. Quite the opposite. It encouraged a nearly constant Psalmody, but not in their Bibles. The Genevan community embraced a new type of Psalmody, first created by Thomas Sternhold (†1549) with secular tunes to facilitate personal devotion during the reign of Edward VI. It was then revised, following Continental tunes and practices by John Hopkins (†1570), to create a metrical Psalter, which became the cornerstone of Genevan congregational Psalmody.⁴⁸ As demonstrated by Quitslund, the metrical Psalter influenced the appearance of the Psalms in the Geneva Bible, which replicated most of the former's arguments, as well as incorporating some of its notes and texts.⁴⁹ However, unlike the Geneva Bible, the metrical Psalter was more attuned to performance. The metrical Psalter printed in 1556 in Geneva (RSTC§16561) omits the biblical superscriptions, while incorporating Latin incipit, argument, and musical notations. The same layout spread beyond the Genevan community. It was often employed in *The Whole Book of Psalmes* (known also as *Sternhold and Hopkins*), which became one of the most popular books in early modern England. The Geneva congregation thus employed two different Psalters for two different purposes: the metrical Psalter for liturgy and private Psalmody, and the Psalms in the Geneva Bible for study and meditation.

The Geneva Bible, despite its popularity, was not printed in England for almost two decades. A more conservative party, led by Archbishop Parker (†1575), opposed its reformed origins and some of its annotations. In its stead, Parker initiated a new Bible: The Bishops' Bible of 1568.⁵⁰ A royal folio, its printing was meticulous and of the highest quality, a world apart from the faded ink and lower-grade paper of the Geneva Bible. Unlike the Geneva Bible, The Bishops' Bible was created with performance in mind. It followed the Bibles of Edward VI's reign, and was meant to fill the need of re-installing Bibles into churches, following Mary's reign. It is therefore equipped with a plethora of liturgical apparatus: a table of lessons, the order of Psalms in morning and evening prayers, as well as an almanac and an extended calendar, all laboriously printed in red and black ink. Its Psalter (Fig. 8), newly translated from the Hebrew, replicates the liturgical layout of Grafton's 1553 Bible, with a title indicating the day and the prayer, accompanied by a marginal note and a major illuminated initial (6–10

---

**48** Beth Quitslund, *The Reformation in Rhyme: Sternhold, Hopkins and the English Metrical Psalter, 1547–1603*, St Andrews Studies in Reformation History (Aldershot: Ashgate, 2008); Ian Green, "Hearing and Reading: Disseminating Bible Knowledge and Fostering Bible Understanding in Early Modern England," in *The Oxford Handbook of the Bible in England, C. 1530–1700*, ed. Kevin Killeen, Helen Smith, and Rachel Willie (Oxford: Oxford University Press, 2015): 272–86; Nicholas Temperley, "'All Skillful Praises Sing': How Congregations Sang the Psalms in Early Modern England," *Renaissance Studies* 29 (2015): 531–53; Green, *Print and Protestantism*, ch. 9, "Mystery of Metrical Psalm."
**49** Quitslund, *The Reformation in Rhyme*, 190–92.
**50** RSTC§2099. Relatively little has been written on this Bible: Margaret Aston, "The Bishops' Bible Illustrations," in *The Church and the Arts*, ed. Diana Wood (Oxford: Blackwell, 1992): 267–85; C. Clair, "The Bishops' Bible 1568," *Gutenberg Jahrbuch* (1962): 287–90; Green, *Print and Protestantism*; A recent monograph adds little new information: Jack P. Lewis, *The Day after Domesday: The Making of the Bishops' Bible* (Eugene: Wipf & Stock, 2016).

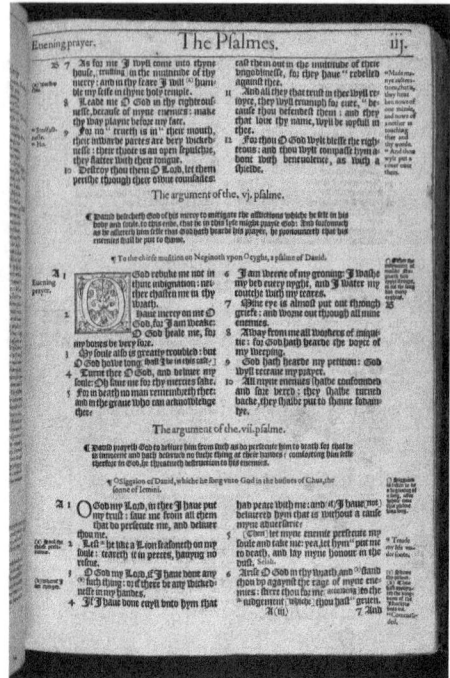

**Fig. 8:** *Bishops' Bible Psalms (The. holie. Bible [London: Richarde Iugge, 1568], pt 3 p.3).* Edinburgh University Library Special Collections.

lines, as distinct from the 2–3 lines medium, non-illuminated, initial for other Psalms), which identifies the beginning of each section. However, much like the Geneva Bible, old ways of knowing the Psalter are omitted: The Psalms reproduce the Geneva verse-numbering, and no Latin incipits are attached to individual Psalms.[51] The Psalms are preceded by an argument and by the superscription, grounding them in biblical history and Christian faith.

The Geneva and Bishops' Bibles are often examined as opposed to one another, embodying the rift within the Elizabethan Church. They could not be more different in appearance – one a small quarto, the other a royal folio that surpassed even the Great Bible in size. The Psalters in their first editions share, however, important similarities. Both broke away from past knowledge and Psalmody: They newly translated the Psalms from the Hebrew, and omitted, by and large, the Psalms' Latin incipits. In both Bibles, however, these transformations proved short-lived, already modified in the second edition of both Bibles printed in England. The second royal folio edition of the Bishops' Bible

---

[51] A brief table at the end of the Psalter (*Numerus secundum Hebreos*, pt 3 fol. 48v) links Latin incipit with Psalm number.

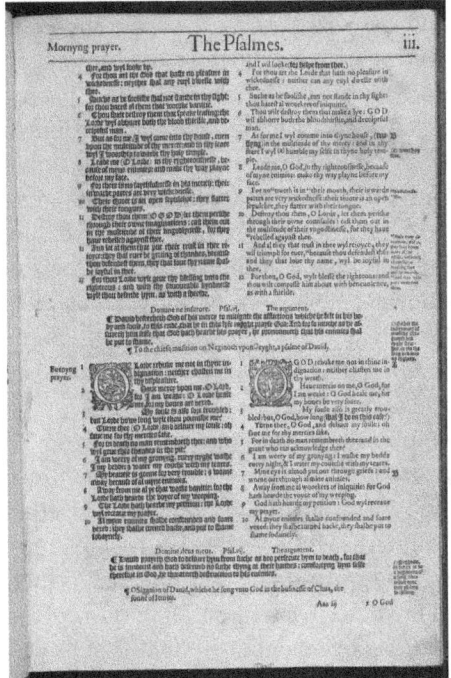

**Fig. 9:** *Bishops' 1572 Psalms (The. holie. Bible [London: Richarde Iugge, 1572], pt 3 p.3).* Edinburgh University Library Special Collections.

bears a strong resemblance to the second edition of the Geneva Bible printed in England following Parker's death.[52] As could be seen in the Psalter in the Bishops' 1572 edition (Fig. 9), this was an attempt to convey the two translations simultaneously, presenting Coverdale's Psalms alongside the newly translated ones.[53] Distinct typographical means separate the two texts. The 'old' Psalter is printed in Black Letter in the inner part, while the 'new' version in Roman type on the outer part. The Psalm is preceded by argument, number, and superscription, written across the two columns. While above the 'new' version appears the title of the argument, the 'old' version is preceded by the Latin incipit, adding to its liturgical applicability. The choice of typeface is not accidental. Black Letter was typically employed in the BoCP, creating not only a textual but also a visual allusion between text and performance; Roman type, innovative to sixteenth-century readers, likewise indicated the novelty of the new translation.[54]

---

52 RSTC§2107; RSTC§2123.
53 This mirrors the dual-Psalters of the High Middle Ages, which presented in parallel columns Jerome's distinct translations.
54 Green, *Print and Protestantism*, 61–65; Molekamp, "Using a Collection".

The dual Psalter enabled the old and the new to share the same space. Its use of two typefaces in two columns, with materials printed across columns in both Roman type and Black Letter, was an impressive feat. It would have proved challenging even for the most accomplished printer and was quickly abandoned. Subsequent editions set the Geneva and Bishops' Bibles once more on separate tracks. After 1573,[55] editions of the Bishops' Bible contained a single translation – that used in the BoCP. The Psalms were thus printed in an inferior translation, but the one used daily in churches. These editions brought the Psalms' performance centre-stage, with a lack of arguments, summaries or notes, a complete removal of superscriptions and the full reintegration of the Latin incipits. Some of these Bibles, such as the 1573 quarto edition (RSTC§2108), are also prefaced by the entire BoCP, enhancing their liturgical applicability.

Subsequent editions of the Geneva Bible followed a similar trajectory, which embodies the influence of the liturgy in a process that was accelerated once printing commenced in England. Still in Geneva, metrical Psalms were inserted alongside other hymns at the end of a quarto edition of *c*.1569 (RSCT§2106). Their translation did not follow the BoCP, but rather that of the metrical Psalter, which grew in popularity in Geneva and England. Two years after printing of the Geneva Bible commenced in England, the above-mentioned dual Psalter was published, but was quickly abandoned. The first quarto edition of the Geneva Bible printed in London in 1579 (RSTC§2126) embraced a new strategy of great longevity. It follows previous editions in presenting a single Psalter between Job and Proverbs – that of the Geneva version with its arguments, superscriptions, headings and annotations. However, a very different Psalter is provided at the beginning of the book. Accompanied by the liturgical apparatus typical of the Bishops' Bible, it encompasses the entire BoCP, alongside a full Psalter. Its Psalms were of the Great Bible's translation, without arguments or superscriptions but preceded by their Latin incipit; rubrics and titles connected the Psalms to their performance in the monthly cycle. Thus, avoiding the complex printing of a parallel edition, this solution preserved the newly translated Psalms for meditative and scholarly purposes, while providing a performance-oriented Psalter as well.[56] The latter's position at the beginning of the volume suggests that it was the liturgical Psalter that served as a first port-of-call. The Geneva Psalms could be located only after leafing through much of the book. This quarto edition was highly influential and replicated in numerous subsequent editions, at times with the *Whole Book of Psalmes* added at the end of the volume.

---

[55] Apart from the folio edition of 1585, RSTC§2143.
[56] This is similar to the modularity of Dutch Books of Hours: Rudy, *Piety in Pieces*.

# 5 Conclusion

The evolution of the Psalms' layout over four hundred years reveals a surprisingly constant pattern: a pendulum move between two ways of conceptualising the Psalter. Innovative layouts and new ways of engaging with the Psalms have been introduced to Bibles across the period. The same phenomenon is revealed in the small mendicant sub-group of the 1250s, in the early manuscripts of the Wycliffite Bible and Coverdale's 1535 Bible, as in the Geneva Bible of 1560 and the Bishops' Bible of 1568. In all these Bibles, the layout of the Psalms was made to accord with that of other biblical books, removing the unique, older, and primarily liturgical features of the Psalms' layout. This was often accompanied by the introduction of a new translation. Without exception, in each and every one of these instances, the change was subdued, modified, or completely obliterated. In later manuscripts and subsequent editions new divisions were removed, older translation re-introduced, and liturgical elements re-embedded. These transformations reveal the power of performance and mnemonics. Lay and clerical audiences alike encountered the Psalms through their chanting in the liturgy. The Psalms were intrinsically linked to their Latin incipits (a primary way in which they had been known and recalled throughout the period under investigation), and to a layout that reflected chant and liturgy. And despite the best efforts of innovators and reformers, the Psalms' layout continued to reflect this knowledge.

A material history of the Bible directs our attention to books less frequently explored by scholars of the English Bible. Studies of texts and Reform often highlight first editions as landmarks in the history of the English Bible. The dynamics of layout, however, are better served by tracing the changes these Bibles underwent over time, especially in dialogue with the English market. Most people encountered the Bible through subsequent editions, which often transformed biblical layout and text. These editions assist in presenting a more nuanced view of English religious history. Most Wycliffite Bibles are far from representing their heterodox inception, and subsequent editions of Coverdale's 1535 Bible omit some of its most reformed features. Latin and English emerge in these editions not as opposing forces, but as converging linguistic spheres. Thus, the LMB and the Wycliffite Bible have much in common, as do the Geneva and the Bishops' Bibles.

Innovative layouts were often the work of Church reformers, attempting to mould new ways of engaging with the Bible. Scholars have indeed attempted to trace the work and intellectual biographies of reformers such as Wyclif (and his followers), Tyndale, and Coverdale. Subsequent editions and later manuscripts, however, draw our attention to a different power shaping English Bibles and religion. Modifications which went back on theological innovation and embraced popular perceptions were often introduced by printers and stationers.

Many LMBs and later Wycliffite Bibles were the work of professional (and lay) stationers; Bibles were printed by a handful of merchants. Many of these were devout, with evidence for Lollard scribes, or the reformed affiliation of Grafton and Whitchurch. They also had to accord with market forces, ensuring that their Bibles would sell and repay the huge investment in ink and labour, paper or parchment. The omission of heterodox articles of faith by London stationers producing Wycliffite Bibles in the early fifteenth century, or the side-lining of Luther's influence when Nicolson reprinted the preliminaries of Coverdale's Bible, attest to the way printers and stationers subdued more contentious materials, thus enhancing their appeal to wider markets. More work is needed to trace the commercial elements behind the production of religious texts, but, as is evident from work on seventeenth-century printers,[57] it has the potential to transform our understanding of English religion.

The period under investigation saw the rise of moveable-type print, religious reform and political upheavals. Through the prism of materiality – and the Psalms' layout in particular – we can identify important continuities: Psalms were known through their Latin incipits long after the introduction of English Bibles, and the layout of early modern Bible owed much to their medieval predecessors. Changes are equally important. In his edition of the BoCP, Brian Cummings addresses the forces opposing the introduction of the new liturgy.[58] The Bibles of the 1570s reveal how the BoCP's Psalters became a new orthodoxy. More accurate translations, conservative and reformed alike, were put aside in favour of the liturgical Psalms. Performance remained key to the way the Psalms were presented and recalled.

## Bibliography

Aston, Margaret. "The Bishops' Bible Illustrations." In *The Church and the Arts*, edited by Diana Wood, 267–85. Oxford: Blackwell, 1992.

Ayris, Paul. "Reformation in Action: The Implementation of Reform in the Dioceses of England." *Reformation & Renaissance Review: Journal of the Society for Reformation Studies* 5 (2003): 27–53.

Berry, Lloyd E., ed. *The Geneva Bible, a Facsimile of the 1560 Edition*. Madison: University of Wisconsin Press, 1969.

---

[57] James Doelman, "George Wither, the Stationers Company and the English Psalter," *Studies in Philology* 90 (1993): 74–82.

[58] "The Book of Common Prayer: The Texts of 1549, 1559, and 1662," xvii.

Betteridge, Maurice S. "The Bitter Notes: The Geneva Bible and Its Annotations." *The Sixteenth Century Journal* 14 (1983): 41–62.

Blayney, Peter W.M. *The Stationers' Company and the Printers of London 1501–1557*. 2 vols. Cambridge: Cambridge University Press, 2013.

"The Book of Common Prayer: The Texts of 1549, 1559, and 1662." Edited by Brian Cummings. Oxford: Oxford University Press, 2011.

Cameron, Euan, ed. *The New Cambridge History of the Bible: Volume 3: From 1450 to 1750*. New Cambridge History of the Bible. Cambridge: Cambridge University Press, 2016.

Carruthers, Mary. *The Book of Memory: A Study of Memory in Medieval Culture*. Cambridge Studies in Medieval Literature. Cambridge: Cambridge University Press, 1992.

Clair, C. "The Bishops' Bible 1568." *Gutenberg Jahrbuch* (1962): 287–90.

d'Avray, David. "Printing, Mass Communication and Religious Reformation: The Middle Ages and After." In *The Uses of Script and Print, 1300–1700*, edited by Julia C. Crick and Alexandra Walsham, 50–70. Cambridge: Cambridge University Press, 2004.

de Mézerac-Zanetti, Aude. "A Reappraisal of Liturgical Continuity in the Mid-Sixteenth Century: Henrician Innovations and the First Books of Common Prayer." *Revue française de civilisation britannique*, no. 1 (2017), http://rfcb.revues.org/1218.

Dijk, S.J.P. van. "Medieval Terminology and Methods of Psalm Singing." *Musica Disciplina* 6 (1952): 7–26.

Doelman, James. "George Wither, the Stationers Company and the English Psalter." *Studies in Philology* 90 (1993): 74–82.

Dove, Mary, ed. *The Earliest Advocates of the English Bible: The Texts of the Medieval Debate*. Exeter: University of Exeter Press, 2010.

Dove, Mary. *The First English Bible: The Text and Context of the Wycliffite Versions*. Cambridge Studies in Medieval Literature 66. Cambridge: Cambridge University Press, 2007.

Duffy, Eamon. *Marking the Hours: English People and Their Prayers 1240–1570*. New Haven, CT.: Yale University Press, 2006.

Frere, Walter Howard, and William McClure Kennedy, eds. *Visitation Articles and Injunctions of the Period of the Reformation. Vol. 2: 1536–1558*, Alcuin Club Collections. London: Longmans, Green, 1910.

Fulton, Thomas. "Toward a New Cultural History of the Geneva Bible." *Journal of Medieval and Early Modern Studies* 47 (2017): 487–516.

Ghosh, Kantik. "The Prologues." In *The Wycliffite Bible: Origin, History and Interpretation*, edited by Elizabeth Solopova, 162–82. Leiden: Brill, 2016.

Green, Ian. "Hearing and Reading: Disseminating Bible Knowledge and Fostering Bible Understanding in Early Modern England." In *The Oxford Handbook of the Bible in England, C. 1530–1700*, edited by Kevin Killeen, Helen Smith and Rachel Willie, 272–86. Oxford: Oxford University Press, 2015.

Green, Ian. *Print and Protestantism in Early Modern England*. Oxford: Oxford University Press, 2000.

Green, William M. "Hugo of St. Victor: De Tribus Maximis Circumstantiis Gestorum." *Speculum* 18 (1943): 484–93.

Greenslade, S.L. *The Coverdale Bible, 1535*. Folkestone: Wm. Dawson & Sons, 1975.

Harper, John. *The Forms and Orders of Western Liturgy from the Tenth to the Eighteenth Century: A Historical Introduction and Guide for Students and Musicians*. Oxford: Clarendon Press, 1991.

Hellinga, Lotte. "Printing." In *The Cambridge History of the Book in Britain Volume 3: 1400–1557*, edited by Lotte Hellinga and J. B. Trapp, 65–108. Cambridge: Cambridge University Press, 1999.

Hudson, Anne. *The Premature Reformation: Wycliffite Texts and Lollard History*. Oxford: Oxford University Press, 1988.

Hudson, Anne, and Elizabeth Solopova. "The Latin Text." In *The Wycliffite Bible: Origin, History and Interpretation*, edited by Elizabeth Solopova, 107–32. Leiden: Brill, 2016.

Hughes, Paul L., and James F. Larkin, eds. *Tudor Royal Proclamations: Vol. 1, the Early Tudors, 1485–1553*. New Haven: Yale University Press, 1964.

Kuczynski, Michael P. "Glossing and Glosses." In *The Wycliffite Bible: Origin, History and Interpretation*, edited by Elizabeth Solopova, 346–67. Leiden: Brill, 2016.

Lacey, T.A., ed. Henry VIII, "The King's Book: Or, a Necessary Doctrine and Erudition for Any Christian Man, 1543." In *Church Historical Society New series*. London: Society for Promoting Christian Knowledge, 1932.

Lewis, Jack P. *The Day after Domesday: The Making of the Bishops' Bible*. Eugene: Wipf & Stock, 2016.

Light, Laura. "Thirteenth-Century Pandects and the Liturgy." In *Form and Function in the Late Medieval Bible*, edited by Eyal Poleg and Laura Light, 185–215. Leiden: Brill, 2013.

Light, Laura. "What Was a Bible For? Liturgical Texts in Thirteenth-Century Franciscan and Dominican Bibles." *Lusitania Sacra* 34 (2016): 165–82.

Longfellow, Erica. "Inwardness and English Bible Translations." In *The Oxford Handbook of the Bible in England, C. 1530–1700*, edited by Kevin Killeen, Helen Smith and Rachel Willie, 626–39. Oxford: Oxford University Press, 2015.

McFall, Lesley. "The Evidence for a Logical Arrangement of the Psalter." *Westminster Theological Journal* 62 (2000): 223–56.

Mirelman, Sam. "Contrafactum in the Ancient near East." In *Herausforderungen Und Ziele Der Musikarchäologie : Vorträge Des 5. Symposiums Der Internationalen Studiengruppe Musikarchäologie Im Ethnologischen Museum Der Staatlichen Museen Zu Berlin, 19.–23. September 2006 = Challenges and Objectives in Music Archaeology: Papers from the 5th Symposium of the International Study Group on Music Archaeology at the Ethnological Museum, State Museums Berlin, 19–23 September 2006*, edited by A.A. Both, R. Eichmann, E. Hickmann and L. Koch, 99–110. Rahden: M. Leidorf, 2008.

Molekamp, Femke. "Genevan Legacies: The Making of the English Geneva Bible." In *The Oxford Handbook of the Bible in England, C. 1530–1700*, edited by Kevin Killeen, Helen Smith and Rachel Willie, 38–53. Oxford: Oxford University Press, 2015.

Molekamp, Femke. "Using a Collection to Discover Reading Practices: The British Library Geneva Bibles and a History of Their Early Modern Readers." *The Electronic British Library Journal* (2006).

Mozley, James Frederic. *Coverdale and His Bibles*. London: Lutterworth Press, 1953.

Peikola, Matti. "'First Is Writen a Clause of the Bigynnynge Therof': The Table of Lections in Manuscripts of the Wycliffite Bible." In *Form and Function in the Late Medieval Bible*, edited by Eyal Poleg and Laura Light, 351–78. Leiden: Brill, 2013.

Pettegree, Andrew. "Publishing in Print: Technology and Trade." In *The New Cambridge History of the Bible: Volume 3: From 1450 to 1750*, edited by Euan Cameron, 159–86. Cambridge: Cambridge University Press, 2016.

Poleg, Eyal. *Approaching the Bible in Medieval England*. Manchester Medieval Studies. Manchester: Manchester University Press, 2013.

Poleg, Eyal. "The First Bible Printed in England: A Little Known Witness from Late Henrician England." *JEH* 67 (2016): 760–80.

Poleg, Eyal. *A Material History of the Bible in England, 1200–1553*. Oxford: Oxford University Press, 2020.

Poleg, Eyal. "Wycliffite Bibles as Orthodoxy." In *Instructing the Soul, Feeding the Spirit and Awakening the Passion: Cultures of Religious Reading in the Late Middle Ages*, edited by Sabrina Corbellini, 71–91. Turnhout: Brepols, 2013.

Poleg, Eyal, and Laura Light, eds. *Form and Function in the Late Medieval Bible*. WWMW. Leiden: Brill, 2013.

Quitslund, Beth. *The Reformation in Rhyme: Sternhold, Hopkins and the English Metrical Psalter, 1547–1603*. St Andrews Studies in Reformation History. Aldershot: Ashgate, 2008.

Rex, Richard. "The Crisis of Obedience: God's Word and Henry's Reformation." *The Historical Journal* 39 (1996): 863–94.

Rex, Richard. *Henry VIII and the English Reformation*, 2nd ed. British History in Perspective. Basingstoke: Palgrave Macmillan, 2006.

Rudy, Kathryn M. *Piety in Pieces: How Medieval Readers Customized Their Manuscripts*. Cambridge: Open Book Publishers, 2016.

Ryrie, Alec. *The Gospel and Henry VIII: Evangelicals in the Early English Reformation*. Cambridge Studies in Early Modern British History. Cambridge: Cambridge University Press, 2003.

Saenger, Paul. "The Impact of the Early Printed Page on the Reading of the Bible." In *The Bible as Book: The First Printed Editions*, edited by Paul Saenger and Kimberly Van Kampen, 31–51. London: British Library in association with The Scriptorium: Center for Christian Antiquities, 1999.

Salmon, Pierre. *Les "Tituli Psalmorum" Des Manuscrits Latins, Collectanea Biblica Latina*. Roma: Abbaye Saint-Jérome, 1959.

Solopova, Elizabeth. *Latin Liturgical Psalters in the Bodleian Library: A Select Catalogue*. Oxford: Bodleian Library, University of Oxford, 2013.

Solopova, Elizabeth. *Manuscripts of the Wycliffite Bible in the Bodleian and Oxford College Libraries*. Exeter Medieval Texts and Studies. Liverpool: Liverpool University Press, 2016.

Solopova, Elizabeth, ed. *The Wycliffite Bible: Origin, History and Interpretation*. Medieval and Renaissance Authors and Texts. Leiden: Brill, 2016.

Spinks, Bryan. "The Bible in Liturgy and Worship, C. 1500–1750." In *The New Cambridge History of the Bible: Volume 3: From 1450 to 1750*, edited by Euan Cameron, 563–78. Cambridge: Cambridge University Press, 2016.

*The Statutes of the Realm, Printed by Command of His Majesty King George the Third, in' Pursuance of an Address of the House of Commons of Great Britain from Original Records and Authentic Manuscripts*. London: Eyre and Strahan, 1817. Reprint, 1963.

String, Tatiana C. *Art and Communication in the Reign of Henry VIII*. Aldershot: Ashgate, 2008.

Sutherland, Annie. *English Psalms in the Middle Ages, 1300–1450*. Oxford: Oxford University Press, 2015.

Sutherland, Annie. "The Wycliffite Psalms." In *The Wycliffite Bible: Origin, History and Interpretation*, edited by Elizabeth Solopova, 183–201. Leiden: Brill, 2016.

Temperley, Nicholas. "'All Skillful Praises Sing': How Congregations Sang the Psalms in Early Modern England." *Renaissance Studies* 29 (2015): 531–53.

Verbraak, Gwendolyn. "William Coverdale and the Clandestine Book Trade: A Bibliographical Quest for the Printers of Tyndale's New Testament." In *Infant Milk or Hardy Nourishment? The Bible for Lay People and Theologians in the Early Modern Period*, edited by W. Francois and A.A. den Hollander, 167–89. Leuven: Peeters, 2009.

Victor, Hugh of St. "The Three Best Memory Aids for Learning History." In *The Medieval Craft of Memory: An Anthology of Texts and Pictures*, edited by Mary Carruthers and Jan M. Ziolkowski, 32–40. Philadelphia, 2002.

Amanda Dillon
# Be Your Own Scribe: Bible Journalling and the New Illuminators of the Densely-Printed Page

## 1 Introduction

Bible journalling is a popular trend of recent times amongst mostly female readers of the Bible in the United States. It involves an active and creative engagement with the material book of the Bible. Readers, empowered with a plenitude of attractive stationery accessories – coloured pens and pencils, watercolour paints, washi tapes, stickers and templates – draw and make typographic designs directly into their Bibles, illustrating verses and passages that have particular personal resonance for them. The name given to this trend is Bible Journalling and it is essentially a devotional practice of reflecting on the Bible – and yet distinctly new as a trend amongst lay readers of the Bible. This paper considers the striking retention and valuing of the iconic material artefact of the Bible at the heart of this practice, as well as the considerable agency taken by the readers (and facilitated by the producers of the Bible journals and stationery) in the making of these creative interventions to the densely-printed and "sacred" page. These readers have become illuminators of their own Bibles. Photographs of these newly illuminated verses and pages are often shared on social media platforms such as Instagram and Pinterest, thereby migrating beyond the material page into the digital realm. Here online communities share their pages and choose common themes to work on, over short periods of time, occasionally with exegetical input from one of the members of the group. A brief introduction to the process of Bible journalling contains distinct echoes of the ancient monastic practice of *Lectio Divina*:

> As you read your Bible, allow God's Word to speak to your soul. It's worth taking time to quiet your heart and be still before beginning. Depending on where you are in your faith walk, you may be drawn to certain passages. Read the passage once to get an overview, and then again to dig deeper into the text. Look for the verse, phrase, or concept that speaks to you. Once you identify scripture that you find meaningful, try to determine what God is saying to you through the passage, so you can begin the process of bringing it to life by lettering, colouring, and/or illustrating its message.[1]

---

[1] Joanne Fink and Regina Yoder, *Complete Guide to Bible Journalling: Creative Techniques to Express Your Faith* (Mount Joy, PA: Fox Chapel, 2017), 8. Cf. Christine Valters Paintner, *Lectio Divina: The Sacred Art* (London: SPCK, 2012), 8–11.

This chapter explores the creative process of Bible journalling, with a specific look at the agency of women readers who take up this practice. Materiality, and the Bible-publishing enterprise, both play considerable roles in this emerging trend. Two Bible journal entries – creative illuminations of different texts by female Bible journallers – shall be considered in depth, in the context of this emerging spiritual practice, among those who value the material artefact of the printed Bible.

## 2 The Practice of Bible Journalling

Bible journalling as a hobby has taken off in the United States and appears to be gaining some traction in Europe, with Dutch Bible-readers most notably.[2] As we shall see, publishers, including Zondervan, Crossway and Thomas Nelson, are now producing dedicated journalling Bibles designed to facilitate this direct, artistic engagement with the Bible. These Bibles have wide margins, sometimes feint-ruled and sometimes blank. Some "interleaf" Bibles leave complete pages blank intermittently throughout the Bible – thereby facilitating expansive artworks stretching across the double page spread. A definition of Bible journalling as it appears in the best-selling *Complete Guide to Bible Journalling* suggests:

> In its simplest definition Bible journalling is a way to express your faith creatively. Putting pen to paper is a great way to remember and record biblical concepts that are meaningful and relevant to your life. Whether you are drawing, colouring, and writing right inside your Bible – the most commonly understood definition – or writing and illustrating scripture verses in a separate book or on to paper alongside your Bible, the essential thing to understand is that Bible journalling is about creating while reflecting on God's Word.[3]

The reader/artist receives a book that conforms to all expectations of what a material Bible is; hundreds of thin pages densely printed with the written text of the Bible. The only exception here is the margin that has been left wider than usual. In most of the journalling Bibles this margin is approximately five centimetres (2 inches) wide and 20 centimetres (8 inches) in length. This extra-wide margin is the area of invitation to the reader to make their mark. It is their piece of "blank canvas" on the page. In a few editions, designs are already featured in the margins for colouring in. However, it appears the preferred versions have blank margins open to the reader's creativity.

---

[2] This is from evidence gleaned from the social media platforms of Instagram and Pinterest.
[3] Fink and Yoder, *Complete Guide*, 8.

Interventions are made, by the reader, to the physical and material structure of the book through the addition of further paper and ink. The edges of pages are lined with coloured and patterned washi tape. There is the addition of tabs, often pre-designed; they may have a textured background, a watercolour appearance, or be patterned; but they are always colourful. These tabs indicate the beginning of a new book of the Bible. There are also theme tabs that relate to particular topics, such as prayer, or hope, for example. There is a trend of marking the first page of a new book with washi tape as well as a tab. Further techniques include "Tip-ins" and "tip outs." A "tip in" is an extra page, conventionally a page of similar thinness to that of the Bible pages, like a tracing paper, that is taped in place along the *inner* margin or "gutter" of the Bible. It becomes an extra page between two pages, held in place most usually with washi tape. The extra page allows for a design to stretch across two pages without interfering with the text of the facing page. A "tip out" is a similar process but here the extra page or piece of paper is taped in place along the *outside* edge of the page and may fold out of the Bible – creating a three-page effect.

Clear gesso is a type of added substrate that comes in a liquid form, and may be applied to a ground on which an artist desires to work – in this instance a page in the Bible.[4] Spread thinly and evenly over the page, possibly with the edge of a plastic (credit) card or some such thin, sharp and hard object, it creates a thin, transparent film, almost like a layer of clear varnish over the page. When the gesso dries, the page is not buckled and is now ready to have other inks and paints applied on over it. The gesso protects the page from buckling with the addition of watercolour washes. This transparent layer of gesso allows the scriptural text to remain visible beneath thin applications of colour, if desired. It is, of course, also possible that the text may be obscured by a darker or thicker application of ink or paint. This use of gesso to make of the page a working surface for other applications is of particular interest. The scriptural text is now layered into a foundation for further addition. It is possible for the artist to move out of the margin and make incursions into the printed page, to occupy the page with their designs. This can be a subversive act. Whilst valuing the text and desiring that it be the ground on which the artwork is created, it is also layered into the art. By subsuming the text into the art, it becomes an integral feature of the art. The text is appropriated as an element of the design, a texture that is altered into the

---

4 Gesso, in its more conventional thicker and opaque white form, is almost invariably applied either smoothly or in a textured, impasto way to canvas and boards before artists begin work on a painting in oils or acrylics. This protects the canvas, adding durability and longevity to the artwork, and allows the paint to go much further, especially if the style is impasto and a thickly textured ground is desired.

artwork. In this sense it functions like a pattern: it symbolises text, its legibility is perhaps slightly obscured, but its iconic function remains to perform the biblical text in the artwork. This approach almost suggests that the text is so familiar that it is no longer required to be completely visible or legible within or beneath the layers of colour.

Paper additions – whether of full page tip ins or tip outs, or the washi-taped edges of pages – have the effect of bulking up the Bible, as do other additions such as adding bits of ribbon and cloth, stickers, and other paper cutouts. Likewise, the use of gesso, paint, fixative – even the covering of pencil crayon – all adds to the thickness of pages and bulk of the Bible and creates a festive, joyful and colourful look to the Bible. Beyond being an appreciation and engagement with the material artefact, these artists also *add their own material*, mostly paper and paint, thereby modifying and extending the material artefact. It is personalised as this extra heft is added to it. This added weight is both literal and symbolic; it signifies a personal investment in this book and its claim on the reader's spiritual life. By adding these material bits, the Bible is invested with personal meaning and value, and a claim is made on the Bible's authority and influence in the reader's life.

The philosopher Lisa Heldke suggests that growing and preparing food are thoughtful practices that both use and generate emotional and erotic energy – not merely as incidentals, but as vital parts of the process.[5] In her challenge to the Western philosophical tradition that valorises "knowing work," while denigrating "hand work" or practical work, she argues that growing, cooking and eating food should be understood as forms of "bodily knowledge."[6] Heldke explains:

> The knowing involved in making a cake is "contained" not simply "in my head" but in my hands, my wrists, my eyes and nose as well. The phrase "bodily knowledge" is not a metaphor. It is an acknowledgment of the fact that I *know* things literally with my body, that I, "as" my hands, know when the bread dough is sufficiently kneaded.[7]

Similarly, Meredith McGuire makes the point that "lived religion is constituted by the practices by which people remember, share, enact, adapt, create and combine the stories out of which they live. And it comes into being through the often-mundane practices by which people transform these meaningful interpretations

---

[5] Lisa M. Heldke, "Foodmaking as a Thoughtful Practice," in *Cooking, Eating, Thinking: Transformative Philosophies of Food*, eds. D.W. Curtin and L.M. Heldke (Bloomington, IN: Indiana University Press, 1992), 204–29.
[6] Heldke, "Foodmaking," 204–229, at 218.
[7] Heldke, "Foodmaking," 204–229, at 218.

into everyday action."⁸ Bible journalling, which may seem "mundane" to some, is a practice that engages the whole person, body, mind and spirit. In the first instance there is the aesthetic delight that is generated in the use of artistic materials attested to by many artists. Van Gogh famously ingested a tube of his favourite yellow oil paint so enraptured was he with the beauty of its colour and texture. We see it too in the ecstatic, bright, paper cut-outs of Matisse's later work, no longer able to paint but still obsessed with the beauty of colour and form. There is a thrill for many in the materials alone before any encounter with the biblical text has even begun. Moreover, sitting hunched over a Bible with a pile of papers and paints, cutting, pasting, rubbing, smoothing are all physical acts that linger in the fingertips. Drawing, colouring and painting are highly tactile processes that involve holding specialised instruments in different ways and making diverse marks with them. The feeling of gently building up colour with a pencil crayon by repeatedly going over the same small area is unlike laying a wash of watercolour over a page. Likewise, cutting with scissors or a craft knife are different processes, they feel different in the hand and produce different results. Gouache has its own distinctive smell, as do oil pastels. This form of journalling is an embodied process that weds an intellectual and spiritual knowledge with a "bodily knowledge." McGuire says of such embodied practices: "their potential to involve integrally a person's knowing body, knowing mind, sensations, memory, emotions, and spirit is evident."⁹

The how-to websites and books are replete with contemporary graphic treatments of certain verses from a biblical text that may be traced over in the margin. These are text-based designs that may be embellished with other graphic symbols, candles or stars, for example. Hearts, butterflies, birds, flowers and other plants, clouds, rainbows, seeds, fish, sea, angels, bunting – these make up the conventional repertoire of visual symbols that have been illustrated as attractive line art for tracing and copying by beginner journallers. Some pages, displayed publicly, contain what appear to be incongruous symbols in the context of the Bible: a VW camping van or a moped, for example. Some appear to be rather bizarrely out-of-place – but is a bear on a bicycle really any more frivolous than a cat running off with a communion wafer, as we see in the Book of Kells and other such delights of medieval illumination – or is it simply a similar sense of humour expressed in a different time and place, and therefore though new visual tropes?¹⁰

---

**8** Meredith B. McGuire, "Why Bodies Matter: A Sociological Reflection on Spirituality and Materiality," *Spiritus: A Journal of Christian Spirituality* 3/1 (2003): 1–18, at 2.
**9** McGuire, "Why Bodies Matter," 11.
**10** Fink and Yoder, *Complete Guide*, 110. The bear on a bicycle in this example illustrates Prov 3:5–6 "Trust in the Lord … and he will make your paths straight." See Amanda Dillon, "The Book

## 3 Bible Journalling and Bible Publishing

Much has been written about the multiplicity of Bibles being published and the niche marketing of Bibles to appeal to every conceivable reader, often aligned with hobbies or personal interests.[11] These types of niche Bibles are frequently designed around gender roles, such as motherhood or fatherhood, and given a thoroughly gendered graphic treatment. There has been little research as yet about what actually happens to these Bibles once bought or received as a gift. How many Bibles does the "average" Christian own and how many do they make use of regularly? What are the emotional relationships a reader might have with the many Bibles in their possession?

I suggest that Bible journalling is, in many ways, an almost natural consequence of this proliferation of material Bibles. For those who hold the Bible to be a sacred book, owning many Bibles means that they may hold less value individually whilst simultaneously offering – or demanding – to be put to use in some way, rather than being allowed to gather dust. Owning many Bibles frees the owner-reader to place less value on the individual, material artefact and therefore to make an intervention to the book. Owning multiple copies of the Bible also means that there are others available and so creative incursions on the text that make it less legible do not matter because there is always another Bible to read if this one is no longer legible. Conversely, I suggest, Bible journalling is *also* precisely about investing a Bible with personal, and significantly, *material* "added value." It's a personal embellishment that individualises a Bible beyond stereotypical niche marketing. It may in some instances be a subtle form of resistance to clichéd designs.

Bible journalling has become a significant driver of Bible sales, and journalling Bibles are a lucrative business. Tyndale Publishers produced their first journalling Bible in 2016. "Our first three journalling Bibles that we published – a leatherlike, hard cover, and soft cover – were all extremely popular from the very beginning, and the first printings sold out quickly, and then over the first year, each additional printing was sold out before the new stock arrived. We have since then expanded to additional designs and features, including *Inspire Psalms, Inspire Praise*, and we will be releasing a girl's edition later this year.

---

of Kells and the Visual Identity of Ireland," in *Ireland and the Reception of the Bible, Social and Cultural Perspectives*, eds. Bradford A. Anderson and Jonathan Kearney (London: Bloomsbury, 2018): 295–312, at 299.
**11** Timothy Beal, *The Rise and Fall of the Bible: The Unexpected History of an Accidental Book* (New York: Houghton Mifflin Harcourt, 2012). Jeffrey S. Siker, *Liquid Scripture: The Bible in a Digital World* (Minneapolis, MN: Fortress, 2017).

We also have several other popular journalling Bibles: *Thrive, Expressions*, and *Reflections*."[12] Tyndale's NLT *Inspire Bible* (The Bible for Colouring and Creative Journalling) which came out in March 2016 was ECPA's (Evangelical Christian Publishers Association) Bestselling Bible of 2016 (the year it was published).[13] It was a Christian Retailing's BEST Award Winner (Bible: Journalling category) at the 2017 awards. The *Inspire Bible* is doing extremely well in the Christian marketplace, retailing at the time of writing at between $33–$40 USD; it has a trendy and colourful illustrated cover. A departure from the formality of black leather and gold lettering, it features a bird and a butterfly collaged alongside large roses and lilies in full colour. Stamped around them are white peonies, over a polka dot patterned background. It has a decidedly "vintage" look, with a hint of typography in the lower third with the French word D'HORTICULTURE standing out. Two other versions of the Tyndale *Inspire Bible* (Silky Vintage and Softcover) featured in the top ten bestsellers for 2016.[14] The NIV Beautiful Word Bible, a journalling Bible published by Zondervan, comes in at number ten on this list, with a further two ESV Journalling Bibles by Crossway in the top twenty.[15] Figures for 2017 show three journalling Bibles in the top twenty, published by Tyndale and Zondervan.[16]

Bible journalling might be said to find its commercial origin in the scrapbooking trend of the last two decades.[17] It was perhaps inevitable that a clever marketer would make the link eventually and something of scrapbooking would find its way into the world of Bible publishing and its seemingly insatiable drive to find ever new ways of selling the best-selling book in the world. "How do you monetise Bibles when so many are freely available?" Timothy Beal asked; his answer being that, "The challenge is to keep reinventing the Bible

---

12 Email correspondence with a Tyndale Publishing marketing executive (25 May 2018).
13 "Inspire Bible NLT," https://www.tyndale.com/p/inspire-bible-nlt/9781496413734.
14 "Bible Bestsellers, Best of 2016. Compiled and distributed by the Evangelical Christian Publishers Association," http://christianbookexpo.com/bestseller/bibles.php?id=BO16.
15 "Bible Bestsellers, Best of 2016," http://christianbookexpo.com/bestseller/bibles.php?id=BO16.
16 "Bible Bestsellers, Best of 2017," http://christianbookexpo.com/bestseller/bibles.php?id=BO17#. Current monthly figures for 2018 show two journalling Bibles in the top twenty: "Bible Bestsellers, September 2018," http://christianbookexpo.com/bestseller/bibles.php?id=0918.
17 Jack Neff, "Scrapbooking Gets Reinvented to Suit New Digital Reality," 25 July 2011. http://adage.com/article/news/scrapbooking-reinvented-suit-digital-reality/228856/. "A study by Scrapbooking.com, an online magazine serving the industry, found industry sales peaked at under $2.6 billion in 2004 and 2005 and then began declining slowly to $1.7 billion by 2009." Current estimates are that there is still a healthy $1.5 billion scrapbooking-supplies industry in the United States.

in new got-to-have, value-added forms."¹⁸ In the instance of journalling Bibles, the added-value far exceeds "innovative packaging and physical format," as it extends its reach into the expansive parallel world of hobby arts and crafts stationery and materials. The combining of these two economic phenomena is explosive indeed.

Interestingly, at the time of writing, the number one bestseller on Amazon in the Christian books and Bibles section is not a Bible but a book about *how to do* Bible Journalling.¹⁹ This is a critical aspect in the marketing of Bible journalling. The journal Bible, with its wide margins, sometimes left blank but usually lined, and designed with the intention that the reader embellish the margin with their own written or drawn notes and doodles, is the core product around which there are a plethora of other "spin-off" or peripheral products. In the main this other merchandise might be termed "stationery" and consists of everything from designed patterned papers, stickers, washi tape (sellotape with either patterns or texts), a phenomenal array of coloured pencils, pens and markers, watercolour kits, gesso, paints, glues, tracing papers, and templates. A quick look at the blogs reveals that those blogging on these matters are in turn working closely with many of the journalling materials companies to promote their products – as they blog their experiments with different gel pens and gessoes. Bookshops hold Bible journalling workshops and in-store events with designers, bloggers and authors giving demonstrations on how to use different products.

## 4 Bible Journalling: Women's Spirituality and Agency

One striking dimension of Bible journalling that is revealed in the public presentation on social media such as Instagram and Pinterest is that it appears to be almost universally practiced by women.²⁰ The blogs and vlogs that teach people how to begin Bible journalling are produced by women for women. The same may be said for much of the merchandising that has been developed: the stationery,

---

**18** Beal, *Rise and Fall*, 49.
**19** Fink and Yoder, *Complete Guide*, with 4.7 stars and 365 customer reviews. This paperback book includes "270 Full-Color Stickers, 150 Designs on Perforated Pages, 60 Designs on Translucent Sheets of Vellum" and presently retails new at between $10–$20 USD online.
**20** In my research I found only a few male Bible-journallers who display their pages publicly (James Presley, Alvin Keyte and Andrew Coates).

washi tapes, stickers, lettering, and templates are clearly oriented towards female consumers, and designed and developed by female artists.[21]

Traditionally, in the history of the Christian (and indeed, Jewish and Muslim) illumination of sacred Scriptures the scribes were men, usually clerical men within the ecclesiastical hierarchy.[22] However, recent research has shown that women of the Middle Ages, especially those in convents, were prolific in their artistic output, and this included beautiful, high quality illumination of Bibles, Books of Hours, psalters and prayer books, but received almost no scholarly attention until the last few decades.[23] The nature of their work, which often included embroidered textiles or miniature illustrations, was deemed insignificant and of little interest.[24] Wealthy medieval laywomen are now also understood to have commissioned and owned books and through such patronage played a vital role in the development of new iconographic forms. Excluded, as they were, from most public religious life and usually literate only in the vernacular, these female patrons stimulated the growth of vernacular language devotional literature.[25] When read in light of these historical precursors, Bible journalling can also be seen as the development of a contemporary, vernacular, devotional, visual language.

Despite the rich history of illuminated Bibles in the Christian tradition, many women beginning Bible journalling express anxiety about drawing directly into a printed Bible. One guide speaks of Valerie, who "was at first unsure about working directly in a book that contains the Word of God."[26] Shanna Noel, now owner of one of the most successful online fora and shops for Bible journallers

---

[21] Examples include "Print and Pray Shop," online at https://www.illustratedfaith.com/shop/, and "Bible Journaling," online at https://www.dayspring.com/bible-journaling, featuring the artwork of many female artists.

[22] Keith Houston, *The Book: A Cover-to-Cover Exploration of the Most Powerful Object of Our Time* (New York: W.W. Norton, 2016), 155–174.

[23] See: *Sermologium*, MS Douce 185. c. 1320–50. Bodleian Library, Oxford. This is an exquisite book of homilies illuminated by a group of nuns in northern Germany.

[24] A review of the literature in this regard may be found in Lila Yawn Bonghi, "Medieval Women Artists and Modem Historians," *Medieval Feminist Newsletter* 12/1 (1991): 10–19.

[25] Susan Croag Bell, "Medieval Women Book Owners: Arbiters of Lay Piety and Ambassadors of Culture," in *Women and Power in the Middle Ages*, ed. Mary Erler and Maryanne Kowaleski (Athens, GA: University of Georgia Press, 2004): 149–87.

[26] Fink and Yoder, *Complete Guide*, 64. Brian Malley writes, "Specific biblical texts are, for the most part, influential because they are part of the Bible, part of 'God's word.' Expressions like 'the word of God,' 'God's word,' and 'the word of the Lord,' refer to a kind of authoritative discourse that includes the Bible, but is seldom limited to it." See: "Understanding the Bible's Influence," in *The Social Life of Scriptures: Cross Cultural Perspectives on Biblicism*, ed. James S. Bielo (New Brunswick, NJ: Rutgers University Press, 2009): 194–204, at 196.

wrote about being worried about being judged for drawing in her Bible: "I was extremely nervous to share my new form of worship as I wasn't sure how people would react to it."[27] Since the demise of the illuminated manuscript over five centuries ago, the densely-printed sacred page has held a particular authority. Whilst verbal additions – the writing of notes in the margin – to this sacred page have been largely sanctioned, especially in personal Bibles, until recently visual additions have been viewed with some suspicion. The hegemony of the verbal mode and the densely-printed page is well documented. This move towards the mode of the visual is consistent with the "visual turn" that is taking place in society generally emerging largely from the digital revolution and its multimodal use of the visual mode. Wide-margin journalling Bibles were initially intended for written notes, inspired by Sunday service sermons, the fruit of Bible Study sessions and personal reflection.[28] The move towards the visual has been initiated by women from within the Bible-reading community and the uptake has been exponential, facilitated largely through online sharing on Instagram and Pinterest. Most of those now posting, writing, blogging and vlogging about Bible journalling became aware of and began to journal themselves as recently as 2014 in most recorded instances.[29] This is a highly significant development in the practice of Bible-reading and the reception of the Bible among "lay" women because women are claiming agency in their practice of Bible-reading and their authority to make visual and material interventions in their Bibles. It is significant that for the first time in over five hundred years women are illustrating and illuminating Bibles. This is a visual reception of and engagement with the Bible that it is led by women and almost exclusively (at this time) practiced by women. Unlike the illuminations of the scribes of the past, these drawings and paintings are about a personal interpretation of the text.

Agency has been facilitated to some extent through the creation of these wide margins in Bibles. Nonetheless, it is a minimal change to the traditional page layout conventions of the Bible as a printed book. The agency claimed by the

---

[27] Shanna Noel, "Our Story," online at https://www.illustratedfaith.com/our-story/.
[28] James S. Bielo, *Words Upon the Word, An Ethnography of Evangelical Group Bible Study* (New York: New York University Press, 2009). Bielo has written a substantive account of Evangelical Bible-reading practice. "Evangelicals throughout the United States emphasise the need for Bible study in their individual and collective lives. [...] Bible study contends strongly for being the most consequential form of religious practice to the ever-evolving contours of American Evangelicalism. From a sheer numerical perspective, it is the most prolific type of small group in American society, with more than 30 million Protestants gathering every week for this distinct purpose. As a matter of substance, it provides individuals a unique opportunity to engage in open, reflexive, and critical dialogue" (3).
[29] Fink and Yoder, *Complete Guide*, 54–96.

artists, on the other hand, is extraordinary, as is their creativity. Breaking out and beyond the prescribed blank margin they make incursions into and over the printed text, frequently claiming the full page in their design. This emerging practice is indicative of a wider, personal authority over biblical interpretation being claimed by women readers and most especially "lay" readers, those with no pastoral or teaching role in a church, nor formal education in Biblical Studies. They are, in ways not dissimilar to the readers of Biblezines – as studied by Susan Harding, "in some fundamental ways making themselves as religious subjects and prying open living spaces for themselves."[30]

Theologian Nicola Slee writes: "As many feminists have argued, one of the key struggles for women in our time is to find a voice and a language to name our experience in terms which are authentic and empowering, against a patriarchal culture in which women's silence and invisibility have been normative, women's experience systematically occluded, and where the only language available for naming has been codified in terms of male meanings."[31] One method that emerged in women's spirituality over recent decades as a way of claiming back this power and of exercising the agency to name spiritual experience has been the process of journalling.

The keeping of a diary or journal is a tradition that dates back at least a thousand years, to the "pillow books" kept by the women of the Japanese court during the tenth century.[32] While most known journals published in the past were written by men, there is reason to believe that women were writing them in equal if not greater numbers. Marlene Schiwy explains: "Often denied a voice in the public realm and the possibility of publication, women have kept diaries in order to communicate with themselves, to explore the meaning of their lives, and to

---

[30] Susan Harding, "Revolve, the Biblezine: A Transevangelical Text," in *The Social Life of Scriptures: Cross Cultural Perspectives on Biblicism*, ed. James S. Bielo (New Brunswick, NJ: Rutgers University Press, 2009):176–193, at 189. Harding argues that the implied "listening position" (of the girl readers) in *Revolve*, a Christian Biblezine published by Thomas Nelson, is not "passive." "The girls have voice and voices" (189).

[31] Nicola Slee, *Women's Faith Development* (Aldershot: Ashgate, 2004), 67.

[32] Jennifer New, *Drawing from Life: The Journal as Art* (New York: Princeton Architectural Press, 2005), 16. One of the most renowned is the "*The Pillow Book of Sei Shonagon*, by a member of the Japanese court in the Heian period at the end of the tenth century. The author of the pillow book described her activity thus: "I set about filling the notebooks with odd facts, stories from the past, and all sorts of other things, often including the most trivial material. On the whole I concentrated on things and people that I found charming and splendid; my notes are also full of poetry and observations on trees and plants, birds and insects."

give form to their creative impulses."³³ In their important study of women's psychological development, *Women's Ways of Knowing*, Mary Field Belenkey and her coauthors cite journal writing as a powerful tool in the evolution of a woman's self, voice and mind.³⁴ The diary is a place where women think and feel their way through key concerns and issues that determine their lives. "Nowhere is the true nature of our psychic development more clearly evident. In journals we see emotion and thought, intuition and experience fused into something quite different from our usual attempts to be logical. What we write and read in diaries is a language of the heart."³⁵ Schiwy continues:

> Women have historically had a different relationship with literature and language than men. We have provided the admiring audience for male linguistic performance; only rarely have we possessed pen and paper of our own. Even when we have, the language hasn't fit our experience; the words have not come out right. But now, more than ever, claims the literary critic Nicole Brossard, "The question for women in playing with language is really a matter of life and death. We're not just playing for fun in a kind of game. We're finding our own voice, exploring it, and making new sense where the general sense has lost meaning and is no longer of use." Through keeping a diary, we begin to find our own words, our own language, our own voices. We start to tell our own stories.³⁶

Bible journalling is far from a feminist movement. Wide margin Bibles predate this visual development in Bible Journalling. They were initially designed to facilitate the taking of notes during sermons and Bible Study classes and groups. And, indeed, this is how they were used, the freehand written text of the reader supplementing the printed text with notes and insights gleaned often under the instruction of others, frequently male pastors. No doubt many Bible journallers would resist this feminist understanding of their contemporary journalling practices. The majority of Bible journalling shared online takes place in what are perceived to be religiously conservative social groups where male elders and pastors continue to hold authority over the interpretation of the Bible (and may claim a biblical mandate for doing so). In many ways these are the most unlikely and incongruous settings for a reflexive practice to emerge that facilitates women claiming agency over their own spiritual experience. And yet, this burgeoning movement enables women to engage with the Bible in a personal, intimate way

---

**33** Marlene A. Schiwy, *A Voice of Her Own: Women and the Journal Writing Journey* (New York: Simon and Schuster, 1996), 16.
**34** Mary Field Belenkey, et al., *Women's Ways of Knowing: The Development of Self, Voice, and Mind* (New York: Basic Books, 1986).
**35** Schiwy, *A Voice of Her Own*, 22.
**36** Schiwy, *A Voice of Her Own*, 23.

and then journal visually back into the Bible something of their own spiritual appropriation of that text in the light of their own life experience. Gleaned from her research into women's written journalling, Slee notes their creative use of metaphor:

> Struggling to overcome the stultifying effects of silencing or false naming which renders their experience and meanings impotent, they reach for images, metaphors and combinations of metaphor which can evoke the reality of their lives. The potency of their metaphoric language is testimony to their linguistic creativity and to the ownership of their lives towards which they aspire. Even when their words assert a sense of spiritual powerlessness, the originality of the images they use to describe this reality gives the lie to its ultimate thraldom. By its very presence, metaphoric creativity – when it is not merely the repetition of stock imagery or unthinking assent to "dead metaphor" is indicative of women's spiritual vibrancy and engagement in the claiming of experience and the naming of the powers that be.[37]

The templates and design ideas presented to beginner journallers are designed to fit, to be contained within the margin given in the page layout. The supplied graphics may also be said, on occasion, to conform to "stock imagery," perhaps even a kitsch sentimentality. Many of the women who engage in Bible journalling may well assent to the patriarchal structure of their religious practice but what is emerging in their artistic journalling practice is frequently striking in its originality and "spiritual vibrancy." One fascinating example is an online community of Bible journallers who have engaged with the female characters in the Bible, selecting one per day for a month, and producing a journal entry, in the relevant place, featuring that female biblical character.[38] Whilst the explicit objective of claiming a voice may not be remotely in the minds of female Bible journallers, that is in fact what is emerging; a new visual illumination of biblical texts that illustrates the interpretation and appropriation of the Bible by female readers for their own personal spiritual growth. This is expressed multimodally, through both image and word, in the most apt metaphors and symbols available to these groups of female Bible readers. As such it is a highly significant development in female Bible reading and reception and, like the illuminated manuscripts of the Middle Ages, is worthy of scholarly attention and analysis.

---

[37] Slee, *Women's Faith Development*, 67.
[38] A group of Dutch Bible journallers took as a project amongst themselves in their online group to focus on a different female character of the Bible every day for a month, under the collective hashtags: #woordvrouw and #31daysofbiblicalwomen. These they then share on Instagram.

## 5 "Red Rain Boots" and "War in Syria": An analysis of two Bible Journal designs

A journalled entry in a Bible that is a good example of a "newly made sign"[39] is a full-page, watercolour painting over a page of text that features Deut 11:4–32 (Fig. 1) by Carol Belleau. From this page a section of text is highlighted within a red border. This is the ESV text for Deut 11:11–14:

> But the land that you are going over to possess is a land of hills and valleys, which drinks water by the rain from heaven, a land that the LORD your God cares for. The eyes of the LORD your God are always upon it, from the beginning of the year to the end of the year. "And if you will indeed obey my commandments that I command you today, to love the LORD your God, and to serve him with all your heart and with all your soul, he will give the rain for your land in its season, the early rain and the later rain, that you may gather in your grain and your wine and your oil."

The final phrase of 11:14b: "that you may gather in your grain and your wine and your oil" is omitted from the bordered selection in this journalled page. The border is red, like the rain boots, and this text is not painted over, it is kept clear and easily legible. It is foregrounded in front of the left boot. There is a further, personal reiteration of Deut 11:14a in black handwritten pen under the boots in a puddle: "*He will give you rain for your land in its season, the early rain and the later rain.*" This is followed by a reference to the longer, bordered section above, from whence it is quoted: *Deut 11:11–14* and dated: *10·24·16*.[40] There is also a digital watermark, *carol@belleauway.com,* which serves both as a signature and contact email address for the artist when she uploads her images to the various online

---

**39** This will be a social semiotic analysis. See: Gunther Kress and Theo van Leeuwen, *Reading Images: The Grammar of Visual Design,* 2nd ed. (London: Routledge, 2006) for a full explication of this analytical approach to multimodal communications. Kress and van Leeuwen explain, "We see representation as a process in which the makers of signs [...] seek to make a representation of some object or entity, whether physical or semiotic, in which their interest in the object, at the point of making the representation, is a complex one, arising out of the cultural, social and psychological history of the sign-maker, and focused by the specific context in which the sign-maker produces the sign. [...] In social semiotics the sign is not the pre-existing conjunction of a signifier and a signified, a ready-made sign to be recognised, chosen and used as is…. Rather, we focus on the process of sign-making, in which the signifier (the form) and the signified (the meaning), are relatively independent of each other until they are brought together by the sign-maker in a *newly made sign*" (7–8, emphasis mine).
**40** The dating of journal entries is recommended by those who write in this area.

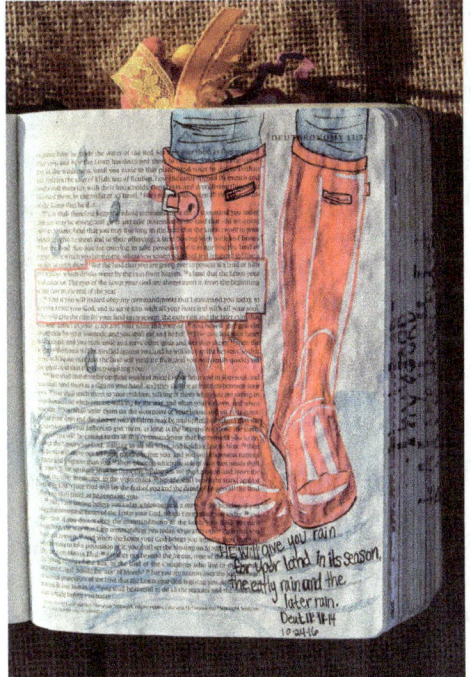

**Fig. 1:** Carol Belleau: *Deut 11:11–14*. With kind permission of the artist.

fora, most notably Pinterest, where she has her artwork on display for others interested in Bible Journalling.[41]

There is a narrowing selection of text operating throughout the page. The text of Deut 11:4–32 appears in the galley of type from top left to bottom right. From this, Deut 11:11–14a has been selected for special attention, surrounded with a bold, red border and further highlighted through the contrast set up with the bright red boot it now appears to overlap. This particular couple of verses is deemed so important it is not painted over – as is the rest of the text in the centre

---

[41] The online sharing of these images raises its own questions about motivations, intentions and privacy. It is repeated vigorously in the books and online fora that no comparison should be entered into at all. There is no competitive element intended and that the online sharing is for mutual enjoyment, inspiration and upliftment. This would be consistent with Bielo's findings of a "collaborative, positive atmosphere" from his observation of Bible study groups, an experience familiar to many, if not most, Bible journallers: "All maintained a good relationship among the members, resulting in a group dynamics that were familiar, amiable, and committed to cooperation. This norm of congeniality does reflect a foundational goal of Bible study – to have a constructive spiritual experience as a group." Bielo, *Words Upon the Word*, 161.

of the page. The red border strongly links the selected text with the red boots and begins the separation and appropriation of this text. Finally, in a further narrowing down, Deut 11:14a, is personally written by hand on the page. It is a quotation taken from the larger text and given special focus. These lines of text are written along, and therefore subtly underlined by, the ripples of water displaced by the boots walking through the rain. A slight change is made to the text by the artist: "he will give *the* rain" becomes "he will give *you* rain."[42] The personal appropriation of the promise made in the text is complete. The promise of rain has literally shifted from the established printed text, the dialogue of Moses with the Israelites in the desert, to the personal life of the reader and artist who has now visually and verbally appropriated this promise of God into her own life and context, here and now.

The scriptural text speaks of the blessing of rain, *"in its season, the early rain and the later rain,"* – both at planting and before harvesting, an ongoing, seasonal blessing. The rain boots strengthen this idea – there will be much rain, puddles; "wellies" will be required. Rain boots are also about comfort in the rain, the rain does not overwhelm, the wearer stays protected and dry in the rain. This is a positive relationship with the rain. The red colour is highly saturated, bright, strong and suggestive of positivity and energy. A link is made between rain and being energised for action. The right foot is slightly raised, indicating movement, a walk or a dance in the rain – the rain is celebrated.

This is an intriguing work of art. A pair of highly salient red rain boots walk through the rain drops plopping around them into puddles on the ground. The viewer is placed up close to the boots, depicted frontally, at the level of the knees, which suggests an intimate and indeed personal experience or appropriation of the legs in the boots. In this way, the viewer is enabled to imagine one's own legs within the boots. There is a high level of engagement facilitated with the shiny boots. There is no perspective or distance or landscape to distract the viewer away from the boots.

There are two primary puddles on the left, a larger and a smaller – perhaps suggestive of the two rains: "early" and "later" mentioned in the text. They appear on the left hand side of the composition, and are closely identified with the scripture passage, layered over the printed text. In visual semiotics, the left hand side of a composition is taken to signify that which is established, or "given", contrasted with the new information or element on the right hand side.

---

[42] This is, in fact, the translation that appears in the NKJV, however, it is not the version that appears on the page here. The NKJV translation of Deut 11:14 is "I will give *you* the rain for your land in its season."

Here, both the biblical text and its visual illustration in the rain is depicted in this "given" position in relation to the receiver of the blessing/rain, wearing the boots on the right, in the "new" position. The promised rain falls and gathers most predominantly over the printed text, the "Word of God," reiterating visually that it is the fulfilment of God's word. These puddles are connected through an "S" shape that spirals around both. Concentric circles ripple outwards, and an underlying spiral dynamism is created through the stronger lines and washes in the painting. The intrinsic symbolic properties of a circular or spiral pattern are indicative of eternity. This is known as a *helical* vector, an "infinity" sign.[43] The rain shall continue; the later rain shall follow the early rain, and this shall repeat and repeat. God's favour has begun and is ongoing. The wearer of the red boots walks in this blessing.

The extremely shallow perspective renders this artwork almost abstract in terms of space and time. The blue, watery wash of the rain fills half the page and appears to run off the edges, as it is free flowing. We are in the "here and now." There is no horizon line, the image bringing us right down to earth and the very immediate area around the boots. The time is this immanent, present moment of raining. It is visually implied, through the strong "S" spiral, that this shall continue. Within the naturalistic coding orientation, the absence of setting lowers modality. In other words, the rain and the boots are treated in a naturalistic way; they are not abstract, yet the absence of a clearly defined environment around them lessens the sense of realism and opens up the possibility of a symbolic interpretation to the rain and boots. The lack of spatial perspective and any context of place imply an interpretation beyond simply the literal meaning. Indeed, this is borne out in the artist's commentary on this work:

> In a spiritual sense my husband and I were ordained as Pastors over the marriage and family ministry at our church in the summer of 2016. That fall we found ourselves praying something similar to this as we were "planting" new "seeds" in our new ministry and asking for God's blessing (rain) over the growth of the ministry and future harvest of restored marriages and families as we tried to serve Him diligently. We want to walk in the direction He is guiding us and in His blessing; feet seemed the appropriate picture as I reflected on this scripture and it's meaning in my life. **The puddles and rain depict His abundant blessing and the red rain boots symbolises our faith to expect and be ready to receive His blessing. You only wear rain boots when you are expecting rain, right?**[44]

The artist's commentary bears out indeed that a rich, personal, metaphorical interpretation has been made; the "land" is their new pastoral ministry, that they

---

43 Kress and van Leeuwen, *Reading Images*, 70–71.
44 Carol Belleau in personal correspondence by email, with kind permission. Emphasis mine.

understand and describe in terms of agricultural metaphors: "planting" and nurturing its growth to the fullness of "harvest". The rain is God's blessing over this work. Neither land, as such (certainly not the "land" referred to in the biblical text) nor their ministry appear in the illustration. The boots symbolise their faith in expectation of God's blessing and their willingness to actively and energetically engage with it. The sense of expectation and immediacy is heightened by the extremely shallow depth and perspective depicted and the viewer's placement right up close to the boots walking in the rain.

The second illumination (Fig. 2) I wish to explore comes from a Dutch Bible-journaller Salomé Vleeming, who uploads her artwork to Instagram, but does not appear to be on Pinterest. It is a good and rare example of a page that moves outside of the personal relationship with God towards those who suffer in the world. This page is labelled "- war in Syria -" (lower left corner) and dated "Jan'18" (lower right corner). The reference "Psalm 112:4" appears under the main lettering element. The biblical text featured extends from Psalm 110:2b to Psalm 112:8. One sentence (112.4) is highlighted, by having an incomplete border, like brackets on either side, placed around the outer edges of the printed verse and no colour wash painted in behind it. It is worth noting that the Bible itself is in Dutch, while the artist has chosen to use English for her designs over the Dutch text. In her descriptor on Instagram, she describes briefly in English and then in Dutch what this journal art is about for her. She also notes in the Dutch explanation that this is her first Bible journalling artwork of 2018, "Mijn eerste pagina van 2018."[45] She writes:

> The LIGHT dawns in the DARKNESS for the upright… i [sic] wanted to do something in my bible with this picture in my head of the war in Syria. So much pain and suffering but in the midst of it all there are people who help and love others, there are children who play like ours… God loves them and He will be with them.[46]

In Dutch she writes: "I had this image in my head for days, but found it difficult to reproduce a picture of war in my Bible."[47] This, along with "My first page of 2018," suggests that this picture may have appeared in the news media around Christmas, a time when a Bible-reader might have been particularly sensitive

---

[45] Salomé Vleeming, "salomebiblejournaling," Instagram post, 9 January 2018, https://www.instagram.com/p/BdvjcZzgqOl/?taken-by=salomebiblejournaling. Salomé Vleeming is a Dutch Bible-journalling artist and may be found on Instagram at Salomebiblejournaling.

[46] Vleeming, "salomebiblejournaling,"https://www.instagram.com/p/BdvjcZzgqOl/?taken-by=salomebiblejournaling. Accessed 6 February 2018.

[47] Vleeming, "salomebiblejournaling,"https://www.instagram.com/p/BdvjcZzgqOl/?taken-by=salomebiblejournaling.

**Fig. 2:** Salomé Vleeming, *Psalm 112:4*. With kind permission of the artist.

to the plight of children, particularly in the Middle East. This is an interesting statement from the artist, reflecting the emotional impact of the original, news-reportage photo upon her, staying with her "for days." Some scholars might find her reluctance to depict an image of war in her Bible a strange and ironic concern considering how much violence and war, often sanctioned or even commanded by God, and indeed in that geographical region, is already present in the text, most especially in the Hebrew Bible.

The font chosen for the words Light and Darkness is a bold, thick, slab-serif letter with a spur (Fig. 3).[48] It has the look of nineteenth century woodcut or hand-stencilled lettering, most readily associated with American pioneer life (cowboy saloons and "Wanted" posters in Westerns). It is also a "display"

---

[48] A slab serif font is characterised by thick, block-like serifs that may be either blunt, angular or rounded. Slab serifs were invented in and most popular during the nineteenth century. A spur is an added serif that projects out horizontally at the midpoint of the height of the letter, or on the curve. Spur slab serif typefaces are also referred to as "Western" typefaces because of their popularity in the US in the nineteenth and early twentieth centuries.

**Fig. 3:** Salomé Vleeming, *Psalm 112:4, detail of lettering.*

typeface that conventionally has only capital letters and is used for large headlines, being unsuitable for body copy. This style of typeface is most frequently referred to as a "Western" typeface. A lawless frontier, populated with ruthless, gun-slinging, trigger-happy "cowboys" (be they soldiers, terrorists or mercenaries) may be implied by the use of this font. In this design, it may be more applicable to the "darkness" than the "light." The grey letters are stickers that contains a polka dot pattern. So within the light grey, in fact further light may be perceived in the white dots. The light grey letters sit on a thin, black, dropped shadow; light on dark, light emerging from darkness – literally.

Two very young children sit amidst a pile of rubble, one has her arm protectively around the shoulder of the other.[49] One child faces out of the picture –

---

[49] The artwork suggests an original photographic reference from news reportage of this conflict. These two little children may be found almost instantly in a Google image search. This is from a UNICEF blog: Rashini Suriyaarachchi, "What if you'd spent your whole life in a war zone?" at https://www.unicef.org.au/blog/stories/march-2016/what-if-youd-spent-your-whole-life-in-a-war-zone. The children are here identified as a little girl, Esraa, 4, and her younger brother,

the other faces away into the distance behind towards a female figure dressed in black, standing in a doorway or on a ledge of a partially collapsed building. The destruction of Syrian cities such as Homs and Aleppo, as brought to us by the media, comes instantly to mind when we see this image. Although not a lot of detail is given, the pile of rubble, the dilapidated building in the distance, and exposed beam, shred of curtain, broken window and crumbling wall all imply the site of recent bombing that has brought down buildings and left peoples' homes without external walls – if they still exist at all. It is an image of chaos and destruction. The figure in the distance may or may not be their mother. Again, we have no way of knowing what social relationships exist between these three figures. The woman appears to stand on a ledge. Possibly, she has no way down to ground level to reach the two little children. Except for this figure, the children are lost and alone, looking anxiously about them, sitting isolated in this devastated city.

The foregrounded boy looks directly out of the centre of the composition at the viewer. He makes eye contact with the viewer and therefore establishes an emotional connection with viewer. Bearing in mind the real-life context of this image, derived from real news coverage of the war in Syria, this may well explain why this image affected the artist and was "in my head for days" – a psychological demand, an emotional connection was established, through the power of the direct gaze, between herself and the little boy in her original viewing of this photograph. The second child engages with the woman in the distance, the only other human being in this picture.

The compositional layout of the various elements in this design are of particular interest. There are three elements worthy of closer consideration. First, the large, vertically diagonal beam on the right. The placement of this beam, leaning against the wall, suggests that the front of the woman's home has been blown away. It also makes it clear that she is not on the ground floor and may herself be stranded in this bombed building. Visually, the beam serves as a divider that separates the children from the woman. It appears they are not physically able to reach one another. Secondly, the beam acts as a vector that connects the last word of the scripture quotation "upright" with the woman. The beam points to the word "upright" and leads the eye to the woman.

Thirdly, the composition is divided up into three clear areas in both horizontal and vertical directions. On the vertical axis, these are: the building overlapping the biblical text; the gap between the buildings; and the buildings in the

---

Waleed, 3, and in Aleppo. The artist has created an original composite image from a selection of media images of the bombing of Aleppo.

distance on the right. A three-way distinction may be observed in the horizontal layout too. The upper third contains the lettering; the middle third, a shred of curtain in front of a horizontal beam; a blank space in the centre; and the buildings with the (almost) silhouetted woman on the right. Finally, the children are in the lower third. This three-way, type of composition sets up zones that recognised as "mediatory", as what happens in the centre mediates between the two outer zones.[50]

The artist has chosen to write her scripture passage in the top third of the composition, referred to in this type of social semiotic analysis as the "heavenly" or divine realm (Fig. 3). She opens her quotation with the word "Light", which she has portrayed with pale grey lettering. Significantly, she has also used the exact same colouring and lettering for the word "Darkness", reiterating the concept carried in the actual meaning of the phrase, "LIGHT dawns in the DARKNESS." The word is spelt "Darkness" but visually it says Light. In this way she shows that the "Light" has literally dawned in the "Darkness", the Darkness is no more, it is now the same as Light. This lettering occurs against a white background with little colour behind it – the lightest area of the page. The white of the paper is largely untouched and also acts as light.

It is not immediately apparent why the journaller chose this particular psalm as it is not a "psalm of lament", nor does it explicitly refer to war, oppression or justice for the innocent victims of such. The psalm recognises that good people may be afflicted and promises God will support and deliver nonetheless. It praises the "upright", and the artist's use of it infers an inclusive understanding of the people depicted as recognised by God as righteous (regardless of their politics). Her choice of and creative rendering of the words "Light" and "Darkness" echo a verse from John's prologue: "The *light shines in the darkness*, and the darkness can never extinguish it" (John 1:5). An intertextual connection is made, I suggest, between this line from Psalm 112:4 and John 1:5a. The "light" is Christ in the latter suggesting that perhaps the reader-artist has intended a Christological inference may also be read in her painting. The psalms are understood as the prayers of believers directed towards God.[51] Here, the use of the psalter, as the ground, the text over which she makes her illustration, relates directly to her personal prayer for these people of Syria and using this text to do so. Apart from a few contemporary details, it is an image that is timeless to many of the conflicts described in the Hebrew Bible – and this deepens its textual resonance in many ways.

---

**50** Kress and van Leeuwen, *Reading Images*, 194–201.
**51** This is an acrostic psalm in the Hebrew but it is not a psalm of lament.

This treatment of a biblical text is unusual in the general body of Bible-journalling art to be found online, as it engages with a major human catastrophe in our time. It looks outward, beyond the self, and reveals a deep compassion for those suffering in the world. The artist has brought the mediated news of the world right into her Bible, committing these particular children and the people of Syria to prayer, placing them "under the word of God," in a literal, but also very moving way. For all it's apparent devastation, it is an image of hope.

## 6 Journalling Sacred Scriptures in Jewish and Islamic Practice

One of the most famous female diarists of all time was, of course, a young Jewish girl: Anne Frank. As it happens, of all the three Abrahamic religions, Judaism is the one with the least apparent take up of the journalling trend at this moment. A search through the online fora of Instagram and Pinterest reveal barely a handful of journallers posting images of their journalled pages.[52] What is certain is that they are not journalling into a material, printed edition of the Torah. There is a small selection of images of scripture passages, being illustrated and "scrapbooked" in blank-page journals – with both English and Hebrew words and verses visible.[53] There is also a growing community of Qur'ān journallers both in the United States and in Great Britain. Again, as is to be expected this journalling happens in separate blank-page journals or diaries and not directly into a printed Qur'ān. These illuminations tend to be text-oriented, as an Arabic Sura is given a beautiful calligraphic treatment with various coloured translations, notes, and reflections written around this featured text. A London-based journaller, Sumayah Hassan, writes of her practice: "All I do is write the date, ayah in Arabic, reference and reflection below that." (Fig. 4).[54]

---

[52] Talia Carbis (@taliamakesart) is one Jewish woman, residing in Brisbane, Australia, who is journalling the Torah and using the hashtag #torahjournaling on her Instagram postings.
[53] An example of the scrapbooking-journal trend within Jewish journalling can be found in the guidebook by Janet Ruth Falon, *The Jewish Journaling Book: How to Use Jewish Tradition to Write Your Life & Explore Your Soul* (Woodstock, VT: Jewish Lights, 2004).
[54] Sumayah Hassan, "What is Quran Journalling? How do you set up your Quran Journal?", November 27, 2016, https://www.recitereflect.com/what-is-quran-journaling/.

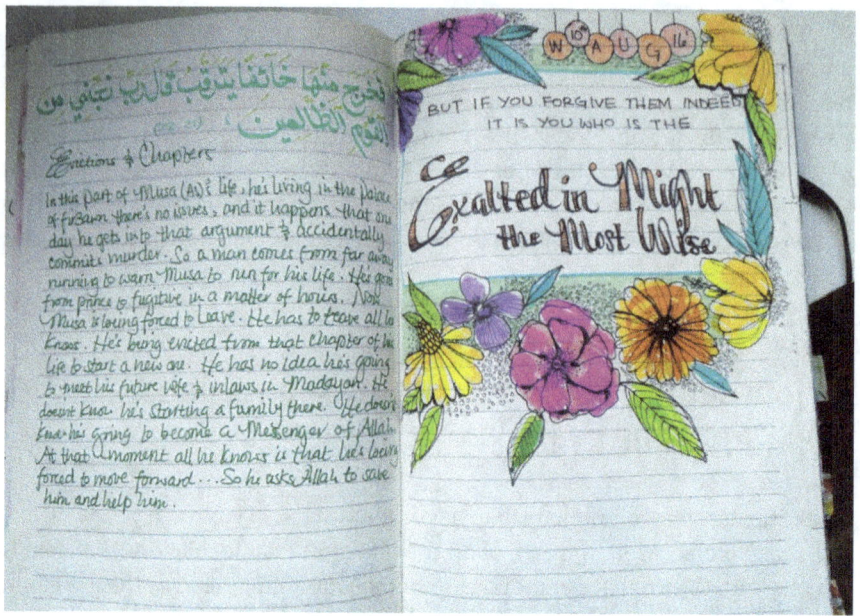

**Fig. 4:** Sumayah Hassan, *A page of a Qur'ān journal featuring Ayah 28 from Surah 21*. With kind permission of the artist.

One US-based designer, Ameenah, is developing graphics that can be bought online, downloaded and printed to adorn journal pages with English words and excerpts from Ayah and Sura.[55] Hassan offers courses and workshops in Qur'ān journalling in London.[56] Her website states the aim of these is to deepen the reader's relationship with the Qur'ān:

> The Recite & Reflect workshops, content, and resources are specifically designed to help people connect with the Quran on a personal level, relate it to their everyday lives and develop themselves through its teachings. To help them ask the right questions, derive lessons and come up with action points, that become the first steps of their journey to being transformed by the Quran.[57]

---

[55] Ameenah, "Quran Journalling: A guide for beginners," https://www.mariampoppins.com/blog/quran-journaling-a-guide-for-beginners. She also has accounts on Instagram at @mariampoppins.

[56] Hassan, "What is Quran Journaling?" She also has accounts on Instagram at @ReciteReflect and @imanillustrated.

[57] Hassan, *Recite & Reflect*, "About" page, https://www.recitereflect.com/about/.

# 7 Conclusion

Far beyond the illustrative nature of medieval illumination where the illumination related to the text it accompanied on the page, what these women are doing is completely unique. They are engaging in a profoundly deep way with the foundational scripture of their faith, this encounter then personally appropriated, creatively interpreted, expressed and embellished, through its material treatment in the iconic artefact of the Bible. This form of journalling invests the Bible with ever greater materiality – a materiality that is now deeply reflective of personal engagement, time, money, energy and prayer spent contemplating the role and place of these sacred scriptures in the reader's life. This new experience and understanding is expressed multimodally, in newly made signs, through the embodied labour of the journaller and with other material substances, paints and textiles, patterns and textures, laid into the printed book. Each Bible journal contains a deeply personal account of a spiritual journey – stretching the spine, adding to its heft – a record in the world, not subject to the vagaries of technological advances and redundancies, it stands as a testament to a personal dialogue with the Word of God.

# Bibliography

Beal, Timothy. *The Rise and Fall of the Bible: The Unexpected History of an Accidental Book.* New York: Houghton Mifflin Harcourt, 2012.

Bielo, James S. *Words Upon the Word, An Ethnography of Evangelical Group Bible Study.* New York: New York University Press, 2009.

Croag Bell, Susan. "Medieval Women Book Owners: Arbiters of Lay Piety and Ambassadors of Culture." In *Women and Power in the Middle Ages*, edited by Mary Erler and Maryanne Kowaleski. Athens, GA: University of Georgia Press, 2004, 149–87.

Dillon, Amanda. "The Book of Kells and the Visual Identity of Ireland." In *Ireland and the Reception of the Bible, Social and Cultural Perspectives*, edited by Bradford A. Anderson and Jonathan Kearney. London: Bloomsbury, 2018, 295–312.

Falon, Janet Ruth. *The Jewish Journaling Book: How to Use Jewish Tradition to Write Your Life & Explore Your Soul.* Woodstock, VT: Jewish Lights, 2004.

Field Belenkey, Mary, et al. *Women's Ways of Knowing: The Development of Self, Voice, and Mind.* New York: Basic Books, 1986.

Fink, Joanne and Regina Yoder. *Complete Guide to Bible Journalling: Creative Techniques to Express Your Faith.* Mount Joy, PA: Fox Chapel, 2017.

Harding, Susan. "Revolve, *the Biblezine*: A Transevangelical Text." In *The Social Life of Scriptures: Cross Cultural Perspectives on Biblicism*, edited by James S. Bielo. 176–193. New Brunswick, NJ: Rutgers University Press, 2009.

Heldke, Lisa M. "Foodmaking as a Thoughtful Practice." In *Cooking, Eating, Thinking: Transformative Philosophies of Food*, edited by D.W. Curtin and L.M. Heldke. 204–29. Bloomington, IN: Indiana University Press, 1992.

Houston, Keith. *The Book: A Cover-to-Cover Exploration of the Most Powerful Object of Our Time.* New York: W.W. Norton, 2016.
Kress, Gunther, and Theo van Leeuwen. *Reading Images: The Grammar of Visual Design,* 2nd ed. London: Routledge, 2006.
Malley, Brian. "Understanding the Bible's Influence." In *The Social Life of Scriptures: Cross Cultural Perspectives on Biblicism*, edited by James S. Bielo. 194–204. New Brunswick, NJ: Rutgers University Press, 2009.
McGuire, Meredith B. "Why Bodies Matter: A Sociological Reflection on Spirituality and Materiality." *Spiritus: A Journal of Christian Spirituality* 3/1 (2003): 1–18.
New, Jennifer. *Drawing from Life: The Journal as Art.* New York: Princeton Architectural Press, 2005.
Schiwy, Marlene A. *A Voice of Her Own: Women and the Journal Writing Journey.* New York: Simon and Schuster, 1996.
Siker, Jeffrey S. *Liquid Scripture: The Bible in a Digital World.* Minneapolis, MN: Fortress, 2017.
Slee, Nicola. *Women's Faith Development.* Aldershot: Ashgate, 2004.
Valters Paintner, Christine. *Lectio Divina: The Sacred Art.* London: SPCK, 2012.
Yawn Bonghi, Lila. "Medieval Women Artists and Modem Historians." In *Medieval Feminist Newsletter* 12/1 (1991): 10–19.

## Webography

Ameenah, "Quran Journalling: A guide for beginners." *https://www.mariampoppins.com/blog/quran-journaling-a-guide-for-beginners*.
"Bible Bestsellers, Best of 2016." Compiled and distributed by the
Evangelical Christian Publishers Association (ECPA). *http://christianbookexpo.com/bestseller/bibles.php?id=BO16*.
"Bible Bestsellers, Best of 2017." Compiled and distributed by the
Evangelical Christian Publishers Association (ECPA). *http://christianbookexpo.com/bestseller/bibles.php?id=BO17#*.
"Bible Journaling: Bibles, Journals, Devotional Kits, Supplies." https://www.dayspring.com/bible-journaling.
Hassan, Sumayah. "What is Quran Journaling? How do you set up your Quran Journal?" November 27, 2016. *https://www.recitereflect.com/what-is-quran-journaling/*.
"Inspire Bible NLT: The Bible for Coloring & Creative Journaling." *https://www.tyndale.com/p/inspire-bible-nlt/9781496413734*.
Neff, Jack. "Scrapbooking Gets Reinvented to Suit New Digital Reality," 25 July 2011. *http://adage.com/article/news/scrapbooking-reinvented-suit-digital-reality/228856/*.
Noel, Shanna. "Our Story." *https://www.illustratedfaith.com/our-story/*.
Noel, Shanna. "Shop." *https://www.illustratedfaith.com/shop/*.
Suriyaarachchi, Rashini. "What if you'd spent your whole life in a war zone?" 21 March 2016. *https://www.unicef.org.au/blog/stories/march-2016/what-if-youd-spent-your-whole-life-in-a-war-zone*.
Vleeming, Salomé. "Salomebiblejournaling." 9 January 2018. *https://www.instagram.com/p/BdvjcZzgqOl/?taken-by=salomebiblejournaling*.

## II Sacred Texts and the Digital Turn

Garrick V. Allen
# Monks, Manuscripts, Muhammad, and Digital Editions of the New Testament

Reaching back to the mythic world of the Library of Alexandria, editors have honed the skills associated with creating editions of texts preserved in various documentary sources, focusing largely on works of literature that are of value to bookish circles (both ancient and modern) and central to the production of culture. These include the Bible (which has become one of the most contentiously edited traditions since the advent of print), the literature of classical antiquity, and other important vernacular works like Shakespeare, the *Song of Roland*, and Dante's *Inferno* among many others.[1] Critical editions represent and weigh the variety of documents that comprise culturally or academically interesting works of literary art; they are powerful cultural machines that negotiate and condense individualities of the documentary sources of a literary tradition into a textual narrative.[2] As such they remain central to the humanities and biblical studies in particular, forcefully shaping forms of scholarly engagement.

The modern editorial process, however, has been fine-tuned in the context of print culture, which is potentially problematic when the object of study is non-typographic. The reliance on print technologies also leads to a necessary selectivity in the presentation of material, a selectivity constrained both by the pragmatics of presentation, and also by editorial choice, curating the breadth of the tradition in an effort to transmit only its salient features. Editions shape perceptions of the works they represent, but they are not immune to the social and technological pressures of the context of their own making. Their representations are shaped by the economics of bookspace and the history of editorial praxis, forces that create a necessary abstraction that distils the relevant portions of a documentary tradition that serves a foundation higher order interpretive activities.

---

**1** For an overview of textual scholarship from antiquity, cf. David Greetham, "A History of Textual Scholarship," in *The Cambridge Companion to Textual Scholarship*, ed. N. Fraistat and J. Flanders (Cambridge: Cambridge University Press, 2013): 17–41. On trends in vernacular editing see Bernard Cerquiglini, *In Praise of the Variant: A Critical History of Philology*, trans. B. Wing (Baltimore: The Johns Hopkins University Press, 1999), esp. 72–82 for his prescient anticipation of the digital edition.
**2** Cf. Jerome McGann, *Radiant Textuality: Literature after the World Wide Web* (New York: Palgrave Macmillan, 2001), 53–97 for an articulation of the prowess and restrictions of the classic critical edition and editorial theory and McGann, *A New Republic of Letters: Memory and Scholarship in the Age of Digital Reproduction* (London: Harvard University Press, 2014).

∂ Open Access. © 2020 Garrick V. Allen, published by De Gruyter. This work is licensed under a Creative Commons Attribution-NonCommercial-NoDerivatives 4.0 International License.
https://doi.org/10.1515/9783110634440-009

When we edit, we create for ourselves pictures of great detail, but not comprehensive representations; key parts of the traditions that we edit become inaccessible in the process.

A notable consequence of editorial practice is that modern print editions of the New Testament, even the new *editio critica maior* (ECM), fundamentally divorce texts from the manuscript artefacts that transmit them, creating a situation in which the works of the New Testament are further abstracted from their material contexts.³ Practically, this means that essential characteristics of non-typographic traditions like segmenting, format, paratexts, marginalia, corrections, diachronic production layers, commentaries and catenae are rarely represented in critical editions in ways that do justice to their diversity and expressive value. These items and others comprise an artefact's bibliographic code, features that fundamentally influence the processes of reading and cognition. Most critical editions of the New Testament are purely *textual* abstractions.

But what happens when the medium and functionalities of the critical edition change? The ECM projects, of which the fascicles of Acts and the Catholic Epistles have appeared,⁴ have also facilitated the development of *digital* editions. For example, a digital edition of Acts was recently launched that reconnects text to manuscripts by providing hyperlinks in the apparatus to corresponding images, transcriptions, and metadata, although the platform is currently designed only for research experimentation and is not yet fully vetted or developed in terms of data or interface.⁵ The ongoing production of the ECM offers a distinctive opportunity to theorise the future of the critical edition of the New Testament since its digital form is still in production and because the fascicle for the book of Revelation will be a "born digital" edition. The media of critical editions is in a state of flux.

In response to these impending fundamental changes to editions of the New Testament this discussion argues that digital editions open unexpected critical avenues when they integrate a critically constructed text with the material

---

**3** This principle is codified in the text-genetic method used in evaluating variation units for the ECM editions called the Coherence-Based Genealogical Method. Cf. Gerd Mink, "Contamination, Coherence, and Coincidence in Textual Transmission," in *The Textual History of the Greek New Testament: Changing Views in Contemporary Research*, ed. K. Wachtel and M.W. Holmes (Atlanta: Society of Biblical Literature, 2011): 141–216 (here 146). On the CBGM, cf. Tommy Wasserman and Peter J. Gurry, *A New Approach to Textual Criticism: An Introduction to the Coherence-Based Genealogical Method* (Atlanta: Society of Biblical Literature, 2017).
**4** B. Aland et al., eds., *Novum Testamentum Graecum Editio Critica Maior IV. Die Katholischen Briefe*, 2nd ed. (Stuttgart: DBG, 2011); H. Strutwolf et al., eds., *Novum Testamentum Graecum Editio Critica Maior III. Die Apostelgeschichte* (Stuttgart: DBG, 2017).
**5** Available at http://ntvmr.uni-muenster.de/nt-transcripts.

artefacts. To illustrate this point in a concise way, I explore the expressive features of the manuscripts of Revelation that comment on the number of the beast and its significance (Rev 13:18), one of the most exegetically contentious texts in the Apocalypse and a text of considerable interest in the history of interpretation. Forty-eight of Revelation's 310 Greek manuscripts[6] contain marginal notes in connection to Rev 13:18 that decode the wordplay embedded in the text, usually drawing from traditional sources like Irenaeus, Hippolytus, Oecumenius, or Andrew of Caesarea, but also upon entrenched cultural anxieties that manifest as anti-Islamic sentiment in the face of Ottoman hegemony in the medieval and early modern periods (see appendix).

These marginal traditions, always omitted from critical editions, are important because they contextualise the relationship between Revelation's textual history and reception history, providing unanticipated information that informs discussions on monastic textual cultures, channels of transmission of ancient interpretive traditions, and the eschatological politics of religious tension and cultural subservience. Digital editions provide the opportunity for researchers to reconnect the expressive and paratextual features of manuscripts with their textual characteristics, creating editions that are not necessarily organized around the idea of the "original" text of the author[7] or "initial" text,[8] but around a more decentralized conception of representing the tradition writ large. Instead of scanning diligently through every image of every manuscript, users of a curated

---

[6] This number does not include commentary manuscripts, marginal notes like those in GA 522 (Oxford, Bodleian, Canon gr. 34), which simply decodes the number abbreviations in 13:18 and 14:11 in Arabic numerals, or now-illegible or tachygraphic marginal notes like those in the margins of catena manuscripts like GA 919 1617 1746 and 2669 that likely also comment on the passage. Other manuscripts, like GA 2046 and 2069, appear to preserve marginal comments, but they simply represent the insertion of Andrew of Caesarea *kephalaia* titles by a later hand, while 2031 simply repeats that "the number of the beast is χξϛ." For a recent overview of Revelation's manuscript tradition, cf. Markus Lembke, "Beobachtungen zu den Handschriften der Apokalypse des Johannes," in *Die Johannesoffenbarung: Ihr Text und ihre Auslegung*, ed. M. Labahn and M. Karrer (Leipzig: Evangelische Verlagsanstalt, 2012): 19–69.

[7] Cf. D.C. Parker, *Textual Scholarship and the Making of the New Testament* (Oxford: Oxford University Press, 2012), 26–29 for a critical evaluation of this approach, which he calls the "authorial fallacy." So also Kathryn Sutherland, "Anglo-American Editorial Theory," in *The Cambridge Companion to Textual Scholarship*, ed. N. Fraistat and J. Flanders (Cambridge: Cambridge University Press, 2013): 57–58; Ronald Hendel, *Steps to a New Edition of the Hebrew Bible* (Atlanta: Society of Biblical Literature, 2016), 271–95.

[8] Holger Strutwolf, "Original Text and Textual History," in *The Textual History of the Greek New Testament: Changing Views in Contemporary Research*, ed. K. Wachtel and M.W. Holmes (Atlanta: Society of Biblical Literature, 2011): 23–41. Cf. more generally E.J. Epp, "The Multivalence of the Term 'Original' Text in New Testament Textual Criticism," *HTR* 92 (1999): 245–81.

digital edition will be able to access the data through a single hyperlink and perceive the innate interrelationships between text and artefact, form and content. This conception of the critical edition views biblical manuscripts as embodied textual objects where the relationship between form and content is inextricable. If the move from print to digital formats is indeed as significant as the shift to print from manuscripts or from roll to codex,[9] then we are only beginning to imagine what the editions of the future can do.

In essence, the following discussion explores the consequences of editing in an age where "original" texts are no longer the express aim of editorial praxis, where editions are no longer proscribed by the modalities of print, and where scholarly attention is returning a philological sensibility that recognised in inherent material value of every witness of a given tradition. Digital editions offer unique pathways to information not prioritised by classic print editions, information that enhances the analysis of the work from both historical-critical and reception-historical perspectives. Analysing Rev 13:18 illustrates the connectivity between text, manuscript, and editions, underscoring the complexity of the New Testament as a diverse aggregate.[10] The questions raised in this analysis are particularly pressing in an era where biblical scholars continue to negotiate the dual imperatives of print and digital culture, an ongoing negotiation that has led to a renewed examination of the ways that media influences message and the ways bibliographic and non-typographic forms are expressive parts of the tradition.

Throughout this discussion we should keep in mind, however, that digital editions are not *prima facie* better or more complex than classic print editions. Digital and print are complimentary mediums structured by a desire to retain our cultural inheritances, and critical editions are among the most complex and powerful progeny of print culture.[11] This examination is about theorizing how digital editions can provide both the textual acumen of classic editions and necessary access to digital and edited forms of the documents that stand behind these editions. As Jerome McGann has eloquently argued,

> digitizing the archive is not about replacing it. It's about making it usable for the present and the future. To do that we have to understand, as best we can, how it functioned – how it made meanings – in the past. A major task lying before us – its technical difficulties are

---

**9** Greetham, "History," 39.
**10** Cf. Neil Fraistat and Julia Flanders, "Introduction to Textual Scholarship in the Age of Media Consciousness," in *The Cambridge Companion to Textual Scholarship*, ed. N. Fraistat and J. Flanders (Cambridge: Cambridge University Press, 2013): 1–15 which emphasises the interrelatedness of material culture and textual scholarship, a relationship that is becoming more tangible in the digital age.
**11** McGann, *Radiant Textuality*, 168–72.

great – is to design a knowledge and information network that integrates, as seamlessly as possible, our paper-based inheritance with the emerging archive of born-digital material.[12]

Before the editorial and technical work on a comprehensive set of digital editions of the New Testament is complete – and I think that this is the task of the next generation of editors – I want to imagine one possible nexus of scholarship that the edition of the future will stimulate: the dynamic relationship between reception history and the materiality of manuscripts.[13] We are currently situated in a time of convergence between two great cultural mechanisms of print and digital culture that the following examples help us negotiate.

# 1 The Number of the Beast in Text, Tradition, and Nestle-Aland[28]

Before approaching the manuscripts, we need to see the larger narrative of which Rev 13:18 is an integral part and better understand how the Nestle-Aland editions have influenced this text's interpretation. Revelation 13 introduces us to the sea beast who has "ten horns and seven heads, and on his horns are ten crowns and on his heads are blasphemous names," "appearing like a leopard and his feet like a bear and his mouth like the mouth of lion" (13:1–2). The beast is given authority and a throne by the red dragon whose assault on the heavenly woman and her offspring in chapter 12 fails, pursuing her until the earth comes to her aid by swallowing up the water that the dragon disgorges. The vision is all the more marvellous since one of the beast's heads has been healed of a mortal wound (a direct comparison to the slain-but-standing lamb in 5:6–8); the whole world marvels at and worships the beast, who blasphemes with his mouth, and takes authority for forty-two months over every tribe, tongue, and nation (13:3–8). The author then steps out of the vision report, offering a word of patient endurance for the saints (13:10).

As if this beast was not menacing enough, a beast arises out of the earth in 13:11 with a similar profile: it has two horns, is zoomorphic (lamb-like), and speaks like a dragon. It is the inimical equivalent of the lamb who receives worship in the heavenly court in chapter 5, its serpentine features connecting it to the red dragon from chapter 12. The cosmic topography of Revelation's protagonists

---

[12] McGann, *A New Republic of Letters*, 22.
[13] As an example of this dynamic in biblical studies, cf. Brennan W. Breed, *Nomadic Text: A Theory of Biblical Reception History* (Bloomington: Indiana University Press, 2014).

and antagonists is complex and interconnected. The land beast reinforces the worship of the sea beast by performing signs, by making fire fall from heaven (13:12–13). It propagandizes for the sea beast, leading humans astray, compelling them to make cultic idols of the sea beast with the miraculously healed head. The land beast is given authority to give voice to the image of the beast, allowing it to speak. Those who do not worship the sea beast are annihilated, and the land beast forces all to take a mark on their right hand or forehead in order to partake in economic activity. The mark of this beast is "the name of the beast or the number of its name" (τὸ χάραγμα τὸ ὄνομα τοῦ θηρίου ἢ τὸν ἀριθμὸν τοῦ ὀνόματος αὐτοῦ; 13:17).

How does the seer then want the reader to decode this cipher? He makes an esoteric identification in 13:18 that actively initiates the hearers in the process of comprehension: "This is a call for wisdom (Ὧδε ἡ σοφία ἐστίν): Let the one who has understanding calculate the number of the beast, for it is the number of a man [or: a human number; cf. Rev 21:17], and his number is 666" (cf. 17:9–11; *Sib. Or.* 5:28–29, 33–34). The number of the beast has been decoded in many ways, the most prevalent of which in modern scholarship is to understand it as a cipher for "Nero Caesar" based on the numeric value of transliterated Hebrew graphemes: קסר נרון.[14] This solution has a certain historical verisimilitude since Suetonius also records instances of bi-lingual (Latin-Greek) coded wordplay that circulated in regard to Nero's despatching of his mother (*Nero* 39.2). Regardless of identification, the text seeks the active participation of the reader, but the fundamental problem of textual variation makes the parameters of this event even more uncertain.

As we read the passage in Nestle-Aland[28], we notice that the number at the end of the verse – ἑξακόσιοι ἑξήκοντα ἕξ – have angled brackets, denoting that the formulation is not entirely stable in the tradition. Based on the material in the apparatus, a collation of the reading looks like this[15]:

---

**14** For the range of possibilities, cf. D.E. Aune, *Revelation*, WBC 52b, 3 vols. (Nashville: Thomas Nelson, 1998), 2.770–73 and Craig Koester, *Revelation*, AYB 38A (London: Yale University Press, 2014), 596–99; G.K. Beale, *The Book of Revelation*, NIGTC (Grand Rapids: Eerdmans, 1999), 718–28. Cf. also Jan Dochhorn, *Schriftgelehrte Prophetie: Der eschatologische Teufelsfall in Apc Joh 12 und seine Beudeutung für das Verständnis der Johannesoffenbarung*, WUNT 268 (Tübingen: Mohr Siebeck, 2010), 109–21, who argues forcefully that the sea beast should be identified with Nero; and Jan Willem van Henten, "Dragon Myth and Imperial Ideology in Revelation 12–13," in *The Reality of Apocalypse: Rhetoric and Politics in the Book of Revelation*, ed. D.L. Barr (Atlanta: Society of Biblical Literature, 2006): 181–203.
**15** In addition to the list H.C. Hoskier, *Concerning the Text of the Apocalypse*, 2 vols. (London: Quaritch, 1929) offers some additional readings: 660 in GA 582 (εξακοσια εξηκοντα) and a number of other abbreviations, many of which are scribal errors (2.364–265). Cf. also M. Lembke et al., eds.

ἑξακόσιοι ἑξήκοντα ἕξ (χξς) A P⁴⁷ 046 051 1611 2329 2377 Ir Hipp] εξακοσιαι εξηκοντα εξ ℵ ||
εξακοσιαι δεκα εξ (χις) P¹¹⁵ C Ir^mss || εξακοσια εξηκοντα πεντε 2344 || εξακοσια εξηκοντα εξ P
1006 1841 1854 2053^vid

The apparatus indicates the existence of two major readings: 666 (including two sub-readings) and 616, which is preserved in only a few, but weighty witnesses. 665 is also preserved as a singular reading in GA 2344. The variation is central to the understanding of the passage, since the audience is asked to decode the beast narrative based on their knowledge of paranomastic practices, the world in which they live, and their ability to do basic arithmetic. The word play is the bridge between the text and their world or at least their world as the author perceives it.

Modern scholarship has approached this problem in one of two ways. First, some have simply asserted that one of the numbers, usually 666, is original and therefore the authentic arbiter of the tradition.[16] This perspective suffers on a number of issues. Not only is the concept of "original reading" problematic, but the variant 616 is ancient, preserved in P¹¹⁵, Codex Ephraemi Rescriptus (C), and other witnesses.[17] Irenaeus is also aware of the variant 616, even though he refers to it as an error and places the blame at the feet of copyists who were confused by the forms of abbreviation (χις and χξς; *Adv. Haer.* 5.30.1–3). For Irenaeus, using 616 to calculate the name of the beast (which he equates with the antichrist) is heretical (5.30.2). The earliest layers of interpretation identify the beast not as the menacing power of the Roman religious, political, and economic systems,[18] but as an eschatological adversary, an idea carried into the commentaries of Oecumenius and Andrew of Caesarea.[19]

---

*Text und Textwert der griechischen Handschriften des Neuen Testaments. VI. Die Apokalypse*, ANTF 49 (Berlin: de Gruyter, 2017), 130–33 (hereafter *TuT*).

16 Also cf. D.C. Parker, "A New Oxyrhyncus Papyri of Revelation: P115 (P. Oxy. 4499)," *NTS* 46 (2000): 159–74 who expresses doubts about the certainty of 666 as the initial reading.

17 Other sources also preserve 616; for example, the *Liber Genealogus* (CPL 2254). For a fuller rehearsal of the versional data, cf. J. Neville Birdsall, "Irenaeus and the Number of the Beast: Revelation 13,18," in *New Testament Textual Criticism and Exegesis: Festschrift J. Delobel*, ed. A. Denaux (Leuven: Peeters, 2002): 349–59. On the reading in P115 specifically, cf. Zachary J. Cole, *Numerals in Early Greek New Testament Manuscripts: Text-Critical, Scribal, and Theological Studies*, NTTSD 53 (Leiden: Brill, 2017), 64–65, 192–94; Peter J. Williams, "P¹¹⁵ and the Number of the Beast," *TynBul* 58 (2007): 151–53, who argues that the abbreviation for 616 (χιϲ) was created to produce a greater graphic similarity between the number and the *nomina sacra* for Christ (χϲ) or Jesus (ιϲ).

18 So Koester, *Revelation*, 599–601 and many others.

19 The name of *kephalaia* that comment on Rev 13:18 also identifies the figure as an antichrist (περὶ τοῦ ὀνόματος τοῦ ἀντιχρίστου). On Oecumenius' treatment of numbers, cf. Pieter G.R. de Villiers, "Numerical Symbolism in Oecumenius's Commentary on Revelation," in *Tot sacra-*

Another approach has been to argue that the variant is the result of the process of decoding itself, especially when transliteration into Hebrew forms an integral part of the process. In this case, 616 was introduced into the tradition because a more Latinizing form of "Nero Caesar" was transliterated into Hebrew as קסר נרו without the final nun (616 = ר = 200; ו = 6; נ = 50; ק = 100; ס = 60; ר = 200). This network of word play is all the more interesting since the word θηρίον ("beast"; cf. 13:1), when transliterated to Hebrew (תריון), also adds to 666.[20]

The data in the apparatus of Nestle-Aland[28] proves invaluable in assessing the tradition, offering a healthy number of variants, even singular readings and morphological deviations. The editors realised that the wording of the tradition in this unit would be of great interest because it has direct exegetical consequence for how historical-critical exegetes reconstruct the world which the Apocalypse was designed to address, in addition to the fact that the identification of a historical figure might help date the production of the work. The edition provides fruitful grounds for historical-critical discussion.

But it does not offer a deeper level of access to the tradition. Interest in the name of the beast extends back to the earliest commentators as I mentioned above, interest that has shaped all pre-critical engagement with this passage. For example, Irenaeus offers three Greek names whose graphemes equate to 666 (ΕΥΑΝΘΑΣ, ΛΑΤΕΙΝΟΣ, and ΤΕΙΤΑΝ) in an effort to quell unrestrained interest. Neither ΕΥΑΝΘΑΣ nor ΤΕΙΤΑΝ are the names of rulers, although ΛΑΤΕΙΝΟΣ might be of interest since it corresponds to the fourth kingdom in Daniel 7, since the Latins (= Rome) are currently ruling (*Adv. Haer.* 5.30.3; cf. Hippolytus *De Ant.* 50). This name also carried special significance in the later Byzantine empire. In spite of the surfeit of information in the apparatus, the hand edition barely scratches the surface of other information that lurks in Revelation's manuscript witnesses and history of interpretation. To understand more fully the way that the manuscript tradition of the Apocalypse received its own text in conversation with the broader tradition, we need to examine further every witness of the book of Revelation that preserve marginal comments or paratextual emphasis on Rev 13:18 to see how the expressive features of these forms speak to the practices of interpretation active in the contexts in which they were produced and read.

The manuscripts that preserve marginal comments can be grouped into three traditional streams, although there are obvious overlaps between them and

---

*menta quot verba: Zur Kommentierung der Apokalypse des Johannes von den Anfängen bis ins 12. Jahrhundert*, ed. K. Huber, R. Klotz, and C. Winterer (Münster: Aschendorf, 2014): 135–52.
**20** Cf. Aune, *Revelation*, 2:769.

variations internal to each. None of these witnesses are particularly venerable in terms of their text and all are medieval or early modern, but they comprise an important group that arbitrates interpretive information on a difficult passage.

## 2 Irenaeus Traditions

As the earliest known commentator on Rev 13:18, Irenaeus' influence is visible across each of these other streams that transmit marginal comments. However, only two manuscripts explicitly point to Irenaeus as their traditional source. GA 1859 (Athos, Kutlumusiu 82; fourteenth century)[21] preserves a conventional form of the text of Rev 13:18. More interesting is the note that appears at the lower margin that is connected to 13:18 via matching supralinear glyphs located above ὁ ἀριθμὸς αὐτοῦ and in the lower margin (135v). The text of the note, reads:

> Εστι δε η ερμενεια του οναματος του θηριου . ευανθας . Τουτο δε ειρηκεν ειρηναιος επισκοπος λουγδοων γαλλιας
>
> And here is the interpretation of the name of the beast: Euanthas, because this was explained by Irenaeus Bishop of Lugdunum in Gaul

The note, included by the initial copyist of the manuscript, identifies the name of the beast as Euanthas ("blossoming," from εὐάνθητος or εὐανθία), a name whose Greek graphemes equate to 666 when assigned numeric values. By making explicit its connection to Irenaeus, the note demonstrates the influence of this tradition as a perduring and authoritative intertext for Rev 13:18. Furthermore, it is interesting that the note keys on Euanthas because Irenaeus himself notes that "for the name Evanthas contains the required number, but I make no allegation regarding it" (sed nihil de eo affirmamus). Instead, Irenaeus prefers Titan (TEITAN) because of its ancient pedigree, royal dignity, and tyrannical implicature, although he demurs at identifying the antichrist's name with certainty (*Adv. Haer.* 5.30.3).

The note in 1859 is valuable insofar as it mediates between the interpretation of the Apocalypse and the interpretation of Irenaeus in the Middle Ages (although it does not betray a close reading of Irenaeus) and interest in decoding the name of the beast, who by this time did not represent a Roman emperor of old, but an eschatological figure yet to come. For good reason the editors of Nestle-Aland[28] omitted this material: it does not quote the text of the Apocalypse, it is an idiosyn-

---

[21] Cf. Spyr. P. Lambros, *Catalogue of the Greek Manuscripts on Mount Athos* (Cambridge: Cambridge University Press, 1895), 1:281 (3151).

cratic witness to Irenaeus, and it is preserved in a late copy that is not textually interesting enough to be utilised as a "consistently cited witness." 1859 corresponds closely to the *Koine* text form,[22] one of Revelation's two Byzantine textual traditions.

The same holds for GA 2027 (Paris, BnF, gr. 491, thirteenth century) whose text is also closely aligned with the *Koine* tradition (Fig. 1). This witness preserves an identical note to the one in 1859, added into the right margin by a later hand who also made selective comments on other texts.

**Fig. 1:** *GA 2027 (Paris, BnF, gr. 491), Comment on Rev 13:18 (289r).* With permission of the Bibliothèque national de France.

Neither 1859 or 2027 boast extended commentary or catena apparatuses and the identity of the beast receives special attention, decoding the name by appeal to one of Irenaeus' possible options. Despite the lack of textual importance of these witnesses, they remain valuable for those interested in the reception of Irenaeus or in the interpretive history of Rev 13:18. Beside combing through digitised images of every manuscript and out-of-print philological works, how else is one to access this material? What other reservoir of information might archive such a scribal note? The answer that I will inevitably give is the digital edition, but there is more material to examine first.

## 3 Oecumenius and Andrew of Caesarea Traditions

The most prevalent form of paratextual comment on Rev 13:18 is closely related to the commentary tradition of Oecumenius, which was adopted and further devel-

---

22 *TuT*, 553.

oped by Andrew of Caesarea in the late sixth or early seventh century. These comments are located in thirty-two manuscripts and fall into three main categories. The first and largest body are excerpts taken directly from the Andrew of Caesarea commentary, although they often differ in their wording, reflecting the high level of textual variation within the Andrew text.[23] For example, take GA 1732 (Athos, Lavra, A 91; copied in 1384; Fig. 2), which preserves the following notation in the lower margin[24]:

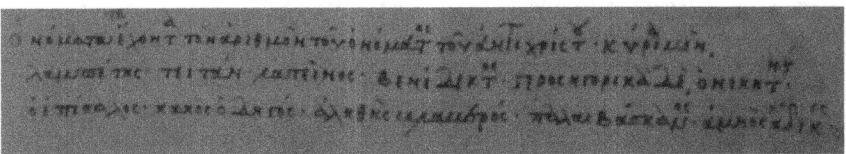

**Fig. 2:** *GA 1732 (Athos, Lavra, A 91) comment on Rev 13:18* (detail, lower margin). Public Domain: Library of Congress Collection of Manuscripts from the Monasteries of Mt. Athos.

Ονοματα ᵗᵃ εχοντα τον αριθμον του ονομοτος του αντιχριστου. κυρια μεν, λαμπετης.[25] τειταν . λατεινος . βενεδικτος . προσηγορικα δε, ο νικητης . ο επισαλος . κακος οδηγος . αληθης βλαβερος . παλαι βασκανος . αμνος αδικος

Names of those that have the number of the name of the antichrist: First, proper nouns: Lampetis, Titon, Lateinos, Benedict. Second, common nouns: The Conqueror; the Rough One; Wicked Guide; True Harm; Ancient Slanderer;[26] Unjust Lamb.

This text extracts all the possible formulations that add to 666 offered by Andrew in the same serial arrangement, with the added addition of ὁ ἐπίσαλος (Rough

---

**23** Cf. the apparatus of J. Schmid's edition *Studien zur Geschichte des griechischen Apokalypse-Textes* (Munich: Karl Zink, 1955), 144–46. On the interpretation of the Andrew commentary, cf. Juan Hernández, Jr., "Andrew of Caesarea and His Reading of Revelation: Cathechesis and Paranesis," in *Die Johannesapokalypse: Kontexte – Konzepte – Rezeption*, WUNT 287, ed. J. Frey, J.A. Kelhoffer, and F. Tóth (Tübingen: Mohr Siebeck, 2012), 755–74; Eugenia Scarvelis Constantinou, *Guiding to a Blessed End: Andrew of Caesarea and his Apocalypse Commentary in the Ancient Church* (Washington, D.C.: The Catholic University of America Press, 2013); Georg Kretschmar, *Die Offenbarung des Johannes: Die Geschichte ihrer Auslegung im 1. Jahrtausend* (Stuttgart: Calwer, 1985), 80–90.
**24** GA 325 2059 2259 retain nearly identical texts in their notes.
**25** The word totals 666 if spelled λαμπετις.
**26** Cf. *Mart. Pol.* 17:1, where the "envious Evil One" (βάσκανος πονηρός) steals Polycarp's body after his immolation.

One), which is found in Oecumenius.²⁷ There are multiple interesting features of this note that shed further light on the reception history of the passage, features that are routinely omitted from critical editions for a host of legitimate reasons. First, the scribe responsible for this note identifies the beast as the antichrist, the eschatological foil of the lamb, following traditional precursors like Irenaeus and Hippolytus. The antithetical parallelism between the beast and the lamb (cf. Rev 5:5–7) is further amplified by the final name in this list, Unjust Lamb, indicating that the tradition here is aware of the broader contours of Revelation's narrative and use of antithetical characters.²⁸

While the sum of the names taken from the Andrew commentary equate exactly to 666, the scribe is not so fastidious in his arithmetic and/or copying. All of the names as copied are within the ballpark of 666, but many are divergent. For example, the graphemes of κακος οδηλος (Wicked Guide) amount to 693, but if οδηλος is corrected to οδηγος, the equivalence to 666 is restored. This mathematical digression suggests that the scribe did not necessarily understand the principles of the inherited tradition.

This exemplar emphasises the importance of Rev 13:18 as a location of intense exegetical activity. The material layout of the leaf points in this direction through the presence of paratextual markers (heavy dots) that bracket the verse in the text and the marginal notation, both of which cannot easily be embedded in conventional print editions. Additionally, both of these features are not expressly textual insofar as they implicitly interpret the text of Rev 13:18 without functioning as witnesses to the text themselves, only to traditions of interpretation.

A second subsection of the commentary stream is represented by witnesses that simply list the proper names listed in the Andrew commentary, and sometimes other traditions. These lack explicit attribution and the relationship between them and the text is assumed. For example, GA 1865 (Athos, Philotheu 38, thirteenth century), a witness to Revelation's Complutensian textual traditions, preserves the four proper names in the Andrew commentary²⁹:

---

**27** The Oecumenius tradition also adds ὁ νικητής (the Conqueror) as an option. Cf. Marc de Groote, ed. *Oecumenii Commentarius in Apocalypsin*, TEG 8 (Leuven: Peters, 1999), 192–93. Cf. also Andrew's similar list of names ascribed to Jesus in his commentary of Rev 19:12b (*keph*. 58), although these names are not paranomastic or tied to the numerical value of Greek graphemes.
**28** For more on antithetical characters, cf. Richard Bauckham, *The Climax of Prophecy: Studies on the Book of Revelation* (Edinburgh: T&T Clark, 1993), 174–98.
**29** Identical traditions appear in GA 1768 and 2723, and other manuscripts contain only single names from this list" GA 2201 (τειταν); 1854 (λατεινος); 2821 (λαμπετις).

λαμπετης³⁰:
τειταν:
λατεινος:
βενεδικτος:

Lampetis
Titan
Latin
Benedict

These four names, the graphemes of which (with the exception of the uncorrected form of λαμπετης, "Arsonist") add up to 666, are also part of the list of names in 1732 and it incorporates two of the three names that Irenaeus mentions in *Adv. Haer.* 5.30.3. But other lists preserve other proper names. The list in the lower-right margin of GA 468 (Paris, BnF gr. 101, thirteenth century) lists five names, including two not mentioned 1865: περσαιος, whose graphemes only add to 656, and the Irenaen ευανθας, along with τειταν, λατεινος, and βενεδικτος. GA 1685 (Athens, Byz. Mus. 155), a manuscript with a handful of marginal scholia, adds other proper names not yet found in other witnesses, including ευινας ("of stout fibres;" "strongly built"), χαιεν (666),³¹ and σαρμεναιος (677),³² names that do not correspond to any known commentary on Revelation. It seems that the tradition inaugurated by Irenaeus of using the numerical value of Greek graphemes to determine the identity of the beast continued, sparking imaginative engagement with the text that led to creation of additional onomastic options, even if their meanings remain obscure.

But the lists expand further, drawing on the material in the Andrew commentary, both the proper names and adjectival formulations, as well as other sources. GA 2073 (Athos, Iviron, 273; copied in 1316) is a copy of the Andrew commentary, copied on 157 leaves, attached to a copy of a work by John Chrysostom (Fig. 3). It contains some additions and marginal comments from other sources, including Irenaeus, Hippolytus, and the Oecumenius commentary.³³ Among these include a ten-item list of names whose graphemes equal 666, located in the upper left margin of the leaf after the lemma that contains Rev 13:18.

---

30 λαμπετις = 666.
31 A corrupt form of χόω "to bury"?
32 For σαρμενος (666), from σαρμεύω, "to dig sand"?
33 Cf. Schmid, *Studien*, Einleitung, 27–28.

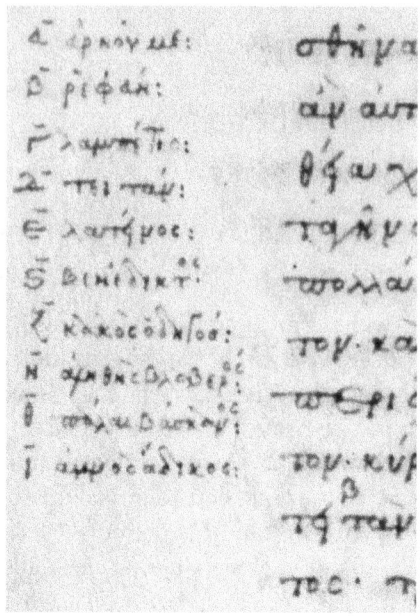

**Fig. 3:** *GA 2073 (Athos, Iviron, 273), Comment on Rev 13:18 (73v)*. Public Domain: Library of Congress Collection of Manuscripts from the Monasteries of Mt. Athos.

α αρνουμε:
β ρεφαν:
γ λαμπετις:
δ τειταν:
ε λατεινος:
ς βενεδικτος:
ζ κακος οδηγος:
η αληθης βλαβερος:
θ παλαι βασκανος:
ι αμνος αδικος:-

1. Arnoume
2. Rephan
3. Lampetis
4. Titan
5. Latin
6. Benedict
7. Wicked Guide
8. True Harm
9. Ancient Slander
10. Unjust Lamb

Many of these names and titles (3–10) are drawn directly from the Andrew commentary, but two new proper names head this list that have been hitherto unknown, the second of which (ρεφαν) adds to 656, although as minor morphological change (ρειφαν) solves this issue. This name is drawn from Amos 5:26, a passage that critiques Israel's cultic devotion to foreign gods, contrasting their faithfulness in the time of wilderness wanderings to their current infidelity. GA 051 (Athos, Patonkratoros, 44, tenth century, Fig. 4), the earliest witness to marginal comments on Rev 13:18, connects the beast explicitly to the text in Amos.

> Αμως προ[φητης] ονειδιζων τους ιουδαιους λεγει οτι ανελαβετε την σκηνην του μολοχ και το αστρον του θ[εο]υ υμων ραιφαν οπερ εχει ψηφον χξς

> Amos the prophet reprimanded the Jews. He said that you took up the tent of Moloch and the star of your God Raiphan, which calculates to 666.

Of all the marginal notes, this is the only one that explicitly identifies an intertext embedded within Revelation, a notoriously allusive text. Despite the fact that the spelling of Raiphan in this note only equates to 662, the scribe responsible for the note and catenae in the manuscript responded to the compositional features of Revelation to make an obscure connection to Amos. This connection, like the other names identified in these notes, is based on the numerical value of the sum of the Greek graphemes in a given appellation.

The name Arnoume ("deny me") appears as an option in the work *De consummation mundi* (28) of Pseudo-Hippolytus,[34] and this descriptive name appears alone adjacent to Rev 13:18 in the margin of a number of manuscripts, almost as a mantra for warding off the antichrist.[35] Although the form of this marginalia differs from the preceding examples in terms of form (enumerative list), it functions identically by connecting Rev 13:18 to traditions of its interpretation. The list also appears to be innovative based on the paratexts that appear in the commentary. The names that appear in the accompanying Andrew commentary preserved in this manuscript are denoted with supralinear Greek numerals, numerals that differ from those in the list. This page in GA 2073 preserves two competing, but overlapping lists: one in the margin and one in the commentary text.

Many other witnesses in this strand preserve similar lists to the one located in 2073, along with other traditional catenae, and even attribute the material to "Hippolytus and others" (κατα τον ιππολυτον και ετερους).[36] These numerous instances of related marginal comments represent a broad body of evidence, with its own internal textual variation, that speaks to medieval perceptions of

---

[34] Cf. Hans Achelis, *Hippolyt's kleinere exegetische und homiletische Schriften* (Leipzig: Hinrichs'sche, 1897), 301.
[35] Cf. GA 699 2024 2079. 452 preserves αρνητης (666), "one must deny" (ἀρνητέον).
[36] GA 35 757 824 1072 1075 1248 1503 1551 1597 1637 1740 1745 1771 1864 2041 2254 2352 2431 2554.

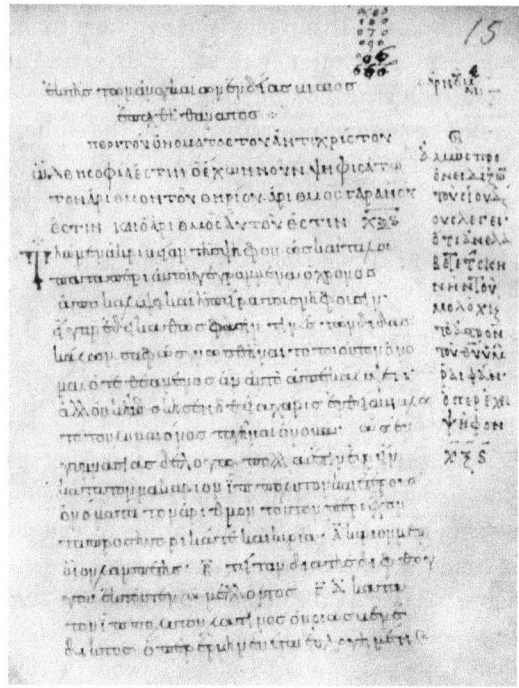

**Fig. 4:** *GA 051 (Athos, Pantokratoros 44) comment on Rev 13:18 (15r)*. Public Domain: Library of Congress Collection of Manuscripts from the Monasteries of Mt. Athos.

the importance of Rev 13:18. It also confirms that the Andrew of Caesarea tradition is the dominant channel of tradition for the interpretation of the Apocalypse in this period since the majority of this material is traceable back to this commentary. Even those examples that mention Hippolytus do so because Andrew himself quotes him explicitly. Before commenting on how a digital edition might incorporate this material and thus increase the editorial flexibility and reception historical value of such a digital artefact, other relevant examples should be highlighted.

# 4 Conflicts with Muhammad and Islam

A third strand of the tradition of comment on Rev 13:18 deals with anti-Islamic sentiments. These comments offer insight not only into traditions of interpretation further untethered from ancient and late antique interpreters, but also into the historical pressures and existential threats that these communities – mostly monastic, Orthodox, and located in Greece – perceived in the waning fortunes of the Byzantine empire. These communities were threatened both by Ottoman political ascension and also by the influence of western Latin Christianity under the auspices of papal power, especially following the sack of Constantinople in 1204 by the Fourth Crusade.[37] Eschatological tensions increased in the late Byzantine period as many saw the growing threat from Islamic groups in the east as an omen of the impending eschaton and theological influence of the Latin church (and threat of unification in the thirteenth century) as evidence of a larger cosmic struggle between orthodoxy and heresy.[38] In this context, interest in Revelation as a work increased dramatically. Over seventy percent of all of Revelation's Greek manuscripts were copied from the thirteenth century onward, spiking following the events of 1203 and the fall of Constantinople to the Ottomans in 1453 (see Table 1). And this is coupled with the fact that although only three Greek commentaries on the Apocalypse had been composed in late antiquity (Oecumenius, Andrew, and Arethas), eleven were produced in the post-Byzantine period between 1600 and 1800, not even considering the numerous works devoted to the exposition of the Apocalypse that were composed during the late Byzantine empire. A primary focus of many of these writings is the interpretation of the two beasts, which appear in Revelation 13, an exegetical emphasis that spills out into the margins of particular manuscripts.[39] Like the notes located in the following manuscripts, these traditions, diverse though they are, tend to interpret Rev 13:18 as the identity of the antichrist, who is either the papacy, Muhammad, or both.

A first example of this type of interpretation is located in GA 1778 (Thessaloniki, Vladaton, 35, fourteenth-fifteenth century), a double commentary that includes material from both the Andrew and Oecumenius commentaries.[40] The comment here appears on the page after the lemmatic text of 13:18, attaching itself to the commentary text (98r).

---

[37] On the messianic and eschatological pressures of the period, cf. Asterios Argyriou, *Les exégèses grecques de l'Apocalypse à l'époque turque (1453–1821): Esquisse d'une histoire des courants idéologiques au sein du people grec asservi* (Thessaloniki: Kronoz, 1982), 9–124. An especially popular seventeenth century text by Anastasios Gordios entitled Βιβλίον κατὰ Μωάμεθ καὶ λατίνων (*Book against Muhammad and the Latins*) adequately expresses these dual pressures posed by Ottoman hegemony in the east and the Latin church in the west.
[38] Cf. Michael Angold, "Byzantium and the west 1204–1453," in *The Cambridge History of Christianity: Eastern Christianity*, vol. 5, ed. M. Angold (Cambridge: Cambridge University Press, 2008): 53–78.
[39] Cf. Argyriou, *Les exégèses grecques*, 113–24.
[40] Cf. Schmid, *Studien*, Einleitung, 64–66.

> εστι δε τις την τοιαυτην
> ψηφον προσαψας
> και εις τον ψευδοπρο-
> φητην μωαμεθ . ε-
> ξεληνιζομενος γαρ
> μαμετιος λεγεται.
> οπερ φερερ την ψηφον
> ανελλιπη:-

For it refers to the calculation of those also attached to the false prophet Muhammad. For in Greek he is called Mametios. The calculation lacks nothing.

Like the preceding streams, this note identifies the number of the beast as a name, but in this case it is not tied directly to a name (μωαμεθ), but a latinized Greek transliteration of the name (μαμετιος) which not coincidentally totals 666. Moreover, unlike the other lists that include names unattached to any particular historical figure, this example identifies Muhammad as the antichrist, demonstrating a rejection of Irenaeus' caution in identifying a particular figure. The stakes of this exegesis are much higher.[41]

GA 2077 (Athos Iveron 644; copied in 1685) also carries a similar reading, offering the name μοαμετις which also adds to 666. The full marginal reading is μοαμετις μετρισα τα ψιφια ("Muhammad: do the math") and μοαμετις is specially emphasised by ornamental penwork frames. The first leaf of this manuscript also preserves the word μοαμετις, signalling the importance of this identification in the context of the manuscript's production. Muhammad was on the mind of our copyist. Again, like the other examples, the concern does not seem to be an effort to understand the beast within the first century world, but to create a decoded synecdoche for Islam by appealing to the name of the prophet. The identification of a specific person increases the eschatological pressure of the text – if Muhammad is the antichrist then the end of the age in certainly nigh.

The association of Muhammad with the beast further illustrates the ways in which Christian communities understood their present through the lens of scriptural interpretation. The threat of Islamic political domination posed an existential threat to the community, and therefore could be identified with

---

**41** Byzantine resistance to Islam and its prophet precedes the presence of these notations by many centuries. Cf. Argyriou, *Les exégèses grecques*, 17–25, especially the practical reasons to emphasise the tradition of Muhammad as anti-Christ: "L'image de Mahomet-Antichrist et du règne de l'Islam-règne de l'Antichrist était effectivement de natur à frapper l'esprit des simples fidèles, à freiner les conversions et à contenir la collaboration avec les ennemis du Christ" (p. 24).

**Table 1:** Chronological Distribution of Revelation's Greek Manuscripts.

| Century | Number of Witnesses |
|---|---|
| II | 1 |
| III | 1 |
| IV | 7 |
| V | 4 |
| VI | 0 |
| VII | 1 |
| VIII | 1 |
| IX | 1 |
| X | 14 |
| XI | 35 |
| XII | 28 |
| XIII | 29 |
| XIV | 69 |
| XV | 59 |
| XVI | 43 |
| XVII | 15 |
| XVIII | 5 |
| XIX | 2 |

Cf. *TuT*, 2–22.

one of Revelation's beasts. This note identifies a specific historic person, in contrast to the previous streams, but its method of identification is identical to that of Irenaeus or Andrew: decoding based on the numerical value of Greek graphemes.

Another manuscript in this strand is GA 2075 (Athos, Iviron, 370, fourteenth century), a commentary manuscript that contains additional layers of marginal comments by later hands. In line with the preceding example, it too identifies the beast as μοαμετις and encourages the reader to do the math. Its text is similar to GA 2814 (Augsburg, Univ. Bib. I.1.4.1, twelfth century), a copy of the Andrew commentary, that preserves a partially cut off note by a later hand.

This note in 2814 identifies the word μαχκε (from μαχάω, "to fight", or perhaps a reference to Mecca), which corresponds to 666, as an interpretation (ἑρμηνεία) of the name of the beast, which is further identified as μ[ω]αμεθ. This witness to the anti-Islamic strand of interpretation does not rely on the Latinised form μοαμετις, but uses an alternative form that corresponds to the scribe's perceptions of a characteristic of Islam, a perception undergirded by Ottoman advances in Asia Minor and the Aegean in the fourteenth century, perhaps also referring to Mecca. Regardless of mathematical strategy, some readers of Revelation were intent on seeing coded reference to Muhammad in the New Testament.

Other subtler forms of anti-Islamic interpretations co-mingle with other traditions. GA 2072 (Athos, Dochiariu, 81, copied in 1789), a commentary manuscript that preserves evidence of editorial intervention by readers over a period of time, includes μοαμετις among other names, even going through the trouble of adding up the value of the graphemes in Arabic script (fol. 413).

It also includes βενεδικτος and λατεινος, names found in Irenaeus, as well as a pair of other words whose graphemes add to 666 – οτμανες ("Ottomans") and ολ οσμανες ("the Ottomans"), both of which are Greek transliterations of Arabic. Although from a much later period, the juxtaposition of λατεινος ("Latin") with μοαμετις draws upon both existential threats to the Orthodox churches in the Byzantine commonwealth in the twelfth to the fifteenth centuries. In fact, the greatest perceived threat to the prestige of the Athonite monasteries in particular was not Islamic ascendency in Asia Minor – even though the monasteries were occasionally beset by Saljuk raiders and some of the monks had previously taken part in military campaigns in the Levant[42] – but in the potential of political alliance with the Latin west, especially following the sacking of Constantinople in 1204. In some corners of Byzantine society, the fall of Constantinople in 1453 was even viewed as divine judgement on attempts to unify Orthodoxy and Catholicism.[43] The publication of numerous lists of the "errors of the Latins" emphasizes the serious perceived theological differences between Christian communities under Roman and Constantinopolitan spheres of influence.[44] The monasteries benefitted from and actively sought out Ottoman protection, and many Christians in the fading Slavic and Russian Byzantine commonwealth donated their estates to the monasteries in an effort keep their wealth within Christian circles of influence. The population of Athonite monasteries also grew in this period as adherents sought to avoid military service. The monasteries thrived in a period of interreligious conflict. Therefore, the identification of Muhammad as the antichrist in this setting is somewhat counter-intuitive in light of the influx of wealth to the monasteries after the fall of Constantinople, and the political alliance of

---

[42] E.g. Peter the Athonite, a ninth-century monk who was once imprisoned in Samara. Cf. Kirsopp Lake, *The Early Days of Monasticism on Mount Athos* (Oxford: Clarendon, 1909), 8–39.
[43] Angold, "Byzantium," 78.
[44] Cf. Tia M. Kolbaba, *The Byzantine Lists: Errors of the Latins* (Chicago: University of Illinois Press, 2000).

the Orthodox patriarchate in Constantinople with the Ottoman sultans.⁴⁵ This specific interpretation of Rev 13:18 did not necessarily reflect the monastics politics of compromise and protection with Ottoman authorities.

A similar pattern is found in GA 1775 (Athos, Panteleimonos, 100, copied in 1847), which is perhaps the latest non-typographic copy of Revelation and the Andrew commentary in existence (135v).⁴⁶

This manuscript preserves a number of tortured calculations and creative attempts to decode the name of the beast. In addition to λατεινος, the scribe includes Muhammad's sobriquet (μοαμετις), even though he first made an error in spelling the name. Other names like μετζιτδ whose graphemes add to 666 are included, referring to the contemporary Ottoman sultan Abdulmejid I (ruled 1839–1861; Αμπντούλ Μετζίτ in Greek). "Ottoman" (οθωμανος) is also calculated even though it adds to 1240. Despite its singularities, this manuscript shows that a consistent tradition from Irenaeus to the nineteenth century existed in which readers of the Greek text were intent on reading the name of the beast as a paranomastic game that concealed the name of the Antichrist, especially when those names could be tied to opponents of Orthodoxy in the Latin west or their Ottoman patrons. Ancient traditions remained venerable, but were also supple enough to take on contemporary concerns and events. Readers relied heavily on the interpretations of Christian antiquity, but also showed various forms of development, especially in the repeated identification of Muhammad and even their Ottoman patrons as eschatological figures. Interreligious conflict, uneasy political alliances, and fear of the other are deep-seated parts of the Christian interpretive imagination, obvious traces of which still exist in many corners of the modern world.

\*

In each these examples of marginal notes that decode the identity of Revelation's beast, it is always equated with the eschatological adversary of God's people – an identification that is not necessarily obvious in the text itself, especially since the majority of modern interpreters attempt to decipher 666 in a way that equates to a Roman ruler from the first century. Each note, however, represents

---

**45** Cf. Elizabeth A. Zachariadou, "Mount Athos and the Ottomans c.1350–1550," in *The Cambridge History of Christianity: Eastern Christianity*, vol. 5, ed. M. Angold (Cambridge: Cambridge University Press, 2008): 154–68; eadem "The Great Church in captivity 1453–1586," in the same volume, pp. 169–86.
**46** The lemmatic text of the manuscript is abbreviated.

traditions that respond to the text's call for reader participation. Scribes record Greek names whose grapheme sums equal 666 or thereabouts. None of these examples resort to interlinguistic gematria, but focus only on Greek equivalents or sobriquets in the cases of Muhammad and Abdulmejid. This fact highlights the ingenuity of modern scholarly attempts to solve this riddle that focus on identifying a first century Roman emperor instead of an eschatological antagonist. These interpreters were not apparently seeking to identify a historical antagonist or emperor, but instead an eschatological figure that remained relevant in their historical context. Using traditions from Irenaeus, Hippolytus, and Andrew as a platform, these comments embedded names into the margins of documents that preserve Revelation in an effort to warn readers that rulers with these names might be dangerous. These types of "prophetic" decoding of Revelation's imagery are not solely the propriety of modern fundamentalist eschatological hermeneutics.

Dating from the tenth to the nineteenth centuries and clustered in the eastern Mediterranean – particularly in Greek Orthodox monasteries – the material evidence emphasises the local nature of this tradition, as well as the influence of Orthodox monasticism and exegetical commentaries and other works of this period that focus on the identity of the antichrist, illuminating particular reading cultures and accentuating the mediated nature of scriptural interpretation.[47] These traditions represent dominant ways of reading Rev 13:18, especially if we consider that numerous other commentary manuscripts include detailed analysis of this text as basic parts of their composition. This information provides insight into the hermeneutics that controlled interpretations of the Apocalypse. This melding of interpretation and textual witnesses in the material culture that encompasses a work's transmission reinforces again the idea that textual history and reception are integrally linked and that critical editions can potentially serve as the medium for melding these parallel facets of a work, especially editions that are as comprehensive as feasible in providing access to the documentary facets of the tradition regardless of the textual value – or lack thereof – of each witness.

---

[47] For example, the post-Byzantine commentary by Christophoros Anghelos (b. 1575) argues forcefully, from many texts including Rev 13:18, that Muhammad is the antichrist, not the Pope, although the Pope is identified as the first beast in Revelation 13. Cf. Argyrou, *Les exégèses grecques* 227–42.

## 5 The Beast and Digital Editions

Admittedly, the marginal notes and images analysed in the preceding section are a persistent, but secondary concern in the big picture of constructing a workable and economically viable critical edition. However, these traditions are important for reception historians and philologists who grapple with manuscripts not merely as text-receptacles, but as cultural artefacts with expressive power. These types of features provide insight not only into reception history, but channels of textual transmission and the mediums through which interpretive traditions are mediated. A major dissatisfaction with common hand editions of the New Testament, when compared with the theorised possibilities of digital texts, is that the peculiarities of these witnesses are lost, due in large part to the herculean task of sifting through the variants offered by thousands of diverse witnesses. But the turn to digital editions and the drive to digitally transcribe witnesses offers an opportunity to rethink the boundaries of the edition without harming the overriding goal of constructing a workable text and textual history.[48] In fact, the digitalness of the edition also enhances textual studies by potentially allowing users to shape the evidence presented. Hugh Houghton and Catherine Smith note that "electronic publishing… allows much more freedom, with the potential for users to customise their views, such as toggling between a positive and negative apparatus, or selecting different witnesses for inclusion."[49] Not only can readers recombine text and artefact, but they can manipulate the textual rhetoric of the edition.

Let us take as a concrete example the ECM of the Apocalypse that is being constructed by Martin Karrer and his team in Wuppertal, Germany.[50] The project is currently designed to be born digital, meaning that every stage, from image aggregation to transcription to reconciliation to apparatus construction,

---

[48] The turn toward digital text has since the 1990s led to a large-scale reappraisal of the materiality of print and manuscript cultures, and not just in biblical studies. The literature of this discourse is vast, but see especially N. Katherine Hayles, *Writing Machines* (London: MIT Press, 2002), 22–33 whose work on digital texts has led her to conceive of books as "material metaphors": "the physical form of the literary artifact always affects what the words (and other semiotic components) mean" (p. 25). See also McGann, *Radiant Textuality*, 1–19.

[49] H.A.G. Houghton and Catherine J. Smith, "Digital Editing and the Greek New Testament," in *Ancient Worlds in Digital Culture*, ed. C. Clivaz et al. (Leiden: Brill, 2016): 111.

[50] Cf. project reports in U. Schmid, "Die neue Edition der Johannesapokalypse. Ein Arbeitsbericht," in *Studien zum Text der Apokalypse*, ANTF 47, ed. M. Sigismund, M. Karrer, and U. Schmid (Berlin: de Gruyter, 2015): 3–15; M. Sigismund, "Die neue Edition der Johannesapokalypse: Stand der Arbeiten," in *Studien zum Text der Apokalypse II*, ANTF 50, ed. M Sigismund and D. Müller (Berlin: de Gruyter, 2017): 3–17.

is fully integrated in a digital format. Any printed edition that results from the project will be entirely derivative of the project's electronic content. Much has already been said about the process of digital editing of the ECM, especially by H.A.G. Houghton and D.C. Parker.[51] However, I am not interested necessarily in the process of editing, but in the value of using a digital platform.

First, I should note that the ECM of the Apocalypse is revolutionising critical editions of the New Testament due to the quantity of textual and material data that have been aggregated in the process of transcription. The project has chosen to transcribe not only the text of the manuscripts, but also a variety of paratextual features, including corrections, running titles, capitals, *ekthesis*, rubrication, structural features (line and column breaks), *kephalaia*, marginal notes, and artwork among others. The manuscripts are transcribed and reconciled in XML format.[52] This means that at the end of the transcription process, a range of paratexts should be encoded into the basic data of the edition. The ECM of Revelation has the potential to press the boundaries of the standard critical edition to go beyond textual matters, and to dabble in material culture, even though textual issues remain at the forefront of work.

Returning to Rev 13:18, although the text of the notes need not be included in the textual apparatuses, the text of the verse could be configured as a hyperlink that brings the reader to a page where transcribed text of the marginal collations could be accessed, juxtaposed to tagged images of the manuscripts. If a user wishes to use the edition in a way similar to traditional print forms, she is able to continue reading without recourse to the additional information. However, the digital platform offers a way to enhance the functionality of the traditional form by offering ancillary materials that are already captured in XML, the only limitation being that not every exemplar of Revelation was collated for the production of the volume.[53] The editors of the ECM are not responsible for the breadth of the paratextual and material features of the tradition, but other projects oriented

---

[51] E.g. Houghton and Smith, "Digital Editing," 110–27; Parker, *Textual Scholarship*, 101–24. Cf. also Tara L. Andrews, "Philology and Critical Edition in the Digital Age," *Variants* 10 (2013): 61–72.

[52] It is becoming more common to include certain paratextual or codicological features in transcription, e.g. Franz Fischer, "All texts are equal, but…Textual Plurality and the Critical Text in Digital Scholarly Editions," *Variants* 10 (2013): 77–91 (esp. 86–88).

[53] Witnesses were selected based on the data from *TuT* and thus artefacts that are relatively late and fall into a fairly obvious text family, e.g. 2259, are unlikely to be selected. However, witnesses not initially selected could be input into the digital edition at a later date as necessity (or leisure) dictates. Including full collations of every reading into the apparatus would certainly clutter the already dense apparatus, but it would provide further data for reception historical research as far as variant readings are concerned.

toward these features could theoretically integrate with the digital ECM fascicles, creating a more deeply curated digital archive, that contains both editorial texts and links to additional information that contextualises particular textual formulations.

All of this could make the edition of the New Testament a more fully integrated interdisciplinary object that appeals to a wider group of users from various fields. A digital edition spurs on the discovery of knowledge and allows us to understand not merely a work's production, but its reception, a point that preponderates in a more comprehensive edition that includes recourse to material culture.[54] This type of functionality reconnects text to its material witnesses, reversing the necessary divorcing of text from its manuscript in the process of aggregating and evaluation the various textual witnesses of a work. These links and other resources need not be integrated at the outset of its publication, but could be continually edited, updated, and expanded by an editorial team indefinitely (or at least until funding bodies get tired of it). In this sense, the collocation "digital edition" is really a misnomer, since its flexibility transcends the illusion of the fixed nature of print editions. A digital ECM, for example, is more like a repository where primary sources, both texts (transcriptions) and manuscripts (images) are presented on a contingent basis by the primary editors.[55] A digital edition is supple and adaptable to the critical whims of other users – it is fundamentally open to experimentation. Modern editors stand in a less authoritative position and, although their critical judgments should be taken seriously and evaluated analytically, they also function now as aggregators and curators of data that represent the tradition writ large, including data that is not textual in the traditional sense. Editors are becoming the heads of "digital scriptoria," to borrow a concept from Parker.[56] The active engagement of users also democratizes editing, allowing users interested in an idiosyncratic exegetical problem like the one I have described for Rev 13:18 to put the book's textual history and material culture

---

**54** Cf. Jerome McGann, "Coda: Why Digital Textual Scholarship Matters," in *The Cambridge Companion to Textual Scholarship*, ed. N. Fraistat and J. Flanders (Cambridge: Cambridge University Press, 2013): 274–88.

**55** So also Parker, *Textual Scholarship*, 139–42.

**56** Parker, *Manuscripts, Texts, Theology: Collected Papers 1977–2007*, ANTF 40 (Berlin: de Gruyter, 2009), 287–303 (repr. *JSNT* 25 [2003]: 395–411). Cf. also Paul Dilley, "Digital Philology between Alexandria and Babel," in *Ancient Worlds in Digital Culture*, ed. C. Clivaz et al. (Leiden: Brill, 2016): 17–34.

to good use, although the task of critical editing will likely remain in the hands of a restricted group of experts.[57]

Although the details of the platform remain contingent and fungible,[58] the possibilities of such a multi-modal digital object have the ability to reinvigorate editorial activity on the New Testament. Such an interactive platform combines the concerns of both "old" and "new" philology. The exemplars discussed above are of little interested when it comes to constructing an *Ausgangstext*; as members of well-defined textual families, or mixed texts thereof, with mostly derivative texts, they are less than useful for classic textual criticism. But connecting the shared features of the textually uninteresting witnesses injects life into the breadth of the textual tradition in a way that does not detract from textual adjudications.

A digital edition enables thinking about the New Testament that transcends the implicit strictures of print culture, allowing a digital text to engross users in the manuscript tradition and its features that are lost in standard print editions. It also emphasises the contingent nature of critical texts since the ideal digital platform should resemble a work space where the raw data can be reconfigured.[59] Digital media bypasses print culture to more fully encounter a tradition indebted in deep ways to the venerable practice of manuscript production. "We need a way of bringing the critical edition and the manuscripts *as* manuscripts back together again."[60] If a critical edition is truly "a tool for understanding the work"[61] or a narrative of the tradition of which the work is a part, then the inclusion of data from material culture, connecting document to text, is surely a desirable benefit of the digital turn. New mediums make new forms of scholarship and interest in the material possible and help us to learn from the peripheries of the tradition, margins like those found in the margins of medieval manuscripts.

---

**57** Cf. Houghton and Smith, "Digital Editing," 124–125; Fischer, "All texts are equal," 77–91.
**58** Cf. David Hamidović, "Editing a Cluster of Texts: The Digital Solution," in *Ancient Worlds in Digital Culture*, ed. C. Clivaz et al. (Leiden: Brill, 2016): 196–213.
**59** Cf. Paul Eggert, "Apparatus, Text, Interface: How to Read a Printed Critical Edition," in *The Cambridge Companion to Textual Scholarship*, ed. N. Fraistat and J. Flanders (Cambridge: Cambridge University Press, 2013): 105–06.
**60** Parker, *Textual Scholarship*, 126.
**61** Parker, *Textual Scholarship*, 105.

# Appendix: Manuscripts with Marginal Comments at Revelation 13:18

| | Irenaeus Stream | | |
|---|---|---|---|
| GA Signature | Library Signature | Hoskier Number[62] | Date |
| 1859 | Athos, Kutlumusiu, 82 | 219 | XIV |
| 2027 | Paris, BnF, gr. 491 | 61 | XIII |

| | Commentary Streams | | | |
|---|---|---|---|---|
| GA Signature | Library Signature | Hoskier Number | Date | Sub-stream |
| 35 | Paris, BNF, gr. 47 | 17 | XI | Andrew Commentary |
| 325 | Oxford, Bodl. Libr., Auct. E. 5.9 | 9 | XI | |
| 632 | Rome, Bibl. Vallicell. B.86 | 22 | XII/XIV | |
| 757 | Athens, Nat. Bibl. 150 | 150 | XIII | |
| 824 | Grottaferrata, Bibl. Della Badia, A.α.1 | 110 | XIV | |
| 1072 | Athos, Lavra, Γ 80 | 160 | XIII | |
| 1075 | Athos, Lavra, Λ195 | 161 | XIV | |
| 1248 | Sinai, St. Catherine's, gr. 267 | 250 | XIV | |
| 1503 | Athos, Lavra, A 99 | 192 | 1317 | |
| 1551 | Athos, Vatopediu, 913 | 212 | XIII | |
| 1597 | Athos, Vatopediu, 966 | 207 | 1289 | |
| 1637 | Athos, Lavra, Ω 141 | 230 | 1328 | |
| 1732 | Athos, Lavra, A 91 | 220 | 1384 | |
| 1740 | Athos, Lavra, B 80 | 229 | XII | |
| 1745 | Athos, Lavra, Ω 49 | 227 | XV | |
| 1771 | Athos, Lavra, E 177 | 224 | XIV | |
| 1864 | Athos, Stravronikita, 52 | 242 | XIII | |
| 2041 | London, Brit. Libr., Add. 39612 | 96 | XIV | |

---

[62] See H. C. Hoskier, *Concerning the Text of the Apocalypse*, vol. 1 (London: Bernard Quaritch, 1929).

(continued)

| | Commentary Streams | | | |
|---|---|---|---|---|
| GA Signature | Library Signature | Hoskier Number | Date | Sub-stream |
| 2059 | Vatican, Bibl. Vat., Vat. Gr. 370 | 152 | XI | |
| 2073 | Athos, Iviron, 273 | 169 | XIV | 2073 |
| 2114 | Athens, Nat. Bibl., 142 | 234 | 1676 | |
| 2254 | Athos, Iviron, 382 | 216 | XVI | |
| 2259 | Athos, Stravronikita, 25 | (213) | XI | |
| 2323 | Athens, Mus. Benaki, Ms. 46 | | XIII | |
| 2352 | Meteora, Metamorphosis, 237 | 202 | XV | |
| 2431 | Athos, Kavsokalyvia, 4 | | 1332 | |
| 2554 | Bucharest, Romanian Academy, 3/12610 | | 1434 | |
| 452 | Vatican, Bibl. Vat., Reg. gr. Pii II 50 | 42 | XII | Proper Names |
| 468 | Paris, BNF gr. 101 | 55 | XIII | |
| 699 | London, Brit. Libr., Egerton 3145 | 89 | XI | |
| 1685 | Athens, Byz. Mus., 155 | (198) | 1292 | |
| 1768 | Athos, Iviron, 771 | | 1519 | |
| 1854 | Athos, Iviron, 231 | 130 | XI | |
| 1865 | Athos, Philotheu, 1801 | 244 | XIII | |
| 2024 | Moscow, Hist. Mus., V.391 | 50 | XV | |
| 2079 | Athos, Konstamonitu, 107 | 177 | XIII | |
| 2201 | Elasson, Olympiotissis, 6 | (252) | XV | |
| 2723 | Trikala, Vissarionos, 4 | | XI | |
| 2821 | Cambridge, Univ. Libr. Dd. 9.69 | 10 | XIV | |

| | Anti-Islam Stream | | |
|---|---|---|---|
| GA Signature | Library Signature | Hoskier Number | Date |
| 1775 | Athos, Panteleimonos, 110 | 236 | 1847 |
| 1778 | Thessaloniki, Vladaton, 35 | 203 | XV |
| 2072 | Athos, Dochiariu, 81 | (168) | 1789 |
| 2075 | Athos, Iviron, 370 | 171 | XIV |
| 2077 | Athos, Iviron, 644 | 174 | 1685 |
| 2814 | Augsburg, Univ. Libr., Cod. I.1.4.1 | 1 | XII |

| Isolated Note | | | |
|---|---|---|---|
| GA Signature | Library Signature | Hoskier Number | Date |
| 051 | Athos, Pantokratoros, 44 | E | X |

| Other Possible Manuscripts (Damaged/Illegible) and Minor Notations | | | |
|---|---|---|---|
| GA Signature | Library Signature | Hoskier Number | Date |
| 522 | Oxford, Bodl. Libr., Canon gr. 34 | 98 | 1515/1516 |
| 919 | Escorial, Bibl. De Escorial, Ψ III 6 | 125 | XI |
| 1617 | Athos, Lavra, E 157 | 223 | XV |
| 1746 | Athos, Lavra, Ω 144 | 228 | XIV |
| 2031 | Vatican, Bibl. Vat., Vat. Gr. 1743 | 67 | 1301 |
| 2669 | Athos, Lavra, Λ′ 74 | | XVI |

# Bibliography

Achelis, Hans. *Hippolyt's kleinere exegetische und homiletische Schriften*. Leipzig: Hinrichs'sche, 1897.

Aland, B., et al., eds. *Novum Testamentum Graecum Editio Critica Maior IV. Die Katholischen Briefe*, 2nd ed. Stuttgart: DBG, 2011.

Andrews, Tara L. "Philology and Critical Edition in the Digital Age." *Variants* 10 (2013): 61–72.

Angold, Michael. "Byzantium and the west 1204–1453." In *The Cambridge History of Christianity: Eastern Christianity*, vol. 5, edited by M. Angold, 53–78. Cambridge: Cambridge University Press, 2008.

Argyriou, Asterios. *Les exégèses grecques de l'Apocalypse à l'époque turque (1453–1821): Esquisse d'une histoire des courants idéologiques au sein du people grec asservi*. Thessaloniki: Kronoz, 1982.

Aune, D.E. *Revelation*. WBC 52b. 3 vols. Nashville: Thomas Nelson, 1998.

Bauckham, Richard. *The Climax of Prophecy: Studies on the Book of Revelation*. Edinburgh: T&T Clark, 1993.

Beale, G.K. *The Book of Revelation*. NIGTC. Grand Rapids: Eerdmans, 1999.

Birdsall, J. Neville. "Irenaeus and the Number of the Beast: Revelation 13,18." In *New Testament Textual Criticism and Exegesis: Festschrift J. Delobel*, edited by A. Denaux, 349–59. Leuven: Peeters, 2002.

Breed, Brennan W. *Nomadic Text: A Theory of Biblical Reception History*. Bloomington: Indiana University Press, 2014.

Cerquiglini, Bernard. *In Praise of the Variant: A Critical History of Philology*, trans. B. Wing. Baltimore: The Johns Hopkins University Press, 1999.

Cole, Zachary J. *Numerals in Early Greek New Testament Manuscripts: Text-Critical, Scribal, and Theological Studies*. NTTSD 53. Leiden: Brill, 2017.

Constantinou, Eugenia Scarvelis. *Guiding to a Blessed End: Andrew of Caesarea and his Apocalypse Commentary in the Ancient Church*. Washington, D.C.: The Catholic University of America Press, 2013.

de Groote, Marc ed. *Oecumenii Commentarius in Apocalypsin*. TEG 8. Leuven: Peters, 1999.

de Villiers, Pieter G.R. "Numerical Symbolism in Oecumenius's Commentary on Revelation." In *Tot sacramenta quot verba: Zu Kommentierung der Apokalypse des Johannes von den Anfängen bis ins 12. Jahrhundert*, edited by K. Huber, R. Klotz, and C. Winterer, 135–52. Münster: Aschendorf, 2014.

Dilley, Paul. "Digital Philology between Alexandria and Babel." In *Ancient Worlds in Digital Culture*, edited by C. Clivaz, et al., 17–34. Leiden: Brill, 2016.

Dochhorn, Jan. *Schriftgelehrte Prophetie: Der eschatologische Teufelsfall in Apc Joh 12 und seine Beudeutung für das Verständnis der Johannesoffenbarung*. WUNT 268. Tübingen: Mohr Siebeck, 2010.

Eggert, Paul. "Apparatus, Text, Interface: How to Read a Printed Critical Edition." In *The Cambridge Companion to Textual Scholarship*, edited by N. Fraistat and J. Flanders, 97–118. Cambridge: Cambridge University Press, 2013.

Epp, E.J. "The Multivalence of the Term 'Original' Text in New Testament Textual Criticism." *HTR* 92 (1999): 245–81.

Fischer, Franz. "All texts are equal, but…Textual Plurality and the Critical Text in Digital Scholarly Editions." *Variants* 10 (2013): 77–91.

Fraistat, Neil, and Julia Flanders. "Introduction to Textual Scholarship in the Age of Media Consciousness." In *The Cambridge Companion to Textual Scholarship*, edited by N. Fraistat and J. Flanders, 1–15. Cambridge: Cambridge University Press, 2013.

Greetham, David. "A History of Textual Scholarship." In *The Cambridge Companion to Textual Scholarship*, edited by N. Fraistat and J. Flanders, 17–41. Cambridge: Cambridge University Press, 2013.

Hamidović, David. "Editing a Cluster of Texts: The Digital Solution." In *Ancient Worlds in Digital Culture*, edited by C. Clivaz, et al., 196–213. Leiden: Brill, 2016.

Hayles, N. Katherine. *Writing Machines*. London: MIT Press, 2002.

Hendel, Ronald. *Steps to a New Edition of the Hebrew Bible*. Atlanta: Society of Biblical Literature, 2016.

Henten, Jan Willem van. "Dragon Myth and Imperial Ideology in Revelation 12–13." In *The Reality of Apocalypse: Rhetoric and Politics in the Book of Revelation*, edited by D.L. Barr, 181–203. Atlanta: Society of Biblical Literature, 2006.

Hernández, Juan Jr. "Andrew of Caesarea and His Reading of Revelation: Cathechesis and Paranesis." In *Die Johannesapokalypse: Kontexte – Konzepte – Rezeption*, WUNT 287, ed. J. Frey, J.A. Kelhoffer, and F. Tóth, 755–74. Tübingen: Mohr Siebeck, 2012.

Hoskier, H.C. *Concerning the Text of the Apocalypse*. 2 vols. London: Quaritch, 1929.

Houghton, H.A.G., and Catherine J. Smith. "Digital Editing and the Greek New Testament." In *Ancient Worlds in Digital Culture*, edited by C. Clivaz et al., 110–27. Leiden: Brill, 2016.

Koester, Craig. *Revelation*. AYB 38a. London: Yale University Press, 2014.

Kolbaba, Tia M. *The Byzantine Lists: Errors of the Latins*. Chicago: University of Illinois Press, 2000.

Kretschmar, Georg. *Die Offenbarung des Johannes: Die Geschichte ihrer Auslegung im 1. Jahrtausend*. Stuttgart: Calwer, 1985.

Lake, Kirsopp. *The Early Days of Monasticism on Mount Athos*. Oxford: Clarendon, 1909.

Lambros, Spyr. P. *Catalogue of the Greek Manuscripts on Mount Athos*. Cambridge: Cambridge University Press, 1895.

Lembke, M., et al., eds. *Text und Textwert der griechischen Handschriften des Neuen Testaments. VI. Die Apokalypse*. ANTF 49. Berlin: de Gruyter, 2017.

Lembke, Markus. "Beobachtungen zu den Handschriften der Apokalypse des Johannes." In *Die Johannesoffenbarung: Ihr Text und ihre Auslegung*, edited by M. Labahn and M. Karrer, 19–69. Leipzig: Evangelische Verlagsanstalt, 2012.

McGann, Jerome. *Radiant Textuality: Literature after the World Wide Web*. New York: Palgrave Macmillan, 2001.

McGann, Jerome. "Coda: Why Digital Textual Scholarship Matters," in *The Cambridge Companion to Textual Scholarship*, edited by N. Fraistat and J. Flanders, 274–88. Cambridge: Cambridge University Press, 2013.

McGann, Jerome. *A New Republic of Letters: Memory and Scholarship in the Age of Digital Reproduction*. London: Harvard University Press, 2014.

Mink, Gerd. "Contamination, Coherence, and Coincidence in Textual Transmission." In *The Textual History of the Greek New Testament: Changing Views in Contemporary Research*, edited by K. Wachtel and M.W. Holmes, 141–216. Atlanta: Society of Biblical Literature, 2011.

Parker, D.C. "A New Oxyrhyncus Papyri of Revelation: P115 (P. Oxy. 4499)." *NTS* 46 (2000): 159–74.

Parker, D.C. *Manuscripts, Texts, Theology: Collected Papers 1977–2007*. ANTF 40. Berlin: de Gruyter, 2009.

Parker, D.C. *Textual Scholarship and the Making of the New Testament*. Oxford: Oxford University Press, 2012.

Schmid, J. *Studien zur Geschichte des griechischen Apokalypse-Textes*. Munich: Karl Zink, 1955.

Schmid, U. "Die neue Edition der Johannesapokalypse. Ein Arbeitsbericht." In *Studien zum Text der Apokalypse*, ANTF 47, edited by M. Sigismund, M. Karrer, and U. Schmid, 3–15. Berlin: de Gruyter, 2015.

Sigismund, M. "Die neue Edition der Johannesapokalypse: Stand der Arbeiten." In *Studien zum Text der Apokalypse II*, ANTF 50, edited by M. Sigismund and D. Müller, 3–17. Berlin: de Gruyter, 2017.

Strutwolf, H., et al., eds. *Novum Testamentum Graecum Editio Critica Maior III. Die Apostelgeschichte*. Stuttgart: DBG, 2017.

Strutwolf, Holger. "Original Text and Textual History." In *The Textual History of the Greek New Testament: Changing Views in Contemporary Research*, edited by K. Wachtel and M.W. Holmes, 23–41. Atlanta: Society of Biblical Literature, 2011.

Sutherland, Kathryn. "Anglo-American Editorial Theory." In *The Cambridge Companion to Textual Scholarship*, edited N. Fraistat and J. Flanders, 42–60. Cambridge: Cambridge University Press, 2013.

Wasserman, Tommy and Peter J. Gurry. *A New Approach to Textual Criticism: An Introduction to the Coherence-Based Genealogical Method*. Atlanta: Society of Biblical Literature, 2017.

Williams, Peter J. "P115 and the Number of the Beast." *TynBul* 58 (2007): 151–53.

Zachariadou, Elizabeth A. "Mount Athos and the Ottomans c.1350–1550" In *The Cambridge History of Christianity: Eastern Christianity*, vol. 5, edited by M. Angold, 154–68. Cambridge: Cambridge University Press, 2008.

Zachariadou, Elizabeth A. "The Great Church in captivity 1453–1586." In *The Cambridge History of Christianity: Eastern Christianity*, vol. 5, edited by M. Angold, 169–86. Cambridge: Cambridge University Press, 2008.

Alba Fedeli

# The Qur'ānic Text from Manuscript to Digital Form: Metalinguistic Markup of Scribes and Editors

## 1 Different Technologies and Similarities in Writing the Qur'ānic Text

Texts necessarily embody and are expressed by different technologies that are available at different times and in diverse geographical and cultural areas. Thus, texts cannot exist divested of their material form and technology, factors which influence the idea of the text itself.[1] The identity of any textual object – but sacred texts in particular – thus seems to include fluidity and invariance, elements which would seem to be contradictory.[2] With regard to the Qur'ānic text, its digital (i.e., computational) encoding allows us to see the richness of the manuscript, in contrast to the fixed and static page of the printed Qur'ān. In fact, during an important time of change like the digital revolution, materiality becomes apparent to scholars who have to face manuscript variance in the new digital paradigm.

Mordenti suggests that a close consideration of pre-Gutenberg systems can shed light on the mechanisms of the post-Gutenberg context.[3] Indeed, the two non-Gutenberg contexts of manuscript culture and digital texts/objects share and overlap at many points and, possibly, the perspective suggested by Mordenti is reciprocal. Indeed, manuscript texts and their mechanisms can be used as a lens

---

[1] Raul Mordenti, "Parádosis. A proposito del testo informatico," *Atti della Accademia Nazionale dei Lincei. Classe di Scienze Morali, Storiche e Filologiche*, Memorie, Serie IX, 28 (2011): 623–91.

[2] Dino Buzzetti, "Biblioteche digitali e oggetti digitali complessi: Esaustività e funzionalità nella conservazione," in *Archivi informatici per il patrimonio culturale*, Convegno internazionale organizzato dall'Accademia Nazionale dei Lincei in collaborazione con ERPANET e la Fondazione Franceschini (Roma: Accademia Nazionale dei Lincei, Bardi Editore, 2006): 41–75, 51–53, i.e. "Il testo è un oggetto mobile e immutabile ad un tempo, mobile per la sua variabilità e immutabile per la sua invarianza."

[3] Mordenti, "Parádosis."

**Note:** I owe a great deal to the inspiring comments I received from Dino Buzzetti about digital encoding, markup, and other puzzling questions. I also thank him heartily for his time in discussing new ideas in my manuscript reading and encoding and his generosity in sharing some helpful references with me.

for understanding digital texts, but the latter horizon can also shed light on the pre-Gutenberg system. Thus, for example, a deep comprehension of diacritical signs in scripts can disclose subtle mechanisms behind the concept of markup in a digital environment. However, in a reciprocal perspective, tools with a diacritical function developed in early manuscripts can be understood through the lens of markup theory in digital editing.

The materiality of manuscripts on which scholars are forced to reflect when digitally encoding Qur'ānic manuscript texts must also be understood in the sense of the physicality of the technology used in the process of writing. A challenging example of such materiality is the ambiguity of the (complex) writing systems in early Qur'ānic manuscripts and the assumptions embedded in our editing and reading activities because of our typographical mindset.[4] In digital encoding, scholars cannot leave ambiguous examples and rely on the "tolerance and perspicacity of the readers"[5] because the simple – binary – system of the machine cannot admit tolerance and perspicacity.

Thus, the aim of the present contribution is twofold. First, it describes several elements of the materiality and technology of the manuscript form of the Qur'ānic text. Second, it suggests reflection on such technology on the part of the editor during the act of digitally encoding the manuscript form, in light of the hypothesis that the computational/digital text has many similarities with the handwritten text of the manuscript tradition and appears to be far from the rigid, fixed, static and closed text of the printed dimension. The idea of a fixed and static text imposed by the Gutenberg revolution is particularly evident in the history of the Qur'ānic printed text.

---

**4** See, for example, Monella and his five Gutenbergian assumptions, connected with the concept of standardization, i.e. standard alphabet, standard graphic system, standard spelling, standard sequentiality and lastly, the correspondence of one grapheme and one alphabeme, in Paolo Monella, "Many Witnesses, Many Layers: The Digital Scholarly Edition of the *Iudicium Coci et Pistoris* (Anth. Lat. 199 Riese)," in *Digital Humanities: Progetti Italiani Ed Esperienze Di Convergenza Multidisciplinare, Atti Del Convegno Annuale Dell'Associazione per l'Informatica Umanistica e La Cultura Digitale (AIUCD) Firenze, 13–14 Dicembre 2012*, ed. Fabio Ciotti (Roma: Sapienza Università Editrice, 2014): 173–206.
**5** D'Arco Silvio Avalle, "I canzonieri: definizione di genere e problemi di edizione," in *La critica del testo. Atti del Convegno di Lecce, 22–26 ott. 1984* (Roma: Salerno Editrice, 1985): 363–82 (380).

## 2 A Long Way to a Static Text, Materialized in Printed Leaves

The encounter between the Qur'ānic text and the movable type printing press was a very slow process that lasted centuries. In the case of Muslims, it passed through the mediation of lithographic technology which allowed for the copying of manuscript texts, while Europeans ventured into printing the Qur'ānic text from the sixteenth century without considering the cultural implications of the new technology.

A formal interdiction to ban the production as well as the trade of printed texts of the Qur'ān was decreed in the territories of the Ottoman Empire. The ban lasted from the first attempt at producing printed copies of the Qur'ān in Europe in the sixteenth century with the business disaster of Paganino de' Paganini, until the decision in the 1870s to produce a lithographic edition of the calligraphic copy of the famous master Hafız Osman. After the introduction of printing, European publishers had ventured into producing Arabic editions of the Qur'ānic text intended for a Muslim audience, looking for a possible successful market in the Muslim world. Thus, in 1537/1538, Paganino de' Paganini printed the first text of the Qur'ān, but it was a business disaster.[6] The unique existing copy was discovered in the library of the Venetian island of San Michele a few decades ago. Its reappearance confirmed the authenticity of this venture and led to the formulation of diverse hypotheses about the existence of a unique copy.[7] The Ottoman sources clarify the mystery of de' Paganini's surviving copy as all the other copies that arrived in Istanbul were confiscated and destroyed by the Ottoman authorities, because the importation of printed books in the Arabic script – Qur'ānic as well as non-Qur'ānic – was prohibited. Paganini was probably saved from being executed thanks to the intervention of a Venetian ambassador, according to the account in the *Colloquium heptaplomeres* by Jean Bodin (1530–1596).[8]

---

[6] It is likely that it was also a disaster in terms of the aesthetic results in reproducing the Arabic alphabet with moveable type.

[7] See Angela Nuovo, *Alessandro Paganino (1509–1538)* (Padova: Editrice Antenore, 1990), 107–31 (chapter on "Il Corano").

[8] The story of the prohibition and subsequent destruction of de' Paganini's copies has been reconstructed in M. Brett Wilson, *Translating the Qur'an in an Age of Nationalism: Print Culture and Modern Islam in Turkey* (Oxford: Oxford University Press in association with The Institute of Ismaili Studies, 2014), 32ff. The reference to the ban on trading Paganini's printed Qur'āns in the *Colloquium heptaplomeres de rerum sublimium arcanis abditis* is very interesting: "il auroit esté puny de mort: mais il en fut quitte pour la perte de ses exemplaires qui feurent bruslez et pour sa main droicte qui luy fut coupée parce que ce livre estoit tout remply de fautes." See *Colloque*

Bodin explicitly mentioned the presence of mistakes in the copies printed by Paganino (i.e., "infinitis erroribus scatebat") as the reason that led the Ottoman authorities to destroy these copies. In fact, the key point in accepting the new technology was its legitimization from the *'ulamā'* who had to be involved in the checking activity and approval of the correctness of the text, thus confirming the chain of transmission of the text. The printing of the Qur'ānic text as a European enterprise lacked that lineage of transmission that is essential in Islam.[9] Thus, in the Ottoman Empire, the embargo imposed on printed copies of the Qur'ān consequently made the calligraphic Qur'ān in its manuscript form the only licit form of the sacred book. The compromise of the photolithographic – though mechanical – reproduction of a handwritten artefact executed according to traditional skills and knowledge allowed the shift from manuscript culture to the emergent printed dimension. The control over the accuracy of the text by religious authorities who can guarantee its lineage in a new technology is a phenomenon that has recently re-emerged in the current period of the shift to the electronic form of the Qur'ānic text which is in circulation on the Web.[10]

---

*entre sept scavans qui sont de differens sentimens: des secrets cachez des choses relevées*, traduction anonyme du Colloquium heptaplomeres *de Jean Bodin (manuscrit français 1923 de la Bibliothèque Nationale de Paris)*, eds. François Berriot, Katharine Davies, Jean Larmat, Jacques Roger (Genève: Librairie Droz, 1984): 352. The reference to the possible presence of mistakes in the printed form of the sacred text is a key point in the history of the transmission of the text embodied through different technologies. See for example the discussions and efforts related to having a text free from mistakes in the online copies of the Qur'ānic text.

[9] Wilson, *Translating the Qur'an*, 37, 40.

[10] See for example the proceedings of the Conference held in 2013 on information technology used for the electronic text of the Qur'ān, i.e. Juan E. Guerrero ed., *Proceedings of 2013 Taibah University International Conference on Advances in Information Technology for the Holy Quran and Its Sciences, NOORIC 2013* (Piscataway, NJ: The Institute of Electrical and Electronics Engineers, Inc., Conference Publishing Service, IEEE Service Center, 2015). In the proceedings, there are proposals for detecting and authenticating Qur'ānic verses by security systems based on authentication agencies such as Al-Azhar or the King Fahd Quran Complex, e.g. Thabit Sabbah and Ali Selamat, "A Framework for Quranic Verses Authenticity Detection in Online Forum," in *Proceedings of 2013 Taibah University International Conference on Advances in Information Technology for the Holy Quran and Its Sciences, NOORIC 2013*, ed. Juan E. Guerrero (Piscataway, NJ: The Institute of Electrical and Electronics Engineers, Inc., Conference Publishing Service, IEEE Service Center, 2015): 6–11; Izzat M. Alsmadi, "Techniques to Preserve the Integrity of the Electronic Versions of the Nobel Quran," in Guerrero, *Proceedings of 2013 Taibah University International Conference*, 52–56 and Mostafa G.M. Mostafa and Ibrahim M. Ibrahim, "Securing the Digital Script of the Holy Quran on the Internet," in Guerrero, *Proceedings of 2013 Taibah University International Conference*, 57–60.

# 3 The Material Embodiment of Early Qur'ānic Manuscripts

Material properties can embody the use and function of a text, sometimes assuming a sociological and symbolic meaning (for more on this, see the contributions from Suit and Anderson in the present volume). The peculiarities of the textual environment express and participate with the textual meaning.[11] Thus, for example, the codex is the format par excellence of the sacred text of Islam, the *muṣḥaf* (pl. *maṣāḥif*), which is defined as a collection of written leaves placed and contained between two covers[12] and materialized in the surviving remains of a codex form attested in (fragmentary) leaves, quires and groups of quires dating from the first centuries of Islam. A reflection on the technology of the early manuscript form of the Qur'ānic text concerns mainly its codex form, its parchment writing surface, and its layout.

## 3.1 Writing Material Surface: Parchment, Papyrus, and Paper

The codex format, already known in pagan Rome, replaced and contrasted socially with the previous papyrus roll in the transcription of the Jewish and Christian sacred scriptures (see the chapters from del Barco and Outhwaite in the present volume).[13] By contrast, in the written transmission of the Qur'ānic text,

---

[11] Jonathan Walker, "Reading Materiality: The Literary Critical Treatment of Physical Texts," *Renaissance Drama* 41 (2013): 199–232 (201).

[12] al-Farrā' considered the word *muṣḥaf* as a passive participle, i.e. "which has been caused to contain written sheets between two end-covers"; see John Burton, "Muṣḥaf" in *Encyclopaedia of Islam*, 2nd ed., eds. C.E. Bosworth, E. van Donzel and W.P. Heinrichs and Ch. Pellat (Brill: Leiden, 1993): 7:668–69. As regards the format of the leaves contained *bayna lawḥayni*, see Abū Bakr Ibn Abī Dāwūd, *Kitāb al-Maṣāḥif*, ed. Arthur Jeffery, 5 (Arabic section in Arthur Jeffery, *Materials for the History of the Text of Qur'ān. The Old Codices, The Kitāb al-Maṣāḥif of Ibn Abī Dāwūd together With a Collection of the Variant Readings from the Codices of Ibn Ma'sūd, Ubai, Alī, Ibn 'Abbās, Anas, Abū Mūsā and other early Qur'ānic authorities which present a type of text anterior to that of the canonical text of 'Uthmān* [Leiden: Brill, 1937]).

[13] Maria Luisa Agati, *The Manuscript Book: A Compendium of Codicology*, trans. Colin W. Swift (Roma: L'Erma di Bretschneider, 2017 [2009]): 129–35, mentioning Cavallo in relation to the sociological and cultural reasons for the use of the codex form in the transmission of the Christian texts. See also David C. Parker, *An Introduction to the New Testament Manuscripts and Their Texts* (Cambridge: Cambridge University Press, 2008), 19, on the codex as the overwhelmingly predominant format in Christianity.

the codex is considered the original and first attested format. The first copies of *maṣāḥif* produced from the seventh century CE were made of parchment leaves obtained from animal skins processed using a special treatment. As parchment is generally considered a very expensive material, the production of copies of the Qur'ānic text is consequently interpreted as a non-personal activity meant for public use and proposing a common visual identity of the written sacred text. However, there is no evidence for suggesting the actual price of parchment leaves or their usage. An interesting aspect of materiality and its cultural implications is the abundance of skins and hides of animals because of the ritual sacrifice of animals whose meat was to be shared with the poor. Moreover, the skins and hides of those sacrificed animals had to be sold and the sum thus realized had to be donated in charity.[14] The surplus of skins during the ritual sacrifice of animals and the order to give the skins or their proceeds to charity implies that large quantities of skins were available to be used in certain periods of the Islamic year, including the use of leather for parchment.[15]

Parchment was the preferred material for writing the Qur'ānic text in the first four centuries of Islam, while papyrus was reserved for documentary materials in the Islamic world. When used for writing pieces of the Qur'ānic text, the latter material embodies the function of talismans, amulets and personal use of the

---

**14** *Ṣaḥīḥ al-Buḫārī*, Book al-Ḥaǧǧ, chapter *al-Ǧilāl li-l-budn* (Beirut: Maktaba Aṭ-Ṭaqafiya), vol. 2, no. 289. In bn Maǧāh, independently from the sacrifice, it is mentioned that the skin of an animal must be used even when animals die from natural causes (Muhammad "commanded that use should be made of the skins of dead animals, if they were tanned") in Ibn Maǧāh, *Sunan Ibn Maǧāh*, Book al-Libās, chapter 25, ed. Muḥammad Fu'ād 'Abd al-Bāqī (al-Qāhira: Dār Iḥyā' al-Kutub al-'Arabiyya, 1952), 1193–94.

**15** As regards the use of skins and hides, see for example Shlomo Dov Goitein, *A Mediterranean Society: The Jewish Communities of the Arab world as Portrayed in the Documents of the Cairo Genizah. Vol. 1, Economic Foundations* (Berkeley: University of California Press, 1967): 111–12; Ahmad Y. al-Hassan and Donald R. Hill, *Islamic Technology. An Illustrated History* (Cambridge: Cambridge University Press, 1986 [1992]): 199–200 (leather products). Maya Shatzmiller, *Labour in the Medieval Islamic World* (Leiden: Brill, 1994) lists a series of professions related to the manufacturing of skins and hides as leather and parchment (112–13, 230–32), e.g. the *ǧallād*, whose use is attested in Iraq, Egypt and Syria in the ninth to the eleventh century to indicate the "leather worker, leather merchant, worker and/or seller of hides"; the *muǧallid* attested in Iraq since the 8th century to mean the leather worker or bookbinder; and the *ruqūqī*, i.e. the polisher of skins, parchment maker (in Egypt in the tenth to the thirteenth century).

Qur'ānic text.[16] An exception is represented by the recently discovered Hamburg papyrus, which is a quire of seven papyrus bifolia.[17]

Papyrus is often thought to be more fragile than the stronger parchment. However, because of the durability of parchment, the ability to remove its ink, and its ability to be reused/modified, parchment has become associated with temporary documents and the modifiability of non-destroyable sacred text.[18] Thus, Grohmann reported that the caliphs' correspondence was preferably written on papyrus as it is impossible to cancel the script by erasure or even to change it without completely destroying the papyrus.[19] Indeed, there are examples of reuse of parchment writing materials in Qur'ānic palimpsests.[20] This peculiar form of recycling concerns Qur'ānic leaves reused to write new Qur'ānic leaves, retaining the original size and vertical format, like in the case of the Sanaa palimpsest; Qur'ānic leaves reused together with several different text for writing Christian Arabic texts destroying the original size and/or vertical format like the Sinai palimpsest; and, lastly, Coptic leaves reused for writing Qur'ānic text, as recently discovered.[21]

In the central area of the Islamic world, parchment was still in use in the tenth century but was gradually replaced by paper, while in the Muslim West, manuscript copyists continued to write on parchment until the fourteenth century and

---

**16** For example Papyrus Mingana 107, Papyrus Duke inv.274 and Papyrus Utah inv.342 show traces of folding to take the shape of small square talismans with amalgams of Qur'ānic text; see Alba Fedeli, *Early Qur'ānic Manuscripts, their Text, and the Alphonse Mingana Papers Held in the Department of Special Collections of the University of Birmingham* (PhD thesis, Birmingham: University of Birmingham, 2015), 135–37, 336–40. See also the recent work by Andreas Kaplony and Michael Marx, eds., *Qur'ān Quotations Preserved on Papyrus Documents, 7th-10th Centuries And the Problem of Carbon Dating Early Qur'āns* (Leiden: Brill, 2019).
**17** The papyrus quire P.Hamb.arab. 68 of the Staats- und Universitätsbibliothek Hamburg is a single quire consisting of seven papyrus bifolia, each page measuring about 20.2 x 16 cm in a landscape (almost squared) format, presented by Mathieu Tillier and Naïm Vantieghem at the series of the *Colloques at the College de France*, i.e. *Le Coran dans l'histoire culturelle et intellectuelle de Fusṭāṭ entre les VIIe et Xe siècles*, in June 2018. Images of the Hamburg quire papyrus are available among the digitised collection online at https://digitalisate.sub.uni-hamburg.de/handschriften.html (the persistent url being https://resolver.sub.uni-hamburg.de/kitodo/HANSh4089).
**18** See Thomas Schmidt, "Greek Palimpsest Papyri: Some Open Questions" in *Proceedings of the 24th International Congress of Papyrology* (Helsinki, 2007).
**19** Adolf Grohmann, *From the World of Arabic Papyri* (Cairo: Al-Maaref Press, 1952), 23.
**20** The reuse of protocols on papyrus cannot be considered a proper palimpsesting process, as the ink of the first layer was not cancelled. Rather, in this form of recycling, the strategy was to use the empty spaces of the protocol.
**21** Paper presented by Eléonore Cellard, "From Coptic to Arabic: A New Palimpsest for the History of the Qur'ān in Early Islam" at the annual *IQSA Conference*, Denver November 2018.

perhaps even later.²² The replacement of parchment is not only evident from the number of paper codices as opposed to parchment codices, but evidence also comes from documents about Islamic social and economic activity. In fact, in her analysis of labour activities in the Medieval Islamic world, Shatzmiller observed that occupations employed in producing leather goods formed ten percent of the labour force in the Islamic city during the first three centuries of Islam but declined to nine percent after this first period, and suggests a possible reason for this decline was the introduction of paper and the elimination of parchment as a writing material.²³

## 3.2 Form: Codex and Roll

As regards the technical format of the written object, it is worth noting that there are extant examples of rolls (*rotulus*) of the Qur'ānic text kept at the Museum of Turkish and Islamic Arts (TIEM) in Istanbul. These are forty-four Qur'ānic *rotuli* transferred from Damascus to Istanbul after the 1893 fire at the Great Mosque of Damascus. They are dated from different periods and written in different writing styles and on both papyrus (ten *rotuli*) and parchment (thirty-four *rotuli*). In her detailed description of the Damascus Qur'ānic *rotuli*, Ory observed the apologetic intention of the content of their Qur'ānic text; this includes, for example, exhortation to convert Jewish people, proclamation of the unity and omnipotence of God, truth of the new message and its connections with Abraham and the prophets, announcement of the Day of Judgement, the punishment of disbelievers, and the reward of righteous believers. Thus, the apologetic nature of the Qur'ānic *rotuli* mirrors the specific interests of Muslim scholars in seventh to twelfth century Damascus, around the Great Mosque.²⁴

It is interesting to note that in the ecclesiastical tradition of the Latin West, the liturgical *rotuli* are dated from the eighth century, and the Greek world had probably already been using liturgical rolls in a variety of offices and ceremonies from the fifth-sixth century onward, until the fifteenth century. The fact that Greek *rotuli* are not decorated while the Latin ones are sumptuously illustrated mirrors a development of the Latin roll as an authentic symbol of power, although there is another hypothesis that explains the richness in illustrating rolls as an

---

[22] François Déroche, "Codicology," in *Encyclopaedia of Islam Three*, eds. Kate Fleet, Gudrun Krämer, Denis Matringe, John Nawas, Everett Rowson (Brill: Leiden, 2017): 1:26–39.
[23] Maya Shatzmiller, *Labour in the Medieval Islamic World* (Leiden: Brill, 1994), 231–32.
[24] Solange Ory, "Un nouveau type de muṣḥaf: inventaire des corans en rouleaux de provenance damascaine, conservés à Istanbul," *Revue des Etudes Islamiques* 33 (1965/1966): 87–149 (146–49).

instrument for transmitting certain messages to the illiterate masses, that is, for illustrating the text and, in a few cases, for adapting the texts to musical formulae.[25] The Qur'ānic *rotuli* with possibly apologetic purposes do not seem to share any of the doctrinal instruments of propaganda expressed by the Latin roll, while its format (vertical *rotulus* against the horizontal *volumen*) is completely different from the typical Jewish scroll. The Qur'ānic *rotulus* has more in common with the roll of the Eastern tradition, devoid of decoration and illustration.[26]

Dying of parchment is another element of the materiality of sacred texts which assumes a symbolic meaning residing in an interplay between neighbouring cultures and traditions. Thus, the famous blue Qur'ān leaves (of a codex) have been interpreted as a counter-project to the Greek and Latin purple manuscripts of imperial rank. Recently, D'Ottone has proposed that the blue Bible of Cava written in the north of Spain at the beginning of the ninth century is perhaps a competitive model for the blue Qur'ān leaves, possibly commissioned by an Umayyad patron in Spain in the context of the local production of the Christian sacred text on dyed parchment.[27]

## 3.3 Layout

The codex format – or at least its leaves and quires – was the original and dominant shape and arrangement of the written transmission of the Qur'ānic text, with traces that reveal a possible influence from other scribal traditions. The prevalent vertical format and single column arrangement are inscribed in what George defined as the visual landscape of Late Antiquity, as they match visual arrangement of Greek, Syriac, Christian Palestinian Aramaic, and Ethiopic manuscripts.[28] A striking element in the main format of early Qur'ānic manuscripts is their relatively monumental size, which contrasts with the smaller format of the objects of the neighbouring traditions. Such large sizes might indicate possible cultural and political implications, intentionally marking the distinct status of the Qur'ānic text in opposition to the codices of the Christian sacred text.

---

25 Agati, *The Manuscript Book*, 126–28.
26 It is worth mentioning an exception that can be connected with the blue Qur'ān, i.e. the eleventh century Greek *rotulus* Borg.gr.27 of the Vatican Library, with its parchments dyed in red and light blue and written in gold and silver letters with the liturgy of John Chrysostom in the new Constantinople redaction. Agati, *The Manuscript Book*, 128.
27 Arianna D'Ottone, "The Blue Koran: A Contribution to the Debate on Its Possible Origin and Date," *JIM* 8 (2017): 127–43.
28 Alain George, *The Rise of Islamic Calligraphy* (London and Beirut: Saqi Books, 2010), 40–49.

A further element of the layout of a few very early Qur'ānic manuscripts is the absence of margins. The lines of script tend to occupy the entire surface of the writing material independently of the density of the script (i.e. dense or sparse script), suggesting that the argument of the exploitation of expensive materials is unfounded. The leaves of the codex Parisino-petropolitanus as observed by Déroche,[29] and the manuscript whose leaves are scattered in Birmingham (Mingana Isl.Ar.1572b), St. Petersburg (NLR Marcel 17) and Doha (MIA MS 67), show examples of the absence of margins. A seemingly similar situation belongs to the Jewish community as expressed in the Cairo Geniza. In fact, in the Jewish documents on parchment, the four edges were not trimmed and the natural curves were initially left, especially on the right and lower edges, while at a second stage these irregular blank spaces of parchment were trimmed off.[30] In the case of the layout of the Qur'ānic leaves mentioned above, the margins were not trimmed off and the script was adjusted to the irregular shape of the parchment material. The terminology designating the margins (*ḥāšiya, hāmiš,* and *ṭurra*) was also used to indicate the content of the matter placed in the margins as scholia and glosses.[31] In fact, space is physically necessary to admit the insertion of annotations, and the space around the text block is the ideal repository for such amendments and comments to the text. Thus, the absence of margins in early Qur'ānic manuscripts may lead to the suggestion that the writing material's surface was totally used so as not to admit space for comments or changes to the text. However, this argument does not seem to be convincing, as the early artefacts turn out to be a repository of amendments and annotations. Moreover, even in later manuscripts featuring a well-organized and ordered use of script and space with generous margins, the expression, for example, of alternative readings is assigned to the space of the writing block by means of a colour-coded diacritic system rather than in the

---

**29** François Déroche, *La transmission écrite du Coran dans les débuts de l'islam: Le codex Parisino-petropolitanus* (Leiden: Brill, 2009), 28–29 ("dès le départ la copie a occupé au maximum la surface disponible sur le feuillet").
**30** Shlomo Dov Goitein, *A Mediterranean Society: The Jewish Communities of the Arab World as Portrayed in the Documents of the Cairo Genizah. Vol. 2, The Community* (Berkeley: University of California Press, 1971), 232.
**31** Adam Gacek, *Arabic Manuscripts: A Vademecum for Readers* (Leiden: Brill, 2009), 157 (s.v. "Margins"); François Déroche ed., *Islamic Codicology: An Introduction to the Study of Manuscripts in Arabic Script*, trans. Deke Dusinberre and David Radzinowicz (London: Al-Furqān Islamic Heritage Foundation, 2005–2006): 177–78 ("Margins"). On *ḥāšiya*, i.e. the supergloss, as a subgenre of *tafsīr*, see for example the enlightening article by Walid A. Saleh, "The Gloss as Intellectual History: The Ḥāshiyahs on al-Kashshāf," *Oriens* 41 (2013): 217–59.

margins.³² Whatever reason lies behind the absence of margins, early Qurʾānic manuscripts still had space to host later additions, changes, amendments, annotations, and – using an *ante litteram* term – to host a markup system of the writing system and its code.

Describing the metalinguistic markup of scribes and thus the similarities between (a) the manuscript textual environment interpreted in light of (b) the digital encoding perspective, necessitates mentioning briefly a few basic features of the two elements.

## 4 The Textual Environment of the Manuscript

The physicality of the script's conditions concerns mainly two key aspects: the mechanism of the bare consonantal skeleton of the Arabic writing, and the markers for indicating the subdivision of the Qurʾānic text – both aspects are considered in connection with the phenomenon of the (alternative) readings of the text.

### 4.1 Diacritics

The Arabic script's system is based on the writing of its essential consonantal skeleton, which is composed of homograph base letters that can be distinguished by means of diacritics. Similarly, the consonantal skeleton can be differentiated by means of diacritics that mark mainly vowel signs.

These two sets of diacritic markers emerged in two distinct stages. The first markers used to disambiguate homograph letters (i.e., *iʿǧām*) are attested in the earliest stages of the development of the Arabic script in the pre-Islamic period. *Iʿǧām* diacritics are attested in documents such as the one-word Arabic inscription engraved in wood found in a Byzantine church in Petra, dated to the sixth

---

32 On the parallel situation in New Testament manuscripts facing the problem of restricted space at their disposal for inserting annotations in the margins, Parker has interestingly commented about the possible connection between the annotation to the Biblical text as interlinear or marginal notes and the gradual evolution toward the text's increasing stability when the annotation/commentate in proper commentaries made alternative renderings no longer necessary. See David C. Parker, *Textual Scholarship and the Making of the New Testament* (Oxford: Oxford University Press, 2012), 41–42. Parker's hypothesis leads to an exploration of whether Qurʾānic manuscripts show a higher degree of text stability in correlation with the opportunity to commentate on the text in separate works.

or the beginning of the seventh century CE[33]; the inscription of Zuhayr in Northern Saudi Arabia, dated 24 AH/644 CE[34]; and in papyrus PERF 558 from Egypt, dated 22 AH/642 CE.[35] Early Qur'ān manuscripts from the seventh century have *i'ǧām* diacritics executed in a stroke-like shape, while later they developed a more rounded shape. Early Arabic documents are not fully supplied with complete diacritic pointing, and previous scholarship has proposed some possible explanations for their distribution and motivation. For example, Kaplony observed that diacritics in a corpus of Arabic papyri mainly occur in specific environments, such as marking affixes and particles, thereby distinguishing grammatical categories similarly to the function of the Syriac dotting system.[36]

The second set of diacritic markers (i.e., *naqṭ*) is used to indicate mainly vowels as well as vowels in connection with nunation as the final ending of words, the *hamza* sign, and liaison between two words. Vowel diacritics were executed in a rounded dot-like shape placed above, below or after a certain letter to indicate respectively /a/, /i/, and /u/ vowels. Vowel dots appear already in the early eighth century, mainly in Qur'ānic manuscripts, and were rarely used in non-Qur'ānic Arabic papyri.[37] Similar to the use of *i'ǧām* diacritics, vowel dots are placed inconsistently in early Qur'ānic manuscripts from the eighth and ninth centuries. By contrast, this system of dots appears to be fully developed in manuscripts from the tenth and eleventh centuries. Consequently, Arabic vowel dots have been explained primarily through the lens of descriptions in Islamic sources from the tenth-eleventh centuries CE.[38] Recently, Muehlhaeusler focussed on

---

[33] Omar Al-Ghul, "An Early Arabic Inscription from Petra Carrying Diacritic Marks," *Syria* 81 (2004): 105–18.
[34] 'Ali Ibn Ibrahim Ghabban and Robert Hoyland, "The Inscription of Zuhayr, the Oldest Islamic Inscription (24 AH/AD 644–645), the Rise of the Arabic Script and the Nature of the Early Islamic State," *Arabian Archaeology and Epigraphy* 19 (2008): 210–37.
[35] Alan Jones, "The Dotting of A Script And The Dating Of An Era: The Strange Neglect of PERF 558," *Islamic Culture* 72.4 (1998): 95–103.
[36] Andreas Kaplony, "What are those Few Dots for? Thoughts on the Orthography of the Qurra Papyri (709–710), the Khurasan Parchments (755–777) and the Inscription of the Jerusalem Dome of the Rock (692)," *Arabica* 55 (2008): 91–112.
[37] Geoffrey Khan, *Arabic Papyri: Selected Material from the Khalili Collection* (London and Oxford: The Nour Foundation, Azimuth Editions and Oxford University Press, 1992), 44. Khan observed three traces of old vocalization with dots, suggesting that the case of two vowel-dots in a word's internal position could be "a loan from Syriac before the later system of Arabic vocalisation became stabilised."
[38] Dutton has investigated the use of coloured dots in some manuscripts; see Yasin Dutton, "Red Dots, Green Dots, Yellow Dots and Blue: Some Reflections on the Vocalisation of Early Qur'anic Manuscripts – Part I," *JQS* 1 (1999): 115–40 and Part II, *JQS* 2 (2000): 1–24. Similarly, Cellard has studied the system of dots attested in some Qur'ānic fragments from the 8th century

reading marks, distinguishing between disambiguating signs (*iʿǧām*-diacritics and vowel dots) and syntactical or phonological markers. He observed that "the Arabic writing system is set up to consider each semantic element in isolation [...] and without regard for actual pronunciation," thus assigning to diacritical signs the function of compensating for this lack.[39] Muehlhaeusler's conclusions are similar to Kaplony's hypothesis that diacritic dots mark grammatical categories.[40]

One of the main developments in the diacritic system of the Arabic script was the addition of a colour-based code which aimed at encoding readings from the perspective of alternative versus main readings. Basically, in the fully developed vowel-dot system, a bare consonantal skeleton like /T Ḥ R Ǧ W N/ was furnished by *iʿǧām* diacritics in the shape of strokes that made explicit the reading of its possible homograph base letters to be read as T Ḥ Ǧ [N] (fig. 1 and 2). This was also specified by vowel-dots according to the encoding system of positioning them above, below, and after the base letter. Thus, T Ḥ R Ǧ W N could be specified through the vowel-dot system, based on a position code and added in red ink, expressing the reading *tuḥraǧūna* in Q. 30:19 (fig. 3). The level of red vowel dots could be further enhanced by placing another level of vowel dots in a different colour, for example in green ink (fig. 4). Thus, the bare consonantal skeleton at the red vowel-dot level indicates e.g. *tuḥraǧūna* (i.e., "you will be brought out," which is the reading of the majority of the readers) while at the green vowel-dot level the same consonantal skeleton displays a further reading, e.g. *taḥruǧūna* (i.e. "you will leave," which is the reading for example of al-Kisaʾī).[41]

The system developed for annotating simultaneously multiple readings in Qurʾānic manuscripts by means of different colours shares, to a certain degree,

---

to the mid-9th century. She mainly investigated the variation between *hamza*, *imāla*, and third person pronominal suffixes (*hu* and *hum*) in comparison with the description of these features in the early Islamic scholarly literature, see Eléonore Cellard, "La vocalisation des manuscrits coraniques dans les premiers siècles de l'islam," in François Déroche, Christian J. Robin and Michel Zink, eds., *Les origines du Coran, le Coran des origines* (Paris: Académie des Inscriptions et Belles-Lettres, 2015), 151–76. George built on Dutton's observations, focusing on manuscripts from the ninth–eleventh centuries. These observations are interpreted through al-Dānī's treatise (*al-Muḥkam*), see Alain George, "Coloured Dots and the Question of Regional Origins in Early Qurʾans (Part I)," *JQS* 17:1 (2015): 1–44 and (Part II), *JQS* 17:2 (2015): 75–102.

39 Mark Muehlhaeusler, "Additional Reading Marks in Kufic Manuscripts," *JIS* 27 (2016): 1–16 (14).
40 Kaplony, "What are those Few Dots for," 100.
41 These are, for example, the two readings expressed by a colour code of red vs. green dots in manuscript John Rylands Ar.688 [11], f.23r (fig. 5). Ibn Muǧāhid reported the reading *taḥruǧūna*, i.e. the green vowel-dot level reading. I heartily thank the staff of the John Rylands Library for their promptness and kindness in helping me during my visiting fellowship at their Research Institute in summer 2015 when I had the chance to study MS Ar.688 [11] and other Qurʾānic fragments.

**Fig. 1:** Bare consonantal skeleton with homograph base letters: *Arabic MS 11(688) f.23r, detail*. *John Rylands Library, The University of Manchester.* Copyright of the University of Manchester. Layer extracted by Alba Fedeli.

**Fig. 2:** Bare consonantal skeleton with explicit reading of possible homographs: *Arabic MS 11(688) f.23r, detail*. John Rylands Library, The University of Manchester. *Copyright of the University of Manchester.* Layer extracted by Alba Fedeli.

**Fig. 3:** Red vowel-dot level (tuḫraǧūna): *Arabic MS 11(688) f.23r, detail. John Rylands Library, The University of Manchester.* Copyright of the University of Manchester. Layers extracted by Alba Fedeli.

**Fig. 4:** Green vowel-dot level (taḫruǧūna): *Arabic MS 11(688) f.23r, detail. John Rylands Library, The University of Manchester.* Copyright of the University of Manchester. Layers extracted by Alba Fedeli.

**Fig. 5:** Red and green vowel-dot levels: *Arabic MS 11(688) f.23r, detail. John Rylands Library, The University of Manchester.* Copyright of the University of Manchester.

similarities with the medieval musical notation system used in Europe.[42] Guido d'Arezzo (b. circa 994), the inventor or at least the developer of the musical staff, proposed distinguishing musical lines by different colours, although the system was already in use in the *Musica enchiriadis* that inspired Guido's staff in the first place. Each line and its corresponding row should be assigned its own colour (i.e. red, green, yellow, and black).[43] Moreover, medieval manuscripts could have most clefs written in the same brown ink as the notes, while further C clefs were drawn in red ink to change the clef. More interestingly, musical manuscripts show cases of green lines that could indicate, for example, a B-flat reference, as a musical act at once proofreading and prescribing how to read/sing a note as alternative

---

[42] I thank Teunis van Lopik for calling my attention to the two references about colour system used in music.

[43] John Haines, "The Origins of the Musical Staff," *The Musical Quarterly* 91 (2008): 327–78 (331).

to the first reading/singing indication.⁴⁴ Thus, the use of red and green colours to express vowel dots can be seen as a mechanism for indicating the corresponding "clef of reading" of the consonantal skeleton of the Qur'ānic text as if colour indicates the "pitch" of written words.

The complexity of the writing code system of early Qur'ānic manuscripts can be seen as a means to express plurality rather than a repository of ambiguous signs that generate ambiguity and variant readings. The seeming imperfection of the system with its variant readings is possibly a necessary instrument rather than an inevitable consequence. In mentioning the problem of the variant readings as discussed in the work of Abū Bakr Ibn al-ʿArabī, *al-ʿAwāṣim min al-Qawāṣim* (i.e. "protections from catastrophes"), Nasser underlines that the collection and codification of the Qur'ān abrogated all the previous (pre-ʿUthmānic) readings. Although copies of the Qur'ān (*maṣāḥif*) continued to be written and encoded without diacritics (*min ġayr naqṭ wa-lā ḍabt*) in the same way as they were written during the time of Muhammad, the Prophet's companions transmitted how to read it and this non-disambiguated script of the Qur'ānic text was a flexible element (*wa-hāḏā amr yasīr*), since the absence of diacritics facilitated the diverse reading(s). This was important as there were already significant differences in reciting the Qur'ān.⁴⁵

The homograph-based consonantal writing system is the basis of the script's fundamental ambiguity, and the flexible/arbitrary and partial use of the diacritics increases the ambiguity of the system. Although such ambiguity is generally considered to be the cause of the presence and diffusion of variants in reading the Qur'ānic text, the manuscript evidence also shows several cases of variant readings that are expressed by a different consonantal skeleton.⁴⁶

---

**44** Anna Zayaruznaya, "In Defense of Green Lines, or The Notation of B-flat in Early Ambrosian Antiphoners," in *Ambrosiana at Harvard: New Sources of Milanese Chant*, eds. Thomas Forrest Kelly and Matthew Mugmon (Cambridge, MA: Houghton Library of the Harvard College Library, 2010): 33–56, 50–51 and 55–56.

**45** Shady Hekmat Nasser, *The Transmission of the Variant Readings of the Qur'ān: The Problem of Tawātur and the Emergence of Shawādhdh* (Leiden: Brill, 2013): 104–05. See Abū Bakr Ibn al-ʿArabī, *al-ʿAwāṣim min al-qawāṣim fī taḥqīq mawāqif al-ṣaḥāba* (Beirut: Dar al-Kotob al-ʿIlmiyah, 2010), 171.

**46** See for example Alba Fedeli, "Early Evidences of Variant Readings in Qur'ānic Manuscripts," in *Die dunklen Anfänge. Neue Forschungen zur Entstehung und frühen Geschichte des Islam*, eds. K.H. Ohlig and G.R. Puin (Berlin: Verlag Hans Schiler, 2005): 293–316; Asma Hilali, *The Sanaa Palimpsest: The Transmission of the Qur'an in the First Centuries AH* (Oxford: Oxford University Press in association with the Institute of Ismaili Studies, 2017); and François Déroche, *Le Coran, une histoire plurielle* (Paris: Éditions du Seuil, 2019).

## 4.2 Subdivision of the Text

Variant readings are also impacted by the subdivision of the sequence of the Qur'ānic text. Scribes used several arrangements of space and layout to indicate the separation between sections of the text. Thus, scribes left one or two blank lines (i.e. *bayāḍ*), which later could be filled in with simple decorations. They could also leave no *bayāḍ* between two *sūra*s. Consequently, they could accommodate the *basmala* (i.e. the incipit written before the beginning of each *sūra* with the exception of *sūrat at-Tawba*) in different ways. In fact, there are examples of *basmala* written at the beginning of a new line as a continuum before the text, or as an independent line before the text starts on the following line or, lastly, placed in and adjusted to the available space left at the end of the previous *sūra*.

Moreover, early manuscripts exhibit the insertion of devices to mark the end of each single verse (*fāṣila*) in the form of clusters of strokes or dots (three or more strokes/dots arranged in a triangular or rectangular shape). Markers of ends of verses have been traced simultaneously or subsequently to the first writing of the text, and scribes could choose whether or not to leave space to accommodate these markers. At a later stage, likely in the same period of the introduction of the red vowel-dot system, special signs were added to indicate the end of a fifth and/or tenth verse, that is, to annotate a five-verse group (a *ḫams*) or a ten-verse group (a *ʿašr*). Considering the fragmentary nature of early Qur'ānic manuscripts, which often contain incomplete sections of the text and thus an incomplete sequence of numbering of single verses, the annotation of a *ḫams* or a *ʿašr* constitutes a clear trace for verifying the counting system according to recognized or unknown numbering systems of the Qur'ānic text.[47]

Because of the presence of two parallel but distinct counting system annotations, first the notation of single verses and later the introduction of groups of five/ten verses, there are situations where alternative numbering systems are simultaneously present. Manuscripts can have signs counting, for example, nine single verses notated by the first hand whereas a later hand counted those nine verses as a group of ten verses. In such a situation, it has to be noted that the later hand marked the group of ten verses without indicating the end of the extra tenth verse. Thus, there are no traces of corrections and additions to the first numbering of the

---

[47] See Anton Spitaler, *Die Verszählung des Koran nach islamischer Überlieferung*, Sitzungsberichte der Bayerischen Akademie der Wissenschaften: Philosophisch-historische Abteilung 11 (München: Verlag der Bayerischen Akademie der Wissenschaften, 1935).

nine verses, but the ʿašr could be considered as an instruction for interpreting the text sequence, a sort of concordance between the two numbering systems.[48]

## 4.3 Interpretation of the Script: Ambiguity of Incomplete or Obscure Disambiguating System

The Arabic writing system in early Qurʾānic manuscripts accommodates simultaneously competing interpretations that imply that the ambiguity of their script is a constitutive ambiguity rather than a contingent one because of the phenomenon of the multiple layers of readings.[49] Similarly, following Ibn al-ʿArabī's interpretation of the non-disambiguated script of the Qurʾānic text as a flexible tool that facilitated the existing different readings, the underspecified consonantal skeleton is a tool for a communication strategy of tolerance for ambiguity rather than an accidental phenomenon.

Moreover, the sophisticated form of the ambiguous script in Qurʾānic manuscripts generates two challenging situations. In fact, in some cases, disambiguating vowel diacritics (naqṭ) and iʿǧām diacritics are partially added to the consonantal skeleton in a seemingly accidental manner or in an obscure way, thus generating further ambiguity. In other words, the resulting ambiguity suspends the disambiguation system.[50]

As regards the first case, the partial addition of disambiguating vowel dots and consonantal strokes, Kaplony – as above-mentioned – observed that iʿǧām diacritics specified grammatical categories in specific environments, primarily marked affixes and particles. Nevertheless, a systematic analysis of the environments in which these diacritics are placed is still a desideratum. As regards vowel dots placed in certain positions, previous scholarship has interpreted them through the lens of the eleventh century Islamic literature on the subject, considering the vowel dots as segmental signs which are physically attached to a single consonantal element. Thus, from this perspective, both classical works and modern studies

---

**48** This is for example the situation in MS National Library of Russia Marcel 17, MS Mingana Islamic Arabic 1572b and MS Museum of Islamic Art in Doha, Qatar, MIA67. Thus, for example, in Q.3, the first hand counts nine verses between Q.3:22 and Q.3:30 and eleven verses between Q.3:31 and Q.3:41, whereas the later red layer counts ten verses in both cases. The black layer counts ten verses between Q.3:22–31 and Q.3:32–41, in agreement with the first hand (MS NLR Marcel 17, f.3). See Fedeli, *Early Qurʾānic Manuscripts, their Text*, 237–38, 250–55.
**49** On the classification of elementary, hermeneutic, and constitutive ambiguity, see Frauke Berndt and Klaus Sachs-Hombach, "Dimensions of Constitutive Ambiguity," in *Ambiguity: Language and Communication*, ed. Susanne Winkler (Berlin: De Gruyter, 2015): 271–82.
**50** Berndt and Sachs-Hombach, "Dimensions of Constitutive Ambiguity," 272.

note that vowel dots could indicate grammatical endings or distinguish homographs. However, this interpretation does not seem to be able to explain all dots in manuscripts as there are vowel diacritics added in unambiguous situations.[51]

An example of a more challenging situation is the *ḥiǧāzī* manuscript scattered between Birmingham, Doha, and St. Petersburg (Mingana Isl. Ar. 1572b, NLR Marcel 17, and MIA MS67). This manuscript features several cases of red vowel dots that cannot be explained through the available literature on Arabic vocalization systems. The manuscript is the result of several writing stages, having three distinct layers of ink. The first layer – written with brown ink – features the consonantal skeleton, a few diacritical strokes, and markers at the ends of verses. The second layer, in black ink, provides some amendments. The third layer, in red ink, does four things. It provides some amendments to the consonantal skeleton, it retraces the text where the ink has faded, it adds vowel dots, and it marks groups of verses. This shows that the vocalization system was added to the consonantal skeleton at a later stage. The *ḥiǧāzī* style of the script can be traced to the seventh or eighth century and it is likely that the red vowel dots were added at least a few decades later. Several dots are placed in positions that are obscure and even (grammatically) impossible. For example, the final *tanwīn* ending of nouns (*-un*) occurs after one verbal form with the feminine perfect tense ending (*-at*). Analysing a fragment of the manuscript (the Birmingham leaves), Dutton identified traces of a Syrian reading tradition, including variations related to the consonantal skeleton, diacritical strokes, and red dot vowels. However, in his interpretation of the variations, Dutton observed that a few red dots are placed in a "non-accurate" way: "Red dots, however, directly above the *mīm*s of *munkhaniqa* and *mutaraddiya* suggest that these vowels may not always have been positioned in what one might consider an accurate way by later standards!"[52]

Here, the theory of markup system as diacritics in digital editing can shed light in understanding first, some obscure examples of diacritics whose main function is supposedly to disambiguate the script and second, the sophisticated nature of the multiple readings that simultaneously exist and which are accommodated by the ambiguous script.

---

51 For example, in MS John Rylands Ar.688 [11], probably dating from the ninth century, a single vowel dot has been added to the entire consonantal skeleton of *lā yaškurūna* (i.e. "[but most of the people] are not grateful," Q.12:38 in f. 2r), i.e. one dot above the final *nūn* to mark /a/. The consonantal skeleton is not specified by means of consonantal diacritics – thus leaving Y Š [N] as ambiguous homographs – and the only added vowel diacritic has been added to the final ending *–ūna*, which seems an unambiguous situation.
52 Yasin Dutton, "Two 'Ḥijāzī' Fragments of the Qur'an and Their Variants, or: When Did the Shawādhdh Become Shādhdh?," *JIM* 8 (2017): 1–56 (22).

# 5 The Digital Encoding Perspective

## 5.1 Textual Space and Active Readers

The text of early manuscripts is multilayered both because of their historical physical strata and their constitutive ambiguity that accommodates and facilitates simultaneous competing readings. This kind of "open text" in early manuscripts overlaps with the idea of the digital text and its hyperdimensions, in particular hypertextuality or multilayered strata. In fact, building upon Barthes, Mordenti reflected on how the Gutenberg textual product constrains the role of the reader, whereas the readers should be entitled to a greater role in understanding the text as they make their way through the meaningful segments of the text.[53] Thus, for example, the active role of the reader in the digital text has a correspondence to the handwritten manuscript culture: we have traces of this process of passing through the text in the examples of alternative readings expressed (tagged) in early Qur'ānic manuscripts. The "hyper" textual space is dynamic and its reader, or user, has an active role in a digital textspace, whereas the book is perceived and used as a static object.[54] The hypertextual digital space and the fluid and multilayered manuscript text overlap at a few points, since both their readers are active in choosing one level of the possible readings of the text.

More specifically, with regard to editing manuscript texts in a digital horizon, technical possibilities allow texts from all of the manuscript evidence to be transcribed, documented and stored. In a traditional (critical) edition, this abundance of details about the history of the production of the documents is limited to the *apparatus criticus* as regards its textual variants, while its linguistic diversity tends to be regularized. The consequence of this different approach in editing due to different technological possibilities (i.e. hyperdimensions and digital space vs. linear text and printing technology) is crucial. The editions produced in digital encoding are digital documentary editions.[55] They are not critical editions in the sense of a reconstruction of the possible original archetype, as they aim to edit and tag the richness of the manuscript text rather than to recover the original text (on similar issues in Christian texts, see the essay from Allen in the present volume).

---

**53** Mordenti, "Parádosis."
**54** Jerome McGann, "Coda: Why Digital Textual Scholarship Matters; Or, Philology in a New Key," in *The Cambridge Companion to Textual Scholarship*, eds. Neil Fraistat and Julia Flanders (Cambridge: Cambridge University Press, 2013): 274–88 (279). See also Mordenti above mentioned as pertains to the active role of the reader in the post-Gutenberg era.
**55** Elena Pierazzo, "Digital Documentary Editions and the Others," *Scholarly Editing: The Annual of the Association for Documentary Editing* 35 (2014): 1–23.

## 5.2 Notational Markup and Inference Ticket

In a digital horizon of editing of early Qur'ānic manuscripts, two aspects of markup are particularly relevant to decoding the system used in these manuscripts: interpretative and diacritical functions.

The fundamental aspect of digitally editing manuscripts lies in tagging the manuscript text and its features. Like scribes, digital editors transcribe and describe the text – and object – adding metalinguistic notes. They can annotate the text following accepted standards of markup languages, thus encoding the text. Editors can use, for example, the standard language of the Text Encoding Initiative (TEI) whose markup data model is based on an embedded XML markup. Markup is the use of embedded codes to describe the structure of a document or to insert instructions related to its layout that can be used by a layout processor.[56]

Thus, in editing Qur'ānic manuscript texts, digital humanists can use: (1) inline additions of categories to word segments using opening and closing elements that circumscribe and describe a section of the manuscript text; (2) markers for encoding the structural unit of the text (e.g. beginning of *sūra* or beginning of verse); (3) entities to mark paratextual elements like the device to indicate the end of a verse; and (4) editorial and local notes to comment on and annotate the text or other features of the object, such as the comparison between a particular reading of the manuscript and a reading recognized in the *qirā'āt* literature.[57]

In editing manuscripts, markup languages make explicit certain features of a text based on codex/leaves technology, and exhibit these features "by bringing them forth visibly into the expression of the text" – markup languages are thus "essentially notational."[58] As markup is able to make evident the various implicit features of the text, it is able to handle the full range of the editor's choices. The markup encoding makes explicit the code of the artefact and its text according to the editor's interpretation without relying on the reader's above-mentioned ability to handle the ambiguity. Markup is an instrument "to make (*license*) certain inferences about passages in the marked-up material"; it thus remains

---

**56** Darrell R. Raymond, Frank Wm. Tompa, and Derick Wood, "Markup Reconsidered," (paper presented at the *First International Workshop on Principles of Document Processing*, Washington, D.C., October 21–23, 1992): 1–20 (1).
**57** This is, for example, the work I did in editing the Cambridge Qur'ānic palimpsest now available in the Cambridge Digital Library (https://cudl.lib.cam.ac.uk/collections/minganalewis/1). See Alba Fedeli, *Edition of the Qur'ānic Leaves of Palimpsest Manuscript CUL Or. 1287* (Cambridge: Cambridge Digital Library, 2016).
**58** Dino Buzzetti and Jerome McGann, "Critical Editing in a Digital Horizon," in *Electronic Textual Editing*, eds. Lou Burnard, Katherine O'Brien O'Keeffe and John Unsworth (New York: The Modern Language Association of America, 2006): 53–73 (61).

interpretative as it reflects the understanding of the text by the transcriber.⁵⁹ The idea of markup as an interpretative act that generates inferences corresponds to seeing it as an "inference ticket" as underlined by Buzzetti.⁶⁰ Both markup and diacritics have a double value of operator and operand. They are, at the same time, operational – as they provide metalinguistic instructions and inference ticket – and referential – as they are signs of the object language.

## 5.3 Suprasegmental Markup and Diacritics

In digital editing theory, markup can be viewed as a diacritical sign. Markup carries out a proper diacritical function with respect to the text.⁶¹ In fact, diacritics can be part of the text or an external comment on it.⁶² Raymond, Tompa, and Wood have compared markup to diacritics in consonantal scripts. They noticed that the earliest types of markup were intended "to facilitate the reading process," giving as examples the diacritics employed to signify vocalic distinction and the decorations that identify breaks and subdivision in a text sequence.⁶³

In relation to the use and function of diacritics in early Qurʼānic manuscripts, it is important to underline the crucial difference between diacritics that, being part of the text, produce a "textual variant" and diacritics that, being external description related to the text, produce a "variant interpretation."⁶⁴ Diacritics and markup can be part of the text – thus object language – or external description to the text – thus metalanguage. What later layers added to an early Qurʼānic manuscript text, whether object text or metalanguage, will be discussed below.

---

**59** C.Michael Sperberg-McQueen, Claus Huitfeldt and Allen Renear, "Meaning and Interpretation of Markup," *Markup Languages: Theory & Practice* 2.3 (2000): 215–34.
**60** Buzzetti uses Gilbert Ryle's locution referring to the licence that the possessor of an inference ticket has to provide explanations of given facts. See Dino Buzzetti, "Codifica del testo e intelligenza artificiale," *Schede Umanistiche* 17 (2003): 171–97 (188–90) and Buzzetti, "Biblioteche digitali e oggetti digitali complessi," 71, and mentioned also by Buzzetti and McGann, "Critical Editing in a Digital Horizon," 66–67.
**61** Dino Buzzetti, "Diacritical Ambiguity and Markup," in *Augmenting Comprehension: Digital Tools and the History of Ideas. Proceedings of a Conference at Bologna, 22–23 September 2002*, eds. Dino Buzzetti, Giuliano Pancaldi and Harold Short (London: Office for Humanities Communication Publication, 17, 2004): 175–88 (178).
**62** Buzzetti and McGann, "Critical Editing in a Digital Horizon," 65.
**63** Raymond, Tompa, and Wood, "Markup Reconsidered," 2.
**64** In digital editing theory, the distinction is underlined in Buzzetti and McGann, "Critical Editing in a Digital Horizon," 65.

Moreover, inasmuch as markup has a diacritical function separable from the text, it can be a metalinguistic description of the structure of the text. Consequently, as stated by Buzzetti, "out-of-line markup [...] is a form of metalinguistic markup independent of the position of the tags in the sequence of codified characters. This enables us to assign to the expression of the text also nonlinear and overlapping hierarchical structures. Distinct *interpretative variants* can thus be assigned to the structure of the text."[65] Here Buzzetti recalls Raymond, Tompa, and Wood's distinction between strongly and weakly embedded tags. Their difference lies in the function of the tags' position. In strongly embedded markup, the position of the markup is information-bearing, while a weakly embedded markup can be placed at any point in the text as its position is not information-bearing.[66] In other words, markup can be segmental or suprasegmental, thus referring to a precise segment of the text or to more segments. If the position is not information-bearing, editors/readers can also assign nonlinear and overlapping structures.

# 6 The Textual Environment of the Qur'ānic Manuscript Interpreted in Light of the Digital Encoding Perspective: Diacritical and Notational Markup

## 6.1 Suprasegmental Diacritics: The Digital Horizon and the Syriac Parallel

Moving to a closer look at the Qur'ānic manuscript textual environment as interpreted in light of the digital encoding perspective, the latter offers interesting insights about diacritical and notational markup, in particular with regard to a few obscure examples of vowel dots added to early Qur'ānic manuscripts. The above-mentioned manuscript scattered in Birmingham, St. Petersburg, and Doha has some puzzling positions in which red vowel-dot diacritics have been placed. Dutton explains these vowel dots in impossible positions as the result of inaccuracy by the person who placed them "in what one might consider an accurate way by later standards!"

---

**65** Buzzetti, "Diacritical Ambiguity and Markup," 185.
**66** Raymond, Tompa, and Wood, "Markup Reconsidered," 3–4.

However, if we look at a few of these inexplicable vowel dots from the perspective of markup theory in digital encoding, their positions may or may not be information-bearing, and thus they can be placed at any point in the text segment. This perspective turns out to be effective, when considering diacritics as suprasegmental signs (operators with operational value) and not as mere segmental signs (operands with referential value), thus coinciding with the perspective of the Syriac dots noted above. In fact, Syriac dots can have both the function of segmental signs bound to a single base graph and suprasegmental signs, so that some dots mark phonemes while others tag entire words or expressions like metalinguistic markup, as observed by Kiraz.[67] Considering the similarities of the Arabic diacritics with the functions of the Syriac dots[68] also solves the chronological aspect of the problem. As stressed by Dutton, some Qur'ānic vowel dots do not correspond to later standards dating from the tenth or eleventh centuries. Thus it seems to be more effective to compare the Qur'ānic dots that were introduced in the eighth-ninth century with contemporary examples such as the Syriac dots indicating *syāmē* or *mḥaydānā,* or those marking a feminine ending. All three of these signs appeared in Syriac manuscripts in the eighth century.

An example of the nonsegmental and nonphonemic value of vowel dots is in Q.6:138: *wa-anʿ(ā)mun ḥurrimat ẓuhūru-ha*, i.e. "(These are) cattle whose backs are forbidden." In MS Mingana Islamic Arabic 1572b, f.8v (the Birmingham portion of the larger manuscript), the two dots at the end of the verb *ḥurrimat* cannot be read as a final nominal *tanwīn* ending (-*un*). As nonsegmental and nonphonemic signs, they could indicate the assimilation between the final *taʾ* and the initial *ẓaʾ* of the following word, thus corresponding to the *mḥaydānā* ("uniting") dotting of Syriac[69] that also coincides with the representation of examples of *alif al-waṣl* (the phonetic liaison between two words) in Qur'ānic manuscripts.[70]

This alternative approach in explaining obscure vowel dots (*naqṭ* diacritics) in early Qur'ānic manuscripts has to be extended to the perspective on the entire system of *naqṭ-* and *iʿǧām* diacritics. If the diacritical system of Qur'ānic manuscripts originated from a nonphonemic suprasegmental function of markup as

---

[67] See George Anton Kiraz, *The Syriac Dot. A Short History* (Piscataway, NJ: Gorgias Press, 2015), 99–102. An example of a suprasegmental dot is the *syāmē*, i.e. the pair of dots referred to an entire word and indicating its plural form that is not bound to a single base graph but is suprasegmental and its position is not information-bearing.

[68] See, for example, Kiraz on the morphological tagging of dots (Kiraz, *The Syriac Dot*, 76, 79).

[69] Kiraz, *The Syriac Dot*, 118.

[70] Recently, I suggested a few readings of vowel-dots in MS NLR Marcel 17, Mingana Islamic Arabic 1572b and MIA67 in light of the metalinguistic markup approach of digital encoding and similarities with the Syriac dotting system. However, a more systematic analysis of the dotting system in Qur'ānic manuscripts in a comparative perspective with Syriac is needed.

operator, this would enable a nonlinear and overlapping structure to be assigned to the consonantal skeleton of words. The phenomenon of alternative and coexisting readings marked by more than one layer of diacritics is an argument supporting the hypothesis of the position of diacritics as non-information-bearing and their similarity to a weakly embedded markup in digitally encoding, mentioned above.

## 6.2 The Nonlinear Structure

Coexisting readings of a single word or a sequence of words as well as parallel counting systems can be seen as overlapping and nonlinear structures of the Arabic script. Thus, as in the example above, the sequence /T Ḥ R Ǧ W N/ can be read following one "clef" as *tuḥraǧūna* and/or following the other "clef" as *taḥruǧūna* (fig. 5). Its consonantal skeleton can be seen as notes on a musical staff in which the red and green colours indicate the pitch of those notes, similar to the use of colours in medieval musical manuscripts. Interestingly, Monella proposed a "musical score" model for digital scholarly editions with three parallel transcriptions of the text (graphical layer, alphabetic layer, and linguistic layer) which are mapped on to one another.[71] This model would help solve the inconsistency of manuscripts at the graphical and alphabetic layers without normalizing the possible significant different orthographies and different ways of diacritization, while also perfectly fitting the digital edition of the coexistent multiple layers of readings as they are expressed – for example – by different colours.

## 6.3 The Notational Markup and the Inference Ticket

The second aspect of markup languages in digital editing that shows similarities with the manuscript situation is the notational function of markup. In digital editing, the difference between diacritical markup as part of the text (object text) and as external comment on it (metalanguage) is evident. Such distinct perspective can shed light on the markup of embedded additions and amendments to early Qur'ānic manuscripts. The perspective on later additions as being metalinguistic rather than only object language that changes the text is connected with the suprasegmental value of diacritics.

---

71 Monella, "Many Witnesses, Many Layers," section 3.

Markup is the use of embedded codes to make explicit certain features of a manuscript text, thus expressing its interpretative nature given by its being an "inference ticket" as mentioned above with reference to Buzzetti's analysis. If we consider, for example, the situation in which a later, different annotation of the numbering system used in counting the Qur'ānic verses is added to the first annotation, the "inference ticket" value of the later annotation is evident. The two markers of the numbering system run parallel and the second layer does not have the function of correcting the first layer of markers. The manuscript is the space of the encounter between two codes. If the person who added a different layer at a later stage had meant to correct the numbering system (thus adding a markup with the value of a text object), they would have added the end of verse marker at the tenth extra verse.[72] It is likely that their intention was to annotate instructions for the interpretation of the numbering system, thus providing a sort of concordance in order to steer readers who had the other numbering system in mind. The second layer of ten-verse groups in the Birmingham, St. Petersburg, and Doha manuscript represents a sort of reading instruction rather than a correction and expresses the life of the manuscript and its changes over time.

Thus, notational function of markup in digitally encoding provides new insight into interpreting some aspects of the manuscript culture.

# 7 Standoff Markup for a Phylogenetic Analysis: Further Directions in Editing Early Qur'ānic Manuscripts

## 7.1 Functionality of Digital Editing

Undeniably, the use of digital scholarly editing influences the approach to the text, and the concept of an original text is replaced by the idea that each manuscript has its own right to be the text. Collecting and displaying as many Qur'ānic manuscripts and their editions as possible is crucially important in Qur'ānic studies from an epistemological point of view because of the different point of view on the idea of an original text and the new focus on the history of the transmission of the text. Nevertheless, the mere visualization of digital editions of

---

**72** On the details about the numbering systems of verses in this manuscript, see Fedeli, *Early Qur'ānic Manuscripts*, 237–38, 250–55.

Qur'ānic manuscripts does not fully relay all that is required in the digital representation of information.

In fact, the final aim of scholars' work in editing and transmitting manuscript texts is not the mere reproduction of the original document, for example in a diplomatic edition, but the provision of a format that is readable and interpretable. Digital representation has to meet two fundamental requirements: thoroughness and functionality. The digital data assembled in editing manuscript texts have to be not only complete and accurate but also functional for computational elaboration.[73]

An example of the functionality of Qur'ānic manuscript editions in terms of the computational analysis of manuscript data beyond their mere online visualization is the phylogenetic analysis of Qur'ānic manuscripts. Phylogenetic software – developed in biology to group species based on DNA sequences – can be used to understand the possible relationships between several manuscripts in order to reconstruct their possible context and production process. Thus, textual studies merged with information technology and biology can contribute to the knowledge of the transmission of the Qur'ānic text by collecting and comparing data from manuscript evidence. In a testing phase of a phylogenetic analysis project on early Qur'ānic manuscripts,[74] I had to face three main challenges, thus envisaging possible solutions and further directions of research in Qur'ānic manuscript studies: (1) removing embedded markup, (2) presenting multi-layered editions like the musical score model, and (3) highlighting the materiality of the manuscript.

In my experience in the digital scholarly editing of Qur'ānic manuscripts, I faced the challenge of removing embedded markup in order to compare editions of different manuscripts in their different layers. Recent scholarship has formulated a hypothesis on the limitations of embedded markup and the advantages of standoff markup in order to guarantee interoperability and standardization.[75]

---

[73] Buzzetti very sharply distinguished between "esaustività e funzionalità della conservazione dell'informazione." See Buzzetti, "Biblioteche digitali e oggetti digitali complessi," 41–43.
[74] Alba Fedeli and Andrew Edmondson, "Early Qur'ānic Manuscripts and their Networks: a Phylogenetic Analysis Project," pre-circulating paper for the Conference "Qur'ānic Manuscript Studies: State of the Field," Budapest May 2017 after the research project *Early Qur'ānic Manuscripts and their Relationship as Studied Through Phylogenetic Software* at the Central European University, Budapest.
[75] See for example Desmond Schmidt, "The Role of Markup in the Digital Humanities," *Historical Social Research* 37/3 (2012): 125–46, and Desmond Allan Schmidt, "Using Standoff Properties for Marking-up Historical Documents in the Humanities," *Information Technology* 58/2 (2016): 63–69.

## 7.2 Edition of Separate Layers: Standoff Markup and Merged Versions

In editing early Qur'ānic manuscripts, I inserted markup codes to express the stratigraphic nature of these objects and observe the presence of comments or amendments (*ante litteram* markup) made by later users. In my phylogenetic analysis project, it was essential to distinguish the different strata of each manuscript in order to compare single images – in Segre's view[76] – of manuscript texts. A standoff markup system and the consequent technical possibility of producing a multi-version document (MVD) model would allow editing of the separate layers of each manuscript as part of a single document, thus representing a text as a set of merged versions in a single digital entity.[77]

Similarly, distinct manuscript strata refer not only to different historical moments in the production and use of the manuscripts, but also to different graphic systems used in different times and places. The main challenge to solve in the already-concluded phylogenetic project has been the treatment of words that approach the use of diacritical signs differently. The constitutive ambiguity of Arabic script based on the possible use of diacritics generates a difficult situation, as phylogenetic software has to process words that potentially convey the same information but are graphically different. The homograph base letter that can be disambiguated by means of a diacritic is processed differently if it is with or without diacritics, although for the "tolerant and discriminating reader" the two different Unicode points are two different pieces of information to be treated and compared. As Unicode is not sufficient on its own in editing early Qur'ānic manuscripts, their richness, and their variety of graphic systems, a solution based on the distinction of the graphical layer, alphabetic layer, and linguistic layer as suggested by Monella seems to be more convincing. This would allow Unicode to be used efficiently and these early manuscripts to be collated and their data searched. The musical score model developed by Monella seems to be a possible new direction for editing manuscripts.

---

[76] "Image of the text" refers to Segre's interpretation that this image is a linguistic structure that performs a system. See Cesare Segre, *Semiotica filologica. Testo e modelli culturali* (Torino: Giulio Einaudi editore, 1979), 64–65.

[77] See Desmond Schmidt and Robert Colomb, "A Data Structure for Representing Multi-Version Texts Online," *International Journal of Human-Computer Studies* 67 (2009): 497–514.

## 7.3 Annotations About Materiality

Lastly, a desideratum that I considered and partially included in my phylogenetic analysis project is the creation of data referring to the materiality of the manuscripts. In my spreadsheet, I introduced not only the transcription of the Qurʾānic text, but also information about the paratextual elements, the layout of the page, and the writing system: this included format (vertical or horizontal); ruling (yes or no); *bayāḍ* (yes or no); size of the leaves; number of lines; and the layout of the *basmala* (independent or consecutive before the beginning of the verse). With regard to the writing system, a typology of characters used for every single letter was introduced. The introduction of these paratextual elements, physical arrangement of the text, and script characteristics was prompted by previous studies which have applied phylogenetic analysis to physical artefacts that can be analysed insofar as they are encoded in an appropriate way.[78]

This consideration of the encoding of elements related to the object's materiality brings into discussion the importance of including annotations about materiality in scholarly editing in order to produce a "social text editing". In his 1999 study *Bibliography and the Sociology of Texts*, McKenzie stressed the importance of the medium in effecting its message and thus supporting the need to include the relationship between form, function, and symbolic meaning in bibliography. Reading and rereading, editing and reediting a manuscript text should take into consideration the history of the readings of that object without borders "between bibliography and textual criticism on the one hand and literary criticism and literary history on the other."[79]

Thus, we return to our starting point that texts cannot exist as divested of their material form and technology, which influence the idea of the text itself. Digital scholarly editions and their computational analyses (for example, using phylogenetic software) likewise cannot disregard the material aspects of manuscripts, with all their cultural and social value.

---

[78] Christopher J. Howe and Heather F. Windram, "Phylomemetics – Evolutionary Analysis Beyond the Gene," *PLoS Biology* 9.5 (2011), e1001069. doi:10.1371/journal.pbio.1001069.
[79] Donald Francis McKenzie, *Bibliography and the Sociology of Texts* (Cambridge: Cambridge University Press, 2009 [1999]), 10, 23.

# Bibliography

Agati, Maria Luisa. *The Manuscript Book: A Compendium of Codicology*. Trans. Colin W. Swift. Roma: L'Erma di Bretschneider, 2017 [2009].

Alsmadi, Izzat M. "Techniques to Preserve the Integrity of the Electronic Versions of the Nobel Quran." In *Proceedings of 2013 Taibah University International Conference on Advances in Information Technology for the Holy Quran and Its Sciences, NOORIC 2013* edited by Juan E. Guerrero, 52–56. Piscataway, NJ: The Institute of Electrical and Electronics Engineers, Inc., Conference Publishing Service, IEEE Service Center, 2015.

Avalle, D'Arco Silvio. "I canzonieri: definizione di genere e problemi di edizione." In *La critica del testo. Atti del Convegno di Lecce, 22–26 ott. 1984*, 363–382. Roma: Salerno Editrice, 1985.

Berndt, Frauke and Klaus Sachs-Hombach. "Dimensions of Constitutive Ambiguity." In *Ambiguity: Language and Communication*, edited by Susanne Winkler, 271–282. Berlin: De Gruyter, 2015.

Bodin, Jean. *Colloque entre sept scavans qui sont de differens sentimens: des secrets cachez des choses relevées, traduction anonyme du* Colloquium heptaplomeres *de Jean Bodin (manuscrit français 1923 de la Bibliothèque Nationale de Paris)*, edited by François Berriot, Katharine Davies, Jean Larmat, Jacques Roger. Genève: Librairie Droz, 1984.

Burton, John. "muṣḥaf." In *Encyclopaedia of Islam, Second Edition*, edited by C.E. Bosworth, E. van Donzel and W.P. Heinrichs and Ch. Pellat, vol. 7, 668–69. Leiden: Brill, 1993.

Buzzetti, Dino and Jerome McGann. "Critical Editing in a Digital Horizon." In *Electronic Textual Editing*, edited by Lou Burnard, Katherine O'Brien O'Keeffe and John Unsworth, 53–73. New York: The Modern Language Association of America, 2006.

Buzzetti, Dino. "Biblioteche digitali e oggetti digitali complessi: Esaustività e funzionalità nella conservazione." In *Archivi informatici per il patrimonio culturale*, Convegno internazionale organizzato dall'Accademia Nazionale dei Lincei in collaborazione con ERPANET e la Fondazione Franceschini, 41–75. Roma: Accademia Nazionale dei Lincei, Bardi Editore, 2006.

Buzzetti, Dino. "Diacritical Ambiguity and Markup." In *Augmenting Comprehension. Digital Tools and the History of Ideas. Proceedings of a Conference at Bologna, 22–23 September 2002*, edited by Dino Buzzetti, Giuliano Pancaldi and Harold Short, 175–188. London: Office for Humanities Communication Publication, 17, 2004.

Buzzetti, Dino. "Codifica del testo e intelligenza artificiale." *Schede Umanistiche* 17.1 (2003): 171–97.

Cellard, Eléonore. "La vocalisation des manuscrits coraniques dans les premiers siècles de l'islam." In *Les origines du Coran, le Coran des origines*, edited by François Déroche, Christian J. Robin and Michel Zink, 151–76. Paris: Académie des Inscriptions et Belles-Lettres, 2015.

D'Ottone, Arianna. "The Blue Koran: A Contribution to the Debate on Its Possible Origin and Date." *JIM* 8 (2017): 127–43.

Déroche, François, ed. *Islamic Codicology: An Introduction to the Study of Manuscripts in Arabic Script*. Trans. Deke Dusinberre and David Radzinowicz. London: Al-Furqān Islamic Heritage Foundation, 2005–2006.

Déroche, François. "Codicology." In *Encyclopaedia of Islam Three*, edited by Kate Fleet, Gudrun Krämer, Denis Matringe, John Nawas, Everett Rowson, Vol. 1, 26–39. Leiden: Brill, 2017.

Déroche, François. *La Transmission Écrite du Coran Dans les Débuts de L'Islam: Le Codex Parisino-Petropolitanus*. Leiden and Boston: Brill, 2009.
Déroche, François. *Le Coran, une histoire plurielle*. Paris: Éditions du Seuil, 2019.
Dutton, Yasin. "Red Dots, Green Dots, Yellow Dots and Blue: Some Reflections on the Vocalisation of Early Qur'anic Manuscripts – Part I." *JQS* 1 (1999): 115–40.
Dutton, Yasin. "Red Dots, Green Dots, Yellow Dots and Blue: Some Reflections on the Vocalisation of Early Qur'anic Manuscripts – Part II." *JQS* 2 (2000): 1–24.
Dutton, Yasin. "Two 'Ḥijāzī' Fragments of the Qur'an and Their Variants, or: When Did the Shawādhdh Become Shādhdh?" *JIM* 8 (2017): 1–56.
Fedeli, Alba. "Early Evidences of Variant Readings in Qur'ānic Manuscripts." In *Die dunklen Anfänge. Neue Forschungen zur Entstehung und frühen Geschichte des Islam*, edited by Karl-Heinz Ohlig and Gerd-R. Puin, 293–316. Berlin: Verlag Hans Schiler, 2005.
Fedeli, Alba. *Early Qur'ānic Manuscripts, their Text, and the Alphonse Mingana Papers Held in the Department of Special Collections of the University of Birmingham*. PhD thesis. Birmingham: University of Birmingham, 2015.
Fedeli, Alba. *Edition of the Qur'ānic Leaves of Palimpsest Manuscript CUL Or. 1287*. Cambridge: Cambridge Digital Library, 2016. Online: https://cudl.lib.cam.ac.uk/collections/minganalewis/1.
Gacek, Adam. *Arabic Manuscripts: A Vademecum for Readers*. Leiden: Brill, 2009.
George, Alain. "Coloured Dots and the Question of Regional Origins in Early Qur'ans (Part I)." *JQS* 17 (2015): 1–44.
George, Alain. "Coloured Dots and the Question of Regional Origins in Early Qur'ans (Part II)." *JQS* 17 (2015): 75–102.
George, Alain. *The Rise of Islamic Calligraphy*. London and Beirut: Saqi Books, 2010.
Ghabban, 'Ali Ibn Ibrahim and Robert Hoyland. "The Inscription of Zuhayr, the Oldest Islamic Inscription (24 AH/AD 644–645), the Rise of the Arabic Script and the Nature of the Early Islamic State." *Arabian Archaeology and Epigraphy* 19 (2008): 210–37.
Ghul, Omar Al-. "An Early Arabic Inscription from Petra Carrying Diacritic Marks." *Syria* 81 (2004): 105–18.
Goitein, Shlomo Dov. *A Mediterranean Society: The Jewish Communities of the Arab World as Portrayed in the Documents of the Cairo Genizah*. Vol. 1, *Economic Foundations*. Berkeley: University of California Press, 1967.
Goitein, Shlomo Dov. *A Mediterranean Society: The Jewish Communities of the Arab World as Portrayed in the Documents of the Cairo Genizah*. Vol. 2, *The Community*. Berkeley: University of California Press, 1971.
Grohmann, Adolf. *From the World of Arabic Papyri*. Cairo: Al-Maaref Press, 1952.
Haines, John. "The Origins of the Musical Staff." *The Musical Quarterly* 91.3/4 (2008): 327–78.
Hassan, Ahmad Y. al-, and Donald R. Hill. *Islamic Technology: An Illustrated History*. Cambridge: Cambridge University Press, 1986.
Hilali, Asma. *The Sanaa Palimpsest: The Transmission of the Qur'an in the First Centuries AH*. Oxford: Oxford University Press in association with the Institute of Ismaili Studies, 2017.
Howe, Christopher J. and Heather F. Windram. "Phylomemetics – Evolutionary Analysis beyond the Gene." *PLoS Biology* 9.5 (2011), doi:10.1371/journal.pbio.1001069.
Ibn al-'Arabī, Abū Bakr. *al-'Awāṣim min al-qawāṣim fī taḥqīq mawāqif al-ṣaḥāba*. Beirut: Dar al-Kotob al-'Ilmiyah, 2010.
Jeffery, Arthur. *Materials for the History of the Text of Qur'ān. The Old Codices, The Kitāb al-Maṣāḥif of Ibn Abī Dāwūd together With a Collection of the Variant Readings from the*

*Codices of Ibn Ma'sūd, Ubai, Alī, Ibn 'Abbās, Anas, Abū Mūsā and other early Qur'ānic authorities which present a type of text anterior to that of the canonical text of 'Uthmān.* Leiden: Brill, 1937.

Jones, Alan. "The Dotting Of A Script And The Dating Of An Era: The Strange Neglect Of PERF 558." *Islamic Culture* 72.4 (1998): 95–103.

Kaplony, Andreas. "What are those Few Dots for? Thoughts on the Orthography of the Qurra Papyri (709–710), the Khurasan Parchments (755–777) and the Inscription of the Jerusalem Dome of the Rock (692)." *Arabica* 55 (2008): 91–112.

Kaplony, Andreas and Michael Marx, eds. *Qur'ān Quotations Preserved on Papyrus Documents, 7th-10th Centuries And the Problem of Carbon Dating Early Qur'āns.* Leiden: Brill, 2019.

Khan, Geoffrey. *Arabic Papyri: Selected Material from the Khalili Collection.* London and Oxford: The Nour Foundation, Azimuth Editions and Oxford University Press, 1992.

Kiraz, George Anton. *The Syriac Dot: A Short History.* Piscataway, NJ: Gorgias Press, 2015.

McGann, Jerome. "Coda: Why Digital Textual Scholarship Matters; Or, Philology in a New Key." In *The Cambridge Companion to Textual Scholarship*, edited by Neil Fraistat and Julia Flanders, 274–88. Cambridge: Cambridge University Press, 2013.

McKenzie, Donald Francis. *Bibliography and the Sociology of Texts.* Cambridge: Cambridge University Press, 2009 [1999].

Monella, Paolo. "Many Witnesses, Many Layers: The Digital Scholarly Edition of the *Iudicium Coci et Pistoris* (Anth. Lat. 199 Riese)." In *Digital Humanities: Progetti Italiani Ed Esperienze Di Convergenza Multidisciplinare, Atti Del Convegno Annuale Dell'Associazione per l'Informatica Umanistica e La Cultura Digitale (AIUCD) Firenze, 13–14 Dicembre 2012*, edited by Fabio Ciotti, 173–206. Roma: Sapienza Università Editrice, 2014.

Mordenti, Raul. "Parádosis. A proposito del testo informatico." *Atti della Accademia Nazionale dei Lincei. Classe di Scienze Morali, Storiche e Filologiche.* Memorie, Serie IX, 28.4 (2011): 623–91.

Mostafa, Mostafa G.M., and Ibrahim M. Ibrahim. "Securing the Digital Script of the Holy Quran on the Internet." In *Proceedings of 2013 Taibah University International Conference on Advances in Information Technology for the Holy Quran and Its Sciences, NOORIC 2013*, edited by Juan E. Guerrero, 57–60. Piscataway, NJ: The Institute of Electrical and Electronics Engineers, Inc., Conference Publishing Service, IEEE Service Center, 2015.

Muehlhaeusler, Mark. "Additional Reading Marks in Kufic Manuscripts." *JIS* 27 (2016): 1–16.

Nasser, Shady Hekmat. *The Transmission of the Variant Readings of the Qur'ān. The Problem of Tawātur and the Emergence of Shawādhdh.* Leiden: Brill, 2013.

Nuovo, Angela. *Alessandro Paganino (1509–1538).* Padova: Editrice Antenore, 1990.

Ory, Solange. "Un nouveau type de muṣḥaf : inventaire des corans en rouleaux de provenance damascaine, conservés à Istanbul." *Revue des Etudes Islamiques* 33 (1965/ 1966): 87–149.

Parker, David C. *An Introduction to the New Testament Manuscripts and Their Texts.* Cambridge: Cambridge University Press, 2008.

Parker, David C. *Textual Scholarship and the Making of the New Testament.* Oxford: Oxford University Press, 2012.

Pierazzo, Elena. "Digital Documentary Editions and the Others." *Scholarly Editing: The Annual of the Association for Documentary Editing* 35 (2014): 1–23.

Raymond, Darrell, R. Frank Wm. Tompa, and Derick Wood. "Markup Reconsidered." Technical Report presented at *The First International Workshop on Principles of Document Processing*, Washington, D.C., October 21–23, 1992: 1–20.

Sabbah, Thabit, and Ali Selamat. "A Framework for Quranic Verses Authenticity Detection in Online Forum." In *Proceedings of 2013 Taibah University International Conference on Advances in Information Technology for the Holy Quran and Its Sciences, NOORIC 2013*, edited by Juan E. Guerrero, 6–11. Piscataway, NJ: The Institute of Electrical and Electronics Engineers, Inc., Conference Publishing Service, IEEE Service Center, 2015.

Saleh, Walid A. "The Gloss as Intellectual History: The Ḥāshiyahs on al-Kashshāf." *Oriens* 41 (2013): 217–59.

Schmidt, Desmond Allan. "Using Standoff Properties for Marking-up Historical Documents in the Humanities." *Information Technology* 58.2 (2016): 63–69.

Schmidt, Desmond, and Robert Colomb. "A Data Structure for Representing Multi-Version Texts Online." *International Journal of Human – Computer Studies* 67 (2009): 497–514.

Schmidt, Desmond. "The Role of Markup in the Digital Humanities." *Historical Social Research* 37 (2012): 125–46.

Schmidt, Thomas. "Greek Palimpsest Papyri: Some Open Questions." In *Proceedings of the 24th International Congress of Papyrology, Helsinki 1–7 August 2004*, edited by Jaakko Frösén, Tiina Purola and Erja Salmenkivi, vol. 2, 979–90. Helsinki: Societas Scientiarum Fennica, 2007.

Segre, Cesare. *Semiotica filologica. Testo e modelli culturali*. Torino: Giulio Einaudi editore, 1979.

Shatzmiller, Maya. *Labour in the Medieval Islamic World*. Leiden: Brill, 1994.

Sperberg-McQueen, C. Michael, Claus Huitfeldt, and Allen Renear. "Meaning and Interpretation of Markup." *Markup Languages: Theory & Practice* 2.3 (2000): 215–34.

Spitaler, Anton. *Die Verszählung des Koran nach islamischer Überlieferung*. Sitzungsberichte der Bayerischen Akademie der Wissenschaften: Philosophisch-historische Abteilung 11. München: Verlag der Bayerischen Akademie der Wissenschaften, 1935.

Walker, Jonathan. "Reading Materiality: The Literary Critical Treatment of Physical Texts." *Renaissance Drama* 41 (2013): 199–232.

Wilson, Brett M. *Translating the Qur'an in an Age of Nationalism: Print Culture and Modern Islam in Turkey*. Oxford: Oxford University Press in association with The Institute of Ismaili Studies, 2014.

Zayaruznaya, Anna. "In Defense of Green Lines, or The Notation of B-flat in Early Ambrosian Antiphoners." In *Ambrosiana at Harvard: New Sources of Milanese Chant*, edited by Thomas Forrest Kelly and Matthew Mugmon, 33–56. Cambridge, MA: Houghton Library of the Harvard College Library, 2010.

Joshua L. Mann
# Paratexts and the Hermeneutics of Digital Bibles

## 1 Introduction

The Christian Bible is increasingly being read in digital form. In 2018, YouVersion's Bible App had been installed more than 340 million times on "unique devices" worldwide.[1] Some of its more than 1,753 Bible versions in 1,134 languages are likely the most read digital Bibles in the world.[2] A 2014 survey commissioned by communications giant AT&T estimates that one in four Americans who regularly attend a worship service have "used a mobile device/internet to connect with faith or inspiration during worship services."[3] Of those who report connecting to faith-based organisations through a mobile device, twenty-nine percent have used mobile devices to "access electronic holy books and/or song books."[4]

The proliferation of digital technology for reading the Bible raises the question: *What hermeneutical difference does it make when the Bible is engaged digitally?* This question might be answered from a number of perspectives, but for the purposes of this chapter, I want to focus specifically on what we might call the hermeneutical effect, or illocutionary effects, of the Bible's *technology*, print or digital. How might the meaning of the texts and/or the Bible as an object be perceived differently because of the medium? To help answer this question, we will look through one primary lens, *paratextuality*, supplemented by another, material culture – each explained in turn below.[5]

---

[1] Available online at https://www.youversion.com/the-bible-app/ [accessed 18 Sep 2018].
[2] I note that in early 2016, youversion.com was reporting just over 1,200 Bible versions in nearly 900 languages, suggesting that in just over two years, around 500 Bible versions and more than 200 languages have been added. https://www.youversion.com/ [accessed 14 Jan 2016].
[3] "Inspired Mobility Survey Results" (AT&T), 4, accessed October 10, 2018; online: https://about.att.com/content/dam/snrdocs/Inspired_Mobility_Research_Report.pdf.
[4] "Inspired Mobility Survey Results," 5.
[5] Much of my work on paratexts and digital Bibles originated in a blog musing I wrote in 2013 and was developed into seminar presentations in 2015 (see: Joshua L. Mann, "Print vs. Digital: The Effect of Pagination on Interpretation," *Joshua L Mann* (blog), March 21, 2013, https://josh.do/print-vs-digital-the-effect-of-pagination-on-interpretation/). Some of the material has been published in an article exploring the hermeneutical effects of a mobile liturgical app (Joshua L. Mann, "Mobile Liturgy: Reflections on the Church of England's Suite of Digital Apps," *Online – Heidelberg Journal of Religions on the Internet* 12 [2017]: 42–59); see also, Joshua L. Mann, "How

∂ Open Access. © 2020 Joshua L. Mann, published by De Gruyter. This work is licensed under a Creative Commons Attribution-NonCommercial-NoDerivatives 4.0 International License.
https://doi.org/10.1515/9783110634440-011

## 2 Paratextuality

One way to compare digital and print forms of a given text is to compare *paratextual* differences. Gérard Genette, who is responsible for the literary use of the term *paratext*, explains:

> A literary work consists, entirely or essentially, of a text, defined (very minimally) as a more or less long sequence of verbal statements that are more or less endowed with significance. But this text is rarely presented in an unadorned state, unreinforced and unaccompanied by a certain number of verbal or other productions, such as an author's name, a title, a preface, illustrations. And although we do not always know whether these productions are to be regarded as belonging to the text, in any case they surround it and extend it, precisely in order to *present* it, in the usual sense of this verb but also in the strongest sense: to *make present*, to ensure the text's presence in the world, its "reception" and consumption in the form (nowadays, at least) of a book. These accompanying productions, which vary in extent and appearance, constitute what I have called elsewhere the work's *paratext*.[6]

Thus paratexts are hermeneutically significant, exercising illocutionary force on the reader: "Far from being an issue that preoccupies only the theoretically minded, the matter of the paratext is always – albeit often imperceptibly – already at work in the hermeneutic process."[7]

In contrast to Genette's conception of paratextuality, which seemed to focus on the print medium, I offer the following qualifications, which I have made elsewhere,[8] in order to accommodate what might be called *digital* paratexts:

> (1) It matters very little in the following analysis whether or not the "author" legitimates (or accepts responsibility) for a paratext[9]; and (2) the *para* of *paratexts* receives the emphasis, not the *texts*. In other words, paratexts are framing features of the text but not necessarily texts themselves.[10] ... I consider paratexts to be productions that accompany, present, or

---

Technology Means: Texts, History, and Their Associated Technologies," *Digital Humanities Quarterly* (2017). Material from both of these articles has been revised and included below.

6 Gérard Genette, *Paratexts: Thresholds of Interpretation*, trans. Jane E. Lewin, Literature, Culture, Theory 20 (Cambridge: Cambridge University Press, 1997), 1.

7 Laura Jansen, "Introduction: Approaches to Roman Paratextuality," in *The Roman Paratext: Frame, Texts, Readers*, ed. Laura Jansen (Cambridge: Cambridge University Press, 2014): 1.

8 The following passage is quoted from Mann, "Mobile Liturgy," 44.

9 Cf. Genette *Paratexts*, 2: "By definition, something is not a paratext unless the author or one of his associates accepts responsibility for it."

10 Whereas Genette seemed to envision that most paratexts were themselves textual (e.g., table of contents, publisher's name, etc.). For a similar approach as I take for digital paratextuality, see Yra van Dijk, "The Margins of Bookishness: Paratexts in Digital Literature," in *Examining Paratextual Theory and Its Applications in Digital Culture*, ed. Nadine Desrochers and Daniel Apollon, Advances in Human and Social Aspects of Technology (Hershey, PA: IGI Global, 2014): 24–45.

contain a text, including productions that facilitate the engagement of a reader.[11] Paratexts may be produced by an author, publisher, software developers, editors, and the like. Paratexts also include visual features associated with typography, page layout, book design or, in software, the interface and its manifold features.[12]

With this in mind, consider the paratexts of a modern, printed Christian Bible, generally a collection of sixty-six or more ancient documents in a single volume. Note that the binding itself is a hermeneutically significant paratext suggesting to the reader or user that these documents *belong* together. This sense of unity is reinforced by other paratextual features, such as uniform typography, page layout, and consecutive page numbering across the bound collection. (It might also be said that these are paratexts inherent to print technology, though not exclusively so). Consider, however, in terms of the text's history, these paratexts potentially obscure the fact that the documents within were completed at various times over the course of a millennium by authors who very likely did not envision that their work would be read alongside all of these other works. Imagine the difference of a user's perception of these texts if, instead, these documents were each individually bound – perhaps 66 thin volumes arranged on a shelf. This is not unlike the arrangement of previous collections of biblical texts as collections of scrolls.[13]

To illustrate further, even a paratextual feature as simple as pagination can have a significant hermeneutical effect. In fact, it was because I had to *turn a page* that I first set off on researching paratextuality and digital Bibles in the first place.[14] In the Gospel of Luke, I came to Jesus' "Triumphal Entry" into Jerusalem which takes place not long before his crucifixion. I came to Luke 19:41 in a Greek New Testament[15] – the last line of the page, a new paragraph, that might be translated into English as: "And as he [Jesus] came near, when he saw the city, he wept

---

[11] Compare a recent narrow definition in reference to the paratexts of biblical manuscripts: "all contents in biblical manuscripts except the biblical text itself are a priori paratexts." Martin Wallraff and Patrick Andrist, "Paratexts of the Bible: A New Research Project on Greek Textual Transmission," *Early Christianity* 6 (2015): 239.

[12] Compare similar approaches to applying categories from traditional bibliography to digital texts, including considerations of hermeneutical significance, in: N. Katherine Hayles, "Translating Media: Why We Should Rethink Textuality," *The Yale Journal of Criticism* 16 (2003): 263–90; Matthew G. Kirschenbaum, "Editing the Interface: Textual Studies and First Generation Electronic Objects," *Text* 14 (2002): 15–51; Marlene Manoff, "The Materiality of Digital Collections: Theoretical and Historical Perspectives," *Portal: Libraries and the Academy* 6 (2006): 311–25.

[13] See Jocelyn Penny Small, *Wax Tablets of the Mind: Cognitive Studies of Memory and Literacy in Classical Antiquity* (London: Routledge, 1997), 43, 48.

[14] Mann, "Print vs. Digital."

[15] Nestle-Aland 28th Edition.

over it...". This is a complete sentence grammatically, an independent clause. No punctuation appears at the end of the line, however, and it appears at the end the main text on the page. The sentence continues, but to move from the last word of verse 41 (αὐτήν) to the first word of verse 42 (λέγων), the reader must *turn* the page. Coming to the end of the page created an extra moment for my mind to process what I had just read, with the result that the line about Jesus weeping became all the more dramatic. It is the note that ends the page, as it were. This brief pause of having to turn the page contributed to the meaning that occurred to me during this reading. The text *struck* me in a new way. And one of the key features that gave rise to this meaning is the layout of the page, a property of the codex book form which we might classify as a *paratextual* property. Imagine for a moment that I was reading the text on a mobile device, scrolling through lines of text rather than turning pages. I would never have come to this moment of pause, this moment of page turning.

What then might be a feature unique to a digital biblical text? Consider how the finality of the Bible is far less acute in its digital form compared with its print counterpart. One can hold a printed book – it is bound and not easily modified.[16] A Bible app, on the other hand, is periodically updated with new features, corrections, etc. In short, the paratextual messages of a printed book and its digital counterpart are in some ways distinct. These and other examples will be elaborated more fully below, but first let us introduce how material culture can provide another angle for understanding the hermeneutical impact of digital technology on the biblical text.

## 3 Material Culture and Digital Texts

A second angle from which to consider the hermeneutics of technology is provided by material culture scholars, who have maintained and interpreted the significance, including hermeneutical effects, of "things" (as opposed to ideas), including religious objects. S. Brent Plate offers a "working definition" of the discipline of material religion:

---

[16] On the physicality of reading in general, see Naomi S. Baron, *Words Onscreen: The Fate of Reading in a Digital World* (New York: Oxford University Press, 2015), 131–56. On the Bible in particular, see: Katja Rakow, "The Bible in the Digital Age: Negotiating the Limits of 'Bibleness' of Different Bible Media," in *Christianity and the Limits of Materiality*, ed. Minna Opas and Anna Haapalainen, Bloomsbury Studies in Material Religion 1 (London: Bloomsbury, 2017): 101–21.

(1) an investigation of the interactions between human bodies and physical objects, both natural and human-made; (2) with much of the interaction taking place through sense perception; (3) in special and specified spaces and times; (4) in order to orient, and sometimes disorient, communities and individuals; (5) toward the formal strictures and structures of religious traditions.[17]

We are interested in the hermeneutical significance of those "interactions" to which the first part of the definition refers. As Colleen McDannell says in *Material Christianity*, "The material world of landscapes, tools, buildings, household goods, clothing, and art is not neutral and passive; people interact with the material world thus permitting it to communicate specific messages."[18] Investigating these *messages* – what a digital Bible communicates by virtue of its technological medium, the technology through which it presents itself to a user – is what we seek to do, and that primarily through the lens of paratexts.

It is important for our purposes not to equate "material" strictly with what is physical in a way that excludes *digital* technology.[19] In fact, as a starting point, let us define technology in its broadest sense. Helpful in this regard is Ferré's definition: "...technology involves (i) implements used as (ii) means to practical ends that are somehow (iii) manifested in the material world as (iv) expressions of intelligence."[20] By referring to technology as "implements...manifested in the material world," the definition applies equally to print and digital media, books and apps, all of which can then be situated comfortably in what we might call *material* culture.

How similar approaches might handle print-digital comparisons of a religious text can be illustrated by the recent respective analyses of Katja Rakow[21] and Tim Hutchings, the latter of whom says, "A material approach to digital religion must consider the differences between digital and physical objects, as well as what

---

**17** S. Brent Plate, "Material Religion: An Introduction," in *Key Terms in Material Religion*, ed. S. Brent Plate (London: Bloomsbury, 2015): 4.
**18** Colleen McDannell, *Material Christianity: Religion and Popular Culture in America* (New Haven: Yale University Press, 1995), 2.
**19** For a critical summary of how scholars of material culture have treated digital media (as either "essentialist," where materiality applies to what is more-or-less physical, or "binary," where materiality is defined in contrast to what it is not) contrasted with theorists of digital media (who take a "functionalist" approach where "material" extends to whatever "acts like a physical object") see Tim Hutchings, "Augmented Graves and Virtual Bibles: Digital Media and Material Religion," in *Materiality and the Study of Religion: The Stuff of the Sacred*, ed. Tim Hutchings and Joanne McKenzie, Theology and Religion in Interdisciplinary Perspective (London: Routledge, 2017): 87–91.
**20** Frederick Ferré, *Philosophy of Technology* (Athens, GA: University of Georgia Press, 1995), 25.
**21** Rakow, "The Bible in the Digital Age."

they have in common."[22] Along these lines, next I will consider what appears to set a digital Bible apart from a printed one, paying special attention to paratexts.

## 4 Mobile Bible Apps: An Analysis

In what follows, first are general considerations of the hermeneutical significance of the paratexts of digital Bibles relative to their print counterparts. Second are observations and reflections of one specific example, YouVersion's Bible App.

### 4.1 Significant Paratexts of Digital Bibles Compared to Print

As explored above, in Bible software, paratexts might be produced by agents such as authors, developers, editors, or publishers, and include features of the interface, text layout, and even functionality. Unlike print books, some paratextual properties may be manipulated by the user in real time (e.g., changing font and spacing, removing verse numbers, subtitles, and page numbers, etc.). Further, some paratexts may be dependent on the user's technical environment (especially the operating system and other features of the device, including hardware).

Consider again that the printed Bible in codex form carries a strong paratextual message of canonicity – that the sixty-six (or more) ancient documents bound together *belong* together.[23] The literal binding conveys a message of a canonical binding. We might ask, what is the "binding" paratext – the boundary paratext – of a *digital* Bible? Technically, a computer file containing the text exists, usually marked (or tagged) at document boundaries. Since a reader is generally unaware of this technical boundary, its hermeneutical significance is more difficult to discern.[24] In terms of the electronic display of a biblical text, boundaries might include titles, title pages, chapter or page numbers that indicate a beginning, or a scroll bar that indicates the user's relative location within the document.[25] One

---

[22] Hutchings, "Augmented Graves," 93.
[23] Cf. Jeffrey S. Siker who, although not employing paratextuality as I have here and elsewhere, likewise points out potential differences between digital and printed Bibles: *Liquid Scripture: The Bible in a Digital World* (Minneapolis: Fortress, 2017), esp. 125–82.
[24] I do not deny that the code underlying the text *is* hermeneutically significant. For the purposes of this chapter, however, I am focusing on the readerly encounter with a text.
[25] Note that the interface typically includes a "window" within which one scrolls or otherwise moves through the text, but this boundary is not *binding* in the same way as a printed book's binding.

can imagine – and scholars have – ways in which digital technology makes possible user-modified Bibles, custom "canons", which could contribute to general textual instability.[26] So far, however, mainstream digital Bibles allow little in the way of canonical manipulation. For example, YouVersion's navigational paratext includes a dropdown menu which has the books of the Bible in modern canonical order and, when a book is selected, also displays the number of chapters in each book.

Consider also the uniformity of modern printed books in terms of typography, page layout, and other elements of book design – paratextual properties according to my definition – reinforcing the message that the documents are related and belong together since each document (or "book" within) looks and feels exactly the same.[27] Similarly, printed Bibles typically have consecutive page numbering *across* the bound collection, another paratextual message suggesting the unity and progression of its contents.[28] An additional numbering system is commonly used for referencing larger units of each document (consecutively numbered "chapters") under which are smaller units (consecutively numbered "verses", per chapter). These paratexts invite a reader to make reference to quite small units of text, a subtle paratextual message that even the smallest units of the text are important, have authority, and may need to be referenced. The consistency of this reference system across biblical texts, including various editions, versions, and translations of modern Bibles, and even anachronistically used in online editions of digitized manuscripts, subtly suggests readerly, possibly even authorial, agreement about the unit-delineation, and therefore the argument, of the texts. These numbering systems are intentionally absent in some printed Bibles, often called Reader's Bibles, in order to present to the reader a text formatted like familiar modern books. Some Bible applications likewise allow the user to "hide" verse and chapter numbers (and manipulate certain other visual paratextual features).

---

**26** Siker, *Liquid Scripture*, 125–83; Claire Clivaz, "New Testament in a Digital Culture: A Biblaridion (Little Book) Lost in the Web?," *The Journal of Religion, Media and Digital Culture* 3/3 (May 14, 2015): 20–38; D. C. Parker, "Through a Screen Darkly: Digital Texts and the New Testament," *JSNT* 25 (2003): 395–411.
**27** Note that while "early printed copies were not all precisely alike…[t]hey were sufficiently uniform for scholars in different regions to correspond with each other about the same citation and for the same emendations and errors to be spotted by many eyes" (Elizabeth L. Eisenstein, *The Printing Press as an Agent of Change: Communications and Cultural Transformations in Early Modern Europe* [Cambridge: Cambridge University Press, 1979], 81); and further: "[Standardization] also involved the 'subliminal' impact upon scattered readers of repeated encounters with identical type-styles, printers' devices, and title page ornamentation" (82).
**28** The covers of a Bible, usually made of durable material like leather, also reinforce that the bound collection is significant and belongs together.

Even so, print and digital versions alike present an extremely *uniform* text with their paratexts.

Similarly, as briefly mentioned above, there is finality to a printed Bible, like any printed book – a paratextual message that suggests a pure, original text.[29] That sense of finality is far less obvious in digital Bibles. Accordance Bible Software, for example, periodically alerts the user to available updates, listing specific modules that might include a biblical text – a text that is updated and changed with the click of a button! Not only does this diminish the sense of finality present in a printed text; it also reminds the user that textual transmission of the Bible is perpetual. One is, as it were, standing in it. As David Parker, a New Testament textual critic, once observed after creating an electronic transcription of Codex Sinaiticus: "textual critics, under the guise of reconstructing original texts, are really creating new ones."[30] Parker suggests that as technologies give more ability to the user to manipulate a scholarly edition of a text (like the New Testament), "The result will be a weakening of the status of standard editions, and with that a change in the way in which users of texts perceive their tasks."[31] Note, however, that even in Parker's advanced software, Collate, there is a smoothing over of textual materiality for the sake of the machine, which requires for its input the reduction of a manuscript's text (and any of its physical features) to *characters*, and ultimately 1s and 0s. This "smoothing over" is not only required of the digitization of manuscript, but is the effect of any attempt to produce a critical edition, creating the tension, described by Alan Galey, "between the surface orderliness of scholarly resources and the stubborn irregularity of textual materials."[32]

Another paratext of a digital Bible is the search interface, which might be categorized as a "navigational" paratext (e.g., page numbers, table of contents, page headings, etc.). One of the early promising features of Bible software, and one of the mainstays, is the ability to search the texts within the software. The searching

---

**29** This notion of a pure "original" text persists in many quarters, but many textual critics of biblical texts prefer to speak of the "earliest recoverable text", "initial text", or *Ausgangstext*. See Bart D. Ehrman and Michael W. Holmes, *The Text of the New Testament in Contemporary Research: Essays on the Status Quaestionis*, 2nd ed. Leiden: Brill, 2012).
**30** Parker, "Through a Screen," 401. Along these lines, Claire Clivaz (in "New Testament in a Digital Culture") has recently suggested some of the ways that digital texts are challenging modern assumptions about text inherited from the printing press, especially an assumed stability of the text.
**31** Parker, "Through a Screen," 404.
**32** Alan Galey, "The Human Presence in Digital Artefacts," in *Text and Genre in Reconstruction: Effects of Digitalization on Ideas, Behaviours, Products and Institutions*, ed. Willard McCarty (Cambridge: Open Book Publishers, 2010): 93.

function itself gives meaning, suggesting that these texts are intended to be interrogated, to be studied in deep and complex ways. Further, search interfaces not only do traditional "concordance" work faster (i.e., finding all the instances of a specific word in Scripture), they enable compound searches to be done virtually instantaneously.

In sum, digital and print Bibles contain both similar and distinct paratexts. These paratexts contribute to the meaning derived from the text by a user/reader. Having considered digital Bibles in general, let us now turn to what is very likely the most popular digital Bible in the world.

## 4.2 Significant Paratexts of YouVersion's Bible App

As stated earlier, YouVersion's Bible App has been downloaded on hundreds of millions of mobile devices worldwide, and it includes more than a thousand Bible versions and languages, respectively. In my own experiences talking with digital Bible users, it is by far the most used mobile Bible app. Rather than simply describe its paratextual features one by one, I want to focus on the user's experience of some specific paratexts when first installing and using the app.[33]

### 4.2.1 Paratexts During Installation and Initial Use of YouVersion

The first thing one notices is that the app icon depicts a brown leather Bible closed with a red bookmarker ribbon extending from the middle of the pages. Prominent on the cover are the words "Holy Bible". One is presented, then, with a very traditional depiction of the Bible, its sacredness made prominent with the imitation of physical paratexts. The user soon discovers, however, that this "Bible" is also quite *unlike* a traditional printed Bible in many ways.

Upon opening the Bible app for the first time, the user is brought to an initial screen where two options are presented via buttons: the first is the most prominent, filled in with green, and says, "Sign up". The second has no fill (it is transparent) and says "Sign in" (obviously designed for those who have already created an account). Upon selecting "Sign up", the next screen presents three options, the first two filled with color: "Sign up with Facebook" and "Sign up with Google". The third is transparent with the words "Sign up with e-mail". This design arguably encourages the user to sign up with Facebook (as it is the

---

33 This procedure was carried out on an iPad and an iPhone, each using iOS.

first listed) and corresponds with other ways the app encourages social behavior amongst its users with its features.

### 4.2.2 Terms of Use and Privacy Policy

Below these three options for signing up is the line, in small print, "By signing up, you agree to our terms and privacy policy" – with the word "terms" hyperlinked to a webpage containing the Terms of Use (hereafter "Terms"), and the phrase "privacy policy" hyperlinked to a webpage containing the Privacy Policy. Whether or not the user actually reads these documents – both are relatively short and simple[34] – the owner and operator of the app, Life Covenant Church, Inc., assumes the user in fact agrees to said terms and policy if in fact (s)he signs up or *uses the app* at all. Importantly, this assumption includes the following: "By using YouVersion, you consent to all actions taken by us with respect to your information in compliance with the Privacy Policy." A responsible user, then, should learn to what terms and policy (s)he is actually agreeing by using the app! The presence of such agreements in using a Bible seems unique in the broader history of the biblical text and worth comment.

In one sense, such legal agreements are hardly surprising to any mobile user who has in fact signed up for other apps and services. Apps usually come with terms that few users actually read.[35] But to contrast this with the use of a print Bible, imagine if a publisher of a printed Bible handed it to someone, saying, "Now if you open this Bible, you are agreeing to the following terms of use... You may do these things; you may *not* do these things." As a matter of fact, most printed Bibles are copyrighted and may even present the reader, albeit briefly, with what is or is not permitted, usually in terms of how many verses may be quoted without written permission. An additional factor complicates the comparison, however: the intellectual property, so to speak, of a Bible app contains a lot of material *other than* the biblical text (e.g., the code that makes the app run, or display text, or allow navigation, etc.). So the question becomes, to what extent is it a *Bible* that one is using – at least in the same sense as a printed Bible? This train of thought is actually quite long and complex, as one can easily ask questions, too, about the mobile device itself and its operating system – *Who owns it, and what are its terms of use, etc.?* Apps, as with all software, have many dependencies. But

---

[34] The "Terms" document is nearly 2,700 words; the "Privacy Policy" is around 5,450 words.
[35] David Berreby, "Click to Agree with What? No One Reads Terms of Service, Studies Confirm," *The Guardian*, March 3, 2017; online: https://www.theguardian.com/technology/2017/mar/03/terms-of-service-online-contracts-fine-print.

given the scope of this chapter, we will simply note the uniqueness in using this digital Bible of an extensive legal agreement, and now limit ourselves to a few of the most interesting Terms to which the user agrees when using the app.

Importantly, the Terms include a section subtitled "Permitted and Unpermitted Use". The first is one of the most significant, prohibiting use of the app "... in any way that violates any federal, state, local or international law or regulation."[36] From a liability standpoint, it seems prudent as an app developer to have such a term; however, to the extent that the app is used as a Bible, it raises an interesting ethical question about whether Christians should encourage the app's use in countries that limit the distribution or use of Christian Bibles (and, in principle, about whether such a prohibition in the Terms is appropriate). Along these lines another section of the Terms state:

> Life.Church, the owner of YouVersion, is based in the state of Oklahoma in the United States. We make no claims that YouVersion or any of its content is accessible or appropriate outside of the United States. Access to YouVersion may not be legal by certain persons or in certain countries. If you access YouVersion from outside the United States, you do so on your own initiative and are responsible for compliance with local laws.[37]

Other terms include the owner's (i.e., Life Covenant Church, Inc.) right to take action against users deemed to be in violation of the Terms, as well as to refer user information to law enforcement. Again, this seems like the sort of thing any developer may include in such a policy to limit their liability. However, it gives the producer of this Bible app significant authority which, given the large numbers of users, is quite alarming.

For the purposes of this chapter, we are really interested in the *hermeneutical* impact of such statements, not the ethical questions, however significant. Thus, to the extent that a user is *unaware* of the Terms, they may make very little difference. However, these terms strongly suggest that the user does not own the Bible on their phone or tablet in any way like they might claim to own a print Bible. Even setting the Terms aside, like any other app on the user's device, it is only ever licensed, not owned. This is technically and legally true, reinforced by reading the Terms of Use, but I think it also *intuitively* true to the user. Although a digital Bible has some of the same paratexts of physical, printed Bibles, one does not *possess* their digital Bible the way they might possess a printed one. The digital Bible user's sense of what the Bible *is* may therefore be impacted by this.

---

36 "Terms of Use | The Bible App | Bible.Com," accessed March 23, 2019, https://www.bible.com/terms.
37 "Terms of Use | The Bible App | Bible.Com."

The other important legal document is the Privacy Policy, which centers on how YouVersion uses personal data.[38] Even without using the App, the Privacy Policy makes it clear to the user that a number of social features are built into the app, such as "friends" with whom you can connect and communicate, "events" which one can opt in to see near your location (using location data), and "posts and contributions" which might be public. As will be further discussed below, these paratexts suggest to users that socializing around the biblical text is positive. Relative to other social apps, the Privacy Policy is fairly standard, informing the user that the app collects data to "personalize" the experience, provide services, and enable analytics. Note the following paragraph:

> Device ID and Location. When you access or leave YouVersion, we receive the URL of both the site you came from and the one you go to next. We also get information about your IP address, proxy server, operating system, web browser and add-ons, device identifier and features, and/or ISP or your mobile carrier. We also receive data from your devices and networks, including location data. If you use YouVersion from a mobile device, that device will send us data about your device and GPS location based on your phone settings and access you have granted YouVersion.[39]

Again, all of this is standard in today's web and mobile environment, but when considered in the history of biblical texts, the data collected by the Bible "publisher" is quite remarkable. As before, these paratexts *remind* the user that the owner/developer of the app retains large amounts of control over the experience, minimizing the sense in which this "Bible" within might be thought of as a private possession analogous to a printed book.

### 4.2.3 Paratextual Features within YouVersion

After signing up, the App opened to John 1 in the King James Version. This choice, which is not made by the user, is a significant one, suggesting to the user that this is a suitable place to begin reading and a suitable translation. Compare this to buying a print Bible with a bookmarker – also a paratextual feature – already placed at John 1 – except in this example the text is automatically "opened" to this location.

Shortly after the app opened to John 1, a notification appeared with the words, "'Bible' Would Like to Send You Notifications," to which the user could

---

[38] "YouVersion Privacy Policy | The Bible App | Bible.Com," accessed March 24, 2019, https://www.bible.com/privacy.
[39] "YouVersion Privacy Policy | The Bible App | Bible.Com."

respond with "Don't Allow" or "OK". In iOS (the operating system for Apple's mobile devices), selecting "OK" permits the App to send alerts via sounds/vibrations much like when a user receives a text message. For example, the app has a "Verse of the day" feature, to which the user can agree to be alerted each day. Such notifications, as well the features that use them such as the Verse of the Day or the Bible reading plans, are paratexts suggesting that the user's encounter with the Bible could be (perhaps *should* be) a regular one, an activity important enough to set alerts for.

Along the bottom of the app is a menu bar with five options: "Home", "Read", "Plans", "Search", and "More". In the "Home" area of the App are two tabs. The first is "For You", where a number of sections appear (which can be rearranged). Near the top, "Bible App Activity" is tracked (e.g., it will track how many consecutive days the user has used the app, akin to tracking one's Bible reading consistency). Next is a carousel of Bible reading plans (each plan represented by square images akin to music album covers). The next two sections are "Verse of the Day" which contains the text of a verse and "Verse of the Day images", which is an image upon which the verse is superimposed. There are options to have these verses sent to the user, as well as to share them with others (including via another app the user might have on the mobile device, such as Twitter). The second tab in the "Home" area is "Community", where the user can select a button at the bottom of the screen, "Add Friends". Above the button is the line: "The Bible makes it clear: We need friends – to encourage, inspire, challenge, and love us. And your friends need you too." Most prominently is an image of a person holding a phone – the person surrounded by four floating "bubbles", each with a person inside. Above the image is the phrase "Surround Yourself". This is perhaps the strongest encouragement to the user yet to make Bible reading social, to involve others, and to engage their social network.

The "Read" option in the bottom menu bar takes the user to the biblical text, opening to the translation and verse they last read. The "Plans" menu option takes the user to an area for choosing various Bible reading plans. The "Search" option brings the user to a new area, at the top of which is a search bar where text can be entered, below which are three interesting additional sections. First is a section with the text "What does the Bible say about…" with twenty possible words to search for, the first five of which are visible and read, "Love", "Peace", "Faith", "Healing", and "Marriage". The second section asks, "How are you feeling?", offering a choice of four yellow-skinned emoticons which roughly appear to be happy, angry, sad, and depressed. Selecting any one of these allow the user to further select a more specific emotion, this time by selecting a word (e.g., "Joyful", "Disrespected", "Ashamed", "Abandoned", etc.). Choosing one of these brings the user to a list of Bible verses that apply to that emotion. The third and final section in the "Search" area is titled "Bible Stories", from which the user can choose one of forty-two Bible stories. The most unique paratext just described may be the emoticon section. This paratext encourages introspection and seeking biblical material to address the way the user feels. The focus on introspection and how one feels may support the argument that the Bible is increasing being used in therapeutic ways.[40] Thus the app encourages both a certain kind of socialization around the Bible as well as an individualized experience, which supports a feature of new media that Heidi Campbell and Stephen Garner call "networked individualism" and "individualized control", where the networked individual is at the centre of the network.[41] In any case, this is one more example of the hermeneutical impact of paratexts.

## 5 Conclusion

In summary, comparing both the similar and distinct material and paratextual elements of digital Bibles to their print counterparts has shed light on the hermeneutical impact of the Bible's technology upon the reader/user experience. We have considered how this is true for both print and digital technology, and we have examined one specific Bible app, YouVersion, in greater detail. Some of the more significant paratextual properties of this app were: (1) the Terms and Conditions and Privacy Policy, extensive legal agreements that diminish the sense in which the user might feel they "own" this Bible; (2) the social features that encourage certain social behaviors around the Bible; (3) the features that allow the app to communicate to the user (e.g., Bible reading alerts); and (4) the introspective emoticons, encouraging users to explore how the Bible relates to how they are feeling. It is called *You*Version, after all, and upon opening the app, the user is brought to the "Home" page and a tab that reads "For You". A personalized experience, a personalized Bible that nevertheless does not belong to "you", as the Terms of Use make clear.

More generally we noted that the sense of finality of a printed Bible, as well as canonicity, may be diminished in digital Bibles. Some researchers suggest that digital Bibles could re-open the canon, promote liquidity, and diminish institu-

---

[40] Peter M. Phillips, *The Bible, Social Media and Digital Culture*, Routledge Focus on Religion (New York: Routledge, 2019).
[41] Heidi A. Campbell and Stephen Garner, *Networked Theology: Negotiating Faith in Digital Culture* (Grand Rapids: Baker Academic, 2016). These concepts are introduced near the beginning of the book and appear throughout.

tional authority. To date, widely used digital Bibles have not. However, their technology is full of meaning and is influencing how readers understand the Bible and its texts. As time goes on and more research is done – and as hindsight produces a clearer view of the changes currently taking place – how digital media affect Bible readers will become clearer. In the meantime, consider the significance of paratexts.

# Bibliography

Baron, Naomi S. *Words Onscreen: The Fate of Reading in a Digital World*. New York: Oxford University Press, 2015.

Berreby, David. "Click to Agree with What? No One Reads Terms of Service, Studies Confirm." *The Guardian*. March 3, 2017. Online: https://www.theguardian.com/technology/2017/mar/03/terms-of-service-online-contracts-fine-print.

Campbell Heidi A., and Stephen Garner. *Networked Theology: Negotiating Faith in Digital Culture*. Grand Rapids: Baker Academic, 2016.

Clivaz, Claire. "New Testament in a Digital Culture: A Biblaridion (Little Book) Lost in the Web?" *The Journal of Religion, Media and Digital Culture* 3/ 3 (2015): 20–38.

Ehrman, Bart D. and Michael W. Holmes. *The Text of the New Testament in Contemporary Research: Essays on the Status Quaestionis*. 2nd ed. Leiden: Brill, 2012.

Eisenstein, Elizabeth L. *The Printing Press as an Agent of Change: Communications and Cultural Transformations in Early Modern Europe*. Cambridge: Cambridge University Press, 1979.

Ferré, Frederick. *Philosophy of Technology*. Athens, GA: University of Georgia Press, 1995.

Galey, Alan. "The Human Presence in Digital Artefacts." In *Text and Genre in Reconstruction: Effects of Digitalization on Ideas, Behaviours, Products and Institutions*, edited by Willard McCarty, 93–117. Cambridge: Open Book Publishers, 2010.

Genette, Gérard. *Paratexts: Thresholds of Interpretation*. Trans. Jane E. Lewin. Literature, Culture, Theory 20. Cambridge: Cambridge University Press, 1997.

Hayles, N. Katherine. "Translating Media: Why We Should Rethink Textuality." *The Yale Journal of Criticism* 16 (2003): 263–90.

Hutchings, Tim. "Augmented Graves and Virtual Bibles: Digital Media and Material Religion." In *Materiality and the Study of Religion: The Stuff of the Sacred*, edited by Tim Hutchings and Joanne McKenzie, 87–91. Theology and Religion in Interdisciplinary Perspective. London: Routledge, 2017.

"Inspired Mobility Survey Results" (AT&T). Online: https://about.att.com/content/dam/snrdocs/Inspired_Mobility_Research_Report.pdf.

Jansen, Laura. "Introduction: Approaches to Roman Paratextuality." In *The Roman Paratext: Frame, Texts, Readers*, edited by Laura Jansen, 1–18. Cambridge: Cambridge University Press, 2014.

Kirschenbaum, Matthew G. "Editing the Interface: Textual Studies and First Generation Electronic Objects." *Text* 14 (2002): 15–51.

Mann, Joshua L. "Print vs. Digital: The Effect of Pagination on Interpretation." *Joshua L Mann* (blog). March 21, 2013. Online: https://josh.do/print-vs-digital-the-effect-of-pagination-on-interpretation/).

Mann, Joshua L. "Mobile Liturgy: Reflections on the Church of England's Suite of Digital Apps." *Online – Heidelberg Journal of Religions on the Internet* 12 (2017): 42–59.

Mann, Joshua L. "How Technology Means: Texts, History, and Their Associated Technologies," *Digital Humanities Quarterly* (2017). n.p.

Manoff, Marlene. "The Materiality of Digital Collections: Theoretical and Historical Perspectives." *Portal: Libraries and the Academy* 6 (2006): 311–25.

McDannell, Colleen. *Material Christianity: Religion and Popular Culture in America*. New Haven: Yale University Press, 1995.

Parker, D.C. "Through a Screen Darkly: Digital Texts and the New Testament." *Journal for the Study of the New Testament* 25 (2003): 395–411.

Phillips, Peter M. *The Bible, Social Media and Digital Culture, Routledge Focus on Religion*. New York: Routledge, 2019.

Plate, S. Brent. "Material Religion: An Introduction." In *Key Terms in Material Religion*, edited by S. Brent Plate, 1–8. London: Bloomsbury, 2015.

Rakow, Katja. "The Bible in the Digital Age: Negotiating the Limits of 'Bibleness' of Different Bible Media." In *Christianity and the Limits of Materiality*, edited by Minna Opas and Anna Haapalainen, 101–21. Bloomsbury Studies in Material Religion 1. London: Bloomsbury, 2017.

Siker, Jeffrey S. *Liquid Scripture: The Bible in a Digital World*. Minneapolis: Fortress, 2017.

Small, Jocelyn Penny. *Wax Tablets of the Mind: Cognitive Studies of Memory and Literacy in Classical Antiquity*. London: Routledge, 1997.

Van Dijk, Yra. "The Margins of Bookishness: Paratexts in Digital Literature." In *Examining Paratextual Theory and Its Applications in Digital Culture*, edited by Nadine Desrochers and Daniel Apollon, 24–45. Advances in Human and Social Aspects of Technology. Hershey, PA: IGI Global, 2014.

Wallraff, Martin, and Patrick Andrist. "Paratexts of the Bible: A New Research Project on Greek Textual Transmission." *Early Christianity* 6 (2015): 237–43.

Natalia Suit
# Virtual Qur'ān: Authenticity, Authority, and *Ayat* in Bytes

All seats in the women's wagon were taken when I got in at Tahrir Square. The stream of in-flowing bodies steered me to the corner where a young woman was sitting with an open mobile phone in her hand. The bright screen displayed lines of ayat[1] – the Qur'ānic verses. Every now and then, she slid her finger over the glass "turning the pages over." Not so long ago the same young woman would have been holding a small paper copy of the Qur'ānic book. Now, to see her gazing at the lit phone screen was nothing out of ordinary.

"I know it's a strange question," I addressed her, "but why do you like reading the Qur'ān on your mobile?"

She looked up at me with a slight surprise.

"Oh, it's just a matter of convenience," she replied, "and I can read it without ablutions even when I have my period." Then, she promptly returned to looking silently at the screen.

This ethnographic vignette of a chance encounter over a mobile phone in a metro can be read in a number of ways. First of all, it serves as an overture to my account of the modes in which digital technology participates in shaping religious practice surrounding the Muslim sacred text in Egypt. Furthermore, it demonstrates that although over the past ten years or so the Qur'ānic message has been increasingly mediated by digital bytes and electronic devices, this mediation should not be perceived as "dematerialization" of the religious text. On the contrary, more and more popular "electronic Holy Qur'āns" still have material bodies that are capable of producing very tangible effects: the new forms of engagement with the Qur'ānic text, the debates over authenticity and textual authority, the realignments of religious tradition, and the constant efforts to create even better virtual Qur'āns. Additionally, by referencing female biology, the vignette reveals gender distinctions in the ways Qur'ānic software technology can be appropriated and applied by Muslim practitioners. Finally, it tacitly points to the link between books and other digital devices that mediate the Qur'ānic text.

## 1 The *mushaf* and the Qur'ān

Many of the practices and conversations surrounding digital copies of the Qur'ānic text are tied to a religious dogma which states that the Qur'ān is a vocally transmitted

---

[1] All translations from Arabic included in this essay are mine.

Open Access. © 2020 Natalia Suit, published by De Gruyter. This work is licensed under a Creative Commons Attribution-NonCommercial-NoDerivatives 4.0 International License.
https://doi.org/10.1515/9783110634440-012

revelation. Etymologically, the word *Qur'ān* is derived from the root word *qara'a* that refers to "reading" or "reciting." More precisely, *Qur'ān* means "the spoken message of Allah." This emphasis on vocal mediation is grounded in the teachings of the Prophet Muhammad himself, who encouraged his companions to memorize and recite the message he received through spoken words. "Chant it, for whoever does not chant it is not one of us," says the Prophet in a well-known *hadith* (account of the deeds and words of the Prophet Muhammad) narrated by Ibn Kathir.[2] There are many accounts like this in addition to verses in the Qur'ān itself that remind Muslims about the importance of recitation, resulting in a long and rich tradition of the art of Qur'ānic chanting that continues to be an important part of the religious education in Egypt and other parts of the Muslim world.

But the Qur'ān is not only mediated by voice. It has also had a less evanescent medium in the form of a book – consisting of pages, binding, and script – that is called a *mushaf* (read with "s" and "h" pronounced separately). The word *mushaf* comes from the root *suhuf* (bound pages) and is primarily understood to refer to the pages that carry the text of the Qur'ān. It is not mentioned in the Qur'ān itself but appears later in scholarly writings about the Qur'ān. Grammatically, unlike the Quran, *mushaf* has a plural form *masahif*, indicating an essential difference between the ontological status of the two. One is divine; the other is not. Despite the fact that reporters covering the memorable Burn-the-Qur'ān Day often used the word Qur'ān in plural – "the Qur'āns" (as it is customarily done with the Bible, where a proper noun denotes both the content and the object that carries it) – in Arabic the word Qur'ān does not have a plural form. There is only one Qur'ān – al-Qur'ān, *the* Qur'ān – mediated by a man-made book, a *mushaf*.

In spite of the emphasis on vocal mediation of the message, Muslims have not neglected the corporeal medium of the Qur'ān, whether to beautify it through calligraphy, or to address it through acts of ritual purity, or to treat it with particular forms of deference. Given the persistent presence of the Qur'ānic book in Muslim religious practice (with millions of its copies being printed now every year in the Middle East alone), it is hard to think of the Qur'ān only in terms of its abstract, ethereal message without addressing the presence of its tangible "carrier."

By looking *at* the Qur'ānic book – not *through* it – and paying attention to its manufacturing, material form, and practical use, I am able to not only track the forms of mediation taking place between the actual object, script, and the message, but also to understand challenges engendered by the new digital technology and the consequences of its use for religious practice. Thus, speaking

---

[2] Abu al-Fada' Isma'il Ibn 'Amr Ibn Kathir, *Tafsir al-Qur'ān al-'Azim*, vol. 7 (Beirut: Dar al-Fikr, 1966), 481.

about virtual Qur'ān necessarily entails speaking about the Qur'ān in print. Moreover, it is one of the underlying theoretical suppositions of this essay that these two forms of mediation of the Qur'ānic text should be treated as enfolded in each other rather than simply in terms of older technology being replaced by newer forms.

The complexity of the process of technological mediation has already been pointed out by Marshall McLuhan who saw technology – and printed books among them – as multilayered environments in which multiple media, like Russian Matrioshkas, "nest" in each other. "The 'content' of any medium is always another medium,"[3] proposed McLuhan, seeing speech mediated by script used in printing and reproduced through books as an example of such a conglomeration of media, each of which had the ability to introduce change into human affairs through its process of mediation. However, as W.J.T. Mitchell has reminded us, we should not see this "nesting" phenomenon as a historical sequence.[4] From a perspective of the book history, the juxtaposition of printed and electronic copies of the Qur'ān highlights the overlapping nature of different forms of text mediation. As much as handwriting did not end with the introduction of printing so digitization does not entirely eclipse presswork. Computers may have produced new forms of text consumption and reshaped the meaning of printing as a dominant type of text reproduction, but the appearance of one medium rarely completely eliminated the older ones. For instance, almost a century of coexistence between the two ways in which the Qur'ānic text was rendered spans the time from the first local print productions in Egypt to the decline of the manuscript economy.[5] During that time both media had an effect on each other, transforming each other's forms and meanings. Similarly, both printed and digital versions of the Qur'ān are nowadays available on the religious market and the growing numbers of both underlie diversification of their users, including generational, economic, aesthetic, or educational differences. And, as in the past, the digitized text of the Qur'ān is in many ways affected by its predecessor – the book. So, overemphasizing the chronology may prevent us from noticing how the older media can become incorporated into the newer ones and vice versa.[6] And therefore, I do

---

[3] Marshall McLuhan, *Understanding Media: The Extensions of Man* (New York: The New American Library, 1964), 23.
[4] W.J.T. Mitchell, "There Are No Visual Media," *Journal of Visual Culture* 4/2 (2005): 262.
[5] Kathryn Schwartz, *Meaningful Mediums: A Material and Intellectual History of Manuscript and Print Production in the Nineteenth-Century Ottoman Cairo* (Ph.D. diss., Harvard University, 2015).
[6] Brinckley Messick makes the same argument in relation to writing and print. Brinkley Messick, *The Calligraphic State: Textual Domination and History in a Muslim Society* (Berkley: University of California Press, 1993).

not separate the forms in which the Qur'ānic text is stabilized by printing (and the practices produced by the materiality of a printed book) from the practices and materialities engender by the digital technology.

## 2 "Etiquette" of the Qur'ānic Book

A quick search online for the word "Qur'ān" shows that in popular English, the Qur'ān is often referred to as the Muslim "holy book" or "Holy Qur'ān." Yet strictly speaking, and as we already know, it is not a book. Nor is it "holy" in the common understanding of this word. Neither the book nor the message are "holy" in the way the Bible is referred to in the Christian tradition. In the Arabic language, the word *muqaddas* (holy) and its derivatives do not index the Qur'ān or its tangible body. Perhaps it is because *al-kitab al-muqaddas* – the "holy book" – is the phrase already reserved by the Arabic speaking Christians to describe their own scripture, the Bible. Muslims in Egypt never speak of the Qur'ān or *mushaf*'s holiness but instead always emphasized the notion of "deference" (*ihtiram*) which should be directed towards the book that carries the text of the Qur'ān. The word *ihtiram* comes from the root *harima* "to be prohibited, to be forbidden, to exclude or withhold, which in some of its derivative verbal forms has the connotation of being set aside or inviolable. But, etymology alone does not help to understand the realities of the *mushaf* and the Qur'ān. Rather than relying solely on the word's semantic field, I suggest we turn to the actual practices of *ihtiram* performed by Qur'ānic users, people who read and handle Qur'ānic copies in the course of daily activities, and to think of them as meaning-making enactments[7] of the Qur'ān expressed through the daily routines of worship and piety known as the etiquette of the *mushaf* or *adab al-mushaf*.

These practices are inseparably entangled with the materiality of the object that mediates the text. Objects do not simply "carry" the Qur'ānic text. They mediate it, which means that they change the ways in which people perceive the meaning of the text and the practices that surround it, changing themselves in the process. A book made of paper is not the same as the Quranic text on the screen of a phone. A text visible on the page does not necessarily appear in the same way as its digitized version under a plastic cover. When the medium of the message changes, the etiquette of the electronic "*mushaf*" changes as well, and practices of *ihtiram* are redefined to accommodate this

---

[7] Annemarie Mol, *The Body Multiple: Ontology in Medical Practice* (Durham: Duke University Press, 2002), 31–33.

new and unprecedented materiality of the text. I will return to this issue, but in order to grasp the challenges of the co-presence of a new medium, I need to briefly describe the forms of rapport long established between the practitioners and their printed *masahif*.

What practitioners know about *adab al-mushaf* comes from lessons at the mosque, education at home, mass media, and self-study, and pertains to multiple situations in the course of daily activities. Over time, I trained myself to pay attention to the small gestures of deference that surrounded the *mushaf* in private and public spaces. I learned to notice that a *mushaf* was not left open turned upside down, was not covered with other books and objects, was not left on the floor or on a table with food. I watched these acts of deferment implemented daily through gestures of *ihtiram*, I saw my friends and strangers uncover a *mushaf*, pick it up, move it, put it away; I learned where and when it could be left undisturbed, at least as much as life in crowded and polluted spaces allowed. In the discussions about the Qur'ān, I was given many examples of what not to do with the *mushaf*: I was warned not to wet my finger with my saliva when turning the pages; not to read it in bed; not to sit, sleep, or lean upon a *mushaf*; not to throw it; not to put anything between its pages except empty sheets of paper; and not to scribble notes on it. Sometimes ordinary acts of respect would take me by surprise or frustrate me. I remember the moment of awkwardness when my friend Rahab's mother conspicuously removed a pair of golden earrings I accidentally put on her *mushaf*. I also remember incidents in one of the libraries, where an anonymous stranger would persistently remove a *mushaf* from the lower shelf where its call number would require it to be to the top shelf, out of cataloging order.

Although the rules of *adab al-mushaf* are quite clear and specific, even classical scholars recognized the difficulty of following the rules of purity in all circumstances and at all times. A well-known example is the case of pupils in the Qur'ānic schools who, if the rules were upheld, would have to perform ablutions after every urination or defecation, which would disrupt the class and take too much time away from instruction. Therefore different provisions and exceptions, such as holding or touching the book with other objects or between the outer parts of one's palms, have been made to reconcile the rules of purity with the daily exigencies. These provisions and exceptions have become incorporated into daily routines, and are even more necessary as transmigratory life in Cairo makes following the rules more cumbersome: for instance, the long hours of commuting to work could be spent on reading the Quran but making the required *wudu'* (ablutions) beforehand is not always possible. It is, therefore, left to the conscience of individual practitioners how to reconcile *adab al-mushaf* with the contingencies of rapidly changing and accelerated urban lifestyle.

Friendships too may make relationships with some objects more complicated, forcing the practitioners to make uneasy choices about whether their allegiances lie with people or things. I know I was at times the cause of such dilemmas. When some years ago, I traveled for the first time with Rahab's family to their cabin on the shores of Marsa Matruh, I was not yet aware of the rules that guided the handling of a *mushaf*. At the end of the day, I sat on a comfortable bed and stretched lazily, not being able to decide whether I was too tired to read anything. Out of the corner of my eye I saw a book on the bedside table and picked it up. It was a *mushaf*. I flipped through the pages absentmindedly. Rahab walked into the room and saw the book in my hands. "Do you mind putting it away?" she said with unease, "you are … you know … your hands are not clean." "I just washed them," I said. "That's not it." She was clearly struggling. "You are … you are not Muslim so … you shouldn't touch it." Rahab did not want me to hold the *mushaf*. But because we were friends, she could openly ask me to put it away, although it was not a comfortable request to make. In my interactions with other people, I occasionally saw a fleeting hesitation and an almost instinctive jerk of the hand in a protective gesture when I reached for a *mushaf*. Once or twice it was silently removed from my hands with a quick, but telling motion.

Yet, Rahab was one of few who candidly referred to my impurity. As non-Muslim, I could never be in a state of *tahara*, but neither was Rahab that evening in Marsa Matruh. At her request, I put the *mushaf* down. She immediately picked up two other books from the coffee table and using them as tongs carried the *mushaf* out of the room. "I'm having my period," she said in a matter-of-fact voice, responding to the surprised look I threw at her contraption. By not touching the Qur'ānic text while menstruating, Rahab followed the rules of handling the *mushaf* habituated by generations of Muslim women. These rules today are taught in a variety of venues, including increasingly popular in Egypt religious websites containing *fatawa* (religious judiciary opinions), such as the one belonging to the al-Azhar university, an important Egyptian religious institution. Under the keywords: menstruating women and reading the Qur'ān there is a following *fatwa*:

> Question: What is the ruling on menstruating woman entering the women's prayer room in a mosque to participate in studying and memorizing the Qur'ānic verses, memorizing the Qur'ān [in general], and touching the Qur'ān during this period?
>
> Answer: Prof. Dr. 'Ali Goma'a [who served as Grand Mufti of Egypt between 2003–2013]
> It is not permissible for a menstruating woman to enter the mosque for any purpose other than passing, because the Prophet (peace and blessings of Allah be upon him) said: "I do not permit a menstruating or impure person to enter the mosque," narrated by Abu Dawood.

> It is not permissible for a menstruating woman to touch the mushaf or to read the Qur'ān. However, the Maliki [school of law] permitts the woman to read a little of the Qur'ān without touching the mushaf, so that she does not forget it.[8]

This is a well-known guideline; nonetheless, not all women take for granted this particular bodily comportment with the Qur'ānic book, as prescribed by the predominant legal schools (*madhab*) in Egypt. The piety movement that has grown in the last two decades among Egyptian women has produced female practitioners who want to learn more about their religion.[9] By rejecting modern and secular values promoted by the Egyptian government, and trying to oppose various social pressures, they turn to religion for empowerment. These women choose to submit to Islamic principles with diligence and conscious decision-making, including judgements about what to do and what to avoid in time of menstruation.

Apart from indicating various levels of religiosity, the reactions of my female friends and acquaintances to the issue of touching a *mushaf* during periodic bleeding indicate modern shifts in the attitudes towards one's own body. Some women, like Rahab, consider menstruation as a state of major impurity and simply accept the ruling that in that state they cannot physically read the Qur'ān. Others are unsure about how to think of their own menstruating bodies, perceiving the prohibition not so much a matter of ritual uncleanliness, but rather a part of general convention that should, nevertheless, be upheld. Some women, conveying that a prohibition of touching the book makes them feel somehow "dirty," question the rationale behind this practice, but still follow the guidelines. And a few, like Dalia, consider menstruation a biological function that should not prohibit a pious woman like herself from cultivating – as she described it – a personal relationship with Allah, including holding the words of the message mediated in a tangible way by a *mushaf* without any restrictions. Regardless of their convictions, with the introduction of new technologies (radio, TV, audio tapes, CDs) women in Egypt have been finding creative ways to negotiate the rules separating them from the Qur'ānic message. However, the advent of the Qur'ānic

---

[8] "Reading of the Qur'ān, handling the *mushaf*, and entering the mosque in a state of menstruation." *Fatwa* no. 406 issued on the 2nd of March, 2005, by Professor 'Ali Goma'a. Website of Dar al-Ifta' at al-Azhar University. http://www.dar-alifta.org/AR/ViewFatwa.aspx?sec=fatwa&ID=11392. See also: "Reading of the Qur'ān and handling the *mushaf* in a state of menstruation." *Fatwa* no. 2841 issued on the 11th of May, 2016, no author. Website of Dar al-Ifta' at al-Azhar University. http://www.dar-alifta.org/AR/ViewFatwa.aspx?sec=fatwa&ID=12343.
[9] Saba Mahmood, *Politics of Piety: The Islamic Revival and the Feminist Subject* (Princeton, N.J.: Princeton University Press, 2012).

phone and tablet applications has opened up for them a whole new way to access the Qur'ān without transgressing the rules of *adab al-mushaf*.

My attention to the corporeal presence of the book articulated so far through this ethnographic material should by no means suggest that the Islamic legal pronouncements standing behind the rules of *adab al-mushaf* assign any priority to the book over the Qur'ānic message. Yet the same pronouncements about the etiquette of the Qur'ānic book attest to the fact that it is very hard to demarcate a clear boundary between the intangible, eternal words of Allah and their material mediators in the form of perishable ink, paint, paper, and script. On a practical level, this complicated relation between the message and its conveyers becomes most obvious when the medium that conveys the message is drastically changed. The introduction of digital technologies in the dissemination of the Qur'ān provides us with an opportunity to ask: how does a change in medium circumscribe the message? In other words, how does one enact a "digital Qur'ān" according to the rules of *adab al-mushaf* and what are the results of this enactment?

## 3 Virtual Qur'ān

The co-presence of the print and the digital has offered new possibilities for transmission of the Qur'ānic text and has produced alternative understandings of interaction between script and its digital medium. It has also engendered a critical change in the ways practitioners perceive Qur'ānic text as an integral part of the *mushaf*. The "virtual Qur'ān" is not a book in the ordinary sense of this word at all. It is a text mediated by the screen of a computer, an electronic device, or a mobile phone, where it shares memory space with other texts and images. An electronic device, especially a mobile phone, can hardly be called a *mushaf* (although on a few rare occasions, I have seen this word being applied in web advertisements). Moreover, electronic devices that mediate digital Qur'ān assume many forms and types: from small, portable, and multifunctional cell phones and tablets, uni-purpose walk-man like mini-players, or pen-like reading devices designed specifically for learning how to recite for non-Arabic speaking Muslims, to laptops and stationary computers with touch screens and CD and DVD players that can display the Qur'ān interactively.[10]

---

**10** The electronic Qur'ānic media – like video and audiotapes circulating on the religious market – also affects the shaping of the Egyptian public sphere and their practices of ethical

The Qur'ānic applications used on phones and tablets are designed mainly for reading and listening. The more specialized software allows not only to read and listen, but also to search for particular words, verses, or exegetic explanations. It may contain a dictionary, translations into other languages and guidelines facilitating proper recitation. Some programs include an option of following the text while listening to one's favorite *qari* – a Qur'ānic reciter. These versatile types of software (in terms of their use) are increasingly popular not only with the University of al-Azhar students, but also with younger Muslims who are interested in studying the Qur'ānic text on their own as a form of piety. The specialized devices containing exclusively the Qur'ānic text are becoming more popular as well, but they are rather expensive on the Egyptian market and the average, middle-class Muslims cannot afford them. The phone applications are by far most accessible, thus constituting the most popular form of digitized Qur'ān in Egypt. They are available for free or for a moderate fee from various websites and Islamic organizations, but they offer a less diversified range of functions. However, because the number of smart phones in Egypt has been steadily rising, reaching at this point about twenty-seven million users, mobiles have become the most popular platform for the display of the Qur'ānic text.[11]

Each of the electronic devices mediates the Qur'ānic text in particular ways and elicits different forms of engagement with the message. The "PenMan Holy Qur'ān" or "Iqra'a Digital Qur'ān" – Korean-made devices which are advertised and available on the Egyptian market – are, perhaps, the most versatile devices in terms of their content, portability, and application. Because of their convenient size, they can be read and listened to in various locations and circumstances. They feature exegetic explanations, tools for memorization (such as automatic repetition of marked passages or different speeds of recitation), and various search options. The most sophisticated ones show *qibla* (the direction of prayer), play the call to prayer at the right times, and include extra supplications and prayers. They also come with extra memory, allowing users to store pictures, create recordings, and convert files. There is even a radio option in some of the newer models. They are advertised as "the best gift for a Muslim learner who wants to study the Qur'ān."

The specialized software available for computers is specifically design for textual study and requires a beyond-common knowledge of the Qur'ānic text, its grammar, orthography, and schools of recitations. Reading the Qur'ān in such

---

self-improvement. Charles Hirschkind, *The Ethical Soundscape: Cassette Sermons and Islamic Counterpublics* (New York: Columbia University Press, 2006).

**11** "Number of smartphone users in Egypt from 2013 to 2019 (in millions)." *Statista*: the Statistics Portal. https://www.statista.com/statistics/467747/forecast-of-smartphone-users-in-egypt/

specialized software presupposes an academic engagement with the text that entails pausing, rereading, and analysing the content, and the emphasis on the "immersion" in the text through sound and vision is not a priority. The applications used on mobile phones, on the other hand, are more likely to promote reading for "immersion" – a form of reading that emphasizes the sound without necessarily pausing to analyse the content. I suggest that we call this form of engagement with the Qur'ānic text an affectual reading – reading that is likely to illicit an emotional response from the reader. It is often connected with the movement of the reader's lips and silent or half-silent recitation that allows the reader to access the text visually and aurally in a way that more fully engages the senses.

Thus, various forms of devices – laptops, "PenMan Digital Qur'āns," tablets, or phones – engender new ways of thinking about the Qur'ānic text by creating a challenge to the traditional forms of *adab al-muṣḥaf*. The gamut of most common questions that highlight the need to revisit the rules of the Qur'ānic etiquette in relation to the new technology include a number of technology-related concerns. These following examples come from *fatwa* websites easily accessible in Egypt (like the one belonging to al-Azhar University) where Muslim practitioners can ask questions about any religious legal guidelines and rules, such as:

- *Is it permissible to use a digital version of the Qur'ān?*
- *Are you supposed to perform wudu (full ablutions) to read the Qur'ān online or a digital Qur'ān?*
- *Is it allowed to listen to the Qur'ān in the digital format (on laptop, mobile, or mp3's form) without wudu?*
- *Is it allowed in Islam to load the Qur'ān into a smart phone as pdf or in an audio format?*
- *Can I touch or keep the smart phone in my pocket if the Qur'ān is loaded in it as pdf or in an audio format when I don't have wudu?*
- *How can I determine whether or not a mobile phone background image is appropriate if my phone has the Qur'ān in it?*
- *Is deleting a "Qur'ān.pdf" destroying a copy of the Qur'ān?*
- *Is it allowed to enter the bathroom when I have the smart phone in my pocket where the Qur'ān is loaded as pdf or audio format?*

The examples above constitute a set of most ubiquitous questions related to the digitized Qur'ān and pop up time and again in different online discussions and private conversations. The last question in particular is an interesting case, as it evoked significant discussion when the first Qur'ānic phone apps appeared on the market. The initial opinions regarding how to act towards an electronic copy of the Qur'ānic text in ritually unclean places – such as bathrooms – were not unanimous. A few scholars insisted that in those places the rules of *adab* should apply in the same way to both objects, the book and the phone alike; others followed the argumentation implied by a well-known anecdotic *fatwa* also circulating the Internet:

> A man asked a sheikh whether it was permitted to bring a mobile phone with the Qur'ānic verses to the bathroom. The sheikh answered, "It is permissible because the verses are in the memory of the phone."
> The man asked again, "But sheikh, we are talking about the Qur'ānic verses and the most beautiful names of Allah, and you are saying that it is permitted to take them to the bathroom?" The sheikh replied, "Have you memorized any verses from the Qur'ān?"
> "Yes," said the man.
> "Well then," retorted the sheikh, "when you go to the bathroom, leave your head by the door and then step in."

Even though a *mushaf*, an actual physical book, should not be brought to the bathroom – and I have seen instances when people removed their copies from bags or pockets before entering such a place – having the Qur'ān on a phone does not call for the same precautions. Yet, although scholars admit that it would be unreasonable to expect people to leave their phones outside the bathroom – unlike inexpensive *masahif*, they could be easily stolen – they surround the permission to bring the digitized Qur'ān to the bathroom with a stipulation: the sound should be switched off and the verses of the Qur'ān should not appear on the screen.

Menstruating women have deployed this interpretation of *adab al-mushaf* in relation to the use of new technology. Since mobile phones and tablets on which the Qur'ān is recorded do not come under the same rules as the *mushaf*, this also means that other rules of purity do not apply in the same way either. The rationale behind both is that the letters of the Qur'ān in these devices are "different" than the letters in the *mushaf*. Thus, menstruating women follow opinions expressed by the sheikhs of al-Azhar that an electronic device constitutes merely a carrier and a barrier for the text. The plastic case or glass screen is a safe barrier, as it cannot be traversed: one cannot directly touch the digital letters, as they – instead of being "fixed" on the page – appear and disappear from display. For that reason, legally menstruation has no effect on the practical use of the Quranic text in a digital device because, from this point of view, digital letters are immaterial.

This opinion has been disseminated not only by *fatwa* websites, but also by electronic women's periodicals and news web portals, such as the popular *Masrawy* that published in 2016 a fatwa by the Grand Mufti Dr. Ahmad al-Tayeb:

> *Question: Is it permissible for a menstruating woman to read the Qur'ān from any source other than the mushaf?*
>
> *Dr. Ahmad al-Tayeb, Sheikh of Al-Azhar, replies: Imam Malik allowed the reading of the Qur'ān without touching the mushaf during the menstrual cycle, so that the inability to read does not lead to forgetting the Qur'ān.*
>
> *Based on this, it is permissible for a menstruating woman to read the Qur'ān from any source other than the mushaf in order to be rewarded [with blessings], even if it is daily. It is known what the answer is to the question, if the case is as stated. And God Almighty knows best.*[12]

A fatwa on this subject which featured on the al-Azhar website is more ambiguous and indicates that the difference between the *mushaf* and an electronic device is still somewhat debatable. The fatwa reminds practitioners that every letter read from the Qur'ān brings the reader ten blessings. This applies to the letters read on the electronic screens as well, even if the reader has not performed the ablution (*wudu*) – with a few exceptions, including menstruation. However, says the same fatwa, reading from the *mushaf* – a paper book – is better than reading from an electronic device and touching the Qur'ānic text on an electronic screen is not the same as touching the *mushaf* because the text on a screen appears there as on a surface of water or a mirror. The purity required for touching the *mushaf* is not obligatory in this case because touching the screen is like touching the Qur'ān's shadow. In the conclusion, the *fatwa* states that reading from the *mushaf* engages the touch and eye more than reading from the phone.[13] The equivocality of this pronouncement leaves some leeway to treat the phone differently which, in consequence, allows for a common conviction expressed by the woman I approached on the metro.

---

[12] "Is it correct for a menstruating person to read the Qur'ān from a source other than a *mushaf*?" (*Hal yusihh lil ha'id an taqra' min ayy masdar ghir mushaf? Masrawy* (16 January 2016); online at: http://www.masrawy.com. This article has been archived since then and is not accessible on the newspaper's website anymore. A note about websites: In Egypt, a lot of religious information is distributed on the Internet. I have used them as sources because they are often accessed by Egyptian practitioners via their phones. Some of those websites are more stable – like the website of Dar al-Ifta at al-Azhar of King Fahd Complex. Others, however, especially the newspaper sites, do not archive their articles beyond a certain period of time. For that reason, many of the articles published during my fieldwork in 2012 are not available online anymore. Yet, their ephemerality does not mean, in my opinion, that they should be excluded as legitimate ethnographic sources, as they have become a common means of religious education among younger and middle-age Egyptians.
[13] "Benefits of reading the Qur'ān from an electronic screen." *Fatwa* no. 3668 issued on the 14th of December, 2016, no author. Website of Dar al-Ifta' at al-Azhar University. http://www.dar-alifta.org/AR/ViewFatwa.aspx?sec=fatwa&ID=13248.

## 5 Digitizing Qur'ānic Orthography

The attempts to reproduce the Qur'ānic text online have been taking place for about two decades now. Yet, only within the last ten years or so have the software companies and app developers begun to offer electronic editions of the Qur'ān in Arabic (English translations have been available in electronic form since mid-to late 1990s). Interestingly, it is the technology itself that for a long period happened to be the obstacle to spreading the virtual Qur'ān. In spite of growing interest in digitization of the Qur'ānic text, boosted by the quick spread of new technology, skills, and digitally encoded Arabic fonts in the Muslim world, rendering the Qur'ān in a digital format presented numerous conundrums for programmers and religious authorities alike. Although practitioners with access to computers and other electronic devices saw benefits of using the digitized Qur'ān, it was the programmers' inability to properly reproduce the Qur'ānic text in an electronic format that impaired its spread online.

First of all, the calligraphic styles used over the centuries for writing *masahif* and reproduced through lithographic and offset printing – that facilitated continuation of many calligraphic traditions in mechanically reproduced texts of the Qur'ān – have produced their own regimes of authority and authentication that were hard to recreate through a font style that did not participate in the tradition of Qur'ānic calligraphy. It is particularly true when we consider how the introduction of typographic print in Egypt disrupted the semantic system of distinct calligraphic styles and their fields of signification by visually unifying texts belonging to different spheres of religious, political and economic practice. With the introduction of printing, a variety of calligraphic styles that communicated different contents were replaced by one uniform printing font that lost its capacity to convey meaning through format. Eventually, Qur'ānic-like typefaces emerged in printing as well, representing their own distinctive visual styles that in many ways was much more grounded in the pre-print scripts than in the then-contemporary secular printing styles, full of innovative "non-Qur'ānic" designs.

When digitization entered Qur'ānic printing and dissemination markets in Egypt at the beginning of the nineties, this technology was initially able to preserve the Qur'ānic calligraphic tradition only by reproducing handwritten or printed *masahif* as uneditable, undividable text blocks or pictures in which fragments of text could not be copied or searched. Although letters of the Arabic alphabet were encoded first in ASCII (the American Standard Code for Information Interchange ASCII) and later in ISO International Standards Organization, they were significantly simplified and the codification did not include any of the additional layers of the Arabic script, including a number of diacritics. A number of bigger corporation (like IBM, for instance) addressed this inadequacy by creating separate encoding systems that represented non-Latin scripts in a more correct way, but the texts written in those coding systems were not easily transferable from one digital environment to another without causing distortion of the text. These distortions included placement of diacritic marks over incorrect letters which changed the meaning of the words. This was, of course, especially problematic for transferring the Qur'ānic text. From this perspective, the ease of transferring text from one format to another, or from one electronic device to another was, ironically, one of the biggest predicaments of dissemination for the digitized Qur'ān. The challenge, then, was to create a program in which the Qur'ānic text would be stable enough, yet editable, not easily manipulated but transferable.

By the end of the twentieth century, the Unicode system emerged as an answer to the confusion. Its major advantage was that it helped to include many more variations of the Arabic letters and a much larger number of diacritics.[14] However, the basis of the digital revolution, the Unicode system used worldwide for encoding texts in different writing systems was, nevertheless, grounded in a typographic, Latin-script based tradition of assigning a particular code to a particular letter in a sequential order. Although finally good enough to represent the contemporary Arabic script, this system still did not support all the variants and diacritics needed to create the Qur'ānic text.

Moreover, by that point, changes in religious visual culture had begun to take place. These were prompted in particular by Qur'ānic printed editions popular in Egypt, such as *Mushaf Fu'ad* or *Mushaf al-Shimarly*, and in general by the modern aesthetics of the secular texts to which the readers became already accustomed. The reading habits of Muslim practitioners had already changed. People desired to read the text of the Qur'ān that was "legible" and "print-like," and they wanted it to be user-friendly like other easily accessible and usable non-religious electronic texts. Therefore, the push to digitize the Qur'ān in Egypt did not come at first from institutions, such as al-Azhar, but through the initiatives of individual practitioners who were interested in both the correct spelling/diacritics and usability of the text. The early attempts to create searchable digitized texts of the Qur'ān were undertaken by computer engineers and programmers, which, in return, prompted religious authorities to step in.

One of the first programs that would allow searching, copying, and pasting the Quranic text without distortion of the position of the letters, or changing them

---

[14] J.R. Osborn, *Letters of Light: Arabic Script in Calligraphy, Print, and Digital Design* (Cambridge: Harvard University Press, 2017), 170.

into numeric signs and symbols, was created at the King Fahd Quran Complex.[15] Its team of engineers has recently released to the public domain a font application that is also compatible with Unicode. The Qur'ānic application is available for free on the Complex's website and has been developed specifically to accommodate the text of the Qur'ān. Also, a Dutch linguist and designer, Thomas Milo, and his company DecoType[16] have been successful in developing new ways of encoding Arabic script strictly following the rules of Arabic calligraphy that allow preparing fully marked Qur'ānic text. They used this software to create the first digital Omani *mushaf* called Mushaf Muscat.[17]

However, the problem of orthographic distortion and control of the text still exists. In order to understand it, we need to understand two issues: the tradition of the Qur'ānic spelling and the ways in which the Qur'ānic text has been historically authenticated (*isnad*).

# 6 How Does One Know that the Text is Correct? Authenticity and Authority

The transition of the Qur'ānic text from handwriting to print did not happen without controversies. One of the important objections at that time was informed by the problematic relation of printing to the past. The introduction of the printing press created an interruption in the chain of authority produced by generations of copiers who learned from their teachers. Before print, what authenticated the accuracy of the text and what gave the text its authority – whether written or recited – was the *isnad*, a method of transmission in which the provenience of a text was traced through a person-to-person, student-to-teacher connection. The introduction of printing interrupted the *isnad* of person-to person instruction. "Printing," writes Wilson, "unlike the calligraphy and writing, could not trace its origins back to the early Muslim community but rather to the fifteenth-century Germany and to the non-Muslim printers who developed the technology. Therefore, printed books lacked a lineage that provided Islamic authenticity and guaranteed the quality of work."[18] Printing was a technology of multiplicity and

---

[15] Available online from *The King Fahd Glorious Qur'ān Printing Complex* at: https://www.qurancomplex.org.
[16] Available online at the company's website: https://www.decotype.com/.
[17] *Mushaf* available online at https://www.mushafmuscat.com/.
[18] Brett Wilson, *Translating the Qur'ān in an Age of Nationalism: Print Culture and Modern Islam in Turkey* (Oxford: Oxford University Press, 2014), 40.

assemblage. Each *mushaf* produced by a less or more accomplished copyist was nonetheless singular and unique, easily checked for accuracy and completeness, and easy to correct if any mistakes occurred in the process of writing. A printed *mushaf* could multiply the same shape of a letter or a space between words – or, indeed, a misspelling – hundreds of times. A missed word in a handwritten *mushaf* – a rare event – was added in the margin of the text. A correction of an orthographic mistake was not difficult either. Correcting hundreds of copies carrying the same mistake defeated the benefits of fast multiplication. In this circumstance, the question of the text's correct spelling was crucial. How could the accuracy of a written text, previously secured by *isnad*, be preserved now? With printing as primary technology of dissemination, the orthographic mediation of the Qur'ānic message was at risk.

The problem of control over the typographic text has been solved in Egypt by the creation of institutional mechanisms to supervise the production and distribution of the Qur'ānic text. Al-Azhar's branch, the Islamic Research Council, is a parent institution to the *Mushaf* Committee (the full name of which is the "Committee for the Review of the Noble *Mushaf*").[19] The Committee includes a chair, two deputies, and over ten members. The Committee oversees all Qur'ānic production and distribution in Egypt by assigning permits to print and sell. Several stages are required to obtain a license. A publishing house must first submit a copy of the Qur'ānic text to be reproduced for inspection. Then ten test copies of printed text are requested. Once proofed and found correct, the Committee grants the house a permit to print. Several random copies of the Qur'ānic text are selected from the run and forwarded for further inspection. Once the house passes this inspection the Committee issues a license to sell the Qur'ānic book. In a private conversation, a calligraphy specialist employed by the publishing house al-Shimarli described the procedure of getting a license in similar terms, emphasizing that because of this rigorous method the house had received very little complaints from the readers about any misprints.[20]

Considering the complexity of the process of authentication for printed *masahif*, how can the problem of correctness be addressed in the Internet, where the circulation of the unlicensed text is possible? Moreover, how can the institutionalized forms of text control – like the procedures described above – be replicated on the digital level? The channels of bureaucratic control over the publishing houses have already been established, but similar ways of authentication are not yet available for the copies circulating the Internet. The most

---

[19] Lagnat muraga'a al-mushaf al-sharif.
[20] Private conversation on 16 May, 2012.

pressing questions that emerge relate to the creation of a new form of *isnad* for electronic versions of the Qur'ān, to the protection of the integrity of the text in the process of transfer from one environment to another, and to the evaluation of existing copies for their accuracy. Two of the most influential Muslim institutions that deal with the Qur'ānic text – University of al-Azhar, Egypt, and King Fahd Complex for Printing the Holy Qur'ān, Saudi Arabia – addressed this challenge by creating their own digital versions of the Qur'ān that are available to download for free from their websites. However, their versions of the Qur'ān compete with those produced by small, for-profit companies attuned to the digital market who offer a broader range of design, functionality, and features. They are also able to upgrade their applications faster.

This discrepancy between the needs and expectations of the consumers of the Qur'ānic text (quick access to a user friendly application) and concerns of the religious authorities (how to control the text's production to make sure that the text follows the correct rules of orthography and design) creates a dynamic field of activities at the center of which lays the materiality of the Qur'ānic text. On the one hand, these activities include discussions between the al-Azhar authorities and the Egyptian parliament about the forms of legal power to penalize both the publishers and electronic and software companies that release the Qur'ānic copies that do not follow the standards prescribed by the al-Azhar. On the other hand, the flaws present in some of the software available in Egypt and beyond undermine in subtle ways the primacy of al-Azhar as a center of the Muslim authority and influence, slowly shifting the power to the Islamic Council in Saudi Arabia which has been quicker than al-Azhar in its efforts to produce a virtual Qur'ān.

# 7 Conclusion

One of the aims of this essay has been to explore how religious practice surrounding a religious text is rethought as a result of the introduction of new technology that mediates this text. I have outlined some of the differences in which the Qur'ān is enacted through the etiquette of the paper book and an electronic copy of the text. As a final point, I think it is important to ask what happens to the Qur'ān when its enactments start quite suddenly differing from the ones carried out by the previous generations of practitioners. Annemarie Mol, an anthropologist of practice, suggests that when we foreground the practices surrounding things we are able to track how those things come into being. If the socio-material practices differ, new things appear and the realities are multiplied. Instead of a passive thing in the middle seen from multiple perspectives we are faced with new things constantly coming into being. Yet the multiple objects do not fall apart, but as she puts it, they "tend to hang together somehow."[21] For Muslim practitioners the Qur'ān in a phone that can be touched without ablutions is not suddenly different from the Qur'ān in a *mushaf* that cannot. This happens because practices that have ability to create new realities are always entangled with practices that stabilize things, give them a kind of inertia, and make them "hang together." However, the accelerating use of technology in accessing the Qur'ānic message begs a question: how much longer will the *adab al-mushaf* be relevant to the Qur'ān and when/if it ceases to be germane to Muslim practice, what will this change mean for the way the Qur'ān itself is understood and interpreted?

# Bibliography

Hirschkind, Charles. *The Ethical Soundscape: Cassette Sermons and Islamic Counterpublics*. New York: Columbia University Press, 2006.

Ibn Kathir, Abu al-Fada' Isma'il Ibn 'Amr. *Tafsir al-Qur'ān al-'Azim*. Vol. 7. Beirut: Dar al-Fikr, 1966.

Mahmood, Saba. *Politics of Piety: The Islamic Revival and the Feminist Subject*. Princeton, N.J.: Princeton University Press, 2012.

McLuhan, Marshall. *Understanding Media: The Extensions of Man*. New York: The New American Library, 1964.

Messick, Brinkley. *The Calligraphic State: Textual Domination and History in a Muslim Society*. Berkley: University of California Press, 1993.

Mitchell, W.J.T. "There Are No Visual Media." *Journal of Visual Culture* 4/2 (2005): [full page numbers for article needed].

Mol, Annemarie. *The Body Multiple: Ontology in Medical Practice*. Durham: Duke University Press, 2002.

Osborn, J.R. *Letters of Light: Arabic Script in Calligraphy, Print, and Digital Design*. Cambridge: Harvard University Press, 2017.

Schwartz, Kathryn. *Meaningful Mediums: A Material and Intellectual History of Manuscript and Print Production in the Nineteenth-Century Ottoman Cairo*. Ph.D. diss., Harvard University, 2015.

Starrett, Gregory. *Putting Islam to Work: Education, Politics, and Religious Transformation in Egypt*. Berkley: University of California Press, 1998

Wilson, Brett. *Translating the Qur'ān in an Age of Nationalism: Print Culture and Modern Islam in Turkey*. Oxford: Oxford University Press, 2014.

---

21 Annemarie Mol, *The Body Multiple: Ontology in Medical Practice* (Durham: Duke University Press, 2002), 4–5.

Bradford A. Anderson
# Sacred Texts in a Digital Age: Materiality, Digital Culture, and the Functional Dimensions of Scriptures in Judaism, Christianity, and Islam

From scroll to codex, and from manuscript to moveable print, sacred texts have long been influenced by technological developments related to the production and transmission of texts.[1] As with all of these material predecessors, it seems as though the shift to digital culture is another such revolution, altering the textual landscape and the way in which people interact with and use sacred texts across religious traditions.[2] What are the implications of these developments in terms of how people engage with and use scriptures?[3] There has been some reflection on these issues in recent years: a good deal of attention, for example, has been devoted to the academic study of sacred texts in light of digital culture and electronic resources, whether in the digitization of ancient texts, or the use of digital tools for studying various aspects of these texts and their content.[4] There has been more limited engagement with questions of how people are using such texts in digital contexts outside of academia; while studies have begun to appear on these themes in recent years,[5] more common has been anxious reflection emerging

---

[1] For a stimulating exploration of these issues from the perspective of the Jewish tradition, see David Stern, *The Jewish Bible: A Material History* (Seattle: University of Washington Press, 2017).
[2] For a penetrating study on the shift to digital culture more broadly, see Jerome McGann, *A New Republic of Letters: Memory and Scholarship in the Age of Digital Reproduction* (Cambridge: Harvard University Press, 2014).
[3] I use the nomenclature of "sacred texts" and "scriptures" interchangeably throughout the essay, and engage primarily with the texts of Judaism, Christianity, and Islam. Further, I focus here on the actual reproduction of the text in a new literary format, though there is room for further reflection on these matters in relation to other formats to which sacred texts are translated, such as audio or visual.
[4] Claire Clivaz, Paul Dilley, and David Hamidović, eds., *Ancient Worlds in Digital Culture*, DBS 1 (Leiden: Brill, 2016); David Parker, "Through a Screen Darkly: Digital Texts and the New Testament," *JSNT* 25 (2003): 395–411. See also the essays from Fedeli and Allen in this volume.
[5] See, e.g., Tim Hutchings, "E-Reading and the Christian Bible," *Studies in Religion/Sciences Religieuses* 44 (2015): 423–40; Tim Hutchings, "Design and the Digital Bible: Persuasive Technology and Religious Reading," *Journal of Contemporary Religion* 32 (2017): 205–19; Kathy Brittain Richardson and Carol J. Pardun, "The New Scroll Digital Devices, Bible Study and Worship,"

Open Access. © 2020 Bradford A. Anderson, published by De Gruyter. This work is licensed under a Creative Commons Attribution-NonCommercial-NoDerivatives 4.0 International License.
https://doi.org/10.1515/9783110634440-013

from confessional contexts about what the implications of this shift might be for religious (often biblical) literacy.[6]

In this essay I explore the use of sacred texts in digital culture in terms of the functional dimensions of scriptures, with a special focus on questions of materiality. My contention is that while we are seeing dramatic changes in some elements of how sacred texts are used, related primarily to the content of these collections, other functional dimensions are closely tied to questions of material forms, and so the shift to digital contexts have been slower to take hold. I begin, however, with some reflections on the diverse ways in which scriptures are used and employed.

# 1 The Functional Dimensions of Scriptures

Recent decades have witnessed a nascent interest in theoretical reflection on scriptures and their use.[7] One such theory has been put forward by James Watts.[8] Watts has proffered a heuristic three dimensional model for understanding the use of scriptures, and here Watts has in mind the notion of scriptures across religious traditions. He notes that such a "functional model of scripture … might help us better understand those religious traditions that are self-consciously 'scriptural' and to evaluate their claims about the role of scripture within their own tradition against historical and comparative evidence both within that tradition and outside it."[9]

---

*Journal of Media and Religion* 14 (2015): 16–28. See also the essays from Mann and Suit in the present volume.

[6] For example, see Sarah K. Patrick, "The Digital Age and Bible Literacy," *Seeds Family Worship*, available online: https://www.seedsfamilyworship.com/the-digital-age-and-bible-literacy/; "Is Technology Making Us Bible Illiterate?," *Beliefnet*, available online: http://www.beliefnet.com/faiths/christianity/articles/is-technology-making-us-bible-illiterate.aspx.

[7] Wilfred Cantwell Smith, *What Is Scripture? A Comparative Approach* (London: SCM, 1993); Miriam Levering, ed., *Rethinking Scripture* (Albany: SUNY Press, 1989); William A. Graham, *Beyond the Written Word: Oral Aspects of Scripture in the History of Religion* (Cambridge: Cambridge University Press, 1987); Brian Malley, *How the Bible Works: An Anthropological Study of Evangelical Biblicism* (Walnut Creek: AltaMira, 2004); Vincent L. Wimbush, ed., *Theorizing Scriptures: New Critical Orientations to a Cultural Phenomenon*, Signifying (On) Scriptures (New Brunswick: Rutgers University Press, 2008); Jonathan Z. Smith, "Religion and Bible," *JBL* 128 (2009): 5–27; James S. Bielo, *Words Upon the Word: An Ethnography of Evangelical Group Bible Study*, Qualitative Studies in Religion (New York: New York University Press, 2009); James S. Bielo, ed., *The Social Life of Scriptures: Cross-cultural Perspectives on Biblicism*, Signifying (On) Scriptures (New Brunswick: Rutgers University Press, 2009).

[8] James W. Watts, "The Three Dimensions of Scriptures," *Postscripts* 2 (2006): 135–59.

[9] Watts, "The Three Dimensions," 139–40.

Watts notes that scholars involved in the academic study of scriptures and religious texts "have devoted the vast majority of their time and publications to explaining the origins and meaning of scriptural texts."[10] Taking biblical studies as an example, he notes that "modern research has focused on describing the process by which the Bible was composed and the original meaning intended by its authors. Biblical scholars have also given considerable attention to the process by which the Bible became scripture. Such studies of canonization, however, still concentrate on the Bible's semantic form and contents, that is, on questions of when particular books became part of the Jewish and Christian scriptures and under what circumstances."[11] What has too often been missing, Watts suggests, has been robust discussion on the functional dimensions of such texts: how and why they have been used, in various contexts through the centuries.

What emerges is a tripartite system, whereby the ritualized use of scriptures can be heuristically classified in terms of a semantic dimension, a performative dimension, and an iconic dimension.[12] The semantic dimension, according to Watts, has to do with the content and meaning of what is written, and engagement with the written word. This "includes all aspects of interpretation and commentary as well as appeals to the text's contents in preaching and other forms of persuasive rhetoric."[13] Further, "most religious communities with written scriptures encourage many of their devotees to gain expertise in their interpretation, not only for personal devotion but also as a means for directing community behavior and for adjudicating conflict."[14] The semantic dimension, then, focuses on engagement with the *content* of sacred texts.

Meanwhile, the performative dimension of scriptures, Watts suggests, is the performance of what is written, be it the performance of the words or the contents of scriptures. This can take the form of ritualized public readings, recitation of texts, musical performance or singing of scriptures, dramatic presentation, and artistic illustration.[15] Watts points out that these modes of performance "often work in tandem to expose devotees to their tradition's scriptures. They hear the text read and sung, and also see it enacted in drama and art."[16]

---

**10** Watts, "The Three Dimensions," 136.
**11** Watts, "The Three Dimensions," 136.
**12** Watts, "The Three Dimensions," 140.
**13** Watts, "The Three Dimensions," 141.
**14** Watts, "The Three Dimensions," 141.
**15** Watts, "The Three Dimensions," 141–42.
**16** Watts, "The Three Dimensions," 141.

Beyond the semantic and performative levels, Watts notes that scriptures function as icons, pointing to something beyond themselves.[17] Because of this, the physical forms of these texts are treated differently from other books. "They are often displayed prominently on podiums or tables, hung on walls, or else hidden within special cases that call attention to them."[18] Such texts are also "carried in religious processions, displayed to congregations, and venerated through bowing and kissing. ... They are also manipulated in political ceremonies – displayed or touched as part of oath ceremonies and waved in political rallies and protests."[19] This iconicity often leads to another factor, which is that scriptures frequently come to be identified with the tradition as a whole, and so also with the legitimization of particular traditions.[20] Giving the example of some contemporary forms of evangelicalism, Watts notes that they take pride in carrying their Bibles, in both sacred and secular contexts. "In their hands, Bibles function as badges of Christian identity."[21]

The issues of scriptural iconicity and legitimacy lead to another issue, which is the potential desecration of scriptures.[22] Watts notes that "the iconic dimension of scriptures ... can be manipulated by anyone who gains access to a copy of the book. ... Ease of access also means that the iconic dimension is most easily attacked by deliberately mishandling the scripture. Such ritual abuse is called 'desecration.'"[23] This helps make sense of "the explosive social power of desecrating scriptures. Insofar as the scripture has become identified with the religion to the point that the tradition's legitimacy is conveyed by ... the material book, its ritual abuse can feel like an attempt to delegitimize the whole religious tradition."[24]

Watts's model draws heavily on ritual theory, including the work of Catherine Bell and Jonathan Z. Smith, amongst others, making the claim that the religious

---

[17] Other works exploring these issues of iconicity include Martin Marty, "America's Iconic Book," in *Humanizing America's Iconic Book*, ed. Gene M. Tucker and Douglas A. Knight (Chico: Scholars Press, 1982): 1–23; Dorina Miller Parmenter, "The Iconic Book: The Image of the Bible in Early Christian Rituals," *Postscripts* 2 (2006): 160–89. See also the collection of essays in James W. Watts, ed., *Iconic Books and Texts* (Sheffield: Equinox, 2013).
[18] Watts, "The Three Dimensions," 142.
[19] Watts, "The Three Dimensions," 142.
[20] This can be seen quite clearly in visual art: "The artistic association of a deity with scripture legitimizes the scripture as authentic, and the association of a human with recognized scripture legitimizes the person's spiritual status" (Watts, "The Three Dimensions," 142).
[21] Watts, "The Three Dimensions," 148.
[22] James W. Watts, "Desecrating Scriptures," *A Case Study for the Luce Project in Media, Religion, and International Relations* (2009); available online: http://surface.syr.edu/rel/3/.
[23] Watts, "Desecrating Scriptures," § 1.
[24] Watts, "Desecrating Scriptures," § 1.

use of scriptures is in fact a form of ritual.²⁵ "By describing the dimensions in terms of *ritualization,* the model explains the similarities and differences between scriptures and other books and writings. ... All books and writings exhibit semantic, performative, and iconic dimensions at least to an incipient degree. Some secular texts (such as national constitutions and theatrical scripts) are also typically ritualized along one or two of their dimensions. What distinguishes scriptures, however, is that their religious communities ritualize all three dimensions."²⁶ Drawing on Smith's work on ritual, Watts comments that "The otherwise trivial practices involved in reading a book are, in the case of scriptures, given sustained attention. Semantic interpretation is ritualized by commentary and preaching. Reading and dramatization both become ritual performances. The book's physical form is decorated, manipulated in public and private rituals, and highlighted in artistic representations. In each case, special attention is given to otherwise routine acts of reading. Thus religious traditions maintain the status of their scriptures by ritualizing normal features of books and other writings."²⁷ As he goes on to note, "The *more* a book or text is ritualized in *all three* dimensions... the more likely it is to be regarded as a scripture. Thus the functional identification of scriptures depends not on a difference in kind from other books and writings, but on the *degree* to which a particular book or writing is ritualized as text *and* as performance *and* as icon."²⁸

## 2 The Functional Dimensions of Scriptures in the Digital Age

As noted above, the rise of digital media has undoubtedly altered the textual landscape and the way in which people interact with sacred texts. What happens, though, when we think about these technological changes in light of Watts's theoretical reflections on the varied use of scriptures? What I want to do here, for the sake of space, is to focus in particular on the semantic and iconic dimensions. How has the digital turn impacted these aspects of scriptural use?

---

**25** Jonathan Z. Smith, *To Take Place: Toward Theory in Ritual* (Chicago: University of Chicago Press, 1987); Catherine Bell, *Ritual Theory and Ritual Practice* (New York: Oxford University Press, 1992).
**26** Watts, "The Three Dimensions," 140–41.
**27** Watts, "The Three Dimensions," 144–45.
**28** Watts, "The Three Dimensions," 146.

## 2.1 Semantic Dimension

As Watts notes, the semantic dimension includes elements such as reading, interpretation, commentary, and preaching. This dimension, I would suggest, is where shifts in digital usage are most obvious. Such developments have spawned countless new endeavours to rethink the use of the Bible and other sacred texts, from pious devotional reading to digital evangelization. A few examples are worth noting.

### 2.1.1 Reading and Devotion

One area where this shift can be seen is in the rise of digital texts of scriptures aimed at reading and devotion. There are now countless websites that have the full text of the Jewish Tanakh, the Christian Bible, and the Qur'ān. There are also a growing number of apps for portable devices that have this same function.

One such example was documented by the *New York Times*, and picked up by dozens of other news outlets: in 2013, a digital Bible app for mobile devices known as the YouVersion passed 100 million downloads.[29] Their website now, several years later, puts the number at over 352 million downloads.[30] Along with the biblical text in hundreds of languages and translations, the group responsible for the app also provides reading plans and challenges for the faithful, YouVersion for Kids, and even YouVersion events for churches that can sync with peoples' phones and tablets. This is summed up by the tagline on their website, "The Bible is Everywhere."

The use of electronic resources is not always a matter of convenience – digital texts have also been used as a way to make the Bible available in places where it might otherwise be difficult to obtain, or in languages where physical translations are uncommon. Thus, Catholic officials in the Indian Archdiocese of Goa recently launched an app containing the entire Bible translated into Konkani, intended for local laity as well as those in the diaspora.[31]

Such resources are not limited to the Christian Bible. The Jewish publisher Artscroll Mesorah has developed a popular app of the Babylonian Talmud to

---

[29] Amy O'Leary, "In the Beginning was the Word; Now the Word is on An App," *The New York Times*, July 26, 2013. See also the chapter from Mann in the present volume.
[30] Number as of 13 December 2018. See https://www.youversion.com/the-bible-app/.
[31] "Now, a Konkani Bible on Your Cellphone," *The Times of India*, May 1, 2018; available online: https://timesofindia.indiatimes.com/city/goa/now-a-konkani-bible-on-your-cellphone/articleshow/63979490.cms.

encourage reading and study. The MyQuran app, meanwhile, has been extremely popular as well, and advertises the opportunities of reading, study, and memorization. How much these apps and programs are being used, and to what ends, is a matter of debate. Nevertheless, there is evidence that opportunities exist for such engagement in reading and devotional use.

### 2.1.2 Commentary, Interpretation, and Study

The arenas of commentary, interpretation, and study have also been affected in significant ways by the digital turn. There are a number of tools that are very popular among both clergy and academics that offer the chance to study scriptures, while also accessing research and lexical tools, commentaries, and other secondary materials right within the programme. BibleWorks, Accordance, and Logos are some of the major players in the world of biblical studies, and the resources and capabilities of these programmes continue to expand exponentially.

Further, in 2016, a new online, digitized repository of the entire Babylonian Talmud was launched, called Hachi Garsinan, which includes all textual variants. The creator's comments are telling: "Our project is totally comprehensive and will help everyone who studies the Talmud …What we have here is no less a revolution than the printing of the Talmud in 1523 in Venice. It is a unique project and will change the way Talmud is learnt within a few years because it has created the ultimate system for Talmud study."[32]

### 2.1.3 Preaching

Finally, we see the use of digital forms making their way into preaching and other forms of exhortation. Preachers are increasingly making use of digital tools such as tablets in their homilies, sermons, and other presentations, as well as using resources such as iPads for scriptural readings during services. This type of use is considered progressive in some circles, where technological innovation is lauded.[33]

---

[32] Jeremy Sharon, "Digitized Talmud and Mobile App to be Launched," *The Jerusalem Post*, May 29, 2016; available online: https://www.jpost.com/Business-and-Innovation/Tech/Digitized-Talmud-and-mobile-app-to-be-launched-455357.

[33] By way of example: this past year I attended a church service in the United States where the preacher asked congregants to open their Bibles or swipe open their phones to their Bible apps.

It remains the case, as Timothy Beal has noted, that physical Bibles, Tanakhs, and Qur'āns continue to be sold and to proliferate, and there are implications of this trend that need to be considered.[34] Nevertheless, it is also clear that the digital turn is having a significant effect on scriptural use in the semantic dimension. Personal reading, study, interpretation, preaching: all of these bear witness to substantial developments in recent years that are directly related to technological change and how people are engaging with these scriptures in the emerging digital landscape.

## 2.2 Iconic Dimension

Let's turn to Watts's iconic dimension. This dimension focuses on how scriptures point to something beyond themselves, are treated with special reverence, and often come to symbolically represent the larger traditions of which they are a part.

### 2.2.1 Digital Usage

In this domain we find far less evidence of the impact of the digital turn than was seen in the semantic dimension outlined above, though examples can be found. To begin, there have been several headline-grabbing cases over the past few years related to the use of digital texts as part of oath swearing ceremonies. For example, New Jersey firefighters were sworn in on an iPad in 2013,[35] while a New York county executive was sworn in using a digital version of the Bible in 2014.[36] The rise in digital formats has also led to discussions regarding the proper disposal of digital texts. In many traditions, for instance, there are guidelines for the proper disposal of scriptures. But what about digital sacred text? How should these be disposed of? There are numerous online discussion forums where these types of issues are raised. One particular Jewish forum had an interesting

---

[34] Timothy Beal, "The End of the Word as We Know It: The Cultural Iconicity of the Bible in the Twilight of Print Culture," in *Iconic Books and Texts*, ed. James W. Watts (Sheffield: Equinox, 2013): 207–24.
[35] Doug Drinkwater, "New Jersey Firefighters Sworn Into Office With iPad," *Mashable*, 11 February 2013; available online: https://mashable.com/2013/02/11/new-jersey-firefighters-ipad/#mT-NZPQIbsPq1.
[36] Salvador Rodriguez, "Elected Official Takes Oath of Office on an iPad," *Los Angeles Times*, 3 January 2014; available online: http://www.latimes.com/business/technology/la-fi-tn-politician-sworn-in-ipad-bible-20140103-story.html.

discussion regarding what to do with an email that contains scriptures including the name of God. A rabbi notes in response to a query that "This issue was discussed in the 1950s regarding audio cassettes. Rabbi Moshe Feinstein ruled that he saw no reason to forbid erasing a tape with Torah content, but still advised 'perhaps not to erase since it appears like erasing G-d's name.' He – and others – therefore advised that it would be ideal to do the erasing in an indirect manner, such as asking a child to do it."[37] The instruction here is based on the fact that an email, like an audio cassette, is an impermanent, erasable format. Consequently, an email containing scripture can be deleted (but better if someone does this for you, to be safe!). One can find, then, instances of the iconic dimension of scriptures being engaged in relation digital formats, though these remain exceptional: swearing of oaths on iPads and the proper disposal of electronic sacred texts are two examples.

### 2.2.2 Continued Physical and Material Use

These few examples notwithstanding, it is also worth noting a series of incidents from recent years which highlight the continued importance of physical, material scriptures as icons in the contemporary world. I offer a selection of scenes and snapshots drawn from the headlines that demonstrate just how prevalent and diverse such material usage continues to be. I have organized these into examples of desecration, oath swearing, public and symbolic usage, talismanic usage, and cases from religious contexts.

### 2.2.1.1 Desecration
(1) In 2010, Terry Jones, the pastor of a small church from Florida, threatened to burn a Qur'ān on the tenth anniversary of 9/11 in protest of what he decried as the text's violent tendencies. There was much publicity, and even President Obama weighed in, citing the possible destructive implications of such an event for international relations. Finally, Jones relented, and did not go through with the burning. On the 20th of March 2011, however, Jones and his family did burn the Qur'ān after holding a court trial in their own church and

---

[37] Menachem Posner, "Proper Disposal of Holy Objects," *Chabad*, 30 July 2015; available online: https://www.chabad.org/library/article_cdo/aid/475304/jewish/Proper-Disposal-of-Holy-Objects.htm. For more on matters of ritual disposal of sacred texts, see the essays in Kristina Myrvold, ed., *The Death of Sacred Texts: Ritual Disposal and Renovation of Texts in World Religions* (Farnham: Ashgate, 2010).

finding the Qur'ān guilty of encouraging violence. As feared, Jones's actions did lead to further violence, as twelve people ended up dying when people took to the streets in Afghanistan to protest this desecration.[38]

(2) In February 2012, several days of protests led to the deaths of thirty Afghans and four American soldiers after it became known that American soldiers had burned Qur'āns at the Bagram Air Base.[39]

(3) In early 2012, Bishop Eddie Long, the pastor of New Birth Baptist Church in DeKalb County, Georgia, was wrapped in an actual Torah scroll by the charismatic messianic rabbi Ralph Messer, who claimed the ritual was an ancient one symbolizing enthronement and new birth. This event led to both publicity and controversy; the story was highlighted on CNN, and after renunciation from a number of sectors, Bishop Long issued an apology to the Jewish community for the mishandling of the sacred text in this way.[40]

(4) Several states in Central Asia came under scrutiny in 2012 and 2013 for state sanctioned destruction of religious texts. In Russia, Islamic theological texts were ordered to be destroyed, while Bibles and other Christian literature were ordered to be destroyed in Uzbekistan and Kazakhstan, after which several human and religious rights watch organizations called for international actions against these countries.[41]

(5) In March of 2016, footage surfaced of what appeared to be ISIS destroying Christian Bibles and books in a bonfire in Mosul. This was seen as deliberate desecration of Christian texts and part of a larger pattern of hostile persecution of Christians in the region.[42]

(6) Police were called to investigate a series of anti-Muslim incidents in Mississauga, Ontario, Canada, including a woman tearing pages from the Qur'ān and placing them on cars in public places. Elsewhere, the woman was seen

---

[38] Enayat Najafizada and Rod Nordland, "Afghans Avenge Florida Koran Burning, Killing 12," *The New York Times*, April 1, 2011.

[39] Alissa J. Rubin and Graham Bowley, "Koran Burning in Afghanistan Prompts 3 Parallel Inquiries," *The New York Times*, February 29, 2012.

[40] Marcy Oster, "Bishop Eddie Long Apologizes for Torah Scroll Ceremony," *Jewish Telegraphic Agency*, 6 February 2012; available online: https://www.jta.org/2012/02/06/news-opinion/united-states/bishop-eddie-long-apologizes-for-torah-scroll-ceremony.

[41] Felix Corley, "Russia: 'I've never encountered the practice of destroying religious literature before,'" *Forum 18*, 21 March 2012; available online: http://www.forum18.org/archive.php?article_id=1682; Mushfig Bayram, "Uzbekistan: Raids, criminal charges and Christmas Bible destruction," *Forum 18*, 31 January 2013; available online: http://www.forum18.org/archive.php?article_id=1797; Felix Corley, "Kazakhstan: Court-ordered religious book burning a first?," *Forum 18*, 14 March 2013; available online: http://www.forum18.org/archive.php?article_id=1813.

[42] Footage is available online at: https://www.youtube.com/watch?v=np3OszSEmiw.

burning pages from the Qur'ān on video. She noted that these actions were part of a larger attempt to have the Qur'ān listed as hate literature.⁴³

### 2.2.2.2 Oath Swearing

(1) For his second inauguration, President Obama used three Bibles while taking his oath of office: a Bible from the Robinson family (his wife's family), Abraham Lincoln's Bible, and Martin Luther King Jr.'s travelling Bible.⁴⁴ These choices received a good deal of attention and critique, including a robust response from Cornel West, who criticized Obama for appropriating King.⁴⁵ Meanwhile, in January 2017, Donald Trump used two Bibles while taking his oath of office: his own personal Bible, and Abraham Lincoln's Bible, choices which again drew comment and critique.⁴⁶

(2) London's mayor, Sadiq Khan, took office as the city's first Muslim mayor in May 2016. At the time of the election, an anecdote from Khan's previous 2009 appointment to the Privy Council was making the rounds. "The next day Buckingham Palace rang about his appointment to the Privy Council: 'You're going to be sworn in before the Queen, what sort of bible would you like?' I said: 'I swear on the Koran, I'm a Muslim'. They said: 'We haven't got a Koran, can you bring your own?' So I went to Buckingham Palace with my Koran and afterwards they returned it and I said: 'No, can I leave it here for the next person.'"⁴⁷

---

43 Stewart Bell, "Pages ripped from Qur'an put on car windshields again, police investigating," *Global News*, 10 April 2018; online edition: https://globalnews.ca/news/4133148/pages-from-koran-car-windshields-mississauga/.
44 Gabrielle Levy, "Obama's Inauguration: Everything You Wanted to Know About the 57th Inauguration and the 56 Before It," *United Press International*, 21 January 2013; available online: http://www.upi.com/blog/2013/01/21/Obamas-inauguration-Everything-you-wanted-to-know-about-the-57th-inauguration-and-the-56-before-it/8011358757175/. For the public inauguration Obama used just two, stacked on top of one another: The Lincoln and King Bibles.
45 Kirsten West Savali, "Cornel West: President Obama Doesn't Deserve To Be Sworn In With MLK's Bible," *News One*. 20 January 2013; available online: https://newsone.com/2153928/cornel-west-obama-mlk/.
46 Erin McCann, "The Two Bibles Donald Trump Used at the Inauguration," *The New York Times*, 18 January 2017; available online: https://www.nytimes.com/2017/01/18/us/politics/lincoln-bible-trump-oath.html.
47 Sarah Sands, "Full interview: As he launches his bid for City Hall, Sadiq Khan says 'I won't be a Zone One Mayor,'" *The Evening Standard*, 13 May 2015; available online: https://www.standard.co.uk/news/politics/full-interview-as-he-launches-his-bid-for-city-hall-sadiq-khan-says-i-wont-be-a-zone-one-mayor-10247056.html.

### 2.2.2.3 Public and Symbolic Usage

(1) In 2014, Trinity College, Dublin, underwent a rebranding initiative. Part of this included removing the Bible from the college crest, which had been there since the sixteenth century. It was replaced with a generic open book signifying scholarship open to all. This received considerable pushback from a diverse and surprisingly large constituency within and outside of the college who felt that the iconic Bible should remain.[48]

(2) In 2014, the Satanic Temple submitted a Satanic colouring book for distribution in public schools in Orange County, Florida. This was in response to a group (World Changers of Florida) that was distributing Bibles in schools. The distribution of religious materials, and the Bible in particular, has remained a contested issue in the United States – now groups such as the Satanic Temple along with atheist organisations are pushing back by asking for inclusion and distribution of their own materials.[49]

(3) In April 2016, Tennessee's state senate approved a bill making the Bible the official state book, even though the state's attorney general said it would be unconstitutional. Here the Bible was being used as an iconic tool in identity politics in the southern United States, under the guise of historical and cultural appreciation, which is how the lawmakers described their bill.[50] The governor vetoed the bill later in the month, agreeing with opponents who said it would trivialize the Bible.[51]

(4) After the US retailer Target announced a new policy regarding use of bathrooms, including a transgender policy, Target faced extreme backlash to this decision. One prominent example showed up on YouTube, as a mom paraded through a Target store, her kids in tow, warning shoppers of the new policy. Interestingly, the entire time, the woman is holding high above her a Bible.

---

**48** Joe Humphreys, "Is nothing sacred? Trinity College scraps Bible from its crest," *The Irish Times*, 29 March 2014; available online: https://www.irishtimes.com/news/education/is-nothing-sacred-trinity-college-scraps-bible-from-its-crest-1.1742490.
**49** Lauren Roth, "Satanic Temple submits coloring book, fact sheets for Orange school distribution," *Orlando Sentinel*, 30 October 2014; available online: http://www.orlandosentinel.com/features/education/school-zone/os-satanic-temple-coloring-book-20141030-post.html.
**50** Joel Ebert, "Bill to make Bible Tennessee's official book heads to governor," *The Tennessean*, 5 April 2016; available online https://www.tennessean.com/story/news/politics/2016/04/04/bill-make-bible-official-state-book-heads-haslam/82625250/.
**51** Matt Pearce, "Tennessee's governor vetoes Bible as state book," *The Los Angeles Times*, 17 April 2016; available online: http://www.latimes.com/nation/la-na-tennessee-bible-20160417-story.html. On the larger phenomenon of Bibles as representative books, see Melissa Chan, "Tennessee Wasn't First State to Attempt to Make the Bible the Official State Book," *Time*, 20 April 2016; available online: http://time.com/4301131/bible-state-book-bill-fail/.

As Brent Plate notes, "there's really nothing 'biblical' in her soliloquy ... What she does do is firmly hold high a bible. ... It stands as a visible beacon that guides them ... But the bible is never mentioned, never quoted from, never used for anything other than a visual display of some, unknown, power."[52]

(5) In 2016 Irish solicitors were told to always carry with them both Bibles and Qurʾāns in case they have to administer an oath for a sworn affidavit, as instructed by the High Court. An exemption can be made if someone chooses to object on religious grounds.[53]

(6) In March 2017, police in Fort Collins, Colorado, arrested a 35-year-old man, suspected of throwing rocks and a Bible at a mosque. Surveillance video captured a person overturning benches, breaking windows and hurling objects into the prayer area of the Islamic Center of Fort Collins, police said.[54]

## 2.2.2.4 Talismanic Properties

(1) In 2016, a story made the headlines in the United States when a man was pulled from his burning car following an accident – along with an unscathed Bible. Here we see the ancient trope of scriptures functioning as a talisman, protecting people and bringing good luck because of their association with the divine. There have been no such stories, to my knowledge, about the survival of iPads with Bible apps installed.[55]

(2) "When a tornado battered southern Mississippi in January 2017, it yanked trees out the ground and tore through buildings at William Carey University. When staffers combed the campus, sifting through the damage, they said they happened upon a stunning scene: An open Bible on the pulpit of the campus church, undisturbed by the surrounding debris."[56]

---

**52** S. Brent Rodriguez Plate, "Waving Bibles, Protesting Bathrooms," *Iconic Books Blog*, 15 May 2016; available online: http://iconicbooks.blogspot.ie/2016/05/waving-bibles-protesting-bathrooms.html.
**53** Mark O'Regan, "Solicitors Told to Carry Bible and Koran," *Irish Independent*, 24 April 2016; available online: https://www.independent.ie/irish-news/courts/solicitors-told-to-carry-bible-and-koran-34654171.html.
**54** Jason Le Miere, "Colorado Mosque Attack: Bible and Rocks Used to Smash Prayer-Room Windows." *Newsweek*, 27 March 2017; available online: http://www.newsweek.com/mosque-attack-bible-colorado-muslim-prayer-574767.
**55** Henry Hanks, "Bible, Driver Survive After Car Bursts Into Flames," *CNN*, 22 February 2016; available online: http://edition.cnn.com/2016/02/22/us/car-in-flames-bible/index.html.
**56** Madeline Holcombe, "Amid the Tornado Wreckage in Mississippi, a Bible is Left Untouched," *CNN*, 25 January 2017; available online: https://edition.cnn.com/2017/01/25/us/bible-survives-tornado-trnd/index.html.

### 2.2.2.5 Religious Contexts

(1) Numerous reports have been made in recent years of sacred texts stolen from religious communities and their houses of worship, some of these gaining a very high profile. These include ancient Torah texts taken from the Samaritan community in Palestine,[57] as well as significant scrolls and Bibles in communities from New York to Hawaii.[58]

(2) On the other side of this equation, stories of reclaimed scriptures have also been noted, including the special role these material texts continue to play in contemporary religious communities. In Kingston, New York, for example, a local Jewish community celebrated their synagogue's new scroll in 2018, a restored scroll that was rescued from Prague after World War II.[59]

Burning and desecration, talismans, oath swearing, protests, official books, stolen and reclaimed sacred texts: in each case, we find a focus on the material and physical dimensions of these scriptures, and the iconic role that they continue to play in the world today. Thus, in spite of the rapid increase in the availability of scriptures in digital formats, it is important to note that the iconic role of scriptures has seen less drastic change, and that physical sacred texts continue to have a significant place in social and religious discourse.

## 2 Sacred Texts in a Liminal Age

When read in light of Watts's reflections on the functional dimensions of scriptures, the examples highlighted above suggest that the rise of digital culture is impacting in diverse ways the use of sacred texts in different domains: engagement

---

[57] Daniel Estrin, "Who Stole the Torahs? An Ancient Sect, A Brazen Theft And The Hunt To Bring The Manuscripts Home," *National Public Radio*, 29 April 2018; available online: https://www.npr.org/2018/04/29/602836507/who-stole-the-torahs.
[58] Rick Daysog, "Sacred Torah scrolls stolen from Oahu synagogue," *Hawaii News Now*, 24 January 2018; available online: http://www.hawaiinewsnow.com/story/37333800/sacred-torah-scrolls-stolen-from-oahu-synagogue; Nicole Hensley, "Thief steals century-old bible, gold staff and challis from historic Harlem church," *New York Daily News*, 1 May 2018, available online: http://www.nydailynews.com/new-york/manhattan/thief-steals-century-old-bible-gold-staff-harlem-church-article-1.3964989.
[59] "Rescued Torah scroll at Kingston temple stands as reminder of Holocaust," *Daily Freeman News*, 11 April 2018; available online: http://www.dailyfreeman.com/article/df/20180411/news/180419922.

with digital culture is much more evident in the semantic domain than it is in the iconic dimension. Is there a way to account for this?

To begin, it might be helpful to situate the present era in light of the work of van Gennep and Turner and their respective theories of liminality, the stage of disorientation or ambiguity that emerges in the life cycle of rituals.[60] Working in anthropology and ritual, van Gennep and Turner highlighted that rites of passage and rituals pass through three stages: separation, margin, and aggregation. As Turner notes,

> During the intervening "liminal" period, the characteristics of the ritual subject ... are ambiguous; he passes through a cultural realm that has few or none of the attributes of the past or coming state. In the third phase (reaggregation or reincorporation), the passage is consummated. The ritual subject, individual or corporate, is in a relatively stable state once more. ... Liminal entities are neither here nor there; they are betwixt and between the positions assigned and arrayed by law, custom, convention, and ceremonial.[61]

Without pushing the issue too far, this is an apt description of the ritualistic use of scriptures in the contemporary world. We are in many ways experiencing a liminal phase between the old and the new: while new digital forms of the text are beginning to take root, a new ordered and stable reality has yet to emerge, and the older, physical forms of sacred texts continue to manifest themselves in very real ways, particularly with regard to the iconic dimension of scriptures.

But pressing beyond this notion of liminality, how might we account for the ongoing employment of material forms in relation to the iconic domain? Continuing with the theme of ritual, Watts has suggested that work comparing scriptures with what we think of as disposable texts such as phone books might be enlightening.[62] He notes,

> To the degree that a book simply serves as an information source, it can be replaced by computer searches without readers feeling any loss. Online phone directories have become readily available and will likely replace material phone books entirely within a generation. Sacred texts have also been adapted for the new media but with very different prospects for the material books. ... the difference between phone books and Bibles lies not in the degree to which they have been transformed and accepted in electronic form, but rather in the fact that the disappearance of physical Bibles is unimaginable because of their ritual uses. It is

---

60 Arnold van Gennep, *The Rites of Passage*, trans. Monika B. Vizedom and Gabrielle L. Caffee (Chicago: University of Chicago Press, 1960); Victor Turner, *The Ritual Process: Structure and Anti-Structure* (Ithaca: Cornell, [1961] 1977).
61 Turner, *The Ritual Process*, 95.
62 James W. Watts, "Disposing of Non-Disposable Texts," in *The Death of Sacred Texts: Ritual Disposal and Renovation of Texts in the World Religions*, ed. Kristina Myrvold (Farnham: Ashgate, 2010): 147–59.

> impossible that e-readers will ever replace traditional codices in liturgical processions and other ritual uses along the iconic dimension, because computers and other kinds of e-readers do not represent particular texts but are generic containers for any content. ... To the degree that people ritualize books and other texts along the iconic dimension – that is, to the degree that they pay conscious attention to how they look and feel, how they carry them and their own posture as they read them – such iconic books will remain features of human culture. The iconic status of various kinds of material books preserves and even enhances their appeal in an age of digital information.[63]

Watts thus suggests that the continued importance of physical scriptures is related to their ritual use, and this seems to be corroborated by several of the examples noted above, particularly those that highlight the continued importance of these texts in for explicitly religious uses. But what about the other, less overtly religious examples noted above?

Here the work of Jonathan Westin is suggestive.[64] Westin, whose expertise is in the field of critical heritage studies and conservation, has drawn on the sociology of translation to develop what he calls the vocabulary of limitations. Westin makes two important observations for our purposes.[65] To begin with, all formats embody cultural values. As digital books have become increasingly common, "questions arise regarding how those cultural values which are negotiated around a physicality translate to a digital sphere. ... few would argue that nothing has been lost in translation when a phenomenon is moved from an analogue to a digital format. Expressed through digital means, the content is detached from the 'culture' to which it was bound by the context of its traditional physicality."[66] This is not some unspecified culture; rather, networks in societies "champion the positive connotations and authenticity of their format, rather than the content itself, by invoking cultural values in a context tied to time and space. This ensures the longevity of the format and consequentially their investment in it, while the content is deemed lessened in other contexts. As a consequence, the cultural values of a format stand in proportion to the cultural values put into that format by the stakeholders."[67]

Second, these cultural values related to particular formats include limitations, and translation to a new format is a negotiation of cultural values, includ-

---

[63] Watts, "Disposing of Non-Disposable Texts," 149–50.
[64] Jonathan Westin, "Loss of Culture: New Media Forms and the Translation from Analogue to Digital Books," *Convergence: The International Journal of Research into New Media Technologies* 19/2 (2012): 129–40.
[65] The sociology of translation draws on the work of Bruno Latour and others who have given a more prominent role to objects in the forming of social and cultural networks.
[66] Westin, "Loss of Culture," 130.
[67] Westin, "Loss of Culture," 135.

ing these limitations. "When the limits of a format's ability to communicate a content is reached, ... there is a detour to another format."[68] Here we come to an interesting point: limitations are often seen as a reason for translating to a new format. This is clearly seen in the history of sacred texts, as the shift to new formats (e.g., from scroll to codex, or codex to digital form) is often to make the text more accessible. However, these limitations embody numerous cultural values, and consequently "these cultural values enter the negotiation as actants, to be enrolled or ignored."[69] Westin suggests that we pay attention to such limitations, and the way in which these aspects shape the cultural use of these objects: what is often seen as a limitation when translating to a new format is in actuality a socio-cultural signifier, and so the new format must eventually negotiate with this to communicate such a limitation. "In the negotiation process, a new format can either follow the absolute limitations of the new format or partially emulate the limitations of the previous format."[70] Accordingly, "While content can be moved from one format to another, the 'culture' present in the combination of format and content must be translated and in that act branches are created that take the content in new directions."[71]

Thus, according to Westin, the process of translating to a digital format is a negotiation that includes cultural values (including limitations) of physical forms. The examples I have noted above suggest that users are indeed attempting to negotiate these cultural values in digital formats – swearing oaths on iPads, for example – but that many of such values are retained in the physicality of printed scriptures. Can a digital text function as a talisman? Can it be invoked in a protest? Can it be revered and processed in a religious ceremony? These are values that have been assigned to particular material texts (scrolls, manuscripts, and print), and translating these elements to digital formats will be a complex task. In this sense Westin's proposal seems to complement Watts's contention that the iconic, ritualized use of scriptures is an important dimension of why physical Bibles continue to play an important role in a changing world: there are cultural traits that have not yet been – and perhaps cannot be – translated to the digital form.

---

**68** Westin, "Loss of Culture," 135.
**69** Westin, "Loss of Culture," 135. Here Westin draws on Latour's notion of actants. See Bruno Latour, "On Technical Mediation," *Common Knowledge* 3/2 (1994): 29–64; and Latour, *Reassembling the Social: An Introduction to Actor-Network-Theory* (Oxford: Oxford University Press, 2007).
**70** Westin, "Loss of Culture," 137.
**71** Westin, "Loss of Culture," 138.

## 3 Conclusions

As digital culture increasingly becomes the dominant frame of reference for how people engage with texts, further analysis of how sacred texts function in a digital age will become ever more important. I close with a few concluding reflections that such work might consider:

The work of Watts and others is a reminder that we need to think carefully about how and why scriptures are actually used, and in doing so, to reflect more critically on these diverse practices. Further, giving attention to the diverse uses of scriptures suggests that while we are seeing a rapid change in the semantic dimension of how sacred texts are used in the emerging age of digital texts, we are also seeing how manuscript and print texts continue to play an important role in a variety of different contexts. Westin's theoretical reflections are helpful, I think, in that they highlight how translating to the digital domain is not a simple task, but is in fact a complex process, and one which must account for the materiality of the texts in question and attendant social and cultural dimensions.

Indeed, just as digital texts must attempt to account for the social and culture values inherent in physical books, so the digital texts themselves are also acquiring social and cultural values. These, too, will become important elements of these digital texts; the social and cultural values that digital texts acquire will also need to be negotiated when translated to yet another (perhaps still unknown) format – and so the complex process of translation will continue.

## Bibliography

Bayram, Mushfig. "Uzbekistan: Raids, criminal charges and Christmas Bible destruction." *Forum 18*. 31 January 2013/ Available online: http://www.forum18.org/archive.php?article_id=1797.

Beal, Timothy. "The End of the Word as We Know It: The Cultural Iconicity of the Bible in the Twilight of Print Culture." In *Iconic Books and Texts,* edited by James W. Watts, 207–24. Sheffield: Equinox, 2013.

Bell, Catherine. *Ritual Theory and Ritual Practice*. New York: Oxford University Press, 1992.

Bell, Stewart. "Pages ripped from Qur'an put on car windshields again, police investigating." *Global News*. 10 April 2018. Available online: https://globalnews.ca/news/4133148/pages-from-koran-car-windshields-mississauga/.

Bielo, James S. *Words Upon the Word: An Ethnography of Evangelical Group Bible Study*. Qualitative Studies in Religion. New York: New York University Press, 2009.

Bielo, James S., ed. *The Social Life of Scriptures: Cross-cultural Perspectives on Biblicism*. Signifying (On) Scriptures. New Brunswick: Rutgers University Press, 2009.

Cantwell Smith, Wilfred. *What Is Scripture? A Comparative Approach*. London: SCM, 1993.

Chan, Melissa. "Tennessee Wasn't First State to Attempt to Make the Bible the Official State Book." *Time*. 20 April 2016. Available online: http://time.com/4301131/bible-state-book-bill-fail/.
Clivaz, Claire, Paul Dilley, and David Hamidović, eds. *Ancient Worlds in Digital Culture*. DBS 1. Leiden: Brill, 2016.
Corley, Felix. "Russia: 'I've never encountered the practice of destroying religious literature before.'" *Forum 18*. 21 March 2012. Available online: http://www.forum18.org/archive.php?article_id=1682;
Corley, Felix. "Kazakhstan: Court-ordered religious book burning a first?" *Forum 18*. 14 March 2013. Available online: http://www.forum18.org/archive.php?article_id=1813.
Daysog, Rick. "Sacred Torah scrolls stolen from Oahu synagogue." *Hawaii News Now*. 24 January 2018. Available online: http://www.hawaiinewsnow.com/story/37333800/sacred-torah-scrolls-stolen-from-oahu-synagogue.
Drinkwater, Doug. "New Jersey Firefighters Sworn Into Office With iPad." *Mashable*. 11 February 2013. Available online: https://mashable.com/2013/02/11/new-jersey-firefighters-ipad/#mTNZPQIbsPq1.
Ebert, Joel. "Bill to make Bible Tennessee's official book heads to governor." *The Tennessean*. 5 April 2016. Available online: https://www.tennessean.com/story/news/politics/2016/04/04/bill-make-bible-official-state-book-heads-haslam/82625250/.
Estrin, Daniel. "Who Stole the Torahs? An Ancient Sect, A Brazen Theft and The Hunt To Bring The Manuscripts Home." *National Public Radio*. 29 April 2018. Available online: https://www.npr.org/2018/04/29/602836507/who-stole-the-torahs.
Graham, William A. *Beyond the Written Word: Oral Aspects of Scripture in the History of Religion*. Cambridge: Cambridge University Press, 1987.
Hanks, Henry. "Bible, Driver Survive After Car Bursts Into Flames." *CNN*. 22 February 2016. Available online: http://edition.cnn.com/2016/02/22/us/car-in-flames-bible/index.html.
Hensley, Nicole. "Thief steals century-old bible, gold staff and challis from historic Harlem church." *New York Daily News*. 1 May 2018. Available online: http://www.nydailynews.com/new-york/manhattan/thief-steals-century-old-bible-gold-staff-harlem-church-article-1.3964989.
Holcombe, Madeline. "Amid the Tornado Wreckage in Mississippi, a Bible is Left Untouched." *CNN*. 25 January 2017. Available online: https://edition.cnn.com/2017/01/25/us/bible-survives-tornado-trnd/index.html.
Humphreys, Joe. "Is nothing sacred? Trinity College scraps Bible from its crest." *The Irish Times*. 29 March 2014. Available online: https://www.irishtimes.com/news/education/is-nothing-sacred-trinity-college-scraps-bible-from-its-crest-1.1742490.
Hutchings, Tim. "E-Reading and the Christian Bible." *Studies in Religion/Sciences Religieuses* 44 (2015): 423–40.
Hutchings, Tim. "Design and the Digital Bible: Persuasive Technology and Religious Reading." *Journal of Contemporary Religion* 32 (2017): 205–19.
"Is Technology Making Us Bible Illiterate?" *Beliefnet*. Available online: http://www.beliefnet.com/faiths/christianity/articles/is-technology-making-us-bible-illiterate.aspx.
Latour, Bruno. "On Technical Mediation." *Common Knowledge* 3/2 (1994): 29–64.
Latour, Bruno. *Reassembling the Social: An Introduction to Actor-Network-Theory*. Oxford: Oxford University Press, 2007.
Le Miere, Jason. "Colorado Mosque Attack: Bible and Rocks Used to Smash Prayer-Room Windows." *Newsweek*. 27 March 2017. Available online: http://www.newsweek.com/mosque-attack-bible-colorado-muslim-prayer-574767.

Levy, Gabrielle. "Obama's Inauguration: Everything You Wanted to Know About the 57th Inauguration and the 56 Before It." *United Press International*. 21 January 2013. Available online: http://www.upi.com/blog/2013/01/21/Obamas-inauguration-Everything-you-wanted-to-know-about-the-57th-inauguration-and-the-56-before-it/8011358757175/

Malley, Brian. *How the Bible Works: An Anthropological Study of Evangelical Biblicism*. Walnut Creek: AltaMira, 2004.

Marty, Martin. "America's Iconic Book." In *Humanizing America's Iconic Book*, edited by Gene M. Tucker and Douglas A. Knight, 1–23. Chico: Scholars Press, 1982.

McCann, Erin. "The Two Bibles Donald Trump Used at the Inauguration." *The New York Times*. 18 January 2017. Available online: https://www.nytimes.com/2017/01/18/us/politics/lincoln-bible-trump-oath.html.

McGann, Jerome. *A New Republic of Letters: Memory and Scholarship in the Age of Digital Reproduction*. Cambridge: Harvard University Press, 2014.

Myrvold, Kristina, ed. *The Death of Sacred Texts: Ritual Disposal and Renovation of Texts in World Religions*. Farnham: Ashgate, 2010.

Najafizada, Enayat, and Rod Nordland. "Afghans Avenge Florida Koran Burning, Killing 12." *The New York Times*. 1 April 2011.

"Now, a Konkani Bible on Your Cellphone." *The Times of India*. May 1, 2018. Available online: https://timesofindia.indiatimes.com/city/goa/now-a-konkani-bible-on-your-cellphone/articleshow/63979490.cms.

O'Leary, Amy. "In the Beginning was the Word; Now the Word is on An App." *The New York Times*. July 26, 2013.

O'Regan, Mark. 2016. "Solicitors Told to Carry Bible and Koran." *Irish Independent*. 24 April. Available online: https://www.independent.ie/irish-news/courts/solicitors-told-to-carry-bible-and-koran-34654171.html.

Oster, Marcy. "Bishop Eddie Long Apologizes for Torah Scroll Ceremony." *Jewish Telegraphic Agency*. 6 February 2012. Available online: https://www.jta.org/2012/02/06/news-opinion/united-states/bishop-eddie-long-apologizes-for-torah-scroll-ceremony.

Parker, David. "Through a Screen Darkly: Digital Texts and the New Testament." *JSNT* 25 (2003): 395–411.

Parmenter, Dorina Miller. "The Iconic Book: The Image of the Bible in Early Christian Rituals." *Postscripts* 2 (2006): 160–89.

Patrick, Sarah K. "The Digital Age and Bible Literacy." *Seeds Family Worship*. Available online: https://www.seedsfamilyworship.com/the-digital-age-and-bible-literacy/.

Pearce, Matt. "Tennessee's governor vetoes Bible as state book." *The Los Angeles Times*. 17 April 2016. Available online: http://www.latimes.com/nation/la-na-tennessee-bible-20160417-story.html.

Plate, S. Brent Rodriguez. "Waving Bibles, Protesting Bathrooms." *Iconic Books Blog*. 15 May 2016. Available online: http://iconicbooks.blogspot.ie/2016/05/waving-bibles-protesting-bathrooms.html.

Posner, Menachem. "Proper Disposal of Holy Objects." *Chabad*. 30 July 2015. Available online: https://www.chabad.org/library/article_cdo/aid/475304/jewish/Proper-Disposal-of-Holy-Objects.htm.

"Rescued Torah scroll at Kingston temple stands as reminder of Holocaust." *Daily Freeman News*. 11 April 2018. Available online: http://www.dailyfreeman.com/article/df/20180411/news/180419922.

Richardson, Kathy Brittain, and Carol J. Pardun. "The New Scroll Digital Devices, Bible Study and Worship." *Journal of Media and Religion* 14 (2015): 16–28.

Rodriguez, Salvador. "Elected Official Takes Oath of Office on an iPad." *Los Angeles Times*. 3 January 2014. Available online: http://www.latimes.com/business/technology/la-fi-tn-politician-sworn-in-ipad-bible-20140103-story.html.

Roth, Lauren. "Satanic Temple submits coloring book, fact sheets for Orange school distribution." *Orlando Sentinel*. 30 October 2014. Available online: http://www.orlandosentinel.com/features/education/school-zone/os-satanic-temple-coloring-book-20141030-post.html.

Rubin, Alissa J., and Graham Bowley. "Koran Burning in Afghanistan Prompts 3 Parallel Inquiries.'" *The New York Times*. 29 February 2012.

Sands, Sarah. "Full interview: As he launches his bid for City Hall, Sadiq Khan says 'I won't be a Zone One Mayor.'" *The Evening Standard*. 13 May 2015. Available online: https://www.standard.co.uk/news/politics/full-interview-as-he-launches-his-bid-for-city-hall-sadiq-khan-says-i-wont-be-a-zone-one-mayor-10247056.html.

Savali, Kirsten West. "Cornel West: President Obama Doesn't Deserve to Be Sworn In With MLK's Bible." *News One*. 20 January 2013. Available online: https://newsone.com/2153928/cornel-west-obama-mlk/.

Sharon, Jeremy. "Digitized Talmud and Mobile App to be Launched." *The Jerusalem Post*. May 29, 2016. Available online: https://www.jpost.com/Business-and-Innovation/Tech/Digitized-Talmud-and-mobile-app-to-be-launched-455357.

Smith, Jonathan Z. *To Take Place: Toward Theory in Ritual*. Chicago: University of Chicago Press, 1987.

Smith, Jonathan Z. "Religion and Bible." *JBL* 128 (2009): 5–27.

Turner, Victor. *The Ritual Process: Structure and Anti-Structure*. Ithaca: Cornell, [1961] 1977.

van Gennep, Arnold. *The Rites of Passage*, trans. Monika B. Vizedom and Gabrielle L. Caffee. Chicago: University of Chicago Press, 1960.

Watts, James W. "The Three Dimensions of Scriptures." *Postscripts* 2 (2006): 135–59.

Watts, James W. "Desecrating Scriptures." *A Case Study for the Luce Project in Media, Religion, and International Relations*. 2009. Available online: http://surface.syr.edu/rel/3/.

Watts, James W. "Disposing of Non-Disposable Texts." In *The Death of Sacred Texts: Ritual Disposal and Renovation of Texts in the World Religions*, edited by Kristina Myrvold, 147–59. Farnham: Ashgate, 2010.

Watts, James W., ed. *Iconic Books and Texts*. Sheffield: Equinox, 2013.

Westin, Jonathan. "Loss of Culture: New Media Forms and the Translation from Analogue to Digital Books." *Convergence: The International Journal of Research into New Media Technologies* 19/2 (2012): 129–40.

Wimbush, Vincent L., ed. *Theorizing Scriptures: New Critical Orientations to a Cultural Phenomenon*. Signifying (On) Scriptures. New Brunswick: Rutgers University Press, 2008.

# Scriptural Index

**Hebrew Bible (Tanakh/Old Testament)**

Gen 1:1  95
Gen 49:8  95

Exod 14:28  95, 103, 105, 114
Exod 14:30  109
Exod 15  25, 96
Exod 15:1–19  103
Exod 15:19  97
Exod 34:11  95, 113

Lev 16:1–18:30  83

Num 24:5  95

Deut 11:4–32  166–167
Deut 11:11–14  166–167
Deut 11:14  168
Deut 17:19  66
Deut 31:19  66
Deut 31:28  95, 113
Deut 32  25, 96
Deut 34:12  113

Josh 12:9–24  96

Judg 5  96

2 Sam 22  96

1 Kgs 8  81

Esth 9:7–9  95

Ps 1  122
Ps 4  141
Ps 6  139
Ps 9  139
Ps 26  122
Ps 29  141
Ps 31  141
Ps 38  122
Ps 40  131
Ps 44  141
Ps 55  141
Ps 74  141
Ps 95  131
Ps 97  122, 125
Ps 104  17–20, 22, 24–26
Ps 104:11  18–20
Ps 110  122
Ps 110:2  170
Ps 112  21, 27
Ps 112:4  170, 172, 174
Ps 112:8  170
Ps 116  28
Ps 118  14, 25–30
Ps 118:1–4  29
Ps 118:1–24  18–19, 27
Ps 118:5–10, 12  28
Ps 118:24  28
Ps 118:25–26  29–30
Ps 118:29  26
Ps 119  14, 17–27, 31, 120
Ps 136  20

Prov 1  25

Ezek 2:8–3:3  66

Lam 3  25

Amos 5:26  195

Zech 5:1–2  66
Zech 14  81

**New Testament**

Luke 19:41  249

John 1  258
John 1:5  174

Acts 4:25  131

Rev 5  185
Rev 5:5–7  192
Rev 5:6–8  185
Rev 12  185
Rev 13  7, 185
Rev 13:1–2  185
Rev 13:3–8  185
Rev 13:10  185
Rev 13:11  185
Rev 13:12–13  186
Rev 13:17  186
Rev 13:18  183–186, 188–197, 201–202, 204–205, 207
Rev 17:9–11  186
Rev 19:12  192
Rev 21:17  186

**Qur'ān**

3  230
3:22  230
3:30  230
3:31  230
3:41  230
3:22–31  230
3:32–41  230
5:88–107  55
5:93  55
7:73–83  56
7:77  56
7:82  59
12:38  231
30:19  225

# Subject Index

Actants 297
Aesthetic(s) 19, 24, 94, 105–106, 157, 215, 265, 276
Aleppo Codex 69, 74, 79, 81–82, 86–88, 99–100, 102
Annotation(s) 5, 39, 49, 51–60, 113–114, 128, 133, 136, 140–141, 143, 146, 149, 222–223, 229, 238, 241
Apocryphal Acts 44
App(s) 23, 247, 250, 252, 255–260, 275, 286–287, 300–301
Arabic 7, 36, 48, 52–53, 60, 68–70, 72–73, 75–77, 82–84, 88, 127, 175, 183, 200, 215, 217, 219, 222–227, 230, 231, 236–237, 240, 242–244, 263–264, 266, 270, 275–277, 280
Art/artistic 21, 51–52, 54, 56–58, 105–106, 115–117, 135–136, 154–155, 157, 161, 163, 165, 168, 170, 175, 178, 181, 251, 264, 283–284, 285
Ashkenaz/Ashkenazi 94, 110–111, 114, 116
Authority 4, 8, 31, 63, 156, 162–164, 185–186, 253, 257, 261, 263, 275, 277, 279

Book history 2, 265
Book(s) of Hours 120, 126, 129, 146, 161
Burning (books) 24, 289–291, 294

Cairo Codex 71–72, 74, 80–81, 86
Canon(ical) 7, 13, 24, 35–36, 38–44, 46–49, 52, 60, 134, 183, 209, 217, 244, 252–253, 260, 283
Christ, see "Jesus"
Codex/codices 1, 3, 6, 8–9, 15, 35, 38, 41, 47–48, 51–52, 60, 63, 66–83, 85–88, 91–95, 97–107, 109–117, 184, 187, 217–218, 220–222, 233, 243–244, 250, 252, 254, 281, 296–297
Codex Sinaiticus 35, 38, 48, 254
Codicology/codicological 40, 53, 55, 60, 70–71, 73, 76, 87, 92–94, 116, 204, 217, 220, 222, 242
Coding/encoding 7, 169, 188–190, 199, 202, 213–214, 223, 225, 232–233, 235–238, 241, 276–277

Column(s) 15–16, 18–20, 26–29, 37, 45, 77–79, 95, 102–106, 109, 113–114, 123, 131, 133, 145–146, 204, 221

Dead Sea Scrolls 5, 13–33, 36, 63, 65, 71, 75, 91, 102, 114, 120–121
Desecration 9, 284, 289–290, 294, 301
Device(s) 1, 247, 250, 252–253, 255–259, 263, 270–276, 281, 286, 301
Diacritic(s) 214, 222–225, 228, 230–231, 233–237, 240, 242–243, 275–276
Didache 44
Digitised/digitisation 110, 116, 184, 190, 219, 253–254, 265–266, 271–273, 275–276, 281, 287, 301

Electronic 8, 140, 150, 203–204, 216, 233, 242, 244–245, 247, 252, 254, 261, 263, 265–266, 270–276, 279, 286, 289, 295
Ethnography/ethnographic 8, 162, 177, 263, 270, 274, 282, 298

Fragment(s) 5, 14–15, 18–20, 26–30, 36, 43–44, 49, 51–55, 57–59, 61, 67, 71–72, 74–75, 77, 81, 83, 88–89, 91, 93, 102, 217, 224–225, 229, 231, 275
Function/functionality 6, 8, 92, 182, 204–205, 238–239, 251–252, 270, 279, 281–283, 285, 294

Gender 7–8, 153, 263, 292
Genizah 6, 63, 67, 71–89, 91–93, 102, 116–117, 218, 222, 243
Gloss(es) 35–36, 60, 101, 110, 116–117, 119, 131–132, 142, 150, 222, 245
Gospel of Thomas 35, 38–39, 42
Greek 36–38, 44, 70, 73, 93, 134, 183, 186–189, 192–193, 195, 197–203, 219–221, 249
Gutenberg (press) 132, 143, 149, 213–214, 232

Hebrew 6, 13, 15, 18, 24, 26–27, 32, 36, 63–66, 68–73, 75–79, 81–83, 85, 87–89, 91–95, 97–103, 105, 110–121,

125, 131, 134, 136, 143–144, 171, 174–175, 183, 186, 188, 210

Iconic/iconicity 2, 8–10, 153, 156, 161, 177, 283–285, 289, 292–298, 300–301
Illuminated/illumination 72, 105, 119, 143–144, 153–154, 157, 161–162, 165, 170, 175, 177
Incipit(s) 122, 125–126, 128–129, 131, 133–136, 138–139, 142–149, 229
Ink 3, 15, 57, 119, 125, 128, 143, 148, 155, 219, 225, 227, 231, 270

Jesus, Christ 121, 131, 141, 174, 187, 192, 198, 249–250
Josephus 46, 64, 85
Journalling, Bible 153–178

Karaite, *see* "Qaraite"

Layout 5–6, 8, 13–33, 68, 91, 93–107, 109–116, 119–129, 131–137, 139, 141, 143, 147–148, 162, 165, 173–174, 192, 217, 221–222, 229, 233, 241, 249–250, 252–253
Latin 37–38, 121, 126–129, 131–132, 134–136, 138–139, 142–149, 186, 188, 193–194, 197–201, 220–221
Leningrad Codex 66, 72, 74, 79, 86, 88, 99–100, 102
Liminal/liminality 1, 3, 10, 294–295
Liturgy/liturgical 6, 13, 16, 39, 64–65, 70–71, 73–74, 79–87, 92–93, 101–102, 115, 120–122, 124–129, 132–133, 136, 138–139, 141, 143, 145–151, 220–221, 247–248, 262, 296

Maimonides 65–69, 79, 81, 84, 87–88, 97–100, 103, 105–110, 112–114, 117
Manuscript(s) 1–2, 5, 7, 10, 13–15, 18, 21–24, 27, 30–31, 35–43, 47–49, 51–54, 58–61, 63–64, 6667, 70–72, 74–80, 82, 85, 87–88, 91–92, 94, 98–100, 102, 105, 107, 109–117, 119–122, 124–129, 130–133, 137–138, 147, 150–151, 162, 165, 181–185, 187–207, 209–211, 213–217, 219, 221–225, 227–245, 249, 253–254, 265, 280–281, 294, 297–299
Markup 7, 213–214, 223, 231, 233–240, 242, 244-245
Moses 64–65, 68–69, 71–72, 80, 84, 87, 96–100, 103–104, 113, 168
Muhammad 7, 181, 196–202, 198, 218, 228, 264
muṣḥaf/maṣāḥif 70, 72, 83, 85, 217–218, 220, 228, 242–244, 263–264, 266–270, 272–278, 280

Oecumenius 183, 187, 190, 192–193, 197, 210
Orthography/orthographic 224, 237, 244, 271, 275, 277–279

Palaeography 21, 30, 40
Palimpsest 52–54, 59–61, 219, 228, 233, 243, 245
Paper 3, 75–78, 83, 88, 136, 141, 143, 148, 154–157, 160, 164, 174, 185, 217, 219–220, 263, 266–267, 270, 274, 279
Papyrus/papyri 5, 35–49, 73, 187, 211, 217–220, 224, 243–245
Paratext(s)/paratextual 3–5, 7–10, 35, 37, 39–44, 46, 182–183, 190, 192, 195, 204–205, 233, 241, 247–255, 257–262
Parchment 14, 55–59, 64, 66–67, 76–78, 80, 102, 122, 217–222, 224, 244
Performance/performative/performativity 2, 6, 9, 119–120, 122, 124–127, 129, 133–134, 136, 141–143, 145–149, 164, 283–285
Pentateuch 64, 66–67, 95–97, 103, 110, 112–113, 115–116, 133
Poem/ Poetry/ Poetic 5, 13, 16–18, 22, 24–25, 27, 29–33, 66, 73, 76–77, 86, 95–100, 103–111, 113–114, 119–120, 122, 163
Print/ printing press 1, 3, 5–6, 8, 51, 70, 87, 119–121, 123, 132–133, 135–141, 143–151, 153–155, 158, 161–164, 168–170, 175–177, 181–182, 184–185, 190, 192, 203–206, 210, 213–216, 232, 245, 247–258, 260–262, 264–267, 270, 275–281, 287–288, 297–298

Prose 16–22, 24–27, 31, 119
Protoevangelium of James 44
Purity (ritual) 8, 73, 264, 267–269, 273–274

Qaraite/Qaraism 8, 63, 67, 80–86, 89, 91
Qumran 8, 15, 18, 22, 23, 25–28, 30, 32–33, 36, 63–64, 87, 91

Rabbinic/Rabbanite 6, 63–64, 68–70, 73, 75, 80–86, 92, 94, 288
Rashi 71, 95, 110
Reception (history) 1, 7, 9–10, 13–16, 31, 35, 48, 119–120, 128, 136, 140, 158, 162, 165, 177, 183–185, 190, 192, 202–205, 209, 248
Ritual 8, 85, 92, 218, 264, 269, 273, 283–285, 289–290, 295–298, 300–301
Roll(s), *see* "scroll(s)"

Sefer 6, 67–69, 81, 83, 112
Sefer Torah 6, 63–68, 85, 88, 98, 113
Sepharad/Sephardic 94, 97–98, 100, 106, 111–112, 116
Scribe(s)/scribal 6–7, 14–19, 22–24, 27–28, 31–33, 36, 38–39, 41–42, 45–49, 51, 53–60, 66–67, 69–70, 75, 77–78, 86–88, 91, 94, 97, 100–103, 105, 108–116, 122, 127–128, 148, 153, 161–162, 186–187, 190, 192, 195, 199, 201–202, 213, 221, 223, 229, 233
Script 7, 13–15, 41, 54–57, 83, 94, 119, 123, 200, 215–216, 219, 222–225, 228, 230–231, 237, 241–244, 264–265, 270, 275–277, 280
Scroll(s) (roll[s]) 1, 3, 5–6, 9, 13–33, 36, 39, 63–71, 73–75, 77, 79, 81, 83–88, 91–95, 97–99, 101–103, 110–117, 120–121, 184, 217, 220–221, 249, 281, 290, 294, 297, 299–301
Shepherd of Hermas 44
Social media 8, 153–154, 260
Subtitle(s), *see* "Title(s)"
Superscription(s) 16, 26, 121, 125, 127, 129, 131–133, 136, 141, 143–146

Synagogue 63–65, 67, 71, 73, 78–79, 82, 84–85, 92, 101, 115, 294, 299

Talmud 64–66, 71, 73–75, 84–85, 93–98, 100–103, 109–110, 116–117, 286–287, 301
Targum 77, 110
Technology(ies)/technological 1, 3, 8, 10, 70, 74, 76, 86, 132–133, 140, 150, 177, 181, 213–218, 232–233, 239, 241–245, 247–251, 253, 256, 260–263, 265–266, 269–270, 272–273, 275, 277–282, 285, 287–288, 296, 299, 301
Title(s)/subtitle 5, 35–37, 41, 45, 78, 121, 123, 131, 134–136, 139, 141–143, 145–146, 183, 194, 204, 248, 252–253, 257, 260
Torah 6, 23–25, 36, 49, 63–71, 74–75, 78–81, 83–85, 87–89, 94, 98–104, 112–116, 175, 289–290, 294
Torah Scroll 6, 63–67, 69–71, 79, 81, 83–85, 94, 98–99, 101–103, 112–116, 290
Transmission 1, 3–7, 9–10, 35, 40, 51–53, 60–61, 63, 69, 77, 86, 94, 182–183, 202–203, 216–217, 221–222, 228, 239, 249, 254, 270, 277, 281
Translation 3, 6, 16, 31, 53, 55, 72, 77, 78, 120, 125–127, 129, 131, 134, 145–148, 168, 175, 253, 258–259, 271, 275, 286, 296, 298
Tyndale, William 132–133, 147, 151
Typography/typographic(al) 6, 93, 136, 145, 153, 159, 181–182, 184, 201, 214, 249, 253, 275–276, 278

Vacat 18, 27, 29
Vulgate 119, 122, 125, 134, 136, 139

Wyclif(fe), John/Wycliffite Bible 120, 126, 127–134, 136, 138, 142, 147–151

YouVersion 7, 247, 252–253, 255–258, 260, 286

www.ingramcontent.com/pod-product-compliance
Lightning Source LLC
Chambersburg PA
CBHW070341240426
43665CB00046B/2325